*Mothers of Massive Resistance*

# Mothers of
# Massive Resistance
## *White Women and the Politics*
## *of White Supremacy*

### ELIZABETH GILLESPIE McRAE

OXFORD
UNIVERSITY PRESS

# OXFORD
## UNIVERSITY PRESS

Oxford University Press is a department of the University of Oxford. It furthers
the University's objective of excellence in research, scholarship, and education
by publishing worldwide. Oxford is a registered trade mark of Oxford University
Press in the UK and certain other countries.

Published in the United States of America by Oxford University Press
198 Madison Avenue, New York, NY 10016, United States of America.

© Oxford University Press 2018

Library of Congress Cataloging-in-Publication Data
Names: McRae, Elizabeth Gillespie, author.
Title: Mothers of massive resistance : white women and the politics of white
supremacy / Elizabeth Gillespie McRae.
Other titles: White women and the politics of white supremacy
Description: New York, NY : Oxford University Press, [2018] |
Includes bibliographical references and index.
Identifiers: LCCN 2017016910 (print) | LCCN 2017039850 (ebook) |
ISBN 9780190271725 (Updf) | ISBN 9780190271732 (Epub) |
ISBN 9780190271718 (hardcover : alk. paper)
Subjects: LCSH: White supremacy movements—United States—
History—20th century. | Women, White—Political activity—United States—History. |
Women, White—United States—Attitudes—History—20th century. | Women,
White—United States—Social life and customs—History—20th century. |
Segregation—United States—History—20th century. |
Racial discrimination—United States—History—20th century. |
Racism—United States—History—20th century. | United States—
Race relations—History—20th century.
Classification: LCC E184.A1 (ebook) | LCC E184.A1 M354 2017 (print) |
DDC 320.56/909730904—dc23
LC record available at https://lccn.loc.gov/2017016910

1 3 5 7 9 8 6 4 2

Printed by Sheridan Books, Inc., United States of America

*In memory of Sam Gillespie*

# Contents

Conclusion: The New National Face of Segregation:
   Boston Women against Busing

# Acknowledgments

FOR YEARS, advisors, colleagues, and friends warned me about the unwieldy nature of this project. I should have listened. Despite my dismissal of their advice, they remained in my corner. I am indebted to their faith and endurance.

I will never measure up to the two scholars who have been most influential to me—James Cobb and Bryant Simon. While his sense of our meeting might be different, Jim Cobb came to Athens just in time for me. His research suggestions, hard-driving comments, Uncle Jim emails, and Lyra Cobb's lessons in grammar have shaped every page of this work. He has remained a steady mentor and friend to me and my family for which I am so thankful. Bryant Simon tried to make me a better writer and drilled me with questions in his office, on runs, and at celebrations. Then he welcomed me into his life and that of his family—my dear friend Ann-Marie, Benjamin, Eli, Bob, and Susan. There are all kinds of families. The Simon-Reardons are our family of the heart.

A scholarly community and one of friends have shaped this project from the beginning. Years ago an email from Jacquelyn Dowd Hall sent me down this path, and she has been supportive ever since. Archivists and librarians at the North Carolina Department of Archives and History, the Southern History Collection, the North Carolina Collection, Charles C. Capps Archives at Delta State University, the South Caroliniana Society, the Mississippi Department of Archives and History, Albert and Shirley Small Library at the University of Virginia, the McClain Library at University of Southern Mississippi, the Harrison County Historical Society, Hargrett Library at the University of Georgia, and Rockbridge County Library helped me collect materials and conduct my research. Donna Huffer generously shared her research on the Clarks of Rockbridge County with me, and Anne House sent me copies of Florence Sillers Ogden's columns, "My Dear Boys."

Trying to nail this story down has meant the best kinds of collaboration and conversation. Susan Ferber has supported this project for years, and her careful reading of the manuscript made it all the better. She also made sure I had careful, insightful readers. At the University of Georgia, I benefited from working with Emory Thomas, Bob Pratt, Chana Kai Lee, Kathleen Clark, Josh Cole, John Inscoe, Ann Short Chirhart, Glenda Bridges, and Mark Huddle. Along the way Karen Anderson, Dan Carter, Laura Edwards, Jane Dailey, Anna Krome Lukens, Marjorie Spruill, Ann Ziker, Andy Lewis, Blain Roberts, Doug Smith, Jim Noles, Nancy MacLean, Kevin Kruse, Joe Crespino, Robin Morris, Laura Edwards, David Cecelski, Glenda Gilmore, Clive Webb, George Lewis, Michelle Nickerson, and Timothy Tyson have provided helpful commentary. When he called to tell me about his wedding, Steve Kantrowitz generously ended up helping me reframe the story instead. Rick and Mary Beth Holcomb, Kat Charron, Adriane Lentz-Smith, and Christian Lentz have brought good conversation, good friendship, good bourbon, and good fun to Cullowhee, and I would not know what to do without them. Along the way Richard and Hani Brooks, Paul and Sally Williams, Etta Seale Powell, and Steve and Peggy Riethmiller provided good company, a roof over my head, and lovely companionship. Carol, Brent, and Scott McRae have remained encouraging throughout.

For the past seventeen years, I have lived and worked in the mountains of North Carolina. The history department at Western Carolina University hired me days after I defended my dissertation proposal and have been supportive ever since. Graduate and undergraduate students—Beverly Ellis, Whit Altizer, Joe Hurley, Kevin Campbell, James Owen, Sarah Beth Lee, Lynn Parmer, Jennifer Scism Ash, Tony Varvoutis, Donna Clausen, Kayla Payne—have helped track down sources near and far. In my first trip through Cullowhee, an older generation of historians piqued my interest—Cliff Lovin, John Bell, Max Williams, and Gerry Schwartz. But the classrooms of Janice Witt and Mary Adams at Richlands High School and those of Richard Zuber, Gayle McCaffery, and James Barefield at Wake Forest University convinced me even earlier that asking questions mattered. More recently, Jim Lewis, Curtis Wood, Robert Ferguson, Tanisha Jenkins, Gael Graham, Annette Debo, Mae Claxton, Chris Cooper, Benjamin Francis-Fallon, Kathy Orr, and Mary Ella Engel talked through ideas, and encouraged me. Andy Denson, Robin Payne, and Jessie Swigger made excellent suggestions as part of our writing group. Richard Starnes and I first met in Cullowhee, and he has been my dear friend ever since. Vicki Szabo has been a constant for me in McKee. Jessie Swigger brought sweetness, support, and dear friendship to

Cullowhee and to us. I owe my dear friend Alex Macaulay for running thousands of miles with me, for regaling me with Walhalla stories, and in between for talking me through many of these passages.

The mountains have brought me all kinds of additional wise counsel—historians Sarah Judson, Dan Carter, and Matt Lassiter. Matt served as a reader, and I benefited from his copious comments and our conversations then and now. If I managed to make this book better, he deserves much credit. My larger community, Eleanor, Eliza, Lee, Kate, and Julia Macaulay, Betty Farmer, Jim Manning, Dawn Gilchrist, and former Whee residents Kathy and Bobby Woollum have made the world a better place to be. The public school community in Jackson County has also been a source of inspiration. The high school students in the Appalachian Oral History project have reminded me how important the stories of everyday people are, and I am indebted to Pam Shuler and Jake Buchanan at Smoky Mountain, Billie Clemens at Swain High School and Denise Davis at Franklin High for passing on to their students that history matters. My best teachers in the mountains, no doubt, have been Betty Sue and Susan Moore. They taught me much about where we live, how to raise children, and what matters in this world. I am honored to know and love them, and I could not have done this without them.

I grew up in the mountains of southwest Virginia on a family farm surrounded by family who read, talked about politics, and worked hard. Both my grandmothers, Elizabeth Ziegler Gillespie and Lucille Seay Campbell, were voracious readers and kept me in books. My parents, Jim Sam Gillespie and Lucy Campbell Gillespie, taught me to take care of your family, the people you love, and the community in which you live. My father has modeled how to maintain joy, even in the face of sorrow, and I am blessed to be his daughter. I am indebted to my grandmother Gillespie for slipping me money to go to graduate school, and to my parents for walking miles with my crying babies, making my children think Pounding Mill was the best place to be. My mother did not live long enough to see this book come out, but she would recognize the parts as she traveled with me to Raleigh, Cleveland, Mississippi, Atlanta, and Charleston, taking care of the girls while I sat in the archives and admonishing me to finish "the damn book." My sister Ann Brett has been a partner in shared sorrow as we imagine what adulthood would have been like with our brother Sam and in laughter as we have tried to figure out together how to rear all of our children—Katy, Lucy, Campbell, Sarah, Charlotte, and Nora Ann.

I used to joke that my daughters, Katy and Lucy Caroline, would be able to read this book by the time I finished. At seventeen and fifteen, I am glad it is not a joke. Nothing will ever be better than being their momma. They are my heart. Steve has been a quiet, patient force in my life—two qualities that I need but do not have. Rather than asking me if the book was done, he tilled my garden annually, believing that this summer would be the one when I could spend my time outside rather than inside. Maybe this is the year for sunflowers.

# Abbreviations

| | |
|---|---|
| AAA | Agricultural Adjustment Act |
| ALACP | American League for the Abolition of Capital Punishment |
| ASCOA | Anglo-Saxon Clubs of America |
| ASNLH | Association for the Study of Negro Life and History |
| ASWPL | Association of Southern Women for the Prevention of Lynching |
| BPWC | Business and Professional Women's Clubs |
| CIC | Commission on Interracial Cooperation |
| CIO | Congress of Industrial Organizations |
| CORE | Congress of Racial Equality |
| CPA | Concerned Parents Association |
| CWA | Civilian Works Administration |
| CWCC | Civil War Centennial Commission |
| CWEC | Citywide Educational Coalition |
| DAR | Daughters of the American Revolution |
| DNC | Democratic National Convention |
| DUPEC | Durham United Political Education Council |
| ERO | Eugenics Record Office |
| FEPC | Fair Employment Practices Committee |
| HUAC | House Un-American Activities Committee |
| KKK | Ku Klux Klan |
| MEA | Mississippi Educational Association |
| NAACP | National Association for the Advancement of Colored People |
| NAG | National Action Group |
| NCTC | National Consumers Tax Commission |
| NEA | National Education Association |
| NFWC | National Federation of Women's Clubs |
| NTWU | National Textile Workers Union (NTWU) |
| ORFIT | Organization to Repeal Federal Income Taxes |
| PAY | Patriotic American Youth |
| PTA | Parent Teacher Association |
| RIA | Racial Integrity Act |

| | |
|---|---|
| RNC | Republican National Convention |
| ROAR | Restore Our Alienated Rights |
| SAR | Sons of the American Revolution |
| SCV | Sons of Confederate Veterans |
| SOS | Save Our Schools |
| UCV | United Confederate Veterans |
| UDC | United Daughters of the Confederacy |
| UMW | United Mine Workers |
| UN | United Nations |
| UNESCO | United Nations Education, Scientific and Cultural Organization |
| UNICEF | United Nations Children's Fund |
| WAYW | Women's Activities and Youth Work |
| WCG | Women for Constitutional Government |
| WEC | Women's Emergency Committee |
| WONPR | Women's Organization for National Prohibition Reform |
| WPA | Works Progress Administration |
| YMCA | Young Men's Christian Association |
| YWCA | Young Women's Christian Association Organization to Repeal Federal Income Taxes |

*Mothers of Massive Resistance*

# Introduction

## SEGREGATION'S CONSTANT GARDENERS

WHEN THE US SUPREME COURT handed down its 1954 *Brown v. Board of Education* decision, a young white mother near Wilmington, North Carolina, received the news with resolve to circumvent the ruling, using "nerve and plenty of hell in the personality." Mrs. Hugh Bell organized the Pender County Association for the Preservation of Segregation and spent the summer circulating a petition to continue segregated schools "no matter the consequences." By August, the association had obtained nearly 5,000 signatures representing over one-third of the county's white population, and an association member delivered it to the governor of North Carolina in October. The next summer, Bell tried to rally newspaper editors and segregationists across the state. In a letter to the *Raleigh News and Observer*, Bell explained her commitment to school segregation as an attempt to protect her two little girls and to secure states' rights. She intended to put her typewriter to use for "the cause." For others, she wrote, "maybe it will take a little violence," glibly noting that "it was too bad about the murder of the fourteen year old negro boy," but wondered if "this could be only a mild beginning." Included with the letter was the lengthy "New Hanover County Preliminary Report" which she had helped compile and distribute. Filled with questionable quantitative and anecdotal evidence, the report cataloged the deleterious effects of school desegregation, predicting the decline of the family, the schools, the state, and the nation. It acknowledged parental fears that their white daughters would marry someone's black sons and that academics would suffer as black students with low IQs and high sex drives diminished the education of white students. These problems would be compounded by "the negro teacher," who subjected to "subversive propaganda," sees the world in a way "antagonistic, to the white philosophy of life." These malignant consequences would ripple across the nation, the report predicted, as integrated schools fulfilled the wishes of communists and infiltrated the minds of America's youth with a "one-world" doctrine.[1]

In one way, Bell's segregationist moment fits well with the familiar story of massive resistance told in textbooks, documentaries, and scholarly works. In that story, white southern opposition to the civil rights movement rises and coalesces in the decade after the Supreme Court's decision when segregationists insisted on separate schools. Pledging to avoid school integration at all costs, newspapermen and politicians named the movement massive resistance. Then in 1956, echoing the desires of their constituents, 101 southern members of Congress signed the Southern Manifesto—a proclamation "to resist forced integration by any lawful means." To legitimize their rejection of the constitutional principle of federalism, congressmen and segregationists revitalized, for a post–World War II world, the antebellum precept of interposition, which held that state legislatures could intercede between the federal government and citizens of their individual state, nullifying federal laws that threatened their residents.[2] About the same time, Citizens' Councils made up of middle-class white professionals, mostly men, who ostensibly scorned the lowbrow Ku Klux Klan (KKK), spread across the South to circumvent desegregation specifically and racial equality generally. In the 1960s, southern governors—George Wallace, Lester Maddox, and Ross Barnett—further galvanized massive resistance by standing in schoolhouse doors, by ranting racist ideologies on the campaign trail, and by calling on states to eliminate support for public education in their constitutions. Bell's prediction of violence came to fruition in the murder of four little girls in a Birmingham church, mobs hurling fists and insults at young men and women at Woolworth's counters and elementary schools, and policemen turning their hoses, dogs, and billy clubs on civil rights activists and bystanders.[3]

Massive resistance, the well-told story has reminded us, was short-lived. In the face of the grassroots activism of black southerners and their allies, the reluctance of white moderates to abandon public schools, and the economic concerns of the South's businessmen, Bell's Pender County organization and Citizens' Councils eventually disbanded, and the efforts of the powerful— the Wallaces and the Barnetts—faded. Helped along by the nation's outrage at the killing of young black and white activists, moderation gradually replaced massive resistance. Meanwhile, the State Department pressured the executive branch to support desegregation and black voting rights in order to augment the nation's Cold War agenda and counter damaging stories of the nation's racist violence covered by the communist press. Total defiance, the position of the hardline segregationists, gave way to token compliance, the position of most white moderates. By the mid-1960s, faced with the black freedom struggle, the Civil Rights Act, the Voting Rights Act, and *Baker v. Carr*, massive resistance met defeat, and its advocates moved to the political margins. The South's segregationists lost, and the southern political landscape shifted.[4]

Bell's activism, however, also points to some flaws in this familiar conceptualization of massive resistance. In the summer of 1954, petitions carrying the signatures of more than 80,000 North Carolinians spoke to a widespread sentiment among local people who did not rely on governors, senators, or political party machinery to direct their immediate and organized opposition to school integration. Bell's plea for North Carolina to reject the Supreme Court decision predated by more than a year the call for "interposition" made by the editor of the *Richmond News Leader* James Kilpatrick.[5] Support for the segregated state existed among everyday people. Maintaining racial segregation was not solely or even primarily the work of elected officials. Its adherents, like Bell and her association, sustained the system with quotidian work and organizations that reached beyond the KKK and the Citizens' Councils. On the ground, it was often white women who shaped and sustained white supremacist politics.

The anti-integration arguments that Bell and others employed had broad and deep roots across the South and the nation. They did not debut in 1954 as a reactionary response to the Supreme Court's decision. Political support for racial segregation was generations in the making, which suggests that truncating massive resistance to a decade obscures its political evolution and renders its activists reactionaries. The New Hanover document that Bell distributed drew on stories from both in and outside the South, pointing to the presence of a national network of committed segregationists. The document also spoke to the multiple locations where racial segregation had been and would have to be maintained—dating etiquette, teacher training, public health policies, sexual customs, civic organizations, and in the stories people told. Federal legislation could hardly combat segregationist practices in places that lay far below legislative halls, judicial chambers, and voting booths. Nor could a chronology of massive resistance that relied solely on federal legislation, judicial decisions, and violent uprisings capture how the daily, mundane, and local resistance to racial equality persisted. Finally, in Bell's defense of segregation were elements that addressed more than the South's legalized racial divide and formed the foundation of a broader political platform informed by the Cold War, communism, housing policies, federal aid to education, tax reform, and calls for limited government.

This book is about that story—the story of grassroots resistance to racial equality undertaken by white women. They are at the center of the history of white supremacist politics in the South and nation. While they toiled outside the attention of the national media (for the most part), white women took central roles in disciplining their communities according to Jim Crow's rules and were central to massive resistance to racial equality. White segregationist women capitalized on their roles in social welfare institutions, public education, partisan politics, and popular culture to shape the Jim Crow order. From there they provided a political education that mobilized generations and trained activists for white supremacist politics. These women guaranteed that racial segregation seeped into the nooks and crannies of public life and private matters, of congressional campaigns and PTA meetings, of cotton policy and household economies, and of textbook debates and day care decisions. Their work shored up white supremacist politics and shaped the segregated state. White women were the mass in massive resistance.

At times, their political activism connected them to a national network of white segregationists. Far from being regional retrogrades and outsiders in the nation, the South's female segregationists participated in the same eugenics movement that social workers in southern California did. Protests against Social Security joined segregationists in Texas with anti–income tax advocates from Massachusetts. In the 1950s, coalitions opposing the United Nations welcomed Mississippi's female segregationists who made political alliances with right-wing West Coast anti-communist organizations. When female segregationists called for limits on the Supreme Court in the aftermath of *Brown*, they received support from conservative organizations in Chicago and Seattle. In a Jim Crow nation, segregation's female activists imbued women's civic duties, womanhood, and motherhood with particular racist prescriptions. For many, being a good white mother or a good white woman meant teaching and enforcing racial distance in their homes and in the larger public sphere. In the 1970s, the anti-busers of Boston echoed earlier activists for massive resistance when they ignored the persistence of structural racism, elevated individual rights, and made sacrosanct the rights of families to determine their children's public education.[6] Decade after decade, the South's female segregationists were part of the widespread political mobilization of American women.

To uncover this re-conceptualized history of massive resistance, the lives of four, educated, politically active women from North Carolina, Mississippi, and South Carolina form the narrative anchor of this book and offer a long trajectory on white supremacist politics. The public lives of Nell Battle Lewis, Florence Sillers Ogden, Mary Dawson Cain, and Cornelia Dabney Tucker paralleled the reign of Jim Crow segregation and were part of a broad and massive network of women across the South and the nation who now populate this story. Their prodigious correspondence exposed the work of the lesser known and the fleeting, like Mrs. Bell, and the better known and well-connected, like conservative activist and Barry Goldwater acolyte, Phyllis Schlafly. It exposed a network of female segregationists that included old and young, college-educated and high school dropouts, career women and homemakers, urbanites, suburbanites, and rural residents. These women were married and single, childless and mothers. They were staunch Democrats, Republicans, and Independents; some were all three. Their formal and informal networks stretched from the rural environs of the Black Belt South to the right-leaning West Coast city of Pasadena; from the bastion of southern liberalism, Chapel Hill, North Carolina, to Boston's working-class Irish neighborhood, South Boston. The Jim Crow South where Lewis, Ogden, Cain, and Tucker worked with their southern segregationist sisters was one expression of a larger, more diverse Jim Crow nation—a nation where garden club members and stay-at-home moms joined newspaper columnists and school teachers in reifying the color line.[7]

Nell Battle Lewis was a single woman with a caustic tongue and a Mencken-like pen who wrote for the *Raleigh News and Observer* from 1920 to 1956. Born to one of North Carolina's leading families, she left the South to be educated in the North and returned as a career-minded, progressive iconoclast to begin her newspaper career from the urban environs of Raleigh. A southern liberal in the interwar period, she moved into the Cold War as one of the central architects of North Carolina's campaigns against racial equality. On the eve of her death in 1956, she celebrated knowing that resignation to the Court's *Brown* decision had morphed into a broad resistance against desegregation.[8]

Born on a cotton plantation along the banks of the Mississippi River, Florence Sillers Ogden remained in Rosedale, Mississippi, with her Chicago-born husband on her family's land. A member of the rural, Black Belt elite, Ogden filtered her politics through the lenses of the old plantation class and the modern agriculturalist. She shifted seamlessly between working with white women in the Daughters of the American Revolution (DAR) and powerful white male landowners in the Delta Council, an economic lobby for the region's cotton growers. In the 1960s, she looked to Chicago as well as Jackson to build membership for the newly formed segregationist organization,

Women for Constitutional Government (WCG). All the while, from 1937 to 1982, she authored "Dis an' Dat," a how-to-preserve white supremacy column in Hodding Carter's *Delta Democrat* and later the *Jackson Clarion Ledger*.[9]

From the New Deal until the Reagan era, Mary Dawson Cain was owner, publisher, and columnist of Pike County Mississippi's the *Summit Sun*. Located in the Piney Woods region bordering Louisiana, Cain's hometown was in timber country. Married to a gas station owner, Cain had her own career and went to the office every day to put out her weekly paper. She was also a kind of conservative everywoman, working with political activists from Massachusetts to California to defeat prohibition, end Social Security, and oppose civil rights legislation. As a conservative among conservatives and a woman among men, she first ran for governor in 1951. She kept up her newspaper and her conservative crusades until her death in 1984.[10]

In the 1920s, Cornelia Dabney Tucker was widowed with four children and left in a financially precarious position in Charleston, South Carolina. Apolitical early, in 1937 she began a national campaign to oppose Roosevelt's court-packing plan and did not stop her efforts to shape the Supreme Court until her death in 1970. By World War II, she called herself "the first Republican southern belle" and spent much of her time looking north to the investors, vacationers, and businessmen who came to her hometown of Charleston to help her craft a politics that served a segregated South. She built relationships with Republican women in New England and the Midwest, and at the same time, she cultivated a long-lasting political partnership with the rabid segregationist senator from Mississippi, James Eastland. In 1938, she left the Democratic Party, worked to build a lily-white Republican Party, and then vacillated in her partisan loyalties before moving permanently into the New Right in the 1950s. Her political work pointed to early fissures in the Solid South.[11]

Broadly, the work of female segregationists occurred in four areas: social welfare policy implemented at a local level, public education, electoral politics, and popular culture. The household production of white supremacy coalesced around the efforts by white women to police the relationships and racial identities of their neighbors. To maintain the "color line," they drew on evidence gathered from their work as registrars, social workers, and teachers and provided by local knowledge, local history, and even rumor. In part, they linked the domestic and intimate matters of sex, marriage, childbirth, and childrearing to white supremacist politics. Noted southern author Lillian Smith recalled that when her mother taught her "to love God, to love our white skin, and to believe in the sanctity of both," she was performing a political act within the intimate confines of the family. Some of the lessons about segregation taught to black and white children were powerful and private, but they were not always private.[12] In the 1920s, white women assumed new roles in the body politic that allowed them to police physical and familial ties between black and white Americans. White supremacy became bureaucratized in a new social welfare infrastructure, and white women regulated intimate matters with the legitimacy of state sanction. In doing so, this new cadre of female workers translated their gender-specific authority as white mothers into public authority as workers for the state.[13]

White women also used public education to ensure that generations of children would be schooled in white supremacist politics. Just as black women understood that schools could be a place to counter the lessons of Jim Crow, white women crafted their own version of citizenship education for a Jim Crow world. As Katherine Charron's work on Septima Clark has shown, "The school as an institution proved essential to the maintenance of white supremacy," and white women provided lessons on the benefits of racial segregation and the work needed to keep it going.[14] When white women censored textbooks or movies, funded summer schools, or conducted essay contests, they upheld segregation through a broad public education that outlasted both legal segregation and its most vociferous proponents.[15]

Suffrage moved white women undeniably into electoral politics where they could use "the weight of their votes" to shape the worlds in which they lived.[16] They worked in primaries and party conventions. As partisan actors, they canvassed neighborhoods, registered folks to vote, and volunteered at the polls. Some even ran for office. Building on their local networks, electoral politics allowed segregationist women to parlay their grassroots political work into state and national policy. Using their votes and voices, they challenged national party platforms, organized the ouster of office holders who did not adhere to their segregationist vision, and mobilized their constituents to rally against domestic and foreign policies that they believed could erode the economic, political, and cultural power of southern whites. They built political platforms that translated political support for white supremacy into broader debates on national sovereignty, genocide, and the fate of developing nations. In the process, they boiled down communism, the rise of the United Nations, and decolonization into the substance of daily life and then offered instruction in how to combat those forces by watching out for what their children learned, whom they married, and even how they trick-or-treated.

White supremacist politics was also produced at the level of culture where the stories white women told reinforced the Jim Crow order. White women perpetuated customary segregation through a broader creation of a popular culture that constructed and celebrated white ethnicity as superior and separate from black ethnicity and that reified black stereotypes. Again and again, they employed their "culture talk" to remind southern whites of the benefits and privileges of white society. They also offered public commentary on the appropriate place of black people in American society, celebrating the black vernacular while diminishing black accomplishments in politics, high culture, and intellectual endeavors.[17] If black southerners were not named as often in the other areas of the production of white supremacy, they occupied central roles in white supremacist popular culture—as mammies, fieldworkers, happy go-lucky men and women, and manual laborers.

Despite white segregationist women's ubiquitous political work, scholars of massive resistance and southern segregation have rarely confronted them. Beyond New Orleans's cheerleaders or Little Rock's Mother's League, the white southern women who have more often been studied were supporters of the civil rights movement. The politics of Virginia Durr, Anne Braden, white Student Nonviolent Coordinating Committee workers, and Little Rock's Women's Emergency Committee, for example, have garnered scholarly attention.[18] The women who censored public school textbooks, raised money for the Civil War centennial, encouraged their children to participate in essay contests, and formed or joined segregationist organizations have, until recently, remained on the outskirts of the story. The reasons for this are twofold. In part, the scholarship has adopted a more top-down examination of massive resistance that focused on laws, congressmen, state legislators, and violent episodes covered by a national media. Recent studies of Jim Crow segregation, however, have taken a more local view and examined how white supremacist politics and Jim Crow laws manifested themselves in communities as diverse as Miami, Florida; rural Mississippi; and northern Virginia; but white women have often remained bit players.[19] Frequently, when white segregationist women have entered the historical narrative, their politics have been explained as either a result of an inherent racism or of their capitulation to patriarchal power that defined their lives, hiding their political independence. In contrast, conservative women outside the South have had their gender-based, class-based, and culturally derived aspects of their politics plumbed in order to explain how they contributed to the rise of anti-radicalism, anti-communism, and the New Right. Their racial politics—a politics often very much akin to that of their southern sisters—however, has been treated as an aberration or a side note of a more legitimate political platform. As a result, the term "segregationist," often freighted with a host of rural, retrograde, demagogic, and masculine meanings, has been reserved mostly for white southerners, disguising both the sophistication and breadth of white southern women's political work and by consequence the connections they cultivated with white supremacists nationwide. It often has also spared white conservative women the label of white supremacist. These scholarly gaps have disguised our ability to see white segregationist women's systematic and nationwide support for racial inequality and the dogged persistence of white supremacist politics, policies, and cultural practices in the decades before and after the civil rights movement.[20]

Focusing on segregationist women as grassroots activists in social welfare policy, public education, partisan politics, and popular culture reframes the story of massive resistance in several ways. First, white women's work exposes massive support for racial segregation that began long before *Brown* and stretches past its legislative dismantling in the 1960s. No longer limited to the years between *Brown* and the Voting Rights Act, massive resistance looks less like an agenda of reactionaries and more like a long-lived, sophisticated political program.[21] Rooted in the South, massive support for various Jim Crow systems never stays put but sends out its activists and its ideas to already active hosts across the nation. The grassroots organizing of white segregationist women becomes part and parcel of the twentieth-century political mobilization of women, linking massive resistance to political movements beyond the South's geographic boundaries. In the era of women's rising political activism, the longer movement of massive resistance was for many women their entrance into public politics and connected some of the South's leading female segregationists to postwar conservative activists. Instead of a defined moment or movement, massive resistance emerges as a kind of overarching defense of a white supremacist regime regularly reproducing support for racial segregation. It is a program that could be national in its reach but local in its practice and prosaic in its work. By looking at white segregationist women over half a century, this story exposes the endurance and shape-shifting capabilities of white resistance.

As the story is reframed, three narrative threads bind it together. At the biographical level, the book traces the political trajectory of four very different white women who worked for a Jim Crow order. Second, the book examines the symbiotic relationship between legal and customary segregation through the work white women did in social welfare, education, electoral politics, and culture. They knew that daily work on multiple levels was needed to sustain racial segregation and to shape resistance to racial equality. A third theme charts the political diversity and various political alliances that segregationist women cultivated. These networks contributed to the rise of early opposition to the New Deal State and later support for the New Right, its far-right wing, and national partisan realignments.

These stories encourage us at a minimum to reconsider and perhaps to cast aside several common practices: separating the limits of the civil rights movement from the persistent grassroots (and often female-led) organizing for white supremacy, segregating southern segregationist women from national segregationist conservatives, and sparing nationally prominent conservatives the label of segregationists. They also suggest that when we focus too much on national legislative victories over legal segregation, we miss the endurance of white supremacist politics and practices in local institutions, in local communities. The political languages white segregationist women employed, in particular, their experimentation with a color-blind conservatism in the rural and urban South means that the Sunbelt suburbs were not the only location for the germination of a new politics that disguised policies supporting racial inequality behind the language of property rights, law and order, good motherhood, and constitutional intent.[22] It also exposes how Jim Crow segregation remade itself decade after decade, courted a variety of political allies, and attracted diverse activists and followers. For too long, focusing on a narrow definition of massive resistance has left the nation ill-equipped to recognize the power of its grassroots persistence.

Moving from the 1920s into the 1970s, the book charts the long era of massive support for racial segregation and the white women who served as its crucial workforce. The chapters are organized around real or perceived threats to racial segregation as envisioned by its female advocates. When white southern women entered the polity, many did so with a pledge to uphold legal segregation, and for generations, female grassroots activists sustained and reproduced segregation in their communities.[23] Their constant work was so interwoven into daily life that it appeared unremarkable. As they worked, some invoked and shaped a particular brand of middle-class motherhood that married gender roles and devotion to racial segregation to a political platform of family autonomy and parental rights—a kind of white supremacist maternalism.[24] Others offered up a citizenship education reliant on racial separation that met, they believed, the nation's needs. Still others told stories that celebrated a Jim Crow order. Throughout the decades, they operated under a constant fear of threats to white supremacist politics and its accompanying Jim Crow system.

Part I told in four chapters examines the interwar period where the work of white segregationist women was shaped by more discrete, local or state-level threats. While they worked to sustain segregation, the reign of the Jim Crow order in the American South seemed relatively secure. The most significant threat to the system of segregation, white women believed, was the apathy of their white neighbors who failed to realize the constant work needed to sustain it.[25] The most dedicated female segregationists feared that white people would be fooled into believing that the all-white primary, the proliferation of segregation laws, stricter prohibitions on interracial marriage, the reluctance of the president or Congress to oppose lynching, the whitening of the Republican Party, and the decisions of the Supreme Court would be enough to secure segregation. Their white neighbors might believe the stories they were told—that segregation was natural and that black southerners were satisfied.

With white apathy constituting the most important threat to the system of racial segregation, the first four chapters uncover the stories of how female segregationists used social welfare institutions, public education, electoral politics, and popular culture to reinforce the Jim Crow order. Each chapter examines the work of segregationists related to one of these institutions in particular locations. Chapter 1 looks at the domestic production of white supremacy in Rockbridge and Amherst counties in western Virginia, where white female registrars, public welfare officers, and social work students did the daily work of cataloging racial identity according to Virginia's new Racial Integrity Law. Chapter 2 begins in Athens, Georgia, and explores how debates on curriculum, textbooks, and teacher training shaped racial segregation. Chapter 3 examines the partisan political organizing of three women in black majority areas. In Mississippi's Delta and Piney Woods regions and in the South Carolina low country, white women—Florence Sillers Ogden, Mary Dawson Cain, and Cornelia Dabney Tucker— weighed in on local and state partisan politics in order to mobilize women and men to uphold segregation through their political parties. Chapter 4 explores the cultural production of white supremacy through the stories—fiction and non-fiction—that the liberal white supremacist Nell Battle Lewis told in the *Raleigh News and Observer* and other public forums.

World War II challenged their work on all levels by introducing discernible regionwide, national, and even international threats to their system. With World War II, the work of southern segregationist women fundamentally shifted, and the war served as a dividing line between massive support for racial segregation and massive white resistance and between the specific communities featured in Part I and broader regional and national concerns that frame Part II. The postwar period led to regional political discussions and rich opportunities for exchange with segregationists across the South and nation. As the South's female segregationists grappled with regional, national, and international calls for a loosening, if not an eradication, of the Jim Crow order, their political conversations coalesced around common threats, even if the intensity of alarm differed from the Black Belt to the Upper South.[26]

From World War II on, the South's female segregationists tried to invigorate support for the system by praising racial segregation but also by cultivating various critiques of political institutions seen as antithetical to both the South's system of segregation and to conservative political ideology in general. Segregation's activists still believed that their white neighbors were too complacent or too moderate in their commitment to racial segregation, but this apathy was accompanied by growing concern that the system was weakening under an onslaught of new threats: the growing "warfare state," expansion of the electorate, competing historical narratives, vigilante violence, black out-migration, the internationalism of the United Nations (UN), and shifting priorities of state and federal governments. The threats to the system turned former allies in segregationist politics into enemies. Demographic shifts had escalated a southern diaspora that intensified during the war. Rising numbers of southern and northern members of the National Association for the Advancement of Colored People (NAACP), black men in military uniforms, black women moving from domestic service to the industrial working class, and black community organizers who challenged white sexual violence alarmed segregation's white activists and led to a new political calculus in the Democratic Party. The mobilization of African Americans forced the federal government to uphold non-discriminatory hiring policies in war industries through the creation of the Fair Employment Practices Commission (FEPC) at the same time that NAACP lawyers challenged the South's restrictive voting system. Labor policies and the Court's decision in *Smith v. Allwright* further alarmed many southern whites who feared that the federal government was no longer on their side. Domestically, Eleanor and Franklin D. Roosevelt and the Democratic Party that they led, white women felt, imperiled racial segregation. Faced with such seismic national shifts, white complacency remained a serious but no longer the most significant or singular threat. Part II of this book examines how the South's female segregationists harnessed their work in social welfare, education, electoral politics, and cultural production to combat what they understood as diverse postwar threats to white supremacist politics—a faltering Democratic Party, an invasive United Nations, an interventionist Supreme Court, and eventually a widespread mobilization of black southerners.

Chapter 5 examines how during World War II segregationist women focused their political efforts on the federal betrayal of white supremacist politics rather than black organizing. They began a long campaign against the executive branch and the Democratic Party. Advertising the failure of partisan politics and the men who ran it, they cataloged the sins of Democrats—southern and nationwide. They cultivated support for segregation by building distrust in the Democratic Party. World War II constitutes the moment when the Democratic Party existed as both the last hope *and* the next threat to the white South. Segregationist women encouraged the election of hardline segregationists and experimentation with partisan dissent, contributing to the rise of the Dixiecrats, the demonization of Henry Wallace, and the defeat of moderate senators in 1950 and 1952.

International threats to white supremacy proliferated with the advent of the Cold War and are the subject of Chapter 6. During the height of the Cold War, segregationist women publicized the threats that international institutions and their political allies posed to racial segregation and to national sovereignty. Focusing on the United Nations and the anti-communist crusade, white southern segregationist women found the opportunity to construct black activism as the result of outside agitation and infiltration, not homegrown organic political organizing. The reactions of white segregationist women to a new conversation on human rights led them in the spring of 1954 to support the Bricker Amendment, a proposed constitutional amendment requiring state legislatures, not the Senate, to approve international treaties. Those fearful of the erosion of states' rights and an erosion of national sovereignty joined those fearful of the decline of racial segregation to argue that the people best situated to protect the nation from internationalists and integrationists were found in state, not federal, office.[27] Couching the UN as a threat to national security, states' rights, and family autonomy, these women drew parallels between attacks on southern style white supremacy and a UN-inspired world where white-ruled nations such as the United States were bent under the weight of the developing, left-leaning, non-white world. The anti-communist crusade that grew out of this Cold War configuration gave white southern women the chance to connect their local politics of white supremacy to a larger conservative political movement, imbuing their daily work for segregation with national as well as international importance.[28]

Chapter 7 begins with the 1954 *Brown* decision and ends with the Southern Manifesto in 1956. Long able to influence public schools, their curriculum, and the children who attended them, white women now faced a direct threat to what they understood to be their private, public, and political authority and their versions of family life and citizenship education. In the wake of *Brown*, they made the family the center of political life and political ideology, with parental authority threatened by a leviathan federal government. They offered a nascent version of racialized family values. Viewing schools as an extension of their home and a place where they wielded particular authority, many white segregationist women claimed that because school integration eroded their ability to secure the benefits of white supremacy for their children it compromised their ability to be good mothers. This political language minimized racial identity and replaced it with a particular gender identity, prioritizing motherhood while burying how whiteness shaped their understanding of it. *Brown* destroyed the fiction so central to racial segregation's reign—that black southerners were content with segregation, were incited only by outsiders, and were politically malleable. It also put black children at the forefront of the conversation, forcing white segregationist women to forego a maternalist language directed at black families in their communities.

In the years after *Brown*, white women were devoted to making white youth political activists and future purveyors of white supremacy even as the legal support for segregation diminished. Chapter 8 examines the continued efforts for racial segregation after the forced federal integration of Central High School in Little Rock, Arkansas. Amid the cacophony of racist rants, many white segregationists focused on training white youth to sustain racial segregation and gradually amplified their color-blind political rhetoric. While moderate voices directed the implementation of integration, southern segregationist women continued to work in various ways and with various political constituencies to secure resistance to racial equality and meaningful integration. If absolute segregation was the mark of victory for supporters of massive resistance, then these years could be seen as the denouement of a movement. But even as the outward expressions of the Jim Crow South faded, the essay contests, the color-blind political language, curriculum debates, and youth programs remained as did those who were raised to follow that vision. Some white conservative segregationists still worked for an updated version of white over black, but they also moved into the emerging New Right and some deeper into the far right, where they constructed a new political homes. Employing a politicized formulation of motherhood, white segregationists across the ideological spectrum practiced a politics that emphasized performing whiteness as synonymous with "good" womanhood, cultivating a politics that minimized their racial identity and privileged their identity as parents and mothers, to continue to sustain various degrees of racial segregation, in practice, if not in law. The end of de jure segregation in no way meant the end of de facto. The lessons that arose from decades of work had taught them that.

After nearly two decades of resistance to school integration, courts across the country demanded its implementation and supported busing and school redistricting as a means to accomplish it. The last chapter moves to the urban North and explores the political similarities and ties between the most committed southern segregationists and those white women who protested busing in the 1970s. Most Americans, including white women and men across the nation who had supported *Brown*, resisted this new government intrusion into their parental authority, their property values, and their vision of school choice. As Mississippi's Florence Sillers Ogden had predicted, when racial integration came on a yellow school bus and threatened to reorder the daily lives of northern and western urban white women, these women reacted much like the South's segregationists. Women's organizations in Boston and Detroit looked South for models of resistance. They were also segregationists, working for various iterations of racial separation in their public schools. Boston's Louise Day Hicks and her supporters echoed the "Cheerleaders" of New Orleans's Ninth Ward, the women of working-class neighborhoods in Nashville, and the mothers in Little Rock. Across the nation, law made busing a reality, while white women's opposition on the ground eroded the power of its implementation.[29]

The terms "segregationist" and "conservative" fill this story and deserve some definition. All the women I write about are segregationists, at least some of the time. They are not all conservatives, and certainly, they are not all conservatives all of the time. Segregationist refers to people, predominantly white southern women in this book but also white women in Boston, Pasadena, Chicago, and Detroit, who work to maintain a system that separates white and black Americans in public life, public institutions, popular culture, and customary practices. Segregationists drew on a democratic politics that upheld white supremacy in various forms, that denied black Americans equal opportunity, and that invoked constructions of race to order society. Segregationist defines people who adhere to policies and politics that further that agenda. Jim Crow's advocates did not look the same all the time. Place and time shaped the particular contours of their segregationist politics. For decades, a segregationist could be a progressive, a liberal, a New Dealer, a conservative, a member of the Old or New Right, or a moderate, a hardliner, a Democrat, a Republican, or an Independent. Unmooring the definition of segregationist from a specific region and time and instead linking the definition to political action and rhetoric, I hope, will be an important contribution of this book.

If this history broadens the use of the term "segregationist," it also reminds us that we need not homogenize American conservatism to recognize that the white supremacist politics of southern segregationist women was a variant of grassroots conservative politics that operated nationwide and among some acolytes for the New Right. Conservative describes a larger political platform and a group of activists who supported policies that changed over time. In the interwar period, conservatives railed against the income tax, the New Deal and New Deal programs (unless they were Delta planters), internationalism, immigration, and dilution of an "American" identity. After World War II, conservative women crusaded against radicalism and communism and the United Nations. Many supported an anemic federal budget, restricted voting rights, state, not federal, control of political and civil rights, sacrosanct property rights, and states' rights. In terms of public education, conservative women campaigned against the influence of John Dewey's progressive pedagogy, rejected multiculturalism in the classroom, opposed the creation of a federal department of education, and remained wed to a curriculum centered on American exceptionalism. They insisted that public schools were an extension of their homes and should reflect their values exclusively, upholding parental authority and patriotism. For the chronological scope of this book, conservatives occupied wings of both the Democratic and Republican parties, although they began a slow departure from the Democratic Party during World War II. Many conservatives also supported white supremacist politics and fought for some version of a racial hierarchy, even if they attributed their support to a belief in states' rights, a dedication to anti-communism, or an opposition to anti-colonialism.[30] For the most part, these various iterations of conservatism did not embrace the Christian fundamentalism that came with the maturation of the New Right. However, debates over prayer in schools and sex education in which some segregationists and conservatives participated suggested that the role of religion in public life would become an important part of the New Right's agenda.[31] Resembling the multidimensional and dynamic nature of the Jim Crow order, conservatism drew its meaning as much from the particular concerns of a specific place and time as it did from ideology.

Segregationists lived across the nation, they talked to each other, exchanged political strategies, and built a local and a national politics for a postwar world. They worked consistently to circumvent the larger politics of racial equality. The southern diaspora that defined much of the twentieth century and that escalated in World War II included the migration of white southerners raised and schooled in the politics of Jim Crow. White supremacist politics were not simply southern politics that arrived on the backs of southern migrants, however; they were of the nation and were not practiced solely by those on the far right. Mainstream conservatives could espouse white supremacist ideas but still believe that a democratic government was the way to ensure white over black. In many ways, the language we have used—conservatives for some, segregationists for others—has functioned to mask a national commitment to different configurations of a Jim Crow nation. This has homogenized segregationists and systems of segregation, left them in the South, and cordoned them off in the civil rights era. This intellectual segregation has made it harder to understand how white supremacist politics has replenished itself, bearing fruit in community after community long after the nation's professed commitment to equality. As Lewis, Cain, Ogden, Tucker, and their networks teach us, white supremacist politics were both of the South and of the nation.[32]

These national networks and connections persisted and strengthened over the twentieth century, but they did not erase some real differences between a region and a nation. Cain, Ogden, Tucker, and Lewis identified as southern, acknowledged specific circumstances that they deemed southern, and worked on a political landscape in which the construction of white womanhood served multiple purposes. The South's female segregationists operated simultaneously as part of the national political fabric and in a particular southern political context crafted out of particular historical circumstances and stories. In the midst of the Jim Crow era, Ralph Ellison wrote, "Southern whites cannot walk, talk, sing, conceive of laws or justice, think of sex, love, the family or freedom without responding to the presence of Negroes." Southern white women lived where a southern legal code made hundreds of claims on the lives of black and white, where the political system disenfranchised black and white opposition, and where an intellectual culture erased powerful stories of segregation's implementation. These conditions bolstered their activism and shaped the political strategies and rhetoric that they employed. In sustaining and shaping their Jim Crow system, they often spoke in a language of southern history to southern audiences, but not always.[33]

Long before the federal government crafted its opposition to legal discrimination and long after it announced its victory over legal segregation, white women helped to sustain segregation at a local level. Disappointed by the integration of schools and the expansion of voting rights, among other policies, they did not quit. With them at the center, massive resistance is no longer solely about maintaining lily-white schools; rather, it is about sustaining white supremacist politics through a system, however modified, of racial segregation. Responding to local conditions and opportunities, a diverse group of segregationists who differed in terms of dedication, singleness of purpose, partisan allegiance, and strategies sustained the Jim Crow order. Focusing only on the hardline segregationists and not those who spoke in a color-blind language or those who found fertile ground outside of the far right makes us miss the widespread commitment to racial segregation and the various ways it continued. Decade after decade, even in the face of apparent defeat, white women remade the Jim Crow order, in part by training new generations of activists and adherents. Their history taught them that white supremacist politics could meet changing political winds to find diverse political allies and court support across the political spectrum. Their work remained important and often beyond federal purview. Their experience told them that white supremacist politics enacted on a local level—in school board decisions, in teacher training, in bureaucratic categorizations, in public welfare policies, and in historical narratives—would prove more difficult to uproot and eradicate than national or even state-level policies.

Massive resistance in the hands of white women also exposes the limits of the iconography the nation has preserved about segregation—a lynched boy, white and colored water fountain signs, Rosa Parks sitting on a bus, and George Wallace standing in the schoolhouse door. Without diminishing the profound importance of these events, these images often elide the fact that racial segregation affected people's lives in vastly different ways. White supremacist women re-created the signs of racial segregation generation after generation, but they often did not take center stage in the media drama that played out on the nation's televisions. These literal signs of segregation, so intrinsic to the story of civil rights and American freedom, do play a powerful role in the history told about the civil rights movement, in part, because they were removed, offering up a story of redemption. But the other markers of a segregated nation stubbornly remained, weeds in our democratic garden. The history of the civil rights movement and the nation must expand to include the stories of everyday opposition—the white women who created a Jim Crow history in the nation's textbooks, the social workers who participated in racial categorization limiting the opportunities for individuals for most of the twentieth century, the students who benefited from a college scholarship earned because of a first-rate essay on maintaining racial segregation, and a mother walking a kindergartner to school that is evidence of de jure, not de facto, integration.

In the end, the history of massive resistance that emerges out of six decades of white women's activism looks different in terms of chronology, duration, geographic boundaries, and political purpose. Working largely outside the realm of vigilante violence and outside the offices where Jim Crow's legislation was written, white women, nevertheless sustained and shaped the nation's racial caste system at the community level. From their homes, newspapers, civic organizations, and social welfare offices, they made sure that their white neighbors knew that daily vigilance was the cost of a white supremacist political order. They participated first in massive support for racial segregation and later, when it was threatened, massive resistance. White women were and remained segregation's constant gardeners.

# PART I

# Massive Support for Racial Segregation, 1920–1941

# I

## *The Color Line in Virginia*

### THE HOME-GROWN PRODUCTION
### OF WHITE SUPREMACY

IN 1924, a twenty-eight-year-old, single, white schoolteacher and local registrar, Margaret Aileen Goodman, ran into trouble when she tried to register Mr. William Clark of Rockbridge County, Virginia, under the rules of
the state's new Racial Integrity Act (RIA).[1] According to the law, individuals
seeking marriage or those born after 1912 had to certify their racial identity
with local officials. The law did not change the definition of black, which
had moved in 1912 from one-quarter "black blood" to one-sixteenth "black
blood," but it did change the criteria for whiteness—not one drop of non-
white blood. Except for those select few Virginians who celebrated their
connection to Pocahontas, any other Indian ancestry translated into a black
identity. Ostensibly, this hard dichotomy reified the color line by continuing
the ban on interracial marriages and preventing the children of those marriages from shifting racial identities and "passing" (as white).[2] Clark did not
claim Pocahontas as an ancestor, but he was part of a community of people
who had been pejoratively called "free issue," "isshys," or "little people"—
names that indicated an indeterminate racial identity and a "colored but free
past."[3] The RIA eliminated the recognition of individuals with black, white,
and Indian ancestors, and Goodman had to classify her neighbors as either
white or black. When Clark, whose family had been classified as alternately
mulatto and white in earlier census records, met Goodman, she told him
that his family was not Indian; they were not white; they were black. Clark
resisted the categorization, and she reported his insubordination to Walter
Plecker, her state supervisor, head of the Bureau of Vital Statistics, and one of
the architects of the RIA.[4]

Goodman's confrontation with Clark pushed her into a maelstrom of local history, political realities, and evolving state policies. Goodman had grown up just down the mountain from the Irish Creek community, home of Clark and a number of families whose racial identities were fluid. Irish Creek lay just below the ridgeline that formed the border between the counties of Amherst and Rockbridge.[5] On each slope were communities whose history reached back to the 1750s when three white traders settled in the Blue Ridge Mountains and married Indian and black, perhaps enslaved, women. Their progeny lived in scattered communities—Bear Mountain and Pedlar Creek in Amherst County and Irish Creek in Rockbridge County—that drew on a free black, white, slave, Cherokee, and Siouan past. Nineteenth-century census records confirmed that families with the surnames Clark, Branham, Sorrels, Johns, and Redcross, among others, had traveled between Indian, "mulatto," white, and black categories.[6] The RIA, however, gave no credence to complex pasts and complicated family trees. Thus, Goodman found herself at the intersection of her community's particular racial practices, the Clarks' interracial past, and Virginia's expanding state bureaucracy.

Goodman reached this crossroads as a child of the Jim Crow South. She was born in 1896, the same year that the Supreme Court decided the landmark case *Plessy v. Ferguson*, which upheld state racial segregation laws for public facilities, establishing the doctrine of "separate but equal." She had come of age when Virginia had passed segregation laws for trains, schools, restaurants, and even prison cafeterias. Each fall, she readied her classroom to teach her allegedly all-white students in an all-white school. In 1920, Goodman and other women cast their first votes, and Virginia's most active period of segregation legislation commenced.[7] When Virginia passed the RIA, it hardened racial lines and overturned more than a century of racial categorizations based on the racial identity of a single great-grandparent or grandparent. When Goodman faced Clark, she had to take into account local history and practices or loyalty to the Jim Crow state.

She chose the state. In writing her letter to Plecker, Goodman invited state intervention and performed vital work for racial segregation.[8] The letter acknowledged the power of a Progressive Era bureaucracy to create an American racial state and Virginia's requirement that its workers maintain the color line. Why Goodman participated in such an endeavor remained unclear. The correspondence about the Clarks failed to tell whether Goodman's act arose from a deep devotion to white supremacist ideology, an inclination for bureaucratic officiousness, or a tendency to follow authority figures. But her 1924 letter as well as one nineteen years later noting that the Clarks continued resistance to a classification of "colored" or "mulatto" pointed to her lengthy commitment to shoring up a biracial world.[9] For nearly two decades, Goodman did not defy Dixie's color line.

Goodman's embrace of racial standardization put her in the company of other white women, who as new bureaucrats embarked on the sorting out of the American population according to race, ethnicity, delinquency, and mental fitness. Goodman joined women like Mildred Covert whose field-work imposed racial classifications and criminality on California's non-white youth as well as "marriage reformers" from Arizona to Georgia, who turned licensing registrars into the "gatekeepers of white supremacy."[10] Goodman's letters also pointed to the patriarchal relationships replicated by the state whereby women on the ground implemented policies crafted by male offi-cials, earning professional accolades, community authority, and some income. For Goodman and others, new state authority born of the Progressive Era had created zones of racial work at the same time it created economic opportuni-ties for many white middle-class women.[11]

Women did more than work for the state. In the quest for racial purity, white women constituted both the subjects of racial integrity and its labor force.[12] Women's bodies were the landscape on which the policing of racial intermixing often took place. If protected from interracial liaison, contem-porary race scientists argued, white women would purify and invigorate the nation. If white women sought out sexual liaisons with non-white men, however, they could also serve as potential transgressors, ruining racial purity and by consequence enervating the nation. Beyond their reproduc-tive capacity to strengthen or weaken the nation, eugenicists argued that women carried in their very genetic makeup the power to recognize race mixing.[13] They were vital to the enforcement of racial purity. The fact that women often had the most access to and knowledge of the places where this racial classification would occur—the bedroom, the birthing room, and the classroom—enhanced their alleged genetic proclivity for detecting "mixed-race" individuals. The midwife had to certify race on birth certificates. Jim Crow state policy instructed the white schoolteacher to report to the school superintendent's office children she suspected of mixed-race heritage. The social worker recorded the racial identities of the families with whom she worked, deciding race based on a host of behavioral and hereditary observa-tions often mixed with a dose of local gossip. The local registrar had to turn in marriage licenses to each state's Bureau of Vital Statistics. The RIA and accompanying eugenic legislation nationwide created public policies that required enforcement by those with familiar female faces.

These jobs fell mostly to women. In the 1920s, between 80 percent and 90 percent of elementary schoolteachers were women.[14] At the time Virginia's RIA became law, there were 6,000 registered midwives and only 1,500 physicians in the state.[15] And women, like Goodman, constituted a significant percentage of the local registrars, public welfare superintendents, and nurses. These statistics signified that white, college-educated women would have to participate in the actual cartography of race. With access to local knowledge and to institutions central to the sorting out of race, women designated racial lines, labeled families, and drew boundaries around black and white in their communities. In doing so, white women made decisions that would affect families for the rest of the century.[16]

The 1924 correspondence between Plecker and Goodman testified to the collusion and cross pollination between Progressive Era state-building and white supremacist politics. From New York's Eugenics Record Office and New Jersey's Vineland Institute to California's Department of Research and Virginia's flagship university, biologists, social scientists, educators, and criminologists in the 1920s offered new theories on race, disease, intelligence, human development, and delinquency that had coalesced into national discussions on citizenship and "race betterment."[17] Popular literature by Madison Grant, Lothrop Stoddard, and others bolstered these research endeavors and made available to the masses concerns over "race mixing" and its alleged role in the hereditary decline of Americans as well as an emergent discourse on race and criminality.[18] Goodman's work in policing the color line exemplified the bestowing of the authority of scientific and "pseudo-scientific" expertise on white women in local communities.[19] Through her work as registrar, Goodman joined a legion of white women who used the new progressive state to give shape to racial segregation on the ground, translating legislation into local practice. Involved in regulating marriage, they worked in such routine and largely invisible ways that the state came to be an expected participant in the most intimate and personal of matters—the making of families. White segregationist women had assumed crucial roles in the domestic production of a white supremacist state.[20]

But in the case of these Blue Ridge mountain communities, local conditions complicated the work of schoolteachers, midwives, and registrars, who were charged with preventing "passing." On the surface, the cultural geography of racial separation in these mountain counties seemed to reinforce the provisions of the RIA. The mountaintops of Rockbridge and Amherst rose above two colleges—Washington and Lee and Virginia Military Institute—where the young white men who attended and the black men and

## REGISTRATION OF BIRTH AND COLOR

Full name .................................................................................................................
(Given name first.  Give full maiden name if married woman or widow.)

Place of birth ...................................................................................... sex..........................

Date of Birth

Name of Husband ...............................................................................................................
(If married woman or widow)

Father
    Full name ........................................................................................................

    Birth place ................................................................ *Color..........................
Mother
    Full maiden name ..........................................................................

    Birth place ................................................................ *Color..........................
Remarks:


*A white person is one with no trace whatever of blood of another race, except that one
with one-sixteenth of the blood of American Indian, unmixed with other race, may be classed as
white.                                             Form 59—3-17-24—65M.


    I hereby affirm that I believe the statements as to color of parents on the
other side of this card are correct and that I am signing this with the knowledge
that the penalty for making a false statement as to color is one year in the peniten-
tiary.

Signature of registrant .........................................................................................

Address of registrant .........................................................................................

Witness to signature .........................................................................................

Address of witness .........................................................................................

*Signature of physician .........................................................................................

If not signed by registrant state kinship of signer.........................................

Place of filing .......................................................... Date of filing.........................

    If the person signing statement cannot write, he or she must make a mark
between the given name and the last name, Thus:  his (her)
*If the doctor present at birth                 JOHN  X  DOE
signs, it will be accepted as to age
for labor, school, etc.                            mark

**FIGURES 1.1 AND 1.2** The birth and color registration form for Virginians under the
Racial Integrity Act. Midwives and doctors submitted these to Virginia's Bureau of Vital
Statistics. Arthur Estabrook Papers, M. E. Grenander Department of Special Collections
and Archives, Albany, State University of New York.

women who served them there—were immersed in the commemoration of
the Confederate past. Local school curricula celebrated native son Samuel
Houston's fight for Texan independence and slavery's expansion, Stonewall
Jackson's sacrifices for the Confederacy, and Robert E. Lee's leadership of the
Army of Virginia. Looking eastward, residents could gaze at the University of
Virginia (the southern eugenics research hub) and the Lynchburg Colony for
the Epileptic and Feebleminded, both institutions that translated new race

science into mental and public health policies that embedded class and race prejudices in the modern state.[21]

Cultural geography aside, the logic of making a Jim Crow state defied the logic of the individual pasts of the Clarks and others.[22] The lived experiences of families residing along Bear Mountain and Irish Creek offered lessons in generational histories of mixed-race communities. Local stories, the census, and court records contradicted a rigid dichotomy of white and black and testified to a history of resistance that Goodman and others faced when they tried to categorize people. Families consisted of sisters who were blond and fair-skinned, brothers with olive complexions and dark straight hair, and cousins who were dark-skinned with curly hair. Within nuclear families, census takers had categorized members as white, black, mulatto, and Indian, and individuals had claimed to be black, tri-racial, Cherokee, and later Monacan—a state, but not federally, recognized Virginia native tribe tracing its origins to 1607.[23] Some family members added an "e" to their last name to deny kinship with their darker relatives and reinforce their whiteness.[24] For those state officials in the 1920s who were trying to create a biracial world, the realities of the region and its past provoked those dedicated to an unambiguous color line.[25]

For Rockbridge County's Clarks, the RIA was just the most recent in a long line of racially restrictive policies that incited their resistance. In the 1840s, various Clarks had challenged the 1823 Virginia law that designated Indians and blacks as mulatto and then prevented marriages between mulattos and whites. In 1845, 1864, and 1875, several members of the Clark family went to court and won the legal label of white on their marriage licenses. But courtroom decisions did not always translate into local practice. In 1890, a W. M. Clark, legally categorized as "white," applied to the Rockbridge County school board to send his children to a local white school. The school board claimed that the Clarks were believed to be part "Negro," and for the good of the community and the schools, they could not admit his children. Refusing to attend a black school, Clark's children did not attend public schools for several decades. In 1921, the school board received a petition from members of the Mountain View school asking that those students suspected of mixed blood be removed from classrooms. Citing legal counsel, the board denied the petition, but the debate spoke to the community's willingness to police the color line. Three years later, if the school board chose to dismiss children suspected of having mixed-race heritage, they would have the force of state law behind them.[26]

William Clark would not be the only resident to challenge the state's workers over racial integrity. The census documented the fluid racial identities of many families on Irish Creek and Bear Mountain. In demographic terms, Rockbridge and the neighboring county of Amherst were similar to the state as a whole, which had a population of about 58 percent white, 36 percent black, and 8 percent mulatto, a category that also included Native Americans and those black and white citizens with Native American ancestors.[27] A look at two families, however, revealed how the implementation of segregation promised to be chaotic if not impossible. The 1880 US Census listed William Clark, a thirty-year-old mulatto resident of the South River district (of which Irish Creek was a part), as the husband of a mulatto woman.[28] The 1880 census also listed the Clark's six children as mulattos. In 1900, census workers eliminated the mulatto designation and also did not list an Indian identity. When they returned to the Clark home, the same William was listed as white, as was his wife and their three children who remained at home. His mother, Margaret Clark, had also moved from mulatto to white. By 1910, William's eight grandchildren living in his home were also listed as white.[29] The Johns families of neighboring Amherst County had a similar history of racial categorization. While earlier censuses had listed the Amherst County Johns as white, mulatto, and black, in 1900, all sixteen Johns were black, and ten years later all twenty Johns were labeled mulatto. Ten years later five Johns were mulatto, sixteen were Indian, and two were black.[30] Kate Johns, a midwife, was black in the 1900 census, mulatto in 1910, and reappeared in 1930 as Indian.[31] Shifting census categories explained some of the racial slides, but the census also revealed a racial fluidity that challenged the hard lines that a Jim Crow world mandated and that dismayed proponents of eugenics. The RIA's denial of those histories set the stage for multiple confrontations.[32]

By 1924, federal Indian law complicated the already messy politics of racial identity. Passed the same year as Virginia's RIA, the Indian Citizenship Act made Native Americans living in federally recognized Indian nations US citizens with the right to vote. The Citizenship Act did not apply to those of Native ancestry in western Virginia, as they were not a federally recognized tribe. And the nation-building among Native Americans like the Cherokee and the Choctaw in the Jim Crow era had meant drawing lines between Indian citizens and "black Indians" often in the language of blood quantum, in effect denying those with black, white, and Indian ancestors the right to Native identity. Banned from full membership in Native nations, mixed-race individuals living outside federally recognized nations were also denied the full rights of US citizenship. But for the enforcers of whiteness in Virginia, "passing as Indian" had nothing to do with Native politics or tribal sovereignty; they saw it as merely the first step in a long-term strategy to "pass as white."[33]

Amid such racial fluidity, white women worked to draw the lines that prevented passing, and their work ranged from recording identities on state documents to propagating the intellectual justifications for racial separation. At the ideological level, Richmond resident Louise Burleigh was at the center of Virginia's white supremacist politics. A Radcliffe-educated New Englander, Burleigh had met John Powell—Richmond resident, classical pianist, and the 1922 founder of the Anglo-Saxon Clubs of America (ASCOA)—through their common commitment to uphold white supremacy through the arts. Burleigh claimed that her touring plays from Richmond's Little Theater League "helped to spread the message that Anglo-Saxonism was the taproot of American civilization." By 1931, she and Powell had organized the White Top Mountain Folk Festival to celebrate Anglo-Saxon folk songs as America's true music tradition, rejecting black music and musicians as "inferior mimicry."[34]

Outside the arts, their political collaboration centered on the ASCOA, where they worked with University of Virginia biology professor and eugenicist, Ivey Lewis, and Virginia's state registrar Walter Plecker. They also sought the support of Amy Garvey, wife of black nationalist Marcus Garvey—both of whom advocated racial separatism—aligning a white supremacist organization with a black nationalist one. Claiming a few black nationalist supporters, the Anglo-Saxon clubs fancied themselves a more rational and learned counterpart to the KKK, even though the officers (all men) who held positions in the Richmond chapter had also been KKK members. Burleigh carried out much of the organizational work for the association.[35] She disseminated literature about the potential decline of white civilization, was a ghost writer for the eugenics books of realtor turned world traveler Earnest Cox, and lobbied tirelessly for the 1924 RIA. She supported follow-up legislation mandating segregation at all public performances and hoped to expand the power of the Bureau of Vital Statistics. She was also a member of Virginia's Board of Censors, where she policed interracial sexual transgressions in film and notified ASCOA members of censors she felt were too lenient in their approval of white and black cinematic relationships. She embodied what historian Gregory Dorr called "the larger masculinist ideals of segregation's science—men talked, women worked."[36]

Beyond the ASCOA, Burleigh was an important link between Richmond's elite white women and the eugenics movement. She played an instrumental role in encouraging some of Richmond's leading ladies to join the Women's Racial Integrity Club (WRIC). The forty-three members drummed up support for the RIA, often referring to the scientific evidence that "justi-fied" eugenics. WRIC member Mrs. Smith Brockenbrough requested leave from her classroom to meet with Powell to discuss lobbying strategies for the RIA. Leaders of the WRIC and the Colonial Dames invited Powell to speak about the importance of the legislation. Another WRIC member Dr. Mary Baughmann tried to convince the American Eugenics Society to have its annual meeting in Richmond, which would have added national legitimacy to Virginia's RIA crusade.[37]

While elite Richmond women lobbied for legislation, undergraduate women from Sweet Briar College in Amherst applied their academic knowl-edge to fieldwork as they recorded racial identities and traits of local resi-dents in their journals. In the early 1920s, Arthur Estabrook, a researcher for the Eugenics Record Office of the Carnegie Institute of Washington, had turned south to research "mental defectives" and to strengthen his evidence for eugenic sterilization as a cost-saving measure for state governments.[38] He called on three Amherst County women—former resident and Red Cross worker Louisa Hubbard, a former Bear Mountain missionary worker Isabel Wagner, and a nurse Miss Theresa Ambler—to help him track down women amenable to such work. Writing from her Red Cross office in Greenville, North Carolina, Hubbard provided him with a list of women contacts, including Sweet Briar College students.[39] Estabrook acted on her suggestions and collaborated with sociologist Ivan McDougle to train white undergradu-ates to conduct research on the deleterious effects of white, black, and Indian mixing in western Virginia counties.

The Sweet Briar students followed the methods articulated by the Eugenics Record Office (ERO) in Cold Springs Harbor, New York. There eugenicists like Charles Davenport argued that women's power of intuition and emotional sensitivity made them more adept at judging and assessing the feebleminded and detecting bad "germplasm," a supposed biological product of interracial mixing.[40] The ERO trained more than 250 fieldworkers, 85 per-cent of them women, to take pictures, conduct interviews, study appearances, compile family histories, and translate opinion on ancestry and behavior into scientific judgments about racial identity.[41] Seven of the Sweet Briar students trained as fieldworkers for eugenics work, including Gwendolyn Watson, Martha Lobingier, and Eleanor Harned, who earned the title of "investiga-tors" for their detailed survey of Amherst families living on Bear Mountain.[42] These young women recorded the size and condition of homes and the com-plexion of children as well as the family's religious practices, literacy, clean-liness, sexual behaviors, income, and work ethic. As aspiring social workers, they collected demographic data and counted, categorized, and disciplined bodies for the state.[43]

McDougle, Estabrook, and the Sweet Briar students also sought out locals to assist in their research. Calling on the Bear Mountain Mission teachers, they turned to a profession long central to the Jim Crow project. As early as 1908, Virginia's Board of Charities and Corrections had sent a survey about "defectives" to public schoolteachers who were to mark behaviors that indicated signs of inbreeding. In addition to spasms and pilfering, the checklist included "carelessness, indolence, and excessive exaggerations."[44] In the 1920s, the Bear Mountain Mission teachers continued this work for the state by describing the "character" of non-white children when they spoke to the fieldworkers.[45] The researchers administered the Stanford-Binet intelligence

I.E. McDougle
Gwendolyn Watson
Martha Lobingier
Eleanor Harned.

"The Investigators."

FIGURE 1.3 "The Investigators." Sweet Briar students in Ivan McDougle's sociology class who conducted the fieldwork in the Amherst county community of Bear Mountain and contributed their research to *Mongrel Virginians*. Arthur Estabrook Papers, M. E. Grenander Department of Special Collections and Archives, Albany, State University of New York.

tests to eleven students, but their most helpful information came from a chart made with the help of classroom teachers that categorized all the children in 1923 and 1924. Among the fifty-five students listed in a chart on capabilities, nine students were described as "fairly capable," "capable," and "average"; twenty-two as "hopeless," "stupid," "feeble-minded," and "dull." Twenty escaped with no added description. In measuring academic performance, four students were deemed "very poor" in schoolwork, twenty-seven as "poor," and nineteen as "fair." Of all the students, only four earned a "good." The single student receiving a "very good" for schoolwork was the only eighteen-year-old, and the teacher described him as "slow mentally," mastering only fifth grade material.[46] In these field notes, students, nurses, teachers, and social workers noted that "in the main they [mixed-race residents] were a defective lot."[47]

In 1926, Arthur Estabrook and Ivan McDougle published this research in *Mongrel Virginians*. The book's subjects resided in the fictional "Coon Mountain" and "Buck Hollow" in Ab County, Virginia, located near Lynchburg, next to an Episcopal mission. The racial classifications reflected typologies used nationwide and were as plentiful as they were unscientific. They included "Indian-negro," "predominately negro," "colored," "typical Indian," "negro-white mixture," "copper colored," "practically white," "the same appearance as a person tanned by the sun," "skin light but spotted like a mulatto," "whiter," and "white." Comments on complexion slid into assessments of behaviors. For example, "Bessie Jones . . . with black hair, dark brown eyes but light skin, of very poor mentality, is unindustrious, shiftless, and permits her home to become so littered that one can scarcely walk across the floor." One young girl was "quick in her actions, but mentally dull." In a more sweeping generalization, the authors argued that the girls who lived there became "boy crazy at the age of nine, ten, and eleven" and "in the next few years become more or less promiscuous, generally with younger boys of the vicinity." As a sort of summary, the authors noted, "the sexual relations of the Wins [White, Indian and Negro] are on a very low plane, almost that of an animal."[48]

The lessons of *Mongrel Virginians* reinforced the rise of "racial integrity" laws across the nation. "Mixed breeding," the research suggested, had rendered a portion of the population less intelligent, less restrained, less industrious, and less moral than their "purer" white or black neighbors. Sex constituted the most dangerous act for eugenic supporters. This pseudo-scientific language joined older narratives of white supremacy that emphasized the sexual appetites of black men and black women and that were used to justify racial segregation and racist violence with new narratives that merged science, citizenship, progress, and nation-building. To McDougle and Estabrook, the remedy was clear. They ended their book with the text of the Racial Integrity Act, granting scientific legitimacy to the white supremacist policies of the Progressive Era. They marginalized communities, making their residents objects of study and candidates for medical treatment and institutionalization, not citizenship. The research also shaped the lives of white female students whose observations were legitimized as social work and and made it into print. The white Sweet Briar women carried certain authority as a result of their higher education, their training, and their work with experts. For the social worker or the schoolteacher, a combination of science, state sanction, bureaucratic authority, local gossip, rumor, history, and prevailing ideas about the benefits of racial separation guided their racial categorizations and shaped the power of the Jim Crow order. Their methods, however, were hardly different from those of white women across the state who lacked the benefit of such formal training.[49]

Using local knowledge instead of formal training Goodman joined the ranks of women who alerted Plecker to possible miscegenation and passing for white among those who sought to register. . With surnames and family histories compiled by his assistant Eva Kelley, Plecker recorded racial identities, made a hit list of common names of mixed-race Virginians, and sent directives to local officials in areas particularly susceptible to mixed-race populations.[50] Armed with Kelley's research and his own knowledge from a childhood in Amherst County, Plecker charged midwives, doctors, registrars, nurses, welfare workers, and teachers with gathering names and informing him of those who tried to circumvent the RIA. And they did. A female hospital worker alerted Plecker to the case of a potential "mulatto" woman injured in a car accident who was admitted to a white hospital. Plecker told her that at times children who were the offspring of interracial affairs "are put with their white brothers and sisters" and that this might explain this patient's case. A nurse inquired if a blood test would help her determine racial identity, and he replied that a blood test could not determine racial ancestry. A public welfare worker asked about the racial identity of a woman whose sexual behavior had caught her attention. Plecker affirmed that no scientific tests could show race, and that race "has to be decided upon what can be seen and learned." Plecker continued, "You and the sheriff, and any other intelligent citizen . . . are as capable of judging from the appearance of the child as the most learned scientists." He also instructed her to evaluate "the habits of the mother as to the association with negroes."[51] A white Richmond schoolteacher looked suspiciously at her students' "features" and asked parents for birth certificates.[52] From Plecker's letters, it was apparent that many of those upholding the RIA were women who needed only the power of their observational skills and a diligent commitment to defining whiteness.[53] Their suspicion and impressionistic evidence decided a person's racial identity. Whether they believed in the science of white supremacy was less relevant than that they did their job, designating folks as white or black and ferreting out transgressors who "passed."[54] If they chose not to adhere to this law, Walter Plecker would only have his surnames compiled by Kelley and the census to guide him. But by alerting him to hospital cases, frustrated registrants, suspect schoolchildren, and untoward sexual behavior, these women helped shape when and where and how whiteness would be defined and preserved. In this case, the Jim Crow order rested firmly on the shoulders of local adherents.

One of his local followers in Amherst County was Mrs. W. R. Robertson, a probation officer who echoed Goodman's complaints about uncooperative people in the mountains. Robertson had notified Plecker of numerous cases of people passing as white. Perhaps as many as forty-seven residents, she claimed, had falsified their identities. Acknowledging the prevalence of mixed-race unions, ancestors, and even marriages, Plecker noted his disappointment but also claimed that the difference in Amherst was "that she is ferreting out these cases, which is not being done elsewhere." Robertson herself was evidently pleased with her ability to expose race-crossing in her home county. But her investigation had a price, as rumors circulated that her efforts almost incited a race riot in Amherst.[55]

It was Goodman's Rockbridge County, however, where the RIA met its legal test. Two court cases heard there revealed the level of local resistance. In each case, clerk of court A. T. Shields, a deacon at Goodman's church, refused to grant a marriage license to an Irish Creek couple who claimed to be white, when local rumor held that at least one of the applicants had black or Indian ancestors. In the first case, Dorothy Johns, allegedly mixed, was denied a license to marry a white man, James Conner.[56] In the September case, A. Willis Robertson, future US senator, represented the state. At the trial, Walter Plecker testified that census records and birth certificates revealed that Johns was black. Local Silas Coleman who claimed to know the Johns family supported Plecker's documentary findings. The court agreed, upholding the denial of a marriage license for Johns and Conner.[57]

In late November of 1924, Judge Henry Holt began another session involving a contested marriage license. In this case, Shields had denied a marriage license to Altha Sorrells and Robert Painter, claiming that Sorrells was black. During the week of the trial, Rockbridge's Tuesday Woman's Club had brought John Powell to town for a concert, and he and Earnest Cox also held a forum at the Lexington High School titled "The Color Line in History." Despite community support for "race purity," this time Judge Holt found the argument of Roberston, who was assisted on the bench by Walter Plecker and John Powell, unsound. In refusing to designate Sorrells as "colored," Holt noted that he was not against the statute but rather the lack of evidence needed for a clerk to deny a license and the seeming impossibility of assuring that the person have "no trace whatsoever of any blood other than Caucasian."[58] In fact, Holt wrote to Powell expressing his support for the act itself and claimed that he had written the opinion to guarantee an appeal. Frustrated by the decision, Plecker wished they had used the probation officer, Mrs. Robertson, as she believed "[her witness testimony] would have changed the outcome of the case." In light of the decision, supporters of the RIA worked to give Plecker ultimate discretion in deciding racial identity. An amendment to the act that failed in 1926 but was passed in 1930 allowed Plecker to alter birth certificates as he saw fit.[59]

Ten years later, in the midst of the Great Depression, white women in these western counties still worked with Plecker to enforce the RIA. Grace David at Amherst's City Bureau of Health requested direction on classifying Filipinos.[60] Lizzie Ware of Amherst County alerted him to the possible passing of Mrs. Warren Ogden's children who attended white schools. As a result of Ware's work, Plecker reported that Ogden's children had been removed from the schools. He was still unsure of their identity, however, and asked Ware to have Ogden fill out a questionnaire. He reminded her to note "the appearance of the woman, her husband, and children," being particularly alert to "any negro characteristics." "Frequently," Plecker told her, "these show in one member of the family and not in another." Ware was also instructed to track down other Ogden children in Richmond's schools and the family of Ogden's sisters in Lynchburg.[61]

At the onset of World War II, the Racial Integrity Act remained powerful, but the war brought another challenge to such segregation. In World War I, Native Americans had served in white units, but Virginia's RIA had erased the Indian identity, and now descendants of Native American World War I veterans were to fight in black units, not white ones. To identify all residents with black or Native American blood, local draft boards called on clerks, teachers, and midwives to provide racial designations, even relying on Eva Kelley's "research": a list of common names of Virginians who had been declared to be mixed race. In some western counties, local draft boards moved to the category "colored" the names of all those who claimed Indian identity.[62]

Obviously the presence of the Clarks and other families made the Racial Integrity Act particularly problematic in Amherst and Rockbridge counties, as clerks, registrars, and probation officers toiled for nearly twenty years to reify race. Met with opposition from the Sorrells, Johns, and others, as well as rebellious midwives and clerks of courts, white women's efforts nevertheless had real consequences. By 1940, the Indian population in Amherst County was significantly lower than it had been in 1920. Many Irish Creek and Bear Mountain residents had moved to Maryland, escaping the laws that left them little power to control the most intimate aspects of daily life. Unwilling to attend black schools, the Monacans who stayed attended school at the Bear Mountain Mission. But by 1940, even the Mission had two schools, one for Indians with "Negroid appearances."[63]

The women who worked for the Racial Integrity Act demonstrated that Jim Crow was only as strong as its local enforcers. Without individual vigilance in determining and upholding racial identity, laws decided in Richmond would have little effect in local communities, and this was true across the South as state legislatures in Baton Rouge and Raleigh enacted similar legislation.[64] As new constituents, as new voters, and as workers for the state, Goodman, Robertson, and Ware made sure that the legislation from the center took hold in two western Virginia counties. Certainly, they were not alone in their efforts. Attorneys, clerks of courts, and chairmen of school boards also carried out the law. However, white women often served as those closest to the subjects, filling out birth certificates as midwives or as nurses, serving as registrars, and peering out over their classrooms to see if a child had characteristics that indicated a less than "pure white" background. In this way, the Racial Integrity Act institutionalized some of the authority that white women had long possessed over education, social mores, and childbirth. The expanding bureaucracy had created new positions for white women to affect public policy and had in turn bureaucratized white supremacy. Customary segregation, with the cooperation of grassroots women and the state, morphed into legal, long-lasting, local segregation.[65]

Aileen Goodman Henry's work on the Racial Integrity Act did not appear in the historical record after 1943. Frustrated by the Clarks again that year, Plecker told her to make the designation of "mixed" to quell their resistance, noting that it "is far better than "Indian" and infinitely better than "white.""He told her that his office will understand mixed 'to mean colored,'" and he had the authority to change the designation. Congratulating Goodman on giving the Clarks "some trouble," he noted that their case "will be of lasting benefit to you and to our office."[66] After World War II, Goodman continued to live in Rockbridge County, to teach school, to work hard in the local presbytery, and to raise money for mission work in Africa.

The efforts of her work and that of women like her lasted well past the interwar period. In the 1980s, when a local genealogist, Donna Huffer, who had married an Irish Creek Clark, began to work on the family history of her in-laws, the power of this act still resonated. She recorded stories about how the 1920s missionary Sally B. Dickerson lined up the Clarks from lightest to darkest. Those who fell on the dark end of the line were not allowed to come to the mission school. Mary Martin, born in 1891, told Huffer a convoluted family history that affirmed her whiteness. She noted that her mother who carried the Southers name was not really a Southers (a surname listed on Plecker's 1943 hit list). Martin's biological grandmother had died, and her grandfather had married a Southers woman and thus his daughter was assumed to be a Southers. During the 1924 trials over marriage licenses in Rockbridge County, Martin said that her mother paid a lawyer $300 for a document that proved she was white. Martin remembered hearing that Plecker had put colored on her birth certificate. In the 1960s, she allegedly used the purchased whiteness certificate to change her birth certificate. Rumors told that after passage of the RIA in 1924, people came selling whiteness certificates for as much as $10,000—a clear accounting of not what individuals actually paid but of what they believed whiteness was worth. As late as 1985, Martin insisted that in 1924 the lawyer affirmed the presence of two branches of Clarks. She asserted that she was no relation to the black Clark line, "none whatsoever." "This is very important," she told Huffer. "Make sure you make that distinction!"[67]

When Monacan Indian Rosemary Clark Whitlock began to collect twentieth-century histories of the Monacan Indian Nation, she interviewed dozens of people on Bear Mountain. One interviewee, Phyllis Branham Hicks, doubted that Plecker "deserve[d] all the blame for trying to force Indians to be registered and known as colored." "I have given this matter a lot of thought and I have questions," she continued. How could he have had "full authority to force clerks of courts and hospital personnel in several chosen areas to falsify records and list Indian births as colored?"[68] She came to the conclusion that more men must have been involved, perhaps legislators and governors.

But fellow Monacan Bertie Duff Branham's story suggested other culprits—female progeny of the work of Goodman and Robertson. In 1992, she noted that her daughter had a baby at Lynchburg General Hospital. The new mother refused to accept the birth certificate that labeled her baby as "negro." In response, a woman from the hospital's business office told her that those were the rules. Still, the mother refused. The next day the hospital official returned with "Indian" typed in the space for race.[69] From the late 1940s to the 1990s, similar stories circulated, and in 2000, the Monacan Indian Nation initiated a lobbying effort to get the legislature to change the altered birth certificates from the 1920s—from negro to Indian. The Racial Integrity Act was long repealed, but it had continued to shape the quest of many who had lived on Bear Mountain and Irish Creek as they sought recognition of a heritage that followers of the 1924 law had erased.[70] Institutional memory, generational instruction, and local prejudices continued the practice of racial segregation and "documentary genocide" long after the law pronounced it dead.

The memory and remnants of classification carried out by neighbors, registrars, draft boards, schoolteachers, bus drivers, and missionaries in the mountains of western Virginia remained as American citizens paid for whiteness certificates, challenged race as recorded on birth certificates, and rearranged their history. Unlike many white Virginians, Monacans know Plecker; their children and grandchildren know of Plecker, too.[71] Their assertions of racially heterogeneous family trees provide definitions of identity that defy blood fractions, scientific phenotypes, and legal boundaries. But even in their stories, there remains historical selectivity. The people who imposed the identity of black on the Monacans disappear, as do the stories of intermarriage between blacks and Indians and whites. Residents remember Plecker as the man who issued the edicts, but they do not call out their neighbors who did his bidding, who turned in their names, and who delivered their babies and marked them as black.[72] Goodman's obituary does not mention the long-lasting legacy of her work as a local registrar. The Sweet Briar eugenics workers remain in scrapbooks and brief correspondence, unnamed in *Mongrel Virginians*. The work of Lizzie Ware and Mrs. W. R. Robertson appear only in census records and brief passages in other people's letters and newspaper articles.

In the end, this historical selection does valuable work, rendering invisible the women and the daily acts that secured white supremacy.[73] What it leaves intact is the myth of a system that persisted with leaders at the center but without local people in local communities. The writing out of white women's efforts to police the racial order promotes the white supremacist fiction that segregation was natural and happened without workers. It also promotes the belief that if the law or the legislature or the government changes, then the practices, institutions, and beliefs that guide those practices will also end.

Both fictions overlook the local practitioners—Goodman, Ware, Robertson, Hundley, Kelley, and others. Every time they turned in a child, denied a marriage, or observed a facial feature, they enforced the state's Jim Crow laws and produced a politics of white supremacy that would last for decades. Their work shaped people's lives and instructed their communities in how to uphold white over black. While the RIA shaped the contours of their particular work in the Blue Ridge mountains, the need to catalog, evaluate, and regulate the nation's citizenry spread beyond the Jim Crow South and connected them to both progressive and reactionary impulses across the country.

## 2

## *Citizenship Education for a Segregated Nation*

IN 1919, Mildred Lewis Rutherford, an aging force for Confederate restoration and longtime educator, announced that her last political crusade would center on the propagation of "the truths of history." As the daughter of a slaveholding Georgian, leader of Confederate memorial activities, and former Historian General of the United Daughters of the Confederacy (UDC), she chose to unveil her "cause" at the annual meeting of the United Confederate Veterans (UCV). There she encouraged them to earmark time, money, and personnel to correct historical untruths. She claimed that 81 percent of southern schools were using biased, Yankee-authored textbooks that threatened the present-day South. Fault fell at the feet of white southerners. Without sufficient support or organization and lacking grit, they had neglected, Rutherford argued, to make history matter. Because of this failure, white southern students continued to learn a history that minimized states' rights, put forth slavery as the cause of the Civil War, rejected the right of secession, glorified Lincoln, and focused on the cruelty and injustice of slaveholders. Rutherford called on the UCV to help her rectify this. They responded by establishing the Rutherford Committee that consisted of five members of the UCV, UDC, and Sons of Confederate Veterans (SCV), and by disseminating Rutherford's pamphlet: "A Measuring Rod to Test Text Books, and Reference Books in Schools, Colleges, and Libraries." Cautioning readers to cast aside individual idiosyncrasies in the censorship campaign, she suggested that they follow her pamphlet's guidelines to determine a textbook's fitness. Condensing her pamphlet into newspaper article length, Rutherford expanded the distribution of her ideas and offered white southern readers a to-do list. They should join her in endowing southern history chairs, sponsoring summer schools for public schoolteachers, and creating textbook selection committees. She implored white Georgians to closely monitor appointees to the textbook selection committees, local school boards, trustees, and public school teachers and superintendents. Finally, she called for a loyalty test for school officials to see if they knew the "South's true history."[1]

Given Rutherford's particular focus on the antebellum period, her devotion to the Lost Cause, and her adoption of Victorian dress, it would have been easy to believe that she was held captive by the past. As a seventy-one-year-old woman speaking to a crowd of older white men, her call for a pro-Confederate education could have been the last gasp of a dying generation. Her work as an educator at the Lucy Cobb Institute, a leading secondary girls' school known for its academic rigor, however, meant that Rutherford was immersed in current debates about the role of higher education. Capitalizing on her authority as an educator, she contended that white schoolchildren and the white South were at risk and that her solutions would shape the future by instilling in them the truth, as she saw it, of the past.[2]

Rutherford knew as well as anyone what historian Katherine Charron noted, "Education was never a politically neutral issue in the Jim Crow South," and she toiled to collapse any distinction between support for segregation and the obligations and duties of national citizenship.[3] She believed that public education helped shape politics and culture, and she focused on improving public education, building bureaucratic state-level structures, censoring textbooks, and centralizing teacher training. She intended to create educational policy that sustained the politics of a newly segregated South, not that restored an Old South. If Jim Crow represented the wisdom of the age, then schools were central to instilling that wisdom. Educators, broadly defined, nurtured the system of segregation, and children were the repositories of their efforts. Rutherford called on white women to guarantee that the school curriculum and personnel taught lessons in white over black, maintained white supremacy, and erased the conflicts endemic to the rise of racial segregation. By encouraging white women to redouble their oversight of public education, she worked to combat white apathy about segregation's security. Rutherford reminded white southern women that they were the daily workers needed to guarantee that white children learned the lessons of segregated citizenship and that they grew up to be white supremacy's future activists. Their focus had to be public schools—the pivotal institution in the creation of a Jim Crow citizenship education.[4]

Rutherford's efforts to sustain racial segregation through schooling and a broad citizenship education dovetailed with the national anti-radical impetus to make sure that schools bolstered patriotic education, 100 percent

Americanism, anti-immigration sentiment, and nativist-based politics.[5] Simultaneously "race scientists" across the country had embarked on the overwhelming and largely illogical endeavor to solidify racial classifications. When Rutherford claimed, "The time has come when the South, the true home of the Anglo-Saxon race, which has stood for truth and honesty and righteousness in the past, should come back to the faith and principles for which their fathers stood," she aligned her crusade for Jim Crow with a national conversation on "race purity" and Anglo-Saxon superiority.[6] Meanwhile, nationwide, school reformers pushed for a more expansive state-level centralization of public education, while many white southerners remained skeptical about federal intervention. Yet Rutherford and other white women encouraged state governments to expand their control over education. In the spirit of the Progressive Era, southern states had already established or expanded child welfare bureaus, departments of public welfare and charities, state hospitals, school committees, public health offices, and home demonstration programs.[7] Many of these new state institutions were part of what historian Robin Muncy termed a "female dominion" that tapped into older traditions of Republican motherhood and separate spheres, parlaying gender-specific duties of women into public authority over social welfare and public education. Literature emphasizing the easy transition from raising one's own children to raising the nation's children had propelled women into the social welfare bureaucracy.[8] Rutherford and others felt it was time for public education to follow suit. Georgia's state government had embraced some progressive educational policies, mandating high school education, establishing teacher licensure agencies, and standardizing teacher training.[9] Education reform did not mean liberal reform, however. Rutherford and others saw statewide control over public schools as a strategy to strengthen an education in Jim Crow and Americanization, enabling public instruction in white supremacy to be institutionalized.

For Rutherford, textbook control was central to this campaign, even though it was neither new nor original. In the antebellum era, white southerners had complained about abolitionist sentiment in historical tracts. In 1855, a Mississippi state legislator called for his state government to encourage southern texts, written by southern authors, and printed in southern publishing houses. The next year, whites in New Orleans protested "abolitionist-friendly" textbooks in their schools. The southern periodical *De Bow's Review* led the charge for the publication of regional historical interpretations despite the fact that the relative paucity of public schools meant that historical textbooks were hardly an issue for most southern parents.[10] After the Civil War, public schooling became more widespread for both white and black southern-ers. The presence of northern-educated teachers increased, but textbooks writ-ten by former Confederates such as Vice-President Alexander Stephens served as antidotes to the influx of outsiders less committed to a racial hierarchy.[11] Censorship continued, and in 1893, Mississippi's state government established the Society for the Diffusion of Useful Information to monitor reading mate-rial and promote white South–friendly texts. By the end of the century, UDC chapters in Oklahoma, Maryland, Georgia, and Texas had tried unsuccessfully to ban textbooks that expressed anti-southern sentiment.[12]

In the late nineteenth century, however, many Americans replaced regional animosities with national reconciliation. The advent of Jim Crow coincided with a widespread acceptance of southern race relations, and many embraced the influential historian William Dunning's interpretation that Reconstruction had failed because of government corruption and black infe-riority.[13] In the context of Social Darwinism and the nation's imperial expan-sion, a belief in racial hierarchies undergirded federal foreign policy, and southern crusades for a white supremacist interpretation of the nation's past seemed redundant. Rutherford did not really need to challenge the prevailing national history. That battle, many historians have suggested, had already been won by the Jim Crow South.[14] By World War I, a national consensus in text-books offered to the nation's schoolchildren the following historical "truths": Reconstruction was a mistake; American imperialism provided uplift to non-white people across the globe; the rise of the nation was a story of good democrats and hardworking Anglo-Saxon Protestants; and broad coopera-tion, not conflict, among all classes of Americans characterized the nation's development. The elevation of this national historical narrative coincided with a decline in the textbook treatments of African Americans. The story of the Fort Pillow massacre serves as one example. A textbook staple since the 1870s, it told of a controversial battle when Confederate troops led by Nathan Bedford Forrest overwhelmed a Union garrison killing mostly black Union soldiers who were surrendering. Accounts of the Fort Pillow massacre had disappeared from history texts by the 1900s. W. E. B. DuBois's observa-tion that "schoolbook narratives were the propaganda of history," rang true as African American history slipped from America's textbooks just as the Jim Crow order rose to power. The narratives that suited the political program of white supremacy filled public schools, and Mildred Rutherford made sure that an education in racial segregation reached Georgia's schoolchildren.[15]

Despite the redundancy of Rutherford's crusade, she could not have picked a more opportune time for it. By the 1920s, she drew on a web of contacts cultivated by decades of work with the UDC, Young Women's Christian Association (YWCA), Georgia Association Opposed to Woman Suffrage, and Lucy Cobb Institute alumni, as she encouraged them all to lobby for "southern" textbooks and pro-Confederate historical interpretations. The rise of the second KKK in Athens and across the country took white supremacist rhetoric to national audiences. Her broader program of patriotic education, southern style, complemented national debates about citizen control over textbooks. In the aftermath of World War I, the Red Scare, and rising nativist impulses drew on the reactionary populist strands at work in a nation uncomfortable with its rising commercial character, its loss of local control and cronyism, the elevation of experts and bureaucrats, and the influx of southern and eastern Europeans. Diverse groups of conservative activists—the Grand Army of the Republic, the New York City Board of Education, the KKK, the School Committee of the City of Boston, the American Federation of Labor, the UDC, the American Legion, the DAR—met in broad agreement as they tried to move the authority of historical narratives away from intellectual elites and professionals and toward the realm of popular approval.[16]

In the interwar period, differentiating between the goals of textbooks and the duties of a historian generated proponents all along the political spectrum. Textbooks became a lightning rod for wide-ranging discussions about citizenship education and its relationship to "official" or "legitimate" knowledge.[17] Conservative organizations emphasized the need for a celebratory story of the United States populated with great leaders and great causes thus producing proud, patriotic citizens. Progressive groups—the International Council of Women of Darker Races, the Women's Committee of the Commission on Interracial Cooperation, the Women's International League for Peace and Freedom—argued that historical interpretations in textbooks played a potent role in the making of American citizens, and they sought more inclusive national narratives. But they were no match for the lobbying of the more anti-radical organizations, and leftist groups found themselves frozen out of the textbook market. Many turned instead to juvenile and children's literature available in public libraries. From the Communist Party to the KKK, organizations developed publications aimed at children; but in schoolbooks, the historical interpretations advocated by conservatives and anti-radicals prevailed.[18]

Because of the shortage of teachers, textbooks carried disproportionate authority in the nation's classrooms. The expansion of secondary public education had outpaced teacher training. As a result, schools across the nation were hiring high school teachers who sometimes had only a year or more of training than their students, and some observers believed that better textbooks might counteract this deficit.[19] Textbooks, many agreed, were no place for questioning the past or evaluating it but were the tools of teachers who needed to provide their young charges with stories of heroes and heroism, individual courage, devotion to law and order, and a "faith in American superiority."[20] Teachers could defer to textbooks if they were the right textbooks. However, anti-radicals argued that those textbooks that focused on problems and solutions or conflicts were insidious purveyors of socialism, Bolshevism, and pacifism. With textbooks occupying such a central place in political debates of the 1920s, the DAR, the American Legion, and fifty other organizations organized censorship campaigns to ensure that patriotic "true American history" was taught. In 1924, forty-three patriotic groups endorsed a New Jersey bill legalizing the censorship of history and civics textbooks.[21] The next year, the Women's Patriotic Conference had added a resolution that decried "attempts to replace wartime heroes with 'civilian and scientific heroes' in public school textbooks."[22]

In the white South, the wartime heroes might have been different, but the message was not. Mildred Rutherford's efforts coincided with national efforts to control and purge questionable material, socialist propaganda, stories of labor strife, and generally "un-American" content from public school textbooks. Her northern counterpart, Margaret Robinson—anti-suffragist, anti-radical, and activist in the Massachusetts Public Interest League and the Women's Patriotic Conference on National Defense—lectured across the nation and published letters and columns in Henry Ford's *Dearborn Independent* as part of her campaign to purge anti-patriotic material from the nation's textbooks. While Robinson did not espouse an overtly white supremacist agenda, she did not have to; the most conservative educational reformers ignored the racial politics of their crusades. Instead, she took to heart then-vice-president Calvin Coolidge's 1921 charge that women played a major part in eradicating subversive materials from public schools, and she practiced constant vigilance. Robinson and Rutherford both agreed that for exposing subversion in education, women were better suited to and more effective at the task than men. In fact, they contended, men just talked while women acted.[23]

While the nation debated textbook content, southern states took the lead in establishing statewide textbook adoption. Rutherford and others had advocated for the state centralization of textbook selection. This Progressive Era reform took root in the South and resulted in the emergence of early statewide textbook selection committees and approval lists in Mississippi,

North Carolina, and Texas. Thereafter, convincing one committee to follow Mildred Rutherford's guidelines meant that the entire state would be
ensured of a pro-white South interpretation in their textbooks. As reported
in the *Confederate Veteran*, Mississippi's textbook commission "set the pace
for all other Southern State Book Adoption Boards," following to the letter the Rutherford Committee's recommendations.[24] Once state committees selected their books, textbook manufacturers soon produced textbooks
that earned the most sales, and statewide adoption—particularly in Texas
or California—guaranteed high sales nationwide. By 1926, state committees prescribed American history textbooks in North Carolina, Alabama,
Florida, Georgia, Louisiana, Mississippi, Texas, and Virginia. New Jersey also
censored textbooks and practiced statewide adoption, but the state selection
was much less common in the North, where local adoptions still dominated.
Textbooks friendly to the "white South," marketed by national publishing
houses proliferated. as publishers responded to market forces, printing texts
that would have the widest adoption.[25]

The erosion of local control and the expansion of the state under the
guise of textbook selection committees bred some dissent. Centralization of
school matters, even at the state level, seemed intrusive to white southerners
who relished local control. Thus, the early decades of the twentieth century
witnessed conflicts across Georgia over the centralization of public education. The county unit system in Georgia meant that most political decisions
occurred in each of the state's 152 counties. Counties worked as autonomous
units which meant elevated power for local elites, but for statewide policy
initiatives, like mandatory high school, the unit system stymied progress. By
the 1920s and 1930s, however, Georgia's educational conservatives no longer
saw the state as inimical to their educational interests. Instead, they saw educational reforms necessary for economic growth frustrated by the county unit
system, local resistance to statewide taxation, and religious denominations
that opposed secular, university training programs. Conservatives and progressives believed that each of these factors hindered the pace of educational
reform.[26]

Other white women feared that the centralization of textbook selection might open up a small space for black women and black educators to
influence state policy. Black women had long seen public education as fertile soil for "race work" that challenged prevailing images of black inferiority
and produced another generation of black, educated leaders. Many avoided
state-sanctioned textbooks and manuals. In Gainesville, Georgia, Beulah
Rucker Oliver incorporated black history and literature into her teaching.

The Georgia Education Board's lackluster and underfunded oversight of black schools and the persistent belief in black inferiority contributed to their autonomy. Therefore, Rucker pushed academic rather than industrial training. Others embraced teaching as an extension of motherhood and celebrated black women teachers for "the successful lifting" they did for their race.[27] Outside Georgia, southern black clubwomen, like Marion Wilkinson of South Carolina, were aware that historical interpretations in general and textbooks specifically were sites where Jim Crow was reinforced. They sought to disseminate black history and black literature as well as pan-African interpretations in schools, north and south. In 1920, the International Council of Women of Darker Races led by Booker T. Washington's widow and the Women's Committee of the Commission on Interracial Cooperation promoted the integration of black history into the public school curriculum for all students, noting that it "was imperative both for self-knowledge and for demonstration to whites."[28] Their efforts for an integrated historical narrative of the United States withered, however, against the political and economic power of white constituents in the DAR, the UDC, and the American Legion. Even more damaging to their efforts was the meager funding that strapped black schools, specifically, and public education, generally, across the South.[29]

White women agreed with black women that schools were central to "race work." Rutherford, for example, worked to ensure that public education reinforced the lessons of a segregated South. White liberal women also linked public motherhood to teaching and envisioned public schools as a terrain to expand democratic citizenship. Georgia's Commission on Interracial Cooperation (CIC), forerunner of the Southern Regional Conference and one of a few white-led organizations trying to alleviate racial strife, circulated materials on "America's 10th Man." In this program, they highlighted black achievement, conducted teacher training sessions on incorporating black history, and held essay contests in 1928. Their results were not revolutionary, and white children were unlikely to learn of challenges to white supremacy through their textbooks, teachers, or curriculum. In fact, an education in Jim Crow citizenship meant that most children left school having learned that the racial order was natural and unchangeable. In the segregated South, Rutherford's vision of education, not that of Rucker or the CIC, found more fertile soil in the new bureaucratic state.[30]

In part, the creation of textbook committees enabled targeted lobbying campaigns, privileging those with the most political capital. In Jacksonville, Florida, the Martha Reid UDC Chapter reviewed textbooks and told publishers that "they could not sell textbooks containing slurring remarks . . . prejudicial to the South."[31] In New Orleans, censorship seized the day, when members of the UDC and SCV successfully petitioned the school board to ban the *History of the American People* by Charles Beard and William Bagley because of its "socialistic tendencies" and "objectionable accounts of the South."[32] One of the more widespread campaigns centered on David Muzzey's popular textbook, *The American People*. Citing their "unabated and everlasting interest in the histories that are to be taught to the children of our state," North Carolina UDC chapters conducted a letter-writing campaign and successfully persuaded the state superintendent of education to eliminate the Muzzey text from the adoption list. Rutherford had attacked it because it claimed that the South's cause in the Civil War was an unworthy one, and the Sons of the American Revolution (SAR) opposed it for its treatment of Revolutionary War heroes, inclusion of the controversial tariff issue, and the general pro-British and socialistic tendencies. Outside the South, labor and ethnic groups in New York lobbied to exclude the textbook because of Muzzey's obvious belief in Anglo-Saxon supremacy.[33] This collaboration between national organizations that were not overt supporters of a white supremacist political, economic, and social order and those that were—the UDC, the UCV, and even the KKK— created a powerful lobby. Soon, North Carolina's State Board of Education reneged on its contract for the book.[34] The Rutherford Committee applauded North Carolina and reminded white southerners to look for textbooks that upheld "the right of secession, legally, morally, and constitutionally." By 1923, the North Carolina legislature had granted the state textbook commission permission to select appropriate histories for elementary grades and civics books for high school students. Those making the list met the criteria of Rutherford's "Measuring Rod." They stressed Lincoln's responsibility for the Civil War, glorified Confederate soldiers, referred to the Civil War as the War between the States, and included slavery as just one of several exploitive systems of labor.[35] To maintain its state contracts, publisher Houghton Mifflin promised to include the North Carolina Constitution in its materials along with prominent biographies of "representative men as [Daniel] Boone, Patrick Henry, [Zebulon] Vance, Walter Page, Robert E. Lee, [Stonewall] Jackson, and Woodrow Wilson." Standing in line with the nation, North Carolina also passed legislation requiring the teaching of "Americanization."[36]

In Mississippi, a primer entitled *The KKK* written by Laura Rose, Rutherford's successor as UDC Historian General, made the state adoption list. In it, Rose argued that the first KKK arose as an antidote to the widespread belief among African Americans that freedom meant they no longer had to labor. Children reading the book would learn that the original KKK had been a necessary counterpart to the African-American led Union Leagues which Rose argued had engendered racial strife and oppressed southern whites. In fact, the Union Leagues were political organizations of African Americans and white unionists in the postwar South who advocated for the black franchise, voter registration, and support for the national government, but students would not learn that from Rose's book. Instead, they would read that the KKK countered the impulse among black men to take white wives. The text reminded schoolchildren that "the best citizens of our country" joined the KKK because they were motivated by "love and protection of the home." Violence was their last resort, and Rose also noted that crimes committed by "mean white men" were often falsely attributed to the KKK. She extolled the Klan for preserving "the purity and domination of the Anglo-Saxon race."[37]

While Rutherford applauded the lessons in white supremacy and racial segregation provided in the textbooks of North Carolina and Mississippi, she continued to call on civic, historic, and commemorative organizations to look for challenges to racial segregation in the South's public schools. She reminded them that when they had not been vigilant, challenges to white supremacy had filtered into school curriculum and public history sites, becoming part and parcel of the intellectual repertoire of white teachers and professors. State committees were important, but Rutherford also maintained that securing the supremacy of white over black was the job of students, teachers, and parents.

In particular, the UDC needed to capitalize on women's authority in public education to ensure that white southerners learned a history that naturalized racial segregation. In 1920, the UDC called on members to use the summer to eliminate histories in schools that were "not loyal to the South."[38] In Macon, Georgia, the chapter president described the UDC as an "educational factor." Virginia UDC member Mary Carter began a new prize for the chapter that bought the largest numbers of Rutherford's pamphlet, "The Truths of History," establishing a 100-copy minimum. Carter's chapter had already placed over 2,000 copies of Confederate books in universities, colleges, normal schools, and libraries across the country. Pointing again to persistent apathy among white southerners, she lamented that her efforts received greater interest from universities in the northwest and west than in her home region.[39] In Raleigh, Children of the Confederacy planned to fill several shelves in their public library with "Confederate-friendly" books, and the UDC asked its members to expand this effort beyond Raleigh.[40] By the 1920s, the UDC had increased its college scholarship fund to over $100,000, hoping that funding white students would secure their view of history. In 1920, Georgia received the most scholarships, with 350 students receiving tuition assistance valued at just shy of $29,000.[41]

Georgia's UDC chapter reports attested to their work in the schools. In 1922, the UDC held an essay contest open "to all white children of Georgia under eighteen years of age," on the topic of "the Conspiracy" that began the Civil War, a topic selected by Rutherford.[42] In 1924, the thirty-four chapters highlighted the achievements of their essay contests, reporting over 1,500 essays written by Georgia schoolchildren on Confederate topics. One chapter began a new prize for the best essay written on Rutherford's pamphlet "The Civilization of the Old South" and another on "what Confederate organizations have done to win the Great War."[43] Lucy McDonald noted that the essay contests had generated "much interest." She also reported that her chapter had placed Rutherford's *Southern Heroes* in the schools and hung pictures of Robert E. Lee and Jefferson Davis in school auditoriums. Without providing direct instruction in white supremacy, as essay contests would in the years following the *Brown* decision, these contests still linked white schoolchildren to a particular historical memory that celebrated white Confederate heroes, reinforced the doctrine of states' rights, and minimized the role of slavery in the Civil War.[44]

However popular, the essay contests were not universally welcomed by school officials. One Georgia school board denied the UDC permission to conduct their contest. Frustrated initially, a Sandersville high school history teacher rescued the UDC mission by taking its materials and essay topics and integrating them into her regular curriculum. Delighted by this circumvention of school board control, UDC historian Louise Irwin credited the teacher with the most effective distribution of material yet. Irwin wrote that the cooperation of the teacher succeeded "each year in having the contest subjects studied by all the pupils in the senior class."[45]

While the UDC focused on essay contests, other white southerners realized that teachers were the linchpin in the propagation of certain historical interpretations. Startling reports of illiteracy among World War I draftees, the rising Americanization crusade, and a nationwide teacher shortage contributed to a national conversation on teacher training. The National Education Association (NEA) campaigned for greater licensure requirements and the establishment of a federal Department of Education. The NEA also called for more opportunities for summer education for teachers, noting that the average age of teachers was under twenty and that more than 300,000 had not finished high school. The problem was particularly acute in rural areas. While the NEA did not flourish in the Deep South, the UDC and the DAR had long supported the education of teachers and echoed NEA concerns about teacher preparation.[46]

In Athens, Georgia, women's organizations had spearheaded fundraising for that city's Normal School—an institution that provided teacher training. By the 1920s, UDC chapters across the state notified Rutherford of scholarships that they provided teachers for summer instruction. Each summer, rural white teachers from across the state came to Athens for short courses. As the summer school grew to over 2,000 students, Rutherford's Lucy Cobb Institute offered its dormitories and dining hall to the visiting female teachers. The Athens Woman's Club hosted receptions for the teachers, and the Woman's Club sponsored a short course for teachers. In addition to coursework, students who attended the six-week summer institute had a choice of evening lectures at either the University of Georgia or its normal school. School reformer Rebecca Latimer Felton, suffragist and infamous defender of lynching, lectured one evening in 1923.[47] The next year, the *Banner Herald* claimed that Rutherford "was at her best" when she spoke to hundreds of teachers on southern history providing material they would carry "home . . . to form the bases of a new interest in history study and a new spirit in history teaching in a hundred counties of the state."[48]

To reach lay audiences and expand her scope beyond the UDC and the state's teachers, in 1923 Rutherford began publishing a periodical entitled *Miss Rutherford's Scrapbook: Valuable Information about the South*. She sought to disseminate a southern history through 10,000 donated subscriptions funded by those who paid $2.50 for a yearly subscription. Hoping that Rutherford's stamp of approval would translate into sales, southern publishing houses supplemented the costs of production as the periodical's primary advertisers. In each of the ten annual issues, Rutherford recommended (white) southern-friendly books to parents, libraries, and schools, including a list of Rutherford-approved textbooks. She noted the achievements of southern states and celebrated white southern luminaries. She instructed her readers to police public libraries, public schools, and boards of education, as well as state textbook commissions. With a list of "Don'ts of History," she instructed her readers to avoid saying "the Civil War" and instead refer to it as "the War between the States" and to say "you know" the South was right, not that "you believe" it to be right. In other articles, she slipped easily between past and present. Amid claims that slaves were called servants and were considered members of the family, she also wrote that "the negro of today is far more a slave than he ever was under the Christian institution of slavery in the South."

Just a few pages later, she celebrated Mississippi's 1890 Constitution—the one that disenfranchised black voters—for being the first to "solve the problem of white supremacy by law." From 1923 until 1927, her periodical served as a primer for how white southerners could strengthen their political, economic, and cultural supremacy through the history they taught their children, the language they used to describe the past, and the dissemination of their ideas to a national and international audience.[49]

In 1924, the *Scrapbook* explored two themes—the history of Reconstruction and the accomplishments of textbook committees.[50] Rutherford's interpretation of Reconstruction excoriated carpetbaggers, scalawags, and the Freedmen's Bureau. She claimed that the South would have treated former slaves better than northern agents did and noted that, when ready, southern men would have bestowed civil and political rights, but never social equality. In addition, "the negroes would have been given school opportunities and an education befitting their needs." Commenting on the present, she claimed that "The South," meaning white southerners, "cheerfully pays their taxes to educate the blacks, and they encourage education." And then returning to the past, she reminded her readers that the KKK saved the South, but "justice has never been given the South for what she did at this time and what she is still doing for negro education." Throughout the *Scrapbook*'s run, Rutherford made good on her admonition never to refer to the Lost Cause, because "our Cause was never lost." Her efforts helped make sure that white supremacy was a cause that would continue to be cultivated in the Jim Crow era.[51]

While her periodical focused almost exclusively on matters of southern history and Jim Crow politics, Rutherford weighed in on national politics and joined anti-radicals when she devoted some space to oppose new legislation on child labor. After two decades of Supreme Court decisions rejecting legislation that regulated or banned child labor, a proposed constitutional amendment sought to grant Congress the ability to regulate child labor. In the summer of 1924, to no one's surprise, the amendment met defeat in Georgia and two other southern states. A surprise, however, was the amendment's defeat in Massachusetts where anti-radical women led by Margaret Robinson argued against the "nationalization of children" and the creation of a pseudo- "nanny state." Robinson, the educated wife of a Harvard professor, edited of the *Woman Patriot*, an anti-radical magazine and supported the eugenics movement. To defeat the amendment, she had organized the Citizens Committee to Protect Our Homes and Children, sought the support of the Catholic Church, and created a grassroots groundswell

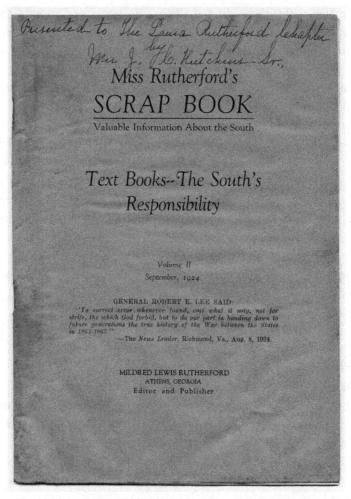

FIGURE 2.1 The September 1924 cover of *Miss Rutherford's Scrap Book*. In the 1920s, Mildred Rutherford called for white southerners to make sure the region's school textbooks upheld white supremacy. Courtesy of Hargrett Rare Book and Manuscript Library, University of Georgia, Athens.

opposing the amendment. Writing in the *Dearborn Independent*, Robinson reached a national audience with her article "Why Massachusetts Beat Child Control: New England Parents Believe They Can Manage Their Own Children." Rutherford celebrated Robinson's work and the efforts of those who campaigned against the legislation and ran an article alerting her readers to the "very serious menace to State Rights now being made through the Child Labor Amendment." Rutherford included long excerpts of Robinson's speeches, highlighting how the amendment's advocates lied about the South's child labor in textile mills, how they were socialists, and how federal control of children was an expression of communism.[52]

Rutherford's opposition to the amendment capitalized on some of the very same alliances at work in the textbook censorship drive. In Virginia, the Women's Constitutional League registered their opposition to the federal regulation of child labor. The New Jersey DAR leadership echoed the national DAR's opposition. In Louisville, Kentucky, a local chapter of the General Federation of Women's Clubs broke from the national organization over its support for the proposed amendment. In standardizing textbook selection, Rutherford and others had felt that the state reinforced good parenting by upholding curriculum materials that made public the instruction in a Jim Crow society. In contrast, they felt that the Child Labor Amendment threatened parental rights by putting children's welfare under federal purview, replacing rather than reinforcing parental judgment.[53] This political alliance between anti-radicals in the name of parental rights and those states' righters opposed to federal regulation was a moment when Rutherford's politics aligned with national conservative trends, and where the white South's broader campaign to secure a Jim Crow order found that a language of parental rights could suit their purposes.

IN THE 1930S, the New Deal provided many more opportunities for broad political alliances to form based on opposition either to federal policies that threatened to reconfigure southern race relations, or to make the federal government more of a presence in state and local schools. The New Deal created tangible and well-publicized enemies of Jim Crow who threatened the educational agendas of segregationist women. The Works Progress Administration (WPA), the Federal Theater Project, and Roosevelt's Black Cabinet strengthened black cultural presence in mainstream American life, even as Depression-era budgets restricted the ability of black history advocates to counter an already entrenched white history. As legal cases wove their way through appellate courts and reached the Supreme Court, it became clear that the gross inequalities between black and white southern schools would bring federal interference to the Jim Crow South.[54] As unequal funding and unequal opportunity became the focus of several court cases, the state-level bureaucratic centralization that Rutherford had schooled white southerners to use to their advantage seemed threatened by a movement to create an independent federal Department of Education. Governors across the nation, but particularly in the South, responded to these threats by pushing for free textbooks and additional funds for school equalization. Rutherford did not live to extend her crusade for historical truths or shore up state bureaucracies.

She died in 1928, but her efforts to enrich the foundations for the educational production of Jim Crow citizenship lived on, as crusades for white supremacy in public schools continued.

Assuring that the South's public schools maintained their lessons in Jim Crow, segregation's educational activists kept up their vigilant work monitoring curriculum and textbooks, even in the face of organizations empowered by the New Deal.[55] Nationwide attention to educational injustice invigorated the efforts of Carter Woodson's Association for the Study of Negro Life and History (ASNLH) fifteen years after its inception. In the 1930s, black pageants made Negro History Week a public event. By 1935, drawing on the recommendations of the ASNLH, black high schools across the South offered courses in black history. Some states even added black history textbooks to their state adoption list. With less than 20 percent of black students attending high schools in the South, Woodson's challenges to the system of segregation were more sporadic than structural. Amid the ASNLH's efforts, textbook censorship and approval remained paramount for the South's segregationists and well within the control of white state legislatures. The Rutherford Committee had moved to the UDC in 1931, as a tribute to white women's work. Miss Marion Salley, the Historian General of the UDC from 1928 to 1931, revised Rutherford's "Measuring Rod" and distributed a new pamphlet called "Errors and Omissions Found in Textbooks." Their persistent work was strengthened by the unintended consequences of the free textbook programs that many states adopted by the end of the 1930s. While providing the state's schoolchildren with free textbooks, the programs also recycled the state-owned textbooks from white schools to black ones, eroding black control over the textbooks in their segregated schools. In Mississippi and Florida, such a shift rendered the black adopted textbook list useless, as black students received hand-me-down textbooks from white schools containing the very historical narratives Rutherford had advocated. At the time of the ASNHL's growing influence, Georgia still had a reputation "for perfection . . . in patriotic education," an accolade that spoke to the state's persistent reinforcement of white over black.[56]

Academic studies during the New Deal attested to the intransigent and imbedded lessons of segregation that kept emerging from public school texts and curriculum. In 1941, a book by Mary Elizabeth Carpenter examined "the treatment of the Negro" in American history textbooks between 1826 and 1939. In 1937, she noted, the NEA found that on a list of thirty-one topics "avoided or tactfully treated" in school textbooks, racial problems were seventh, with mention of African Americans virtually absent. Citing other studies, she noted that textbooks diminished the appeal of the North for African Americans and justified the South's treatment and attitude toward black Americans. Most of the eighty-six textbooks she surveyed included no pictures of African Americans and made no notice of their presence in American life after Reconstruction. The interpretation of slavery had changed somewhat, emphasizing how the North and the South profited from it and how even white southerners considered slavery a problem. But the story of Reconstruction remained one of freedmen lacking fitness for citizenship and their susceptibility to exploitation and corruption. The black codes were mentioned by only three of the eighty-six books, with one noting that they were no harsher than northern laws. Textbooks described the "Negro problem" as a "national rather than only a southern concern." Carpenter noted that Muzzey's textbook, the one so vilified by Rutherford, traced the trade of slaves from West Africa to the West Indies to the United States; explained their denial of citizenship rights; and discussed anti-slavery efforts and colonization's failure. Carpenter noted that Charles Beard, whose work had also suffered censorship, was the only one to mention Harriet Tubman. Meanwhile, six authors echoed Rutherford's contention that "slave life was pleasant for master and slave." Carpenter's study revealed the power of textbook censorship. The elimination of Muzzey's textbook from statewide adoption removed the one text with any specific attention to slavery. The elimination of Beard's book meant that schoolchildren would not meet Harriet Tubman. White southerners could point to textbooks suggesting that black Americans were a national problem, not a southern one. Rutherford and other women, it seemed, had done their work well.[57]

A 1938 study by the Mississippi Educational Association (MEA) found that a student who mastered all the textbooks provided from elementary through secondary school could in all likelihood never meet in his or her reading one black person who had contributed in a significant way to the nation's development. Careful to sidestep any suggestion that they advocated racial equality, the MEA had solicited the help of white students at Millsaps College and the State Teacher's College to conduct an objective study of what the state-approved textbooks taught about "the Negro" and what effects this whitewashed history might have on white students. Allegedly, this study began after a white high school boy proudly recounted to his teacher how he had punched a black girl who had not stepped off the sidewalk for him. His failure to act with either a recognition of basic human rights or even white paternalism startled the teacher who wondered if his schooling might have contributed to this poor behavior. After working eight years on the study, researchers found that in their history books, elementary students would find no mention of black men or women, only of slavery. The world geography texts featured pictures of black men doing agricultural labor in Puerto Rico, Costa Rica, and Africa, not the United States. In literature, if children had two of the approved texts, they might read the story of "Little Black Sambo" or another one entitled "Discharging the Cook." Otherwise, the report noted, "there are no readings from Negro authors, no readings about Negroes, no references to Negro poets, short story writers, novelists, or artists." There was almost complete erasure of black history and black Americans from Mississippi's textbooks. This era-sure certainly had damaging effects on black students, but they had their fami-lies, their churches, and their schools to tell them stories that challenged such hegemony. White southerners raised on a segregated history and living in a segregated society only had stories that upheld a natural order of white over black.[58]

The MEA study also found that the broader historical interpretations offered suited the goals of a white supremacist citizenship education. The treatment of slavery was more idyllic in history texts than in civic ones, but the only consistent treatment of black life were passages about the Nat Turner Rebellion emphasizing the murder of white women and children. In the one book covering US government, there was not a single reference to the "Negro," suggesting that black men and women had no active role in American politics. In all, black men and women were discussed in terms of property, "not personality." The researchers concluded that the texts did not contain misinformation and that there was not direct "animus against the negro in the textbooks." But "the limited portion of the truth told results in a picture decidedly warped," and "The Negro is simply ignored save when problems of white people bring him to the center of attention, and then his treatment is in terms of the white man's advantage."[59]

Rutherford could not have asked for anything more—the exclusion of a black past from textbooks. While such an education suited the Jim Crow order, it also satisfied anti-radical women like Margaret Robinson of the Women's Patriotic Conference on National Defense and conservative men like Charles Horne of the American Legion, both of whom had sought the erasure of con-flict in American history. Without the presence of black Americans in history books, conflicts such as the Camp Grant massacre which marked the end of Republican power in Reconstruction Louisiana, the Populist Party's ascen-sion in North Carolina, and the Wilmington, Tulsa, East St. Louis, and the Rosewood race riots aimed at reducing black political and economic inde-pendence disappeared. Textbook authors like the racialist Muzzey, who had believed deeply in Anglo-Saxon supremacy, were vindicated by textbooks that created a narrative where only white Americans were worthy of historical treatment and acknowledgment.[60]

Given that so many groups vied for control of textbook content, it is hard to quantify the impact of Rutherford's work or measure the role of the UDC or of white women in shaping the resulting interpretations in history textbooks.[61] Rutherford's efforts do suggest that many white women remained concerned and committed to shaping what their white children learned in public schools. The essay contests that white women's organizations conducted, the summer school classes they offered to teachers, and the textbooks they tried to censor established public education as a venue where white women had multiple opportunities and obligations to uphold white supremacy.

The work of Rutherford, the UDC, the DAR, and their progeny did speak to two trends that shaped white women's relationship to white supremacist politics and in turn molded the course of Jim Crow segregation in the South. First, Rutherford instructed white women on the eternal vigilance needed in maintaining public instruction in Jim Crow. In the face of school centralization, of dying Confederate veterans, and of a rising northern textbook industry, it was their duty to make sure that southern history was taught in a way that lauded white southerners, that upheld the supremacy of states' rights, that warned white children about the encroachments of the federal government, and that assured the reinforcement of "the southern way of life" generation after generation. With careful attention, these women could continue to create an education that buried the ugly aspects of slavery, segregation, and racial violence and that breathed life into the myths of Anglo-Saxon origins, benevolent plantation mistresses, and happy black slaves. At the very least, they could police what their children were learning, guaranteeing that they would grow up with few questions about the reign of racial segregation. Working in public education also trained women to support segregation even when it seemed secure. Rutherford, the UDC, and the DAR addressed white apathy by training white activists for a Jim Crow nation. Their work instilled in southern white youth an education that made them resist subsequent revisions to the history they had learned—a history that had situated racial equality as outside the trajectory of American political development. The normative nature of yearly essay contests celebrating the Confederacy became a routine that instilled the lessons of white over black. Each time white women participated in the creation of a public instruction in white supremacy, they increased their authority as political actors in charge of the

white youth, affirming that they were political activists for racial segregation. They also confirmed their status as good white mothers, maintaining
an academic kind of segregation through schools that created social distance
between white and black.

Second, the erasure of individual black achievement and individuals from
both history and the present took deep root not only in the public schools of
the South but also in schools across the nation. In 1973, the pages of *The Black
Book*, a pathbreaking scrapbook-like publication of African American history and culture in the United States, told a story of black achievement and
black struggle unknown to many white and black Americans. White women
across the South were part of the reason people did not know this history.
When Rutherford wrote history, she used language that homogenized the
black population and erased lessons in black leadership, business, art, and
education. In her text, the Mississippi Constitution of 1890 did not attempt
to destroy a black political tradition symbolized by the 3,878 black elected
officials across the post–Civil War South or erase the fragile interracial alliance of the late nineteenth century; it simply solved "the Negro problem."[62]
The textbooks that proliferated in the 1920s and 1930s and beyond helped
continue this erasure. In rendering black lives invisible in school curriculum,
white women perhaps did more lasting damage than the crass negrophobia
articulated by the South's most vitriolic politicians. It was not that the textbooks had to preach black inferiority and white supremacy; they just had to
erase African Americans from American history in all but the most decora-
tive moments, and in those moments they became inferior historical subjects,
not worthy of individual attention. Jim Crow politics relied on the stories it
told and the symbols it created, which were replicated decade after decade
in public schools. The textbooks for which Rutherford lobbied helped tell
that story to white schoolchildren across the nation, reinforcing the "naturalness" of white over black. And when states centralized public school policy
and began offering free textbooks, white schools passed on their textbooks
to black schools, ensuring that black children got to read those stories too.[63]

## 3

# Campaigning for a Jim Crow South

IN 1935, writer David Cohn described the southern landscape as a "whole system of codes and criteria of conduct set up to preserve the status quo based upon the plantation tradition, the one-party political order, and white domination of a numerically black majority."[1] Forged in the specific context of Mississippi's Delta counties, Cohn's assessment resonated in various pitches across the region, particularly in those southern states where contested November elections for statewide office were rare. In the decades after Jim Crow's disenfranchisement victory, the Deep South states of Alabama, Georgia, Louisiana, Mississippi, and South Carolina emerged as a landscape defined by vociferous political demagogues and entrenched purveyors of white supremacy. The Deep South was home to the most authoritarian, undemocratic partisan political systems in the nation.[2] Presidential elections from 1920 to 1940 brought out only between 10 percent and 20 percent of the voting age population. From 1900 to 1944, those who did vote in South Carolina and Mississippi cast over 90 percent of their votes for the Democratic presidential candidate reflecting the Democratic Party stronghold. In those two states, civic mobilization remained lower than in other southern states, and black participation in elections fell below 1 percent of those of voting age. In terms of voting and of electoral politics, there was no real threat of "daunting black insurgencies" in these Deep South states before World War II.[3] In fact, there was no threat of an electoral insurgency of any kind.

In 1920, woman suffrage could have reinvigorated the nation's democratic spirit, but low proportionate participation at the polls, particularly in the Deep South, suggested that women voters did not halt the Jim Crow South's democratic demise. White southern women did expand the electorate, however, and in their first decades of enfranchisement, the overall number of voters in presidential elections steadily rose. From 1916 to 1932, South Carolina and Mississippi, respectively, witnessed 63 percent and 69 percent increases in voters in presidential elections. While some increase resulted from population growth, it did not account for the entire expansion. Woman suffrage did open up the political system. In many cases, white southern women also made good on their promise that as full citizens, they would uphold, not weaken, the Jim Crow order.[4] Their participation in the polity did not substantially challenge racial segregation nor did they need to shore up the Jim Crow order with their votes since it was relatively secure. But electoral politics provided them with a platform around which to mobilize their organizations for particular policies, to encourage white women to go to the polls, and to push male officials to promote more issue-centered politics. Deep South politics were in no danger of upending racial segregation, but like public education, electoral politics gave white women a platform to shape the segregated South. As voters, segregationist women could use partisan politics as a training ground for political engagement preparing to be an antidote to the complacency or the challenges that threatened the racial order.

Three white women—Florence Sillers Ogden, Mary Dawson Cain, and Cornelia Dabney Tucker, all segregationists operating in Deep South states—capitalized on their enfranchisement to mobilize voters, white women in particular, to make electoral politics shape and sustain the system of Jim Crow. They exposed the diverse political paths and strategies available to create local and state networks of segregationists and national networks of conservatives. Responding to their local communities and their relationship to the New Deal, their political methods were as varied as the Jim Crow order they sought to serve. Some cultivated support for the New Deal while others engineered opposition to it. Many remained dyed-in-the-wool Democrats while a few committed acts of political apostasy and turned to the Republican Party. Others avoided partisan labels and instead leveled blistering critiques at state-level officials for sacrificing conservative political principles for political gain. Ogden, Cain, and Tucker represented all these positions, and each one of them, at various times, nourished the seeds of partisan dissent in the allegedly Solid South.[5] Despite their divergent partisan paths, they organized in states—Mississippi and South Carolina—where a two-party system was a charade and where Democratic Party candidates held little real debate on core political issues. With less than 20 percent of eligible voters in the South bothering to go to the polls at all, Ogden, Cain, and Tucker were a minority speaking to a minority. Given their intense political commitment, they were hardly representative of southerners of any kind.[6]

During the interwar years, white segregationist women adopted varying political positions on lynching, prohibition, the Supreme Court, the Works Progress Administration, and European refugees that reflected both their ideological and geographical differences. They experimented in political organizing and political dissent. In the Mississippi Delta, Ogden remained a diehard supporter of President Roosevelt and the New Deal. In south Mississippi, Cain lost her affection for Roosevelt's Democratic Party and became a Jeffersonian Democrat, rejecting the national party for an amorphous branch that celebrated states' rights. In the Low Country, Tucker left the Democratic Party for the Republican Party and then proceeded to purge the black and tan members from South Carolina's Republican Party rolls. In their political work, they forged political alliances beyond the Deep South. Periodically, they employed a political rhetoric that edged toward "color-blindness," minimizing overt appeals to white beliefs in black inferiority while maintaining policies that secured racial inequities. They positioned themselves as "principled" political actors, not minions of party platforms, unwilling to sacrifice devotion to a cause for party patronage. They did not seek statewide elected offices in the interwar period but did seek to elevate the interest of their constituents—white segregationist and white conservative women in the South and nation. Their work exposed the diverse political organizations and paths available to those who supported white supremacy and revealed experimentation in the political languages employed to defend segregation.

In the cotton-rich, black belt county of Bolivar, Mississippi, Florence Sillers Ogden began the 1930s much as she would end it—a devoted Democrat, a New Deal advocate, and a Franklin Delano Roosevelt fan. She was the dutiful daughter of the politically powerful Sillers family, an Ole Miss fan, an aspiring but frustrated writer, the wife of a Chicago man who had come south and stayed and an aunt, not a mother. If she had been a Sillers man, she would have attended the University of Mississippi, studied for the bar exam, and run for statewide political office. Instead, she had attended Belmont College for Young Women in Nashville, Tennessee, where "the womanly graces, the essential elegancies, the refinements that distinguish the genuine from the shoddy gentility," the catalog read, would not be "neglected." In a non-degree program, she studied "expression" and trained in "cultivated originality" and "refined naturalness."[7] At school, she did not pursue her passion, politics. When she returned to the Delta, she consumed politics and was consumed by it—in the journals and papers she read at night and in the morning, at the multiple meetings she attended, in her copious correspondence, and later in the weekly column she wrote.

Like her mother Florence Warfield Sillers, Ogden's earliest political education took place within women's clubs—the DAR and UDC. In the 1920s, the DAR served as her political seedbed and pushed Ogden beyond the local politics of historic preservation and commemoration and into discussions on national defense, subversive foreigners, and anti-radical activism. Over the decade, the DAR had shifted from progressive albeit hegemonic Americanization programs to anti-radical campaigns stressing ethnic nationalism, immigration restriction, the suppression of subversives, and support for the "security state."[8] Many of the 161,000 members welcomed the creation of the DAR National Defense Committee and joined the effort to protect the nation through increased state-sanctioned surveillance, education programs, and the blacklisting of "doubtful" speakers, reformers, and peace activists.[9] While there was some crossover between Ogden's UDC chapter and the DAR's national defense and patriotic projects, the DAR remained cautious of embracing the UDC's race-based nationalism.[10] For Ogden, the conflict was of little concern, and the DAR served to connect her to white women across the nation interested in anti-radical agendas that she saw as aligned rather than in conflict with her commitment to a Jim Crow order.

In Mississippi, Ogden concentrated on educating her contemporaries on the dangers of immigration, which she said "works under cover, like a cancer, eating away at the very vitals of our country." Meshing her DAR and UDC philosophies, Ogden worked to keep other "races" out of the United States, claiming that "into our hand has been placed a precious heritage, a sacred trust . . . to have and to hold for our children and our children's children so long as the race shall endure." As a state DAR leader, Ogden translated immigration into a local threat that weakened white women's authority to run the home, influence their children, and control the education of America's youth. Her anti-immigration stance had a pragmatic side. Bolivar County required separate schools not only for African Americans but also for Chinese, Mexicans, Italians, and Choctaw Indians. Foreign immigration not only threatened national security as the DAR contended, but it could cost her county valuable funds as it doled out money for separate schools and social services.[11]

Despite her civic activism, Ogden yearned to write, and in Roosevelt's second term, she found an outlet in Hodding Carter Jr.'s *Delta Star*. Her earlier efforts to become a published writer had met with meager success, as critics of her fiction had rejected her first person vernacular, her "reliance on humorous quirks of expression with satirical intent," and her use of stereotypical characters.[12] Carter, who was on his way to a Pulitzer prize for editorial writing, was a newspaper man who made his reputation on his journalistic investigation of Huey Long before coming to the Delta, and he hired Ogden to write a weekly column that she entitled "Dis an' Dat." The name came from a conversation with one of her black tenant farmers who had asked to borrow $.50. According to Ogden, he said his wife needed a "lit'l of dis an' dat." While the column affirmed early critiques of her writing, it merged all her interests—literary, historical, political, and economic—into a weekly opinion piece that reached a regional and later a statewide audience. The column ran for more than thirty-five years. By ignoring the social context of economic exploitation that undergirded the tenant's request, by erasing the identity of his wife, and by appropriating black dialect for a column that was often dedicated to the continued subjugation of black laborers in the Delta and beyond, her column's title served as a weekly reminder of the segregated social order she sought to preserve.[13]

The debut of "Dis an' Dat" coincided with the formation of the House Un-American Activities Committee (HUAC), an event that gave Ogden a chance to merge her interest in national defense with national public policy. HUAC investigated foreigners, communists, subversives, and Popular Front organizations that allegedly weakened the United States, but it ignored the KKK and spared white supremacists from subversive status. In an early column, Ogden claimed that Martin Dies, Texas congressman and chairman of HUAC, "is doing more for the ultimate good of this country than any single-handed person in America."[14] By this time, the influx of Europeans fleeing the expansion of Nazi Germany coupled with the congressional debates on abolishing 1924 immigration quotas had revived the immigration restriction discussion of the 1920s. Long schooled in anti-radical, anti-immigrant rhetoric, Ogden alerted her readers to the "political carnivores"—European political refugees—who were seeking to destroy democracy from the havens of American universities by indoctrinating unsuspecting undergraduates. Her solution: "American-born teachers, Americans who love our country, understand our background, revere our history, and respect our ideas and philosophies." "All of the isms of Russia, Poland, and Czechoslovakia rolled into one" could not compare to the democracy crafted "by men who rode horses, fought Indians, hewed forests, tilled land, and marched to battle so that America might be free." Establishing what would become an increasingly common critique of educators, she derided the civic contributions of "scholars shrouded in caps and gowns" and "poets who would steal from the rich and give to the poor." By ignoring subversive teachers, American parents,

Ogden claimed, had failed to protect the nation's youth and let "these wolves in sheep's clothing prey upon their eager young minds."[15] Soon her columns made it into the *Congressional Record* when Mississippi congressman Will M. Whittington read to the chamber Ogden's opposition to an expansive political refugee policy: "If we are to keep our country for ourselves . . . we must guard our principles of government with a jealous eye."[16] To counter a dangerous influx of ideas, Ogden called on women to write letters to their representatives encouraging restrictive immigration laws and to educate themselves on immigration policy. Ogden volunteered to help by pledging to to schedule women speakers on foreign relations and immigration for her DAR chapter.[17]

By the end of the 1930s, Ogden's political concerns extended beyond immigrants and subversives and focused more and more on the cotton economy. Many mornings when Ogden headed to her plantation at Beulah, she looked out over 1,200 acres shrouded in white cotton. The Mississippi River that lay just beyond the levee held the power to flood her land and wash away her profits. On the other hand, the river served as the Delta's economic lifeblood, cheaply transporting her cotton to an international market and enriching the already rich. But in the 1920s, the story had been hardship, not wealth. If the 1920s had seduced many Americans with consumer goods and easy credit, it apparently had skipped over most of Ogden's neighbors— white and black—whose livelihoods rose and fell with the price of cotton. By the 1930s, Ogden was no stranger to economic decline, global competition, natural disasters, or the intertwined relationship between racial segregation and cotton profits. The rollercoaster of cotton prices in the 1920s left behind debt, bank failures, and depleted state coffers.[18] As late as 1927, cotton prices had held at $.20 per pound, and then in April, the raging Mississippi had broken through the levees, ruining cotton crops, displacing tenant farmers and sharecroppers, and leaving the cash-strapped state with the job of rebuilding and shoring up the levee system. Even in the midst of such tragedy, white Deltans held fast to the system of white supremacy first by forcing black laborers to sandbag the levees and then by forcing them (sometimes at gunpoint) to build the tent villages for the Red Cross to house them in.[19] Six years later, cotton had fallen to just $.04 per pound, and economic stress defined Ogden's community.[20]

When President Franklin Delano Roosevelt took to the radio to spread his message of economic recovery, Ogden was ready to hear it. With her brother in the state capitol and her husband involved in rebuilding the levees, she had taken over running her family's cotton plantations. Working under the legacy of her grandmother Matilda Sillers who had prevented the plantation from being occupied by the Union forces and saved it from being mortgaged during the Civil War, Ogden tried to save it from another economic disaster.[21] She recounted learning the "three things of first importance": "how to handle negroes, how to spend your money, and what to do to make cotton." Even though Ogden believed that "all Negroes look alike until you learn them," she professed to know her workers and took care of what she deemed were their needs—food, clothing, medical expenses, and housing. By her own estimation, she was a fair, benevolent, and successful manager of her sharecroppers. Ignoring her own records, she proclaimed to have "very little difficulty with my labor," even though she also had written that her tractor drivers had gone on strike for higher wages. Continuing her paternalistic narrative, in 1936, she noted that "I make them work and they like me," and "they are satisfied. . . . But I treat them like human beings." She also measured her success with her laborers by "very little impudence and 'back talk'" which she found remarkable "from a race only a few generations removed from the savage jungle."[22] As she crafted her own success story by harnessing a historical narrative celebrating white paternalism and black inferiority, she established herself as a woman capable of directing the care of the Delta's black sharecropping and tenant families. Her role as an active plantation owner also earned her the opportunity to move in predominantly men's organizations—the Farm Bureau, the Staple Cotton Association, and Oscar Johnston's Delta Council, all groups dedicated to maximizing the profits of the cotton economy. Beginning in 1937, she could also use her newspaper column to publicize the agenda of the Delta Council and to debate cotton prices, trade policy, taxes, and American farm policy, solidifying her reputation as a planter.[23]

Trying to preserve the property and labor interests of the planters topped the list of Ogden's political priorities and that meant keeping black labor cheap and property taxes low. Since the 1920s, state budgets had tightened and legislative debates had pitted sales tax advocates in the Delta against higher property tax proponents in the rest of Mississippi. Before Roosevelt, Ogden had witnessed the 1927 resurgence of "redneck liberal," governor Theodore G. Bilbo, a hill country "reformer" who sought to make the Delta pay more for state services to help poor white Mississippians. Fearing continued increases in Delta property taxes and inflamed race relations, Ogden took her most public role in the 1931 gubernatorial campaign. Seeking to preserve "conservative government" and find a state executive who privileged their interests over the "hill interests" of southern Mississippi, Ogden and other Delta whites found their man—the wealthy lumberman Martin Sennett "Mike" Conner--among the "business progressives" of south Mississippi. Conner promised to reduce property taxes, and Ogden rewarded him by organizing Delta women for his campaign.[24] In an effort to build support for Conner, Ogden delivered a speech to Bolivar County women praising his political experience, his unmortgaged plantation, and his integrity. For those whose political interests were not married to planter concerns, Ogden stressed that Conner's tax policy would enrich the local infrastructure by supporting the hospital. Conscious that both men and women might doubt her political acumen, she advertised her brother, state legislator Walter Sillers's support for Conner.[25] Yet she called on white women to organize each precinct, to visit every elector, to distribute literature and bumper stickers, and to establish well-marked headquarters. Exploiting white femininity, Ogden told the women to "be peppy," and when they manned the polls to "look their best." Aware that women canvassing door-to-door might offend some men, she also implored the women to be smart. "If there is someone on the list that some man can see best," she directed, "then ask him to go in person." The contradictions in women's political roles were all too evident, but Ogden believed that they were also manageable. As long as her political interests upheld rather than challenged the rule of whites in the Delta, the place of white women in the political debate was assured, and Ogden could charge white women with political responsibilities without challenging the patriarchal foundations of the political system.[26]

No political neophyte, Ogden capitalized on her campaign work and her family connections as soon as Conner took office. In a lengthy letter, she reminded him of the unjust nature of the property tax and painted the Delta planters as benevolent, sacrificing citizens who had contributed to the point of insolvency for the greater good of Mississippi. Now, mired in depression, drought, and excessive taxation, these public-minded citizens faced state confiscation of their lands. To Ogden's delight, Conner honored his campaign promise and introduced a 3 percent sales tax that he called a "consumption tax," easing the burden on Delta landowners by transferring it their tenants. Unlike the property tax, the sales tax, Conner claimed, would bring black Mississippians into the taxpaying fold. Ignoring the woeful record of state services for black Mississippians, he claimed that this tax would make them pay for the services they enjoyed. Like Ogden, white Deltans anxious both to improve their economic standing and to reinforce white supremacy embraced Conner's proposal. On May 1, 1932, the sales tax went into effect.[27]

By 1933, Ogden's desire for pro-landowner economic policies meshed with the federal government's New Deal farm policy, and Ogden became a vocal New Deal supporter. In July, Henry Wallace, Secretary of Agriculture, came south selling his Agricultural Adjustment Act (AAA) cotton plow-up agreement, which was a plan to compensate landowners and theoretically the workers for land kept out of cotton production. The AAA benefited large landowners disproportionately by authorizing them to disburse, voluntarily, the federal funds to their fieldworkers, leaving intact repressive labor relations. Ogden's family would be among the AAA's primary beneficiaries in the Delta, perhaps receiving more than $200,000 and thus were kept financially solvent by the New Deal. As a result, Ogden and other Delta planters remained some of Roosevelt's staunchest supporters.[28]

The AAA was just one of the New Deal programs linking federal expenditures to the architecture of white supremacy. Ogden supported the Works Progress Administration, the Federal Emergency Relief Agency, and the Civilian Works Administration (CWA). The CWA built a library in Rosedale for whites only; Ogden served on its board of supervisors. After Walter Sillers Jr. orchestrated special legislation, the WPA contributed $25,000 to augment the town's $10,000 allotment to build a municipally owned hospital that served white residents only.[29] These federal programs assisted white Deltans more than black Deltans, by strengthening racial segregation and increasing the funding gap in segregated public services.

One of the more spectacular ways Ogden harnessed the New Deal to bolster Jim Crow's infrastructure came when she secured federal funds to build a white-only country club for Rosedale's residents. Worried about the dangers faced by local white children swimming in mud holes near the levees, Ogden called on white mothers to formulate a solution. At the meeting, the mothers decided to circulate a petition calling for the WPA to sponsor the creation of a local park. Ogden knew that the WPA was involved in building recreation centers across the country and proceeded to get government approval for the construction of a nine-hole golf course, tennis courts, a clubhouse, and a swimming pool. She contacted state legislator Walter Sillers, US Senator Pat Harrison, Congressman Will Whittington, and the head of the women's division of the WPA, Mississippian Ellen Woodward, to ensure support for the proposal. With $10,000 in federal money, $3,000 of town money, and land donated by Florence Warfield Sillers, the park, named after Ogden's father, opened in 1936. According to Jim Crow custom, blacks and whites did not socialize together in public facilities, and the federally funded Rosedale "country club" was no different. While black townspeople were denied access to the park, Ogden solicited their help to fund the park's upkeep—the annual Delta mule races. In this "exciting sport," black jockeys rode unsaddled plantation mules for thousands of spectators who bet, drank, and cheered on the Delta's workforce.[30] With the federal government's largesse, this WPA project ended up enlisting black labor to better the lives of white residents, reinforcing racial segregation.

Ogden's devotion to the farm policies and broader New Deal agenda of Roosevelt continued in her support for the president's court-packing plan. When the Supreme Court overruled the constitutionality of the AAA and its crop reduction subsidies, Ogden accused them of ignoring the plight of the people. "If something isn't done to allow the president to continue his policies," Ogden wrote, "we Delta farmers are liable to wake up next fall and find we've planted five cent cotton."[31] While some other southern Democrats painted Roosevelt's proposed expansion of the US Supreme Court as unconstitutional, Ogden declared "he is always right." While she would have preferred a constitutional amendment, circumstances demanded immediate action, and she joined the majority of southerners who supported an expanded Court, even while Americans outside the region tended to oppose it.[32]

Ogden maintained her political praise of the New Deal through Roosevelt's third election. In her column, she drummed up support for the Democratic executive. She called him a leader of "great courage" who "never falters" and would be most capable of addressing the important issues of the day. As the 1940 campaign took shape, she continued to praise the WPA for rescuing "fine men and women, who had always contributed their share toward a great civilization." "We have seen the haunting fear dispelled from the faces of old people," because the WPA had saved people "worth saving."[33] As other Democrats wavered, Ogden remained a defender of the New Deal, a proponent of deficit spending, an appreciative recipient of federal aid dollars, a staunch segregationist, and a white supremacist.

If her reliance on cotton made her welcome an economic policy built on federal intervention and money, she adopted a harder conservative line about matters of state funding for initiatives that served black Mississippians or poor whites in the hill counties. Her support for the national New Deal did not translate into support for Mississippi governor Paul Johnson's "Little New Deal." Against the expansion of black suffrage, she opposed Johnson's proposal to repeal the poll tax. As states moved to bolster public education with free textbook initiatives, Delta whites resisted Johnson's proposal for several reasons.[34] Publicly, Ogden wrote about her fear that higher property taxes would come with the measure and suggested that the state government supply books to families below certain income brackets. She also couched the measure as an intrusion on parental and domestic autonomy. In 1940,

Ogden campaigned against the governor-appointed Textbook Rating and Purchasing Board. She warned that "the surest way to arouse the indignation of the populace is to strike through their children."[35] What she really wanted was an exemption for Delta counties so black students would not receive civic textbooks that explained democratic rights. But she also resented the possibility of a new state textbook censorship board that would be composed of white men, threatening to usurp the roles of white women. Ogden denounced Johnson's reforms as an erosion of white women's autonomy and authority and couched his educational policies as attempts "to try to regulate the little things of our everyday life."[36] Men, as Ogden groused to her readers, were less concerned with children's education than they were reelection.

Ogden's long-lasting devotion to Roosevelt and the New Deal was not echoed by another Mississippi newspaper woman, Pike County's Mary Dawson Cain. By 1937, Cain had rejected both Roosevelt and the New Deal, even though she had begun the decade as a vehment Franklin Delano Roosevelt fan. As a young married women, Cain lived in the southwest corner of Mississippi where the landscape was defined by a thriving timber industry and small farms owned and worked by a 58 percent white majority. Pike County was a not a land of genteel, large-scale cotton planters surrounded by an impoverished but majority black workforce. In fact, only 3 percent of the county's land was in farms larger than 500 acres, in contrast to Bolivar County where at least 20 percent of the county's acreage was held in 500-acre farms.[37] Pike was a hardscrabble county of tough men and tough women that was home to both an early Mississippi NAACP chapter and a thriving KKK presence. It was a county where blacks would go to C. C. Bryant's barber shop for black newspapers and where whites could stop by John Cain's gas station for his wife's white weekly.[38]

At the time of Roosevelt's election, Mary Dawson Cain had a reputation as a young newspaper woman, a local beauty, and a maverick. In 1925, after she and John lost their only child just after childbirth, she had turned to journalism and politics. She was a devout Baptist but believed deeply in the separation of church and state. Religion, she believed, had no role in discussions of freedom and liberty. She held important roles in the Mississippi Business and Professional Women's Club (BPWC) as well as the General Federation of Women's Clubs. By the 1930s, she was a well-known leader in the state's Democratic Party. As early New Deal Democrats, Cain and her husband had been perhaps the first residents of Pike County to sport the Blue Eagle, symbolizing the cooperation of business, labor, and government under the New Deal's National Industrial Recovery Act.[39]

For Cain, the national campaign to end prohibition, not the New Deal, served as her political training ground, providing her with national contacts and statewide exposure. She derided women for their overwrought political drama when they marched to the state capitol with loaves of bread lost to them because their husbands drank their wages. Instead, she argued that prohibition violated the Constitution, made criminals out of decent men, and put following the law above people's welfare. It was not the state's business to regulate individual morals and doing so only criminalized the non-criminal. Her commitment to states' rights also engendered opposition to a federal amendment. As a "wet," she was out of step with a majority of Mississippians. Outside the South, Cain had built connections with men and women like Pauline Sabin of Chicago, founder of Women's Organization for National Prohibition Reform (WONPR), and Walter Liggett, a journalist famous for his articles on prohibition and corruption in the national magazine *Plain Talk*. Cain joined the WONPR, becoming the Mississippi branch's first vice-president. To build the repeal effort, she tapped into the membership of the BPWC and the General Federation of Women's Clubs, both organizations in which she played a major role. As a result, in 1933 the Mississippi branch of the WONPR grew more rapidly than any other state branch, enrolling nearly 5,000 members and winning a membership drive at the national meeting.[40]

Cain's anti-prohibition stance strengthened her political credentials in Mississippi. In 1932, she had endorsed Pat Harrison for the US Senate in part because of his anti-prohibition efforts. When Governor Martin S. Conner took office, he refused her request for what he called a "beer" meeting, but Speaker of the Mississippi House Thomas Bailey did agree to call for a referendum, and Cain would support his campaigns for the rest of his career. But Cain had powerful opponents. Democrat Vivian Franklin offered Walter Sillers the support of the "drys" if he ever ran for a Senate seat, and the Mississippi press also supported prohibition. Undaunted, Cain gave speeches to American Legion and Veterans of Foreign Wars chapters and urged Frederick Sullens, editor of the *Jackson Daily News,* to publish anti-prohibition pieces. Dismissing prohibition as a fight among women, Sullens initially refused, but he later excerpted part of her article, "Prohibition Should Have Been Raped." Cain's politics were not popular, and in a 1934 public referendum, voters supported prohibition by a margin of almost two to one. Officially, at least, Mississippi was so dry that it would be the last state in the nation to end prohibition, allowing the sale of liquor in 1966.[41]

Cain's loss, however, translated into statewide recognition in partisan and press circles. She became the editor for the local *Summit Sentinel,* the publicity director for the women's division of the state Democratic Party, editor of the Business and Professional Women's state publication, and a leader in the General Federation of Women's Clubs. In July 1936, she unveiled her own "newspaper with personality," the *Summit Sun*. Following Sullens's advice, she built her paper around community news, filling it with as many local names as possible. As part of this effort, she even began a column about Summit's African American community. One year later, the Mississippi Press Association recognized the success of her paper.

In 1936, her newspaper supported President Roosevelt's reelection. A year later, she had left Roosevelt and was on her way to leaving the Democratic Party. The combination of Social Security, the WPA, the anti-lynching bill, and the court-packing plan was too much for Cain's brand of conservatism, which emphasized limited government and fiscal restraint and opposed social welfare spending. The specific timing of her break with the New Deal Democrats, however, coincided with the congressional debate on anti-lynching bills. On the floor, Michigan's representative Earl Michener had read aloud the gruesome account of a Mississippi lynch mob's double murder of Bootjack McDaniels and Roosevelt Townes, both of whom were killed with blow torches, a gasoline-fed fire, and chains. Just as a white mob built the fatal fire, a few counties away Mississippi governor Hugh White was delivering an address on the decline of lynching. This apparent blindness to racial violence eroded congressional faith that the South could stop lynching, and the House passed the bill. Only 17 of 123 southern congressmen, however, voted to make "mobsters and law officials . . . liable to stiff Federal prosecution." Cain's faith in states' rights meant that she was on the side of the bill's opponents.[42]

The anti-lynching bill overlapped with the circulation of Roosevelt's court-packing plan. Differentiating between the New Deal Democrats and "Jeffersonian Democrats," a term she adopted in 1938 to describe her politics, Cain opposed the Court's expansion. Refering to herself as a "Jeffersonian Democrat" indicated her whiteness; her unwillingness to be a Republican; her rejection of the national Democratic leadership; and her distrust and disapproval of the New Deal welfare state—Social Security, the WPA, and federal education and civil rights policies. While Dixiecrats would adopt the term in 1948, by that time Cain had used it for a decade. Despite Cain's disdain for the national party, in 1938 Mary Louise Kendall asked Cain to become the publicity director for Mississippi's Women's Division of the Democratic Party. Cain declined the post, citing her inability to support the New Deal Democrats or Roosevelt. Kendall assured her that the national party was broader than one president and asked Cain to reconsider. Cain did and remained active in the state party as the publicity director and as an opponent of its highest ranking official.[43] Cain's abandonment of Roosevelt and her allegiance to Jeffersonian Democrats presaged her ultimate departure from the Democratic Party, the 1944 schism among Mississippi's Democrats, and the dramatic exit of the Dixiecrats in 1948.

Cain's embrace of Jeffersonian Democrats was just one of the rifts she had with the Democratic Party's mainstream. In 1939, she rankled the national leadership of the Women's Division of the Democratic Party when she supported the National Consumers Tax Commission (NCTC). The NCTC claimed to be a network of consumers, farmers, housewives, and businessmen who lobbied for a reduction in business taxes. In the 1930s, consumer organizations proliferated across the political spectrum, all seeking to influence policy or buying habits of Americans. Some, like the League of Women Shoppers, focused on how goods were produced, connecting goods with discussions on labor rights and working conditions. Others, like Consumer's Research (forerunner of *Consumer Reports*), separated consumption from labor and offered evaluations and reviews of products. Cain supported a third type—a lobby founded by the very business it sought to promote. The NCTC argued that higher taxes on businesses were passed on to the consumer, raising the prices on essential goods like groceries. In reality, the grocery chain A&P sponsored the NCTC, hoping to build opposition to an anti-chain store movement seeking legislative redress nationwide. While the name suggested consumers' rights, it was really a business lobby in disguise.[44] In 1939, May Thompson Evans, the assistant director of the Women's Division of the Democratic National Committee, reprimanded Cain for her support of NCTC. Evans suggested that as the publicity director for Mississippi, Cain might encourage women to investigate the money behind certain organizations before they are "taken in." Cain stood her ground, claiming that she was "sick to death of the so-called Democratic party." In a subsequent speech, she said that in "this God-forsaken, Roosevelt-ridden America of today" federal spending must have a cap. She concluded with "I AM A DEMOCRAT AND PROUD OF IT . . . NOT A SOCIALIST."[45] Invoking her identity as a business owner, Cain rejected "the taxation imposed on us today to keep up a nation of people dedicated to a life in the WPA."[46]

By 1940, Cain assured her readers that she was and would always remain a member of the "true" Democratic Party, just not the party of Roosevelt.[47] While she couched her opposition to Roosevelt in primarily economic terms, her embrace of "Jeffersonian" Democrats attested to her support for white supremacist politics. In a 1938 letter to Kendall, Cain called for a separate party for New Dealers, leaving the Democratic one to followers of "local self-government, and the sovereign right of states to manage their own affairs, not to mention the protection of white civilization."[48] While many Democratic officeholders were unwilling to make a clean break with a popular president, such a breach could be most easily accomplished by white women who had little to lose in the way of elected posts or partisan perks. Along with Cain, some white southern conservatives began a nascent crusade to move their communities, their women's networks, and their states out of what they considered a blind and damaging loyalty to the Democratic Party, demonstrating early fault lines in the Solid South.[49]

Cornelia Dabney Tucker was one of these women. She lived in the black majority region of South Carolina's low country. As a Charleston resident, she was surrounded by slave blocks, slave markets, and Gullah people, descendants of slaves who had worked the rice plantations before the Civil War. In 1917, the city had welcomed W. E. B. Du Bois, whose visit energized the local NAACP and led it to successfully protest the practice of hiring all-white teachers for all-black schools. But Tucker, along with Charleston's white elite, buried those stories of the past. She rarely discussed black-white relationships, a shared and complicated local history, or Jim Crow legislation. Instead, she looked toward the beaches, where she envisioned a business-centered, consumption-oriented, real-estate driven southern city. There, she could celebrate a more cosmopolitan Charleston that came with its winter people—wealthy northern and midwestern folks who came to escape harsh winter climes and soak up the sun.[50]

Tucker's life differed markedly from those of Ogden and Cain. She had married Robert Tucker, a real estate man who sought to make his fortune from tourism and who sold South Carolina as a sportsman's paradise. But he was no businessman, and when he died in 1921, he left Cornelia with five children and no fortune. Tucker immediately went to work in real estate and antiques. While she did not vote until the late 1930s, Tucker described herself as a Roosevelt woman for much of the New Deal. But at a 1937 dinner party, she claimed to have had a political conversion when her hosts lamented the inevitability of Roosevelt's Supreme Court reorganization bill.[51]

The next morning Tucker began what would become a national campaign to defeat the Court's expansion. She picked up the phone, called meetings for women across the city, and planned a nationwide petition drive. She called her organization the Supreme Court Security League and welcomed both Democrats and Republicans. She placed petitions at businesses, contacted the leader of South Carolina's Republican women Essie L. Messervy, and gathered

Charleston's winter residents to help nationalize her crusade. Within a week, she telegrammed President Roosevelt to tell him that her committee of mostly "loyal Democrats" believed him "to be so great a man that you will voluntarily abandon this plan if convinced it is not the will of your people."[52] Daily, the Security League sent special delivery petitions opposing court-packing to the offices of every United States senator. Volunteers polled Charleston businesses and found that 50 percent opposed the plan and the other 50 percent were swayed by their admiration and devotion to the president. Given Roosevelt's popularity, some businessmen feared losing customers if news of their opposition to court packing spread. While over 50 percent of those signing the petitions were men, Tucker targeted women and implored them to save the country from the forces of radicalism and communism that were behind such a plan:

> Women of Charleston! Women of South Carolina! Women of the entire South! Wake up and obey the clarion call to arms to save our country from an impending dictatorship, which will eventually plunge us into a communistic form of government.  Drop your luncheons, your bridge, your golf, your cocktail parties, and teas and work as you have never worked before, to save your country from this disaster.[53]

Tucker reminded them that they had only until the hearings on March 9 to reach their congressmen, senators, and the president himself.

The 166 signatures she gathered in the first twenty-four hours paled in comparison with the hundreds of thousands of signatures that poured in over the next three weeks. In twenty days, more than 150,000 telegrams opposing court packing arrived at Congress. When legislators agreed to oppose the bill, Tucker offered to cease the daily deluge. For the recalcitrant, she kept up the harassment by mail. Women across the nation joined her campaign. In newspapers and organizational correspondence, she listed women contacts in South Carolina's upstate and in New York, Georgia, Connecticut, Pennsylvania, Ohio, Tennessee, Virginia, Alabama, Michigan, Massachusetts, Illinois, and Florida. A newspaper headline read "Charleston Fires First Shot Again," noting that Tucker's campaign was the talk of Washington's ladies luncheon circuit. Other newspapers charted the rise of this "women's movement from nationwide protest against the proposed Supreme Court change." Tucker's campaign had galvanized women, led to rising disaffection with the national Democratic Party, and revealed the power of a well-organized group. That summer, Tucker reflected that while men had supported the cause, "by far the majority of letters and petitions came from women."[54] In a few months, she had gone from political neophyte to the creator of a nationwide network.

The following year, she left the Democratic Party to remake South Carolina's Republican Party, an unheard of partisan conversion. South Carolina was widely understood to be the most Democratic state in the nation, outdistancing Mississippi and Georgia with over 95 percent of votes cast going to Democratic presidential candidates.[55] In 1936, just over 1,600 votes were cast in the entire state for the Republican candidate, Alf Landon, and some counties counted no votes at all.[56] On a southern tour, one northern journalist wrote that in South Carolina "everybody he meets socially or other-wise, is a Democrat."[57] To register as Republican meant giving up any voice in state politics. Unlike forty-seven other states, South Carolina had not gone to a secret ballot. At the polls, South Carolinians picked up either a Democratic ballot or a Republican one. As a new Republican, Tucker could not vote for a Republican presidential candidate and at the same time for a Democratic candidate for governor, for the state legislature, or for the US Senate. In fact, there would not be a single legislator from the Republican Party in the entire state again until 1962.[58] To ask for a Republican ticket meant choosing to have no voice in the only party that mattered in the state. It was one thing to fight against a president who seemed to violate the Constitution, but it was quite another for a white woman to take on an entrenched Democratic machine by joining a political party long associated with black citizens and white "Negro lovers." According to her children, her partisan conversion had a cost. As a Republican, Tucker neglected fashion, took up smoking cigarettes and drink-ing bourbon, and lost her ability to talk about anything but politics.[59]

Believing that Roosevelt had betrayed the white South, Tucker sought to break the Democratic Party's hold on the region, translating her tactics from the Supreme Court campaign into breaking up the Solid South. She courted the Chamber of Commerce which was interested in business investment in South Carolina, anti–New Dealers who fundamentally opposed social wel-fare programs, southern Democrats who were chafing at the loss of influence in the Democratic National Committee, and Republican Party officials who believed that a lily-white party could make some headway in the Palmetto state. Above all, she reached out to women voters. She first predicted 10,000 recruits and then 100,000 willing South Carolina women, believing they were less bound by partisan structures and less concerned with the costs that going Republican would have on their businesses. She organized county chapters, publicized contacts, supported efforts to attract young Republicans, and trav-eled up the East Coast to cultivate Republican ties. In the months after the new Republican Party emerged, Tucker met with Mrs. Coolidge, former first lady, and spoke at numerous Republican women's clubs in Massachusetts and Connecticut. She also met with Republican men on Wall Street. As a unique and unknown white South Carolina Republican, she earned press coverage wherever she went.[60]

Unlike Cain who separated the New Deal Democrats from the "true" Democrats, Tucker collapsed the Democratic Party and the New Deal, courting disaffected Democrats with the label anti-New Dealers. In part, she exposed how the Democratic Party no longer represented the South by highlighting the 1936 convention rule that altered the presidential nomination process from a two-thirds majority to a simple majority. In effect, the new rule minimized white southern control over presidential nominations and platform tenets. Under the old rules, the South, which sent 23 percent of the delegates to the Democratic National Convention, could effectively block a presidential nominee. This rule had long allowed white southerners to exercise leverage over Democratic candidates, policies, and platforms. It had also made the presidential balloting at the Democratic National Convention akin to a side show curiosity. While Republican presidential candidates could be chosen in as few as six ballots, Democratic presidential balloting reached a peak of 103 ballots in 1924 but often hovered in the forties. In a 1936 voice vote with Roosevelt virtually unopposed, the Democratic National Committee moved to a simple majority to nominate presidential candidates. Tucker anticipated that the effect of this procedural change would be starkly evident in 1940 when southern opposition to Roosevelt's third term meant very little, particularly compared with the rising power of labor unions.[61] What Tucker did not mention about the 1936 convention, but what white South Carolinians knew, was that in addition to changing the nominating rules, party leaders had allowed black delegates to be seated at the Philadelphia convention, and a black minister had delivered the invocation. In protest, Senator Cotton Ed Smith of South Carolina had stormed out of the convention center and had gone home to tell his "Philadelphia story" about waning southern influence and integrationist sentiment in Democratic Party leadership.[62]

Armed with stories of Democratic Party betrayals, Tucker drew on her earlier networks from the court-packing fight to build county organizations for her new Republican Party. While men would serve in the top positions in this new committee, Tucker served as publicity chairman and Essie Messervy, long a Republican activist and mentor for the state's young Republicans, served as a national committeewoman. However, a host of obstacles hindered their cause. In part, Tucker noted that Republicans had to overcome the history of the party that tied it to the Union during the Civil War and Reconstruction, a social and economic structure that assured Democratic solidarity, and the lack of a secret ballot. The new Republican Party also had to counter an effort to create a third independent party by C. Norwood Hastie, who called himself a "Lincoln Democrat." [63]

To counter the public memory of the past that linked Republican rule to black majorities, white northern influence, and disfranchised white elites, Tucker and Messervy highlighted their Confederate credentials. Tucker celebrated her uncle General Stephen Ramseur, a Confederate general who died fighting the Union Army, and her grandfather, who had sold all his slaves prior to the war. Messervy reminded South Carolinians that her grandfather served in Wade Hampton's brigade and had tried "to rid South Carolina of scalawags and carpetbaggers." "Through the medium of the Republican party," Messervy claimed that she would carry on "my grandfather's work."[64] Tucker also noted that Lincoln was not in favor of political equality of white and black due to alleged evolutionary differences. She concluded that Lincoln's "entire political career and life were motivated by one dominant purpose: To preserve the Union of Sovereign States in representative government." In a magnificent revision of the past, she argued that Lincoln, so often credited with preserving the union, was in most cases a states' rights man. Finally, she contended that white South Carolina Democrats were really Republicans in disguise.[65]

To get her state "out of hock" to the Democratic Party, Tucker also had to change the Republican coalition that represented South Carolina at the Republican National Convention (RNC). She notified the RNC that her Republicans were a separate and distinct party from the Joe Tolbert faction and renounced his "Union Republican" party. Tolbert, a resident of Ninety-Six and Greenwood, was reviled by many South Carolinians for "trafficking with Negroes for political purposes." An imposing force, he had served as a delegate to the RNC ever since 1908, weathering an attempted ouster during Herbert Hoover's campaign. He fell in the face, however, of Tucker's campaign. Citing their appeal to the business class, her Republicans, Tucker claimed wore neck ties, not overalls; did not seek black supporters; and advocated white supremacist politics in the name of states' rights, moving to serve the lily-white impetus in the national party. In 1940, Tolbert's faction lost their convention credentials paving the way for Tucker's colleague Essie Messervy to serve as a delegate to the RNC, with Tucker as an alternate.[66]

But the real structural hindrance to a new Republican party was the lack of a secret ballot that would permit residents to participate in Republican campaigns for national office and continue to participate in Democratic politics at the state level. To fight this campaign, Tucker utilized a host of political strategies. She touted the importance of a secret ballot for business and investment in her home state and asked the RNC to support her efforts. In South Carolina, she named Clara Harrigal of Aiken as the chairman of the women's division of the South Carolina Republican Party. Tucker noted that Harrigal would organize Republican women in each county to speak to all non-partisan women's groups about the problems with the open ballot. This decision was made after Tucker met Miss Marion Martin, head of the National Republican Women, and after a radio poll indicated that less than 10 percent of South Carolina's women knew that their state's elections differed from those of every other state. Tucker praised Harrigal, not as a Republican, but as a woman who realized that "as a whole [women] have not met their political obligation to the nation since we were granted the suffrage."[67]

In addition to making South Carolina's open ballot a national story, Tucker used the Republican Party to educate South Carolinians, particularly women, about their failure to follow election rules that were the norm nationally. She began her letter-writing campaign, reminiscent of the anti–court-packing campaign, writing to all 170 state legislators, the governor, and others about the secret ballot. In March 1939, she was granted the floor in the state legislature by Senator Taylor Stokes. Arguing that as a Republican in an all-white Democrat legislative hall, an invitation to take the floor was the only way she could get a hearing, Tucker recounted how on election day everyone at the polls knew how individuals voted because they had to pick up either a Democratic or a Republican ballot. The state's constitution guaranteed a secret ballot, she claimed, so this practice violated state law. Then she tried to shame lawmakers, telling them that the *State*, South Carolina's leading newspaper, compared this practice to undemocratic elections in the Sudetenland. If they did not institute secret ballots, she insinuated that perhaps the federal government would have to intervene, evoking the ghost of Reconstruction and black voting. Finally, she noted that one day Palmetto State congressmen could be kicked out of the capitol because of fraudulent voting practices, leaving her state with no federal representatives. She urged state legislators to demand one ballot with all candidates listed.[68]

A year later she returned to the legislature, this time uninvited. Nevertheless, she took over the podium as the presiding state senator J. Wilfred Zerbst beat his gavel to drown her out. The chaplain even began a prayer that brought everyone but Tucker to silence. Explaining her irreverent behavior days later in newspapers, Tucker was pictured sitting with one of her

## She Held the Floor

FIGURE 3.1 After seizing the microphone during a prayer to lobby for a secret ballot at the state legislature, Republican Cornelia Dabney Tucker sought to rehabilitate her image by posing as a respectable grandmother who inadvertently disrupted a statehouse ritual. Without a secret ballot, she still contended that her interruption was the only way a Republican could make their voice heard. *News and Courier*, March 21, 1940, Charleston, South Carolina.

seven grandchildren, a doting grandmother who said that she did not know a prayer was being said. She offered an apology for her interruption. She did not, however, apologize for her speech, which she insisted was necessary because she had no representation in the legislature.[69] She returned to the state capitol steps in early May dressed with a banner saying "Legal Ballot 1940" and held a placard that said "Justice, Queen of Virtue, Columbia," a more subdued outfit than her previous paper dress made entirely of newspaper clippings endorsing the secret ballot. Marching in front of the capitol, newspapers noted that this time, she did not "invade" the building but instead stood on the steps posing for photographers.[70]

Tucker's efforts bore little immediate fruit. While she invigorated a new Republican Party that would pave the way for Democratic dissidents in 1948 and 1952, the modern Republican Party did not rise in South Carolina until the late 1950s. Just as Tucker predicted, as soon as South Carolina

**Clothed in a Political Issue**

FIGURE 3.2  As publicity chairman for the Republican Party of South Carolina, Cornelia Dabney Tucker dressed in newspapers endorsing a secret ballot. She adopted this costume as a means of protest when she attended a Business and Professional Women's Club meeting. *News and Courier*, November 26, 1939, Charleston, South Carolina.

implemented a secret ballot, which they did after the 1950 state elections, Republican numbers rose, bringing votes to presidential candidate, Dwight D. Eisenhower. But her victory for the secret ballot had been delayed for more than a decade, as South Carolina held on to its status as the sole state still using an open ballot.

During the 1930s, Ogden, Cain, and Tucker came to prominence as members of the white elite who practiced politics in Black Belt states. In South Carolina and Mississippi, electoral politics resembled a parlor game bereft of real issues, real conflict, or a popular following. Low Country and Delta constituencies controlled state legislatures. In these states, black protest had little room to operate and white critiques of the Jim Crow order from organizations such as the Southern Tenant Farmers Union, Highlander Folk School, the YWCA, or the Southern Conference for Human Welfare remained relatively easy to combat.[71] Yet Ogden, Tucker, and Cain used this period to cultivate political networks built on issues that reached beyond the confines of their state. Less concerned with state-level elections than prohibition, national defense, or the secret ballot, they used the DAR, the WONPR, Jeffersonian Democrats, the Supreme Court Security League, and the Republican Party to organize politically and to build connections to conservatives nationwide. These efforts allowed them to practice early iterations of a kind of color-blind political rhetoric that offered broader political platforms built on states' rights, immigration restriction, a rejection of the New Deal state, or electoral reform.

Whether Roosevelt supporter, Jeffersonian Democrat, or white southern Republican, these women charted a new path that promised to change partisan politics in the South. Time after time, their political organizing drew from the pool of white women voters, white women's civic and business organizations, and white women's partisan auxiliaries. Fully incorporated into the electoral system, Ogden, Cain, and Tucker positioned themselves as moral arbiters of a wheeling and dealing male-centered politics and as full-fledged partisans who cared about issues, not officeholding or a partisan quid pro quo. They had found other white women willing to be politically active, signing petitions, organizing phone trees, canvassing door-to-door, and publishing their political opinions week after week. Relying on the freighted term of "states' rights" when convenient, they forged networks of conservatives without directly invoking the white supremacist political order that their policies upheld. Yet they had opposed anti-lynching legislation, made sure that New Deal monies found white constituents more often than black ones, urged states to reject some federal inroads into social welfare, and purged African

Americans from South Carolina's Republican Party. In each case, their—New Deal–era politics, however divergent, ensured that in their communities racial segregation would not fall victim to a changing political terrain. They also guaranteed that when the time came to save segregation, white women would have the political experience to conduct such a crusade.

# 4

# *Jim Crow Storytelling*

IN THE LATE FALL OF 1923, a young Nell Battle Lewis decided to spend an evening at the Superba Theater in downtown Raleigh, North Carolina, watching *Birth of a Nation* for the fifth time. Reviewing the film in her *Raleigh News and Observer* column "Incidentally," Lewis noted that each time D. W. Griffith's movie came to town, she had to see it. This was her sort of "religious observance." *Birth of a Nation*, she wrote, was "the best movie we've ever seen." It made her weep and drove her to exclaim, "This is my native land." She went on to claim that the first KKK was "a necessary tour de force effected by some of the leaders of a . . . civilization in danger of its very life."[1]

Her devotion to such a film at first seemed incongruous. Lewis had returned to her hometown after years as a southerner living outside the South. After a brief stint at Goucher College in Maryland, she attended and graduated from Smith College in North Hampton, Massachusetts. At Smith, she sat in integrated classes, heard black and white political leaders, debated woman suffrage, and studied a curriculum that challenged the conservatism, reactionary impulses, and, to some extent, segregated and sectarian currents of the South.[2] After a year in Manhattan, she had gone to France as part of the YMCA's "Y-Girl" program to support the American Expeditionary Force. In 1921 Lewis had returned to Raleigh and interviewed with the *News and Observer* editors while dressed in jodphurs, a blazer, boots, and a hat. Her androgynous presentation gave pause to the editor, but he hired her anyway, as an embodiment of the "New Woman"—single, independent-minded, and career-oriented with world experience. As the newspaper's first female staff writer, she set out to challenge the hidebound traditionalism of white southerners, pedestal-residing white women, and greedy industrialists. In economics, she rejected the trappings of the New South creed and disdained the materialism and business practices of the textile industry. In her early politics, she seemed to identify more with white women of the working class than those like her former St. Mary's School classmates. Instead of joining the Daughters of the American Revolution and preaching Americanization and anti-immigration, she made fun of their reactionary politics and condemned their red-baiting. Opposing evangelical Christians, she parodied creationists and defended the study of evolution. When H. L. Mencken pronounced the South "the Sahara of the Bozart," Lewis expressed her intellectual alliance with him, noting that he was "a heady stimulant . . . and effective purgative for intellectual inertia and dry-rot complacency."[3] As her prominence grew, southern commentators called her an iconoclast and a radical. Her enemies

FIGURE 4.1 A young Nell Battle Lewis serving with the American Expeditionary Forces in France before she returned to Raleigh to begin work at the *News and Observer*. Kemp Plummer Lewis Papers, Southern Historical Collection, Wilson Library, University of North Carolina at Chapel Hill.

called her a communist; her father and brothers characterized her as abnormal, eccentric, and perhaps even mentally unstable.[4]

Considering the widespread influence of the second Klan, her relentless attacks on them might have merited such judgments. A national organization with professional fundraisers and advertising executives, the KKK proclaimed Anglo-Saxon superiority, recruited record numbers of members, sponsored candidates for southern legislatures, and intimidated their political opponents. More than a few southern leaders lacked the moxie to publicly condemn the Klan, yet Lewis castigated them for their contribution to mob justice and racial violence and told her readers that the KKK was ignorant of the very race science it claimed to follow. In her published poem, she ridiculed their cowardice and intolerance in her opening stanza: "The Kautious Klan Klandestinely. . . . Kwarrels Konstantly with those; Who Kannot Like their Kourse DesPotio."[5] When the Klan threatened to send one of its female members to take Lewis's job, she gleefully wrote of her anticipation and then attacked them for their criticism of professional women and flappers.[6] She deplored most of all that KKK activity put North Carolina in the company of its less progressive southern neighbors—Georgia and Alabama. Each time the KKK reared its ugly head, Lewis felt it testified to the failure of North Carolina's white leaders who had promised a more humane, compassionate, and just state. Still, she wept through *Birth of a Nation*, a film that she knew the second KKK had exploited.[7]

Taken together, these seemingly dissonant reactions were in fact not anomalous but rather typical outcomes of Lewis's work in the cultural production of white supremacist politics. As Lewis put pen to paper, she celebrated a world led by educated white progressives, white female reformers, and black elites and populated by oppressed white industrial workers and black southerners receptive to enlightened white leadership. In the *News and Observer* and other periodicals, she crafted public narratives that created a cultural landscape of a more "affectionate segregation."[8] Her fiction and non-fiction reinforced specific historical interpretations, invoked black stereotypes, and celebrated white liberals and exceptional black men and women. Her feature writing often highlighted white women who called on social reform for white and black North Carolinians, noting white women's gendered affinity for cleaning up politics. She praised white and black progressives and condemned those who participated in racist violence and who justified the neglect systemic to racial segregation. Lewis did not erase the black South or ignore black achievement. For example, she celebrated the poetry of Harlem Renaissance writers, congratulated North Carolina's black collegiate choral groups, and lobbied for state-run girls' homes for wayward black youth. She also wrote a piece that attributed the impoverished state of the black neighborhood Haiti Alley to the suspect character of those who lived there and ignored structural poverty. When she returned from her travels, she celebrated seeing the first shacks of black sharecroppers because they told her that she was home, romanticizing economic outcomes of segregation. In fact, the stories she wrote offered up both the black elite and the black folk, but such writing often served to educate white people about the appropriate "place" of blacks and whites in a Jim Crow world. In crafting her narratives, she encouraged her readers to follow cultural practices that reinforced racial segregation. She was a storyteller for Jim Crow.[9]

In telling these stories, Lewis did important political work for the segregated South. Culture was one of the central levels where everyday experience could be translated into support for the larger social system, joining social welfare policies, educational practices, and electoral politics as critical sites where the Jim Crow order was shaped and sustained.[10] Her writings offered a template for segregation to be modern and long-lasting—a system grounded in new cultural and scientific arguments more than older biological ones.[11] For Lewis, North Carolina's segregated order would be a product of a progressive state that adopted national reforms. Educated, liberal white supremacists, not mean reactionaries, would control race relations and mitigate the worst abuses of the system. Relying on the "best" white people, Lewis was a female counterpart to Howard Odum, who, as historian Glenda Gilmore noted, served as one of the "hydraulic engineers at Jim Crow's watershed" urging white liberals to be the engines of gradual incremental change.[12] With so many stories of mean-spirited and violent segregationists abusing black women and men, rarely did Lewis or Odum or progressives nationwide have to confront how their liberal reforms reified racial inequities. A broad agreement on white supremacy among white social reformers meant that Lewis could easily balance her progressive ideas with her devotion to a society of white over black. To her readers, she delivered lessons on a racial etiquette that upheld racial segregation, gendered ideas about female citizenship, paternalism, and devotion to social reform. For all the stories she told celebrating North Carolina's enlightened race relations, she served the Jim Crow order by suppressing those that challenged the authority of liberal-minded, middle-class, educated white men and women. Lewis knew that the segregated order was never as secure as it might seem.[13] White people needed instruction in how to maintain white supremacy. White apathy and white misuse of racial authority threatened the very system that guaranteed their political, economic, and cultural authority. In the 1920s and 1930s, her stories criticized the way segregation as practiced departed from the way she wanted and believed it should be. Right up to 1954, Lewis kept calling on fellow white southerners to live up to separate but equal, not abandon it.[14]

Lewis's brand of white supremacist politics clearly took root in the particular conditions of her home state where she could bring her beliefs in progressive era reform, modern science, eugenics, and women's civic participation to bear on her work for racial segregation.[15] North Carolina's champions held the state apart from the racial violence of the Deep South, advertised its black educational institutions, embraced voices that challenged the material greed that undergirded the New South creed, and condemned the rawness and rage that characterized other southern demagogues. Politically, a relatively active state government had earned North Carolina its progressive reputation.[16] Throughout the 1920s, rising public expenditures for state services inspired broad political discussions on economic development, social welfare, and education. Some white political and religious leaders even talked about improving black facilities, held interracial conferences, and welcomed black participation in a community of Christian humanitarianism. For the state's leaders, North Carolina's black population of nearly 30 percent figured in their vision of the state, where black moderates like James Shepard, president of North Carolina College for Negroes, could urge black North Carolinians to challenge inequality gradually and cautiously, exemplifying the "politics of respectability."[17] Josephus Daniels, once an architect of the 1898 white supremacy campaigns, owned the *News and Observer,* which served as a voice of moderation and modernization. The University of North Carolina at Chapel Hill recruited to its faculty such luminaries as sociologists Howard Odum and Guy Johnson and moved to national prominence under the leadership of Harry Chase and Frank Porter Graham. Progressive reformer Kate Burr Johnson headed the state's Bureau of Social Welfare. In the interwar period, Bertrand Russell, Gertrude Stein, James Weldon Johnson, Langston Hughes, Frances Perkins, and Eleanor Roosevelt spoke at the University of North Carolina or Duke University, bringing some of the cosmopolitan energy Lewis had experienced in Manhattan and France.[18]

At the *News and Observer,* Lewis first contributed feature pieces, edited the Society Page, and wrote a children's page. Despairing at the limitations of these forums, she nevertheless made her first mark in "Kiddies Corner." In this full-page feature, Lewis encouraged literacy and imagination, reinforced the social order with black dialect stories and caricatures, and promoted the study of North Carolina history. An early story entitled "Patrick, the Rollin' Possum," was written in dialect and included a Nell Battle Lewis original cartoon with the caption: "then the nigger held Patrick up by his long skinny tail and said: Ef dis heah' possum ain't sho' nuff fat, den I dunno fat w'en I sees hit."[19] The next week, she encouraged young people to have their mothers read to them about their home state so they would "not only . . . feel that North Carolina is the best State, but to know why it is."[20]

Soon she introduced her weekly column "Incidentally," which would run almost uninterrupted for the next forty-five years. Prophetically, her column began with a scene in a park, depicting two black men and one black woman whose "contented laughter broke forth frequently, and the red meat of the melon disappeared rapidly." Later her caricatures acknowledged the calming comfort offered by "deferential Negroes who wave to you even when they don't know you."[21] Contented black North Carolinians joined Lewis's frequent romanticized depictions of black-white relationships embodied in her print tributes to "mammy." She noted that the ties between mammy and her white children were "more than imaginative gossamer," as she lamented a system based on paternalism that was "now passing with the changing times." In return for their loyalty and love, Lewis said that mammies would receive no earthly reward but the same spiritual reward "as the white folks they worked for." In fact, the mammy of her childhood, she claimed, "came as near being a Christian as anyone who ever lived." For Lewis, "Mammies" embodied the epitome of black leadership—serving in a position of deference, devotion, and dependency to white middle-class women.[22] While she attacked her state's social ills, she had established her column by trotting out minstrel-like black characters that assured herself and others of the satisfaction of the state's black population. Under the helpful hands of the state's white progressives, Lewis believed, black North Carolinians would take childlike steps forward.[23]

But as Lewis paid homage to the Mammy in print, she was participating in a larger cultural production of white supremacy in which the iconic black domestic took center stage. In the immediate aftermath of the 1922 dedication of the Lincoln Memorial, the UDC's Washington, DC, branch gained congressional support for a granite tribute to black mammies. Mississippi's Senator John Sharp Williams proposed and received appropriations of $200,000 for it, and North Carolina's Charles Stedman introduced the funding bill to the House of Representatives. At the peak of its membership, the UDC seemed poised to build a monument that imposed its historical interpretation on the national cultural landscape. Some black newspapers responded with outrage. Newspaper owner, editor, and art historian Freeman Henry

Morris Murray argued that "public sculpture was not merely reflective . . . but also productive of new publics and power relationships." Encouraging his readers to be more critical in interpreting the meaning of sculptures, he asked them to evaluate "its obvious and also . . . its insidious teachings." Black newspapers published their own renditions of a mammy statue that spoke to sexual aggression and assault coupled with long hours and no wages. For the UDC, the Mammy monument offered a racialized household that put white women in positions of authority, allowing them "to recast their own citizenship" and create a more "affectionate segregation."[24] While the monument never materialized, "mammy" did not need to be cast in bronze to function as an important symbol of segregation. Inked in Lewis's columns, she remained both important and politically flexible in propagating the cultural infrastructure of segregation.

Lewis did not just deliver black characters of white mythology in her storytelling but also offered up black literary luminaries and black educational leaders. Lewis had long noted that she read the NAACP paper, *The Crisis*, and celebrated the artistic achievement of "Negro poets" like Claude McKay and James Weldon Johnson. Her favorite Harlem Renaissance novelist was Jessie Fauset, whose upper-class African American characters condemned passing as white and interracial marriage, themes that would have fit well with Lewis's belief in eugenics and white supremacy.[25] Lewis's book reviews also upheld a racial hierarchy. In 1924, Lewis wrote a joint review of Walter White's *A Fire in the Flint* and E. M. Forster's *A Passage to India,* declaring that Forster's work was art and superior in form and tone to White's *A Fire,* "a more melodramatic piece along the lines of propaganda." With omissions and exaggerations, White's book, she claimed, made for a biased treatment of the "Southern White" and the "Southern Negro." Like Forster's work, there were similarities in the ruling people of each area who did not understand the colonized—blacks or Indians. She also saw parallels in that the rulers were ruling for "their own good," not the common good. What bothered her most, however, was that "the Negro mind," which she assumed to be distinct, appeared in White's book as "not one whit different from that of the white man." White's black man acted just like a white one would under similar circumstances. "Can the Negro author who speaks for his race in this novel give us something more distinctive than that? . . . With all the mystery of Africa and all the darkness of slavery behind him, is there nothing unique in the Negro, after all?" she asked.[26]

Lewis's question exposed the cultural and geographic underpinnings of her racial ideology. Proud of her association with social reform, informed by scientific data, and assured of white women's authority because of their particular racial and gendered identity, Nell Lewis rejected the pedestal and the pulpit but believed in Anglo-Saxon superiority. She rooted her hierarchical beliefs in "race science," a position superior to those southerners whose racism rose from raw emotion. To educate her readers, she ran a crossword puzzle about eugenics, celebrating modern scientific thought. But as her review of White suggested, her racial liberalism left no space for discussions of an equality born of commonalities. Modernism had educated her, and there were differences—biological, cultural, historical differences—she believed, that should shape public policy and culture. It was not anti-modernism or economic gain that drove her racial politics, but a Progressive Era devotion to social reform, women's gendered contributions to society, and modernity itself.[27]

While Lewis's attention to black accomplishments reflected a kind of racial moderation to both her white readers and her black readers, it simultaneously stung some black readers. In the winter of 1925, she attended a production of Shakespeare's *Twelfth Night* put on by the Shaw University Players. Despite the technical perfection, Lewis noted that "the general effect of the performance was strikingly artificial." Instead of Shakespeare, which black students must perform, she claimed, in their "adopted language," she advised them to focus on folk drama. While the KKK had carried "racial consciousness and racial pride . . . to excess," she conceded, "I am a great believer in trying to be what you are." Lewis advocated an emphasis on "their own distinct racial character." Lamenting that the "advancement of the Negro has been largely imitative," she was anxious to witness "a genuine drama of their own."[28]

Willing to engage with her critics, Lewis published the objections of two black North Carolinians who lamented how white supremacist ideology infiltrated her public narratives. Shaw University dean William Turner appreciated her "to some degree complimentary criticism" but disagreed with her assessment of English as an adopted language for African Americans. He instructed Lewis that black and white babies learn language in the same way and that there was no "racial predilection for any particular language." Black social heritage in the United States, he continued, was the English language. At the State Department of Public Instruction, W. A. Robinson also noted that her comments solicited much discussion among those who "admire your usually broad attitude toward thought in general and concerning the Negro in particular."[29] He also disagreed with her suggestion that black Americans just imitated white Americans, noting that black Americans had long legacies of their own American traditions.

Two years later, Lewis again sparred with her critics after she reviewed black musical performances at the governor's mansion. When black performers sang "Negro-folk songs," Lewis praised them because they "sang like Negroes." In the middle of "Cotton need a-pickin so bad," the Fayetteville singers even "did a little shuffle . . . exactly right," she wrote. This time a University of North Carolina professor reminded her that the "cultured Negro . . . is not the freedman of 1867." Eavesdropping on a conversation about her review among black college girls, he heard them comment that "the white audience had a taste for music that was satisfied in direct proportion as the program descended toward more clownish setting."[30] For Lewis, the Jim Crow South meant black southerners occupied a particular cultural place, and this meant deference, dialect, and slave spirituals, not Shakespeare, "correct" English, or political participation. Her reviews and accompanying criticism reminded her readers—both black and white—that white supremacy reigned even among white southern liberals.

Lewis's views on social reform, however, held some real possibility for positive changes to the justice and prison systems. She worked together with Howard Odum and the *Journal of Social Forces* to publicize reform proposals for mental health and penal facilities. This work connected her to nation-wide efforts that rooted reform in social science research and simultaneously reified an American racial hierarchy.[31] Condemning capital punishment for those suffering mental disabilities, Lewis wrote about "a lone man behind the grim gray walls of the State's prison, with a pitifully jangled brain [who] will pass swiftly and mercilessly and forever into death's dark silence." In 1925, she told her readers how prison guards murdered a "mentally defective Negro prisoner." Lewis blamed this state-sanctioned killing on politicians who cared more for the bottom line than prisoner well-being, an impulse that also shaped an unwillingness to fund a segregated institution for the "feeble-minded." Thirsty for revenge, state officials would rather have a rape trial and lynching of a black man "with a mind of a 10 year old," Lewis wrote, than "provide adequately for the mentally ill." Lewis was incensed that "mental defectives"—particularly those who were black—were often left in society to commit crimes and then put to death without ever receiving treatment. Lewis argued that without the "exercise of disinterested public spirit and intelligence" that might consult sociological rather than economic studies in the pursuit of a fair and just legal and penal system, the state's political leaders would fail to uphold North Carolina's progressive image. Subsequently, Lewis feared that North Carolina would never rise above the South's reputation of "savagery" and "backwardness."[32]

Her outrage about capital cases of mentally ill prisoners in 1921 and 1925 coalesced in her study entitled "Capital Punishment in North Carolina." Full of data about age, region, race, economic standing, and crimes of those put to death by the state, her research connected her to the American League for the Abolition of Capital Punishment (ALACP) and the work of its secretary Vivian Pierce and lawyer Clarence Darrow. Pierce praised Lewis's report on capital punishment as unmatched and asked her for permission to publish parts of the report. While Lewis worked with the League and other reform organizations, she did not join the ALACP, the southern-based Commission on Interracial Cooperation, or the Association of Southern Women for the Prevention of Lynching (ASWPL).[33] In 1930, when a black man was lynched for the alleged rape of a white girl in Edgecombe County, Lewis did not sign the petition circulated by the North Carolina ASWPL. She did write a blistering article that blamed South Carolina's former senator Coleman Blease, known for inciting racist violence among the white working class, for the particular brand of vitriolic racism now circulating in her home state. She criticized the barbarity of a mob that took no account of either the evidence or the mental condition of the accused.[34] Lewis worked closely with white female reformers, public health officials, and the League of Women Voters to upgrade mental health facilities, youth reformatories, and prisons, and to make the state's judicial system administer justice that met the spirit of separate but equal. From this liberal political platform, Lewis managed to continue to craft North Carolina's position as a progressive southern state even in its commitment to racial segregation.

Central to Lewis's vision of social reform and segregation were white women. She celebrated women's newfound political clout and their gendered responsibilities to the public. She cast white women as the real custodians of justice, reform, and a more responsible state. These multiple political duties merged in her attacks on North Carolina's textile industry in which she unrelentingly criticized the state's industrial elite and attacked the rampant materialism of the New South order. By 1923, nearly 200,000 women were working in the textile industry, and the North Carolina Federation of Women's Clubs (NCFWC), the YWCA, the League of Women Voters, the North Carolina Federation of Business and Professional Women, the State Nurses' Association, and the North Carolina Congress of Parents and Teachers lobbied for a survey on conditions. But the survey promised by the executive secretary of North Carolina's Child Welfare Commission, E. F. Carter, never materialized.[35]

Despite these defeats, Lewis maintained her calls to regulate the textile industry and to limit child labor. Her commitment to a child labor law, however, could not overcome her wariness of federal intervention. Like Mildred Lewis Rutherford, Margaret Robinson, and Florence Sillers Ogden, she remained "dead against the Federal Child labor amendment" because it would "make the director of the Children's Bureau in the Department of Labor . . . the super-parent." Establishing the link between parental authority and state sovereignty, Lewis opposed outside interference in North Carolina's economic and social system, burying her reform impulses below her devotion to states' rights. In 1925 the State Legislative Council of Women called for a state-sponsored child labor eight hour day law, but on the floor, the law received only one vote. The rejection of the state child labor law disappointed Lewis and revealed to her the "gross and blatant materialism" of her state. "It was probably very presumptuous of the women," Lewis sarcastically observed, "to think that any manufacturer should be inconvenienced for the sake of the welfare of children."[36]

Enumerating the ills of the southern textile industry—an industry in which two of her half-brothers were leaders—Lewis contended that industrialization had created a working-class consciousness, exploited a native labor force, and forced women to neglect their families. It also prevented white women from doing the important work of childrearing. Her calls for industrial reform continued to fall on deaf ears, but in April 1929, workers at Loray Mills in Gastonia and then in Marion went out on strike, which attracted statewide and national attention. The National Textile Workers Union (NTWU), the Communist Party, and other labor radicals came to North Carolina to assist in these homegrown labor strikes. As Lewis had feared, working-class frustration slipped into violence.[37] While workers organized, set up tent villages, and distributed food, two murders complicated their efforts and pushed local events into international headlines. Management responded to the strike by evicting the families of the strikers and forming a Committee of One Hundred that meted out vigilante violence, poisoned wells, and raided the workers' tent colony. On June 7, police responded to a strikers' march. Shots were fired, and four police officers and one strike organizer were hit. Chief of Police Orville Aderholt, whom many considered sympathetic to the strikers, died of his wounds the following day. The court charged fourteen strike leaders—three of them women—with the murder of the policeman. While the textile owners blamed communist infiltration, not disaffection of their workers, Lewis noted that for a decade, they had dismissed the calls for industrial reform.[38]

Amid the labor strikes, murders, and shoddy trials, Lewis got a chance to shape the public narrative of the strike into, among other things, a Jim

Crow story. She cast both the communist presence and the labor insurrection as desperate reactions of a group of forsaken citizens. "For arrogance, pigheadedness and general social blindness," the state had let its manufacturing interests sacrifice its workers, including the fifteen accused of murder, eight of whom she claimed were "regular" North Carolina textile workers.[39] She condemned law enforcement for failing to keep order and protect the strikers. To Lewis's dismay, the national coverage of mobs using bayonets and black-jacks on women strikers reinforced the barbarity of her home state. Lewis called on lawyers to do "a public service of very high order" by taking the case, and she became a charter member of the Fair Play to the Gastonia Strikers Committee. She defended her involvement on the grounds that she was not "a participant in the class war" but "an interested citizen of North Carolina anxious to see these workers get a square deal and equally concerned for the honor and good name of my 'capitalistic' State."[40]

Covering the events for the newspaper, Lewis was in the western part of the state when the murder trial of those accused of killing Gastonia's police chief commenced in August 1929. That month, one juror had a mental break-down, and the trial was suspended until a later date. Frustrated company men roamed the region, anxious to mete out their own justice. Unaware of a roving posse of angry anti-unionists, on September 14, Bessemer City union members loaded up in a pickup truck and headed to a union rally. In the back rode unionist Ella May Wiggins, a textile worker who had lost five of her ten children to malnutrition. Denied repeated requests to work the night shift in order to take care of her remaining children, she was a prominent member of the tent city and a frequent singer at union rallies.[41]

Wiggins had also reached across the color line when she worked with black organizer Otto Hall to build an interracial group of strikers. Raising class interests above the New South rhetoric of white supremacy, Wiggins's work with Hall, other organizers felt, had left her a marked woman. When confronted on the road by several cars full of angry men, the truck Wiggins was in turned around. But the company men continued. One car deliberately crashed into the truck, and shots echoed from others. Blood spilled from Wiggins's chest. No one other than Wiggins was killed that day, and all but one of the men arrested for her murder were Loray Mill employees. The ninety-minute acquittal of the nine men who had killed Wiggins dashed Lewis's optimism that the judicial system would provide class-blind justice. Disgusted by the power that the textile industry held over state officials, Lewis noted that for Ella May, "the union . . . [was] hope for herself and her children, the possibility of a fuller life." Emphasizing Wiggins's identity as a mother, Lewis asked, "Who in her own state had ever tried to help her?" "The children," Lewis wrote, ". . . Dear Jesus, what will happen to them now?" The state's failure to intervene on the workers' behalf had resulted in violence and had left five orphans in a state that had refused to implement industrial reform.[42] According to Frank Porter Graham, Lewis's rhetoric had "burn[ed] the wrong of Mrs. Wiggins' death into our social consciousness."[43]

Lewis's accounts of the strikes, trials, and murders, however, offered several narratives for the state's citizenry. Despite her despair over the death of Wiggins, Lewis's greatest sorrow, it seemed, came from the public statement the murder made about her North Carolina. Once again the state's leaders— male and female—had failed to protect their weakest citizens, women and children. She faulted not only the negligent mill owners and the "mad police" with their deaths, but also "the prevailing sentiment of a state which has sacrificed its humbler citizens in its new worship of wealth."[44] Because of such negligence, Lewis argued that the workers logically turned to those who would help them, communist or not, and she interviewed union officials to tell their story. In Gastonia, Nell Battle Lewis interviewed Ellen Dawson and Fred Beal, both NTWU officials, who told her the union was not "a Communist organization" but that it received help from the Communist Party. In her newspaper columns, Lewis recounted these interviews and argued that the protest of textile workers fit with their first amendment freedoms and American political tradition. In July, Lewis had returned to Raleigh and attended a rally assembled by communist organizers Sophie Melvin and Julie Poyntz. Denied a forum at the North Carolina Federation of Labor, Melvin and Poyntz held the rally at the Wake County Courthouse. Lewis had spoken with communist organizers, attended rallies, and had even been given journalist and author Mary Heaton Vorse's notes to help her with her articles. Deeply knowledgeable about the labor organizers, Lewis argued that the presence of communist operatives resulted from the abdication of leadership among the state's economic and political elite.[45]

Beyond her critique of greed and materialism, Lewis's narrative whitened the strikers and erased interracial organizing. Anxious for white strikers to win, the stories she told had whisked black organizers off the political stage, buried the communist platform of interracial cooperation, and left elite white North Carolinians as guardians of the state's working white poor. As her handwritten notes attested, she had been in Gastonia in April right around the time black organizers John Owen and Otto Hall were there. On July 12 in Winston-Salem, she noted that the American Communist Party's candidate for president in 1924 and 1928, William Foster, and "Negro speakers" worked to organize a branch of "Southern trade unity." She scribbled that the "Southern Conference of National Textile Workers Union at Charlotte, continued and that on Oct. 12, Negro speaker [was] loudly applauded by . . . 300 [attendees] composed largely of N.C. textile workers." She also wrote that Foster said, "I believe in full social and political equality for the Negroes with all those terms imply"[46] But these notes remained just notes and did not make it into her articles on the strike. Nevertheless, the *Gastonia Gazette* pilloried Lewis's involvement with the communists, and David Clark, mill owner advocate and editor of the *Southern Textile Bulletin*, repeatedly made the connection between the communist agenda and racial equality.

Opponents of the textile union collapsed distinctions between economic justice and communism and racial equality in order to delegitimize workers' demands. Lewis wanted North Carolina's workers to get a fair hearing and some economic redress so she did just the opposite. In her published pieces, she erased the interracial organizing of Wiggins, Ellen Dawson's support of black organizer John Owen, and Sophie Melvin's working relationship with African American Otto Hall. She adhered to the public demand for racial segregation at the same time she supported the very individuals committed to an interracial workers' revolution. Even as she transgressed the barriers of class in North Carolina politics and suffered public criticism, she did not publicly challenge the other tenet of New South industry: racial segregation. Her efforts to tell a story of Gastonia that would engender reform had to uphold the politics of white supremacy and, as such, reinforced the gradualist, paternalistic rhetoric of many white southern reformers.[47]

Lewis's most radical moment exhibited her skills in telling stories that upheld white supremacy. As an expression of her deeply held racial beliefs or her desire for the strikers to win, her story of Gastonia suggested what would define the limits of cooperation.[48] Either unable to admit or unwilling to disseminate the possibility of a working-class, interracial, political alliance, Lewis grappled with what brand of white supremacist politics served the state best and in whose hands race and class relations lay, not about its very existence. While she witnessed a grassroots political movement rising up from the working class, she could not permit black North Carolinians, working class or otherwise, to reject the guiding and paternalistic hand of educated, enlightened, progressive whites. Lewis, white liberal women, and like-minded men, such as Howard Odum, shaped a less violent, more maternal, more moderate white supremacist state where leaders took care of their workers, white and black. Racial segregation could be sustained only if domesticated by white liberal women and men overseeing a state that strove to honor "separate but equal."

After Gastonia, a few more political defeats—her own unsuccessful run for a state legislative seat and her campaign for presidential candidate Alfred Smith—did not soften Lewis's tongue or weaken her attacks on the most reactionary voices in the state.[49] In 1931, the editors of the Chapel Hill magazine, *Contempo*, Lewis's friend Paul Green, and social scientist Guy Johnson invited Langston Hughes to the University of North Carolina for a reading of his scathing poem "Christ in Alabama," about the false accusations and shoddy trial of the nine Scottsboro boys. Hughes came to town, read poetry, and charmed many Chapel Hill residents simultaneously earning the ire of industrial and political leaders across the state. While Nell Lewis applauded academic freedom, her brother, Kemp Lewis, led a campaign to punish those who sponsored Hughes. He wrote to UNC president Frank Porter Graham claiming that Hughes's poetry, particularly the poem he referred to as "Black Christ," was "enough to make the blood of every Southerner boil to have a man like this . . . given any attention or consideration whatever by decent white people." Kemp Lewis asked "if this Negro was allowed to use the buildings" or if he had "any recognition whatever by the faculty?" He then questioned Graham about the students who authored *Contempo* and accused them of "striking at the very foundations of our civilization and our social relationships." Not satisfied with alerting only Graham, Kemp Lewis proceeded to notify Governor O. Max Gardner and included clippings of Hughes's poetry in his letter. He then asked the governor to speak to Graham about this attack on white supremacy.[50]

The turmoil over Hughes alerted the state's white elite to "subversive" activity at their university. By early 1932, more than 300 people had signed the Tatum Petition that called on Graham to curb "the alleged evil influences of the University of North Carolina upon the youth of the State." Though convalescing from oral surgery and bouts with mental illness at Tucker's Sanatorium in Richmond, Nell Lewis did not let this attack on academic freedom pass silently.[51] She wrote her brother Kemp that she hoped "all is well at the University" and asked "Is 'Contempo' still uncensored?" "I wish you would run David Clark out of that State," she continued, as he was "behind that petition . . . as sure as the world, and is nothing but a public nuisance." Kemp Lewis did not sign the Tatum Petition, but he continued his protest and broadened his attack to include the university's leniency on socialism. In her weekly column, Lewis ridiculed the Tatum Petition, describing it as "foolishness, just plain foolishness—I don't care how many mayors, ministers, and manufacturers have signed it." She defended the presence of both Russell and Hughes and claimed sarcastically that "although that [the Hughes visit] was in the ticklish realm of race relations in the South, lynching still seems to me out of order." While Kemp continually referred to the "nausea that came to me over the Langston Hughes incident," Nell Lewis wrote, "Black or white . . . Hughes is a poet and like it or not, his works are part of current American literature."[52]

When Lewis returned to health and to North Carolina, she became less vitriolic in her calls for reform and more indebted financially to the very brothers she had excoriated. The cultural landscape of white supremacy that she continued to shape from her columns, however, was not decidedly different than before, even with the New Deal. She still condemned racist violence and an unresponsive judicial system, and she upheld what she believed could be a sanctified and responsible system of white over black. Far from challenging this position, architects and leaders of the New Deal helped her cultivate this space for social reform in the hands of an enlightened white elite. Thus, Lewis's friend Frank Porter Graham could belong to the Southern Conference for Human Welfare and deny Pauli Murray, an NAACP member and civil rights activist, admission to University of North Carolina's graduate program in social work. Even as African Americans realized the subversive potential of the New Deal, liberal white supremacists, like Lewis, saw few national challenges to southern race relations from the federal government, the Democratic Party, or black southerners. The challenges she did see she could still manipulate, just as she had done to the stories of Otto Hall and John Owen in 1929. The public erasure of interracial radical organizing remained possible.

She still worked to expose her state's failures to meet the equal part of separate-but-equal and attacked reactionaries who condoned exploitative and cruel public policies. Lewis's commitment to prison reform and her public commentary on the deplorable conditions faced by the state's black and white incarcerated demonstrated that she still had room to critique the implementation of white supremacy without threatening its foundation. She exploded with characteristic fury and sarcasm when two black prisoners, Woodrow Wilson Shropshire and Robert Barnes, lost their feet to gangrene. Sentenced to "serve short terms" on the state highways for larceny and drunk and disorderly conduct, respectively, Shropshire and Barnes suffered frostbite after being "hung up" in marginally heated cells during twenty-degree nights. After nine days of such treatment, they worked eighteen days in the prison camp until they received medical treatment for "the flesh of their gangrenous feet rotting and dropping off the bones." At ages nineteen and twenty, the two black men had their feet amputated and were left crippled.[53] When the case reached the courts, the unfairness of the judicial system compounded the tragedy, reinforcing how Jim Crow courts equaled injustice. The jurors failed

to find the guards and the prison physician guilty of cruel and unusual punishment. Lewis claimed that this case revealed how African Americans were
often denied the right to ask for justice in the state's courts. Lewis noted that
the state-appointed attorney presented a lackluster case for the prosecution.
Even though an indictment could not help the prisoners, she noted that it
could have shown them that justice was available to African Americans in
North Carolina. Instead, she claimed, the trial "actively says to them—and to
an admiring world . . . Just a couple o' niggers—so we should worry." Taking
an even sterner stand, Lewis proclaimed that black North Carolinians had
not "a ghost of a chance in its [the state's] white man's courts . . . because they
were poor Negroes without influence."⁵⁴

Read as a defense of black civil rights, Lewis's condemnation of prison
abuse would earn her a place among some of the most liberal activists of the
1930s. The all-white court system—a product of segregation—was partially to
blame, contended Lewis. This was a bold assertion in 1935; it was not a damning one. For Lewis, whites failed to uphold a legal system that guaranteed
their superiority, not their infallibility. Segregation laws did not prohibit a
just conviction of white criminals. The white prison guards and physicians
deserved jail time for their crimes and for compromising the myth of white
superiority. Whites had failed to uphold the law and in doing so had threatened the entire rationale of white supremacy. In failing to carry out its legal
responsibility, the courts of North Carolina, not Lewis's critique, jeopardized
the system of racial segregation. In fact, she was all too aware that incidents
such as these earned her beloved state the condemnation and condescension
of outsiders and perhaps threatened to incite the spirits of the state's black
citizens.

Her blistering attacks fell short of condemning racial segregation. Neither
did she support the Southern Committee for People's Rights, a Chapel Hill
group led by her friend Paul Green and other white radicals who called for
the dismantling of racial segregation. Lewis's commitment to social reform did
not apparently push her this far. The committee rebuked the system and also
defended the rights of the prisoners as individuals. In advance of a national discussion, they spoke of human rights and tied their efforts to those working for
African American civil rights. Lewis did not adopt the human rights discourse
but maintained a tone of parental remorse and paternalistic regret when she
affirmed that even in the face of injustice, "it seems to me that the Negroes of this
State, as a whole, are remarkably well-behaved, remarkably patient." In her open
statement to North Carolina's black population, she reassured them that "many
other white people in North Carolina are shamed by this verdict . . . [and] we

consider it a disgrace to the State." She admitted, however, that her "many" was really more like a few.[55]

The Shropshire and Barnes incident also suggested the strength of the Jim Crow system during the New Deal era. At this time, white southerners including Lewis could still critique the racist abuse of black southerners and advocate the "advance of the Negro" without threatening the foundation of white supremacy, in part because 1930s liberalism focused more on economic and political problems that plagued the South than on racial ones. Because Lewis believed that the greatest threat to segregation arose from white inattention, criticism about its implementation was not heresy. The myth that segregation satisfied black southerners persisted, and her writings only reinforced that myth. For Lewis, it was only when white southerners failed to act properly that problems arose. And it was often white men who precipitated these problems, leaving white women as the real guardians over a racial segregation that could last.[56]

Outside of social reform, Lewis's storytelling for white supremacy was particularly evident in her reviews of theater, art, and fiction. At St. Paul's AME Church, the home church of her childhood "mammy," she delivered an address on opening night of the pageant *Heaven Bound*. This pageant, written by two Sunday school teachers at Atlanta's Big Bethel AME church, was originally a religious drama rendered in modern hymns that told the story of twenty-four pilgrims trying to reach heaven but tempted individually by Satan. Twenty of the twenty-four reject the temptation, and in the end a black soldier in the Army of the Lord kills Satan at heaven's gate. The production was built around audience participation, clapping, and stylized performances.[57] On opening night at St. Paul's, the original hymns had already been replaced with spirituals, which suited Lewis. She claimed "that in this form of art the genius of your people have a good channel of expression." "As a race," she continued, "you have both dramatic and musical talent, and of course, you have, too, a strong religious bent." "So it is appropriate," Lewis said, "that you should express yourselves in this way." Following such praise, she closed by saying that "in relation to religious truth . . . there can be no fundamental distinction of race. There is neither Caucasian nor Negro, white nor black, but we are brothers in that mystical body of which Christ is the head."[58] By suggesting the absence of segregation in heaven, Lewis bolstered her reputation as a racial moderate. Speaking of racial difference and genetic predispositions to drama and music, Lewis also upheld her belief in separate and distinct races. In the interwar period, Lewis could be both a liberal and a defender of racial segregation.[59]

Lewis's comments on the art of North Carolina's W. A. Cooper, a black painter, exemplified the balance Lewis struck. She noted that his conventional portraits of leading black businessmen and educators were "only mediocre." When Cooper painted a black washerwoman, a "youthful yellow bootblack," and a black "Little Brother," he moved to the exceptional. Lewis's favorite painting was of Cooper's father who, she said, represented "a familiar type of patient, faithful Negro whom we all respect." It is with these "distinctive Negro types," she wrote, that Cooper "has special sympathy." Upholding Jim Crow politics through black artistic achievement, Lewis championed artistic renditions of mammies and bootblacks because they upheld the social order, reinforcing the believed necessity of a racial stratification. For whites, they depicted non-threatening black southerners, contented and happy in service to white superiors.[60]

Efforts to perpetuate such a Jim Crow fantasy received a huge boost when Margaret Mitchell's *Gone with the Wind* appeared on screen in 1939. In 1936, Nell Battle Lewis had pronounced Mitchell's novel the best book on the Civil War and Reconstruction. Publicly, she claimed that in it "was everything you've been hearing all your life, the whole story, nothing left out." She reminisced about the "old friends"—white and black—who filled the text. Rarely heavy-handed in her praise, Lewis gushed that Mitchell's book deserved the Pulitzer Prize. Privately, Lewis wrote to Mitchell, *Gone with the Wind* "is the novel I'd like to have written but couldn't."[61] White women and men across the nation praised the book, bombarded Mitchell with fan mail, and called for an early transition to the screen. Mitchell herself blurred the line between the fictional and historical in her work and "often boasted of the novel's historical accuracy." She claimed to have read diaries, unpublished letters, and memoirs and accounts from Generals Sherman, Johnston, Hood, and Cox. Claiming that "the history in my tale was as water proof and air tight as ten years of study and a lifetime of listening" could make it, she also attributed her inspiration to Thomas Dixon's fictional works that inspired *Birth of a Nation*.[62]

For Lewis, *Gone with the Wind* served as a needed antidote to the widely disparaged picture of the South that had emerged in Erskine Caldwell's *Tobacco Road*. Mitchell's pen celebrated the Old South in a way that served the New Deal South in immeasurable ways. It affirmed Lewis's long-held position that deep federal involvement in the affairs of individual states most often resulted in disaster. In the midst of the New Deal, the rise of the Popular Front, and interracial organizing, the novel reinforced the mindset that black southerners were ill-equipped to participate as equal partners in the South's political and economic life. Mitchell's work reiterated the Jim Crow fiction that southern whites knew best how to treat their black neighbors and that the federal government's intervention in social relationships was ineffective. For a segregationist or "ardent Confederate," as Lewis described herself, it trotted out stock characters of Mammy, a black woman whose dependency is central to southern white womanhood, and Prissy, "a lazy, triflin' negro girl," who reinforced black women's subservient place in a world segregated by labor, race, and rearing. Lewis wrote that she would walk through Oberlin and find a better "Prissy," simultaneously criticizing the Harlem actress who played the part and erasing the individuality of her black neighbors. Mitchell also offered up Scarlett, a rebellious white woman who disregarded conventions that prevented white women from entering politics or the economy and who ultimately saved the South. Finally, the novel and film justified the conservative political rebellion against the New Deal by highlighting inept government and heroic individual effort.[63] In her 1940 review of the film, Lewis proclaimed that "the current decay in self-reliance has a by-product of wistfulness. . . . Too often we yield, but some of us still have manhood enough to wish that we didn't, to know that we shouldn't, and to admire someone, even a character in a book, who does not."[64]

By the end of the 1930s, Lewis had made her mark as just such a character. While many North Carolinians and students of the 1920s would remember her radicalism, advocacy for industrial reform, and opposition to the region's most reactionary moments, her most long-lasting work had been in the cultural production of white supremacy. Carefully balancing her political radicalism in other areas with a relatively liberal position on segregation, Lewis had emerged as an incisive storyteller for segregation and the political project that undergirded it. Her reputation as a "truth-teller" only reinforced the lessons she offered about white over black in the Jim Crow South. Her racial politics also offered educated, progressive white southerners a politically palatable way to digest the politics of white supremacy. Lewis was not out of step with more progressive views of women's political activism. Her efforts connected her to reform projects across the nation—prison reform and social science–based policies hatched in universities across the nation and published in academic journals. Rooted in this modern political context, she offered white southerners stories to take them forward in terms of the white supremacist political project.

THE INTERWAR PERIOD had provided possibilities for women's political activism and for their work in an expanded bureaucracy. It also witnessed a kind of equilibrium in the politics of white supremacy. By the time women got the vote, the ferocious and violent battles to institute racial segregation and disenfranchisement as the law of the land—like the Wilmington Riot of 1898—were twenty years in the past and in the process of being erased from the historical memory of many white southerners. In Tulsa, Oklahoma; Rosewood, Florida; Elaine, Arkansas; Detroit, Michigan; and Chicago, Illinois race riots continued to ravage the nation following World War I. These violent uprisings reflected postwar tensions, economic upheavals, labor organizing, and resistance to the reverberations of the Jim Crow order, not to its initial implementation. While radical black and white activists defied the dictates of Dixie in this period, there were no longer black officeholders or viable Republican or Fusion party threats to white control in the South.[65]

From 1920 to 1940, many white southerners created networks and sustained or participated in policies that created a landscape reifying white control and touting the satisfaction of black southerners. Backed by the Supreme Court, a powerful and sympathetic Democratic Party, and presidents who bowed to a southern model of race relations, white southerners seeking to preserve white over black could count on powerful allies. But the political project of white supremacy took a most intransigent form in communities where local people implemented legislation and practiced customs that sustained racial segregation. Layers of political strategies emerged courting everyday white women to participate. Capitalizing on white women's gendered authority over schools their children attended, some had focused on public education. Other women used their local knowledge of their neighbors, their classmates, their students, and their patients to try to render impermeable the lines between white and black. White women interested in exercising their new political power in the formal political sphere could work to get out the vote of white women, pressure legislators to appoint women to public welfare offices, push for legislation that minimized government authority, or support policies that shaped government funding designed to serve white constituents, not black ones. Finally, from newspaper columns to stump speeches, white women told public stories that revealed how good white southerners knew best how to take care of their black brethren, articulating a politics that simultaneously spoke of uplift and immutable racial hierarchies and left power in the hands of the elite few.

White women built these political networks—locally and nationally— making it white women's duty to be Jim Crow's gardeners, public housekeepers, and guardians of public schools. They touted themselves as the moral conscience of politics, the beacons of social reform, and the caretakers of those less fortunate than they—poor white and poor blacks. Their political activity could be radically diverse, but it rarely separated them from the national mainstream. In these two decades, their approaches portended great differences among white southerners' efforts to ensure racial segregation. It also suggested the possibility of alternative political paths, even if Ogden, Cain, Tucker, and Lewis did not take them. For some, it meant undying support for Roosevelt and for others vehement opposition to him. It meant the tightening of state funds for black institutions or the expansion of state funds to equalize white and black schools, prisons, and reformatories. It meant acknowledging black genius of the present and ignoring it in the past or erasing it all together. It meant labor laws that kept black tenants poor and funding for separate black institutions that trained black doctors, lawyers, and teachers. Both the "affectionate segregation" that Lewis professed and its more vicious manifestations took root and grew in the same rich soil that nurtured various strains of massive support for racial inequality.[66]

# PART II

# Massive Resistance to the Black Freedom Struggle, 1942–1974

# 5

## Partisan Betrayals

### A BAD WOMAN, WEAK WHITE MEN, AND THE END OF THEIR PARTY

FOR DECADES, white segregationist women had worked to combat white apathy, training whites to support a Jim Crow world through their social, economic, political, and cultural interactions. Working largely unopposed, they had counted on national and state-level institutions—the Democratic Party, the federal and state judiciaries, Congress, laws, and customs—to be at least complicit if not co-workers in their white supremacist project. Even with wayward whites, the system of segregation seemed fairly sturdy, rarely threatened, and very well maintained. But World War II solidified and expanded federal intervention in the economy and opened up economic opportunities for working-class Americans, prompting a southern diaspora. Fighting Nazi Germany engendered national conversations on the ideological kinship between fascism abroad and America's own white supremacist practices. Black Americans capitalized on their new electoral power outside the South, their greater economic stability, and their military contributions to wage the Double V campaign (for black Americans, a victory at home and a victory abroad). An international revulsion at extreme state-sponsored racial and ethnic discrimination intensified their resistance to persistent and widespread inequality, political and economic disfranchisement, and lack of access to equal facilities. White southerners responded with a cacophony of the oft-repeated fiction of a content black population in need of white oversight—a fiction as crucial to the reign of Jim Crow as laws and lynch mobs. The Democratic Party surveyed wartime economic needs and new demographic realities and realized that a new national political calculus was in the making. The segregated South watched warily as one of its most reliable institutional allies courted new constituencies, supported an expanded warfare state, and shifted to the left, equivocating in its support of their Jim Crow system.[1]

With most whites nowhere near ready to admit that black southerners were dissaffected with the South's racial hierarchy, segregationists turned their ire toward the Democratic Party, accusing them of wavering in their devotion to a Jim Crow nation. They argued that the Democratic Party had slighted white southerners for a new political coalition filled with northeastern intellectuals and newly urbanized African Americans and unionized industrial workers. Many segregationists feared that when the Democratic Party sacrificed the Solid South they would also sacrifice segregation. How to address such a political betrayal by their former ally mobilized many white women across the South, even if it produced little strategic cohesion among them. Some white women segregationists embraced the business conservatism that welcomed federal money for economic growth but not social change. Others held a hard-line opposition to an expanding federal government, no matter the loss of funding, continuing a larger critique against the New Deal.[2] Still others remained "separate-but-equal" liberals, arguing for the expansion and improvement of black facilities. In the wartime years, however, that position lost its viability.[3] A few white southern liberals quietly believed in a more equitable world but doubted that segregation would disappear. And then there were those who feared it would and moved to combat the threat by working on all the political terrains they had cultivated in the interwar period—social welfare, public education, electoral politics, and storytelling.

In the interwar years, white segregationist women had played a creative role in reinforcing, shaping, and even building their South's system of segregation. The threats of the wartime years moved white segregationist women to a position of defense, seeking allies, exposing enemies, and being extra vigilant. They still worked to sustain the system, but they also moved to protect it, worrying as much about outside threats as they did about apathy among their neighbors. For many, the Democratic Party destabilized racial segregation. In their quest to defend the segregated South, the most dedicated segregationists married their opposition to the Democrats to national conservative organizations lobbying for their own partisan interests. Massive support for segregation transformed into massive resistance.[4]

Southern white women reconfigured white supremacist politics during this time in three ways. First, they understood Eleanor Roosevelt as embodying the political betrayal of the Democratic Party. For some women, the fractures in their partisan loyalty became salient in their wartime critiques of the First Lady. She served as a gendered threat to racial segregation and a racialized threat to white southern womanhood. Second, segregationist women couched the labor policies of the federal government as threats to the segregated economies, homes, and hometowns they were preserving for their white soldiers. Third, various white women sought to remedy the Democratic Party's betrayal by breeding political dissent. Their opposition to the national Democrats served as an early sign of partisan disaffection and pointed to the eventual southern partisan realignment that has often been located with uprisings of a later date—the Dixiecrats, Eisenhower's southern appeal, and Goldwater's popularity. In their partisan critiques, they contributed to the rehabilitation of a national conservatism, the weakening of the Solid South, and the persistence of a politics of white supremacy.[5] In August 1942, white and black club women and church ladies of Salisbury, North Carolina, prepared for the visit of the First Lady Eleanor Roosevelt. *Time* magazine reported that white residents, still reeling from efforts of black Boy Scouts to integrate the July 4 parade, had not wanted her to come. But on August 14, she boarded a train for the cotton mill town where she toured the YMCA and the YWCA and visited Cannon Mills, a non-unionized factory with 16,000 workers. Afterward she met Livingstone College's black students and faculty with whom she would spend the remainder of the day. That evening she addressed a crowd of nearly 2,000 at the General Convention on Christian Education of the American Methodist Episcopal Zion Church.[6] During her visit, she ate lunch with various DAR, UDC, and Parent Teacher Association (PTA) members, and at night she dined with black women and men. Breaking white southern rules of racial etiquette outside the South was one thing, but such a move even in the self-styled progressive state of North Carolina was quite another. Having chosen to take interracial dining south of the Mason-Dixon line, the First Lady was an affront to segregation's customs. As a result, the white women of Salisbury, ministers' wives, YWCA women, and the Cannons refused to provide overnight accommodations for Mrs. Roosevelt. In fact, not one middle-class or elite white woman in Salisbury opened her home to the First Lady. At the end of a long day, Eleanor Roosevelt boarded the train and headed back to the nation's capital. For the sake of her "colored friends," one Salisbury resident surmised, she had "insulted the whole state."[7]

This was not the first time Roosevelt's dining habits had provoked criticism among white segregationist women. During the New Deal, some white southerners believed that Eleanor Roosevelt was a bellwether for the administration's domestic policies, particularly those having to do with race. As such, she was worth monitoring. In 1941, columnist Florence Sillers Ogden had commented on the First Lady's attendance at Harlem Hospital's graduation ceremonies for "colored" nurses.[8] Ogden had noted that a few of the nurses came from Mississippi and Texas, and four had accepted southern posts to serve black communities from segregated hospitals. In this way, Harlem Hospital's nursing school accommodated itself to the South's Jim Crow order. When Mrs. Roosevelt went to Mother Zion Church, she could have behaved, Ogden wrote, as "a queen . . . condescending to her subjects" which would have aligned with white southern practices of attending a black church fundraiser, going to a black performance at Hampton Institute, or mourning at the funeral of a black acquaintance. But Roosevelt had not bid the nurses farewell at the ceremony's end. Instead, she had gone home with some, had mingled with their families and friends, and then, she had written, "we all had supper." In Ogden's view, the First Lady "had gone too far." Hovering high on the hierarchy of sins against Jim Crow, breaking bread across the color line was heresy, perhaps as much a threat to Jim Crow as interracial consensual sex. In her column, Ogden wondered if Roosevelt knew that "she is advocating quite another thing for the rest of us."[9]

Even so, the First Lady's Salisbury or Harlem dining arrangements could hardly have constituted a substantial threat to racial segregation, but by 1942, the political allies that white southern women had long counted on to help them maintain racial segregation had begun to slip.[10] Eleanor Roosevelt functioned as a lightning rod on whom white women could locate the threats to Jim Crow without acknowledging black resistance.[11] For segregationists, she served simultaneously as a symbol of the Democratic Party and of the power white women had either to cultivate or to destroy the white supremacist South. In the racialized civic life of the South, threats to racial segregation were often couched in specifically gendered terms, tying constructions of white womanhood to political policies that supported white over black. In fact, white motherhood and womanhood had become a kind of racial performance inseparable from upholding the color line. Good white mothers reared children who maintained appropriate racial distance, made sure that schools taught a curriculum in line with white supremacist politics, and told stories that educated the larger public on the "naturalness" of racial segregation. Respectable white womanhood relied on the cultivation (at times) of physical, political, and social distance from black men, women, and children. Good white motherhood came to be defined by the same complicated rules except that white mothers had to guarantee that their children learned and adhered to the lessons of segregation. Their duties to the Jim Crow order rested on their progeny. Conversely, if white women and mothers did not follow segregation's dictates, then they threatened the foundation of white supremacy.

Eleanor Roosevelt stood in stark contrast to this formula, imperiling not only white southern women's gender roles but also the very system of segregation itself.

For newspaperwoman Mary Dawson Cain, the subversive racial power of the First Lady had national repercussions. In October 1942, Cain published an open letter to Eleanor Roosevelt blaming her for the three brutal lynchings of two black teenage boys and a Laurel, Mississippi, farmer. Calling Roosevelt the "ring leader of . . . racial agitation" and one of the "Southerner-haters," Cain imputed this wartime resurgence in lynching to Roosevelt. Unlike Eleanor Roosevelt, who seemed to court social equality, most black southerners, Cain noted, remained in the South—a testament, she believed, to their fondness for white southerners and their satisfaction with segregation. Cain quoted a black Mississippi man who claimed that "the Negro is not interested in social or racial equality," and reported a conversation between Clayton Rand, a conservative newspaper publisher in Gulfport, Mississippi, and a black janitor in which Rand asked the custodian if he was a member of the "Eleanor Equality League." The janitor responded "that lady don't know her place."[12] To celebrate southern racial harmony, Cain ignored the exodus of black southerners seeking wartime jobs, rising NAACP membership, and an emergent civil rights movement. When racial strife erupted in northern and western cities teeming with new southern migrants, Cain attributed the urban violence to the First Lady's willingness to socially mingle with African Americans. Dismissing persistent structural problems and wartime overcrowding, Cain said that Roosevelt had caused the violence by raising expectations for social equality. Cain's letter blaming Eleanor Roosevelt for urban violence found readers across the nation. In November, she received a copy of the *Black Dispatch*, Oklahoma City's African-American newspaper, which had reprinted Cain's letter and called it "absurd." Cain responded by taping the *Dispatch* article on the window of the *Summit Sun*'s office so "all my colored friends here see how my effort in their behalf was rewarded."[13] As evidence that black southerners liked segregation, Cain noted that two of her black friends had brought her flowers in the wake of her letter and lamented that Roosevelt had "revived the ghosts of the KKK." In the same month, Cain denounced the federal government for forcing public officials to eat and to share restrooms in federal buildings with black citizens. She attributed the mixing to Roosevelt and her communistic cronies who had cast aside "States Rights and white supremacy." Exhibiting the political shift that some white women across the South had made, Cain had taken Eleanor Roosevelt's social visits with black men and women and connected them to a betrayal of an organic order that "protected" blacks and whites and then accused the Democratic Party of failing to support the white South.[14]

Other white women, even young girls, made their own connections between Eleanor Roosevelt's actions and the relative security of racial segregation. In 1944, Roosevelt attended the opening of a canteen for soldiers in Washington, DC, sponsored by the Congress of Industrial Organizations (CIO). Following the CIO's non-discriminatory policy, black and white soldiers and their dates danced and dined together. Subsequently, accusations flew around the South that Eleanor Roosevelt encouraged such interracial mingling, and Louisiana congressman Charles McKenzie asked the First Lady if she sponsored interracial dancing. She claimed that he was misinformed but noted that when an interracial union sponsored a canteen, they could not exclude one group. People, she wrote, had the right to choose their own friends. Two twelve-year-old white girls from Rayville, a country town in McKenzie's congressional district, wrote Roosevelt to complain of her interracial activities. Claiming that "I usually do all my own thinking," one girl wrote, "What I think about white girls dancing and associating with the colored, and your entertaining them at the White House, I am not able to put into words." Writing on a school day, both girls reminded the First Lady that they would not attend integrated schools, and one said that she would rather "finish her education at home." News of Eleanor Roosevelt's attendance at a CIO function had traveled over 1,000 miles in less than two weeks, and by the time it arrived in Richland Parish, at least two girls at the local segregated elementary school knew that Roosevelt's actions meant the erosion of their Jim Crow world. It meant more than dancing. It meant integrated schools.[15] In 1944, a decade before *Brown*, they had internalized arguments that linked black and white physical contact to political and economic equality brought about by school integration.

While the two Rayville girls were younger than most, white women across the South had absorbed similar lessons about Roosevelt's damage to the Democratic Party. Some suspected that her actions would result in the white South voting against President Roosevelt. From Trenton, Alabama, to Lakeland, Florida, white women concluded that Eleanor's actions hurt her husband, were politically selfish, and were even those of a traitor, a crime punishable by death.[16] Others turned from the political to the personal and expressed doubts about the health of the couple's marriage, linking Roosevelt's interracial politics to her own desire for interracial sex. Puzzled by Roosevelt's "inexplicable" association with African Americans, one woman wrote that the president did not "pay any attention to you or you wouldn't be preaching what you are."[17] An "outraged" Florida woman wondered if the First Lady would "have enjoyed seeing your daughter Anna being hugged by those negroes," while another predicted that Eleanor Roosevelt would welcome the marriage of her sons to black women.[18] In the ultimate challenge to racial segregation and to the national proliferation of one-drop rules, one woman predicted that Roosevelt's behavior would lead to interracial marriage and flood "the nation with mulattoes."[19]

For the white women and girls who wrote to the First Lady protesting her racial transgressions, their letters spoke to the inextricable link between intimate matters and white supremacy. How they thought about the futures of their children or their childhood, their bodies, their sexual desires, their physical health, their school days, and their Saturday nights merged into ideas about white motherhood, white womanhood, and interracial democracy. In many ways, the segregated social order defined them. The emotional intensity of their letters and their resolve to prevent change spoke to an investment in racial segregation that was deep and volatile.[20] Constructions of white womanhood denied the possibility of a white woman's desire for black men while simultaneously making such desire an act of political sabotage on the Jim Crow system by a "bad" white woman. At the most individual level, the bodies of white women functioned as repositories of Jim Crow's rules. In racializing womanhood, white women embodied a political system that elevated whiteness and imbued women with political power based on their exclusion of African Americans.[21] Ideally, this separation protected and preserved their bodies, in direct contrast to the open access to black bodies for labor, sex, and violence. When Eleanor Roosevelt dissolved the physical distance between white and black, she threatened not only white womanhood but also the white supremacist order. If the wife of a Democratic president would do such things, the political boundaries that protected their identity as women and the racial order in which they lived threatened to dissolve. The result of that erosion at its most basic was interracial marriage and interracial children, the ultimate rebuke of white women's segregationist work.

But maintaining segregation was not only about politics and sex. White women across the South also framed the wartime threats of industrial and domestic labor in terms of Eleanor Roosevelt. Some white women complained that domestic servants kept leaving for the promise of better jobs to the north and west. Others, as Howard Odum's *Race and Rumors of Race* indicated, discussed wartime domestic labor shortages in terms of "Eleanor Clubs." These allegedly secret organizations of black domestic workers sought to invert the social and economic order by making white women wait on them. Throughout the wartime years from Washington, DC, to the Deep South, rumors proliferated that the war would get black women out of white women's kitchens and put white women to work cooking and cleaning for their former black employees. From Virginia, Mrs. James C. Cowan criticized Eleanor Roosevelt and a Democratic administration for reviving "the servant question in Washington" and for lobbying for social equality. Talking about Eleanor refocused broad political, economic, and social changes into individual homes. By naming these underground activities "Eleanor Clubs," white southern women were able to recast what was black women's rising labor independence and more generally an emerging, powerful, civil rights campaign as the work of a white female authority figure.[22]

Collectively, the critiques that white southern women levied at Eleanor Roosevelt suggested that her power to upset the racial order was limitless, and some concluded that her interracial social engagements jeopardized "the natural order." Many segregationists still spoke in ways that linked white supremacy to evolutionary development, even in the face of Hitler's genocidal use of such theories. For many white supremacists, the race science still taught at flagship universities in the South and the nation granted them intellectual legitimacy in justifying racial segregation.[23] A Louisiana business woman noted that "at this stage of their [African Americans'] advancement, we still find it unfit and unsafe for our race to deal with them loosely."[24] Echoing the comments of biologist and race scientist Ivey Lewis, Ogden contended that "next to the mother instinct, the instinct of race is the strongest in nature."[25] Betraying the "scientific" order as Eleanor Roosevelt did, they argued, not only compromised white supremacy but also imperiled African Americans. In considering the Detroit Riots in the summer of 1943, segregationists ignored the city's conflicts over residential housing patterns, lack of equal access to parks, the powerful historic influence of the KKK in city politics, and a rising frustration among black youth. Instead, they and blamed the riots on the First Lady. In her disregard for "racial instinct," Roosevelt, Ogden concluded, would "reduce [African Americans] to dust and tears by her unbounded and unwise ambitions." Adopting a paternalistic tone, Ogden wrote that the black rioters were not at fault. Instead, Washington bureaucrats and the First Lady held responsibility for "try[ing] to improve on God's plan."[26] A Memphis woman seconded this position, and a Mississippi man claimed, "Outside the Holy Bible, we have read nothing that contained more logical reasoning than Mrs. Florence Sillers Ogden's article," which deserved national syndication.[27] A Houston mother of two soldiers disliked Roosevelt's "meddling" while another predicted that she "will be responsible for a racial war." Anticipating the outbreak of racist violence against African Americans in the aftermath of World War II, a rural South Carolina woman presciently claimed that when white soldiers returned home "the negro's [*sic*] will get the daylights knocked out of them if even they talk back to even one boy."[28] In blaming Eleanor, white southern women diminished the validity of black protest, took away black-initiated violence as a political strategy, and elevated the role white women played in a segregated nation.

As southern white women accused Eleanor Roosevelt of undermining segregation when she dined with and visited African Americans, they also used her policy positions on education to discuss additional threats to white supremacy. Ignoring grassroots efforts among black teachers, black club-women, and black intellectuals to challenge historical narratives that upheld the status quo, white women claimed that it was the First Lady who threatened segregated education when she advocated federal funding for public schools.[29] After a 1938 presidential committee report on the state of public education recorded the deplorable conditions in black schools and the disparities between them and white schools, Congress and state legislatures, with uneven success and commitment, had adopted measures to improve public education. Mississippi senator Pat Harrison had even sponsored a 1938 bill that promised a lion's share of the federal equalization monies to southern schools. In the spring of 1943, Congress renewed its debates on federal aid to education.[30] While many of the South's elected leaders believed that their legislative wrangling and state-level restrictions could bring in federal education money while not disturbing segregated schools, others interpreted federal aid to education as a loss of state control. Long an opponent of Governor Paul Johnson, who had taken some initial steps to equalize black and white schools, Mary Cain wrote to Mississippi Senator James Eastland warning him of the dangers to state control that federal aid would bring. In his response, Eastland acknowledged the wedge that federal aid posed for segregated schools, writing that eventually "limitations could be passed which would prohibit Mississippi from getting any of the money unless we had mixed schools in the state."[31] As the discussion escalated, Ogden equated federal aid with the erosion of parental authority, of states' rights, and consequently of white supremacy. She pointed to the list of federal aid proponents who had also condemned segregated education—the National Education Association, organized labor, the NAACP, and the National Congress of Parents and Teachers.[32] "Don't think for a moment," Ogden warned, "that Federal Aid means anything but control of your schools and your children."

As a result, parents "will have nothing to say in the policies of a government-paid system."[33] Out of step with many national Democrats, Ogden and Cain offered an early version of what by the late 1940s would be mainstream conservative opposition to progressive education that took shape in coffee klatches from New York to California.[34]

In the wartime climate, school curriculum remained as much an issue as actual student integration. In "My Day," her nationally syndicated newspaper column, Eleanor Roosevelt had praised Chicago schools for integrating curriculum from Negro History week into their lessons, leaving southern white women certain that their children would soon be introduced to topics that the southern public school textbooks and teacher training had largely excluded.[35] Challenging the dominant historical narrative that served the white South, this "new" curriculum, Ogden claimed, had immediate political consequences. Namely, it would brainwash white children to accept the demands of black Americans for greater civil rights. White women—as mothers, voters, and southerners—must control curriculum and thus sustain segregation, for the link between education and elections was clear. In Chicago, Ogden argued, an integrated curriculum was a politically opportunistic move of city officials courting a minority vote. In the South, Ogden remained wary of weakening the white supremacist curriculum, doubting that greater funding for education could ever counterbalance the loss of local or state control. Over the course of the 1940s, the Federal Aid to Education bill repeatedly met defeat. Northern senators doubted that southern state legislatures would distribute funds to black schools, and southern senators sought guarantees that federal funding would not come with the attached strings of civil rights.[36]

Despite her challenges to the etiquette, curriculum, labor, and civil rights policies of white supremacists, ironically Eleanor Roosevelt served also as a gift to white female segregationists. By painting the First Lady as a "bad" white woman and therefore a "bad" Democrat, segregationists mobilized their readers, their clubs, and their political parties to contemplate her actions as a partisan betrayal.[37] They could vehemently protest her integrationist practices and reinforce the familiar tale of meddling outsiders, Yankee infiltrators, and "South-Savers." In highlighting Roosevelt's activities, southern segregationists obscured the activities of black southerners, helping to erase southern black men and women from the political terrain and to maintain the fiction of black satisfaction. Consequently, African Americans became the subjects of debate among white women and men rather than historical actors. For white southern women, the First Lady's physical proximity to black women in their homes, to black men on podiums, and to black

leaders at White House functions eroded the social distance and by consequence the political distance that served to bolster white women's authority.
For segregationist purposes, Roosevelt offered white southern women lessons
in how not to act and reminded them of the potentially revolutionary repercussions if they failed to police segregation in their daily lives.

In the Upper South, Nell Battle Lewis also recognized Eleanor
Roosevelt's crossing of the color line, but unlike some other white southern women, she felt that these actions did not make it necessary for all
southerners to abandon the Democratic Party or make a partisan switch.
From the South's self-styled progressive capital, Lewis believed that World
War II required white southerners to address race relations differently.
Striking a more moderate pose than Ogden or Cain, she also separated
herself from what she termed the " 'hush, hush' school" of white southerners who ignored problems in an attempt to deny their existence. Devoted
to states' rights, however, she called for South-led changes, noting that
outside intervention only hindered the peaceful "progress of the Negro."
Instead, the guidance of white southerners who "know it [the problem]
best by daily association" and "continue to direct an improvement in the
condition of black southerners" was best, said Lewis. Agreeing with southern journalist John Temple Graves, Jr., Lewis reprinted his comment that
segregation only became an issue when "Negro leaders outside the South,
with the apparent backing of Mrs. Roosevelt, and the possible support of
the Administration, made the war an occasion for the most intensive campaign ever launched against any and every differential, minor or major,
between white men and black." While Lewis disagreed with Roosevelt on
those efforts, the threat the First Lady posed to segregation, Lewis felt, was
still manageable. Plenty of white and black southerners, she believed, toed
the color line. The First Lady's lack of respect for it did not require Lewis
to exit the Democratic Party.[38]

While the First Lady received the lion's share of the criticism of segregationist women, they also railed against President Roosevelt's wartime labor
policies, believing that he needed to reel in industrial unions. Weary of labor
uprisings, by 1943 over 80 percent of citizens, some polls showed, supported
limiting wartime strikes. President Roosevelt had often validated the concerns
of workers about wage stabilization, inflation, and their anemic purchasing
power. While affirming their economic rights, he also condemned those who
participated in wildcat strikes. In North Carolina, a state with a substantial number of industrial workers and a vibrant discussion on labor reform,
wartime labor demands raised the ire of its white citizens.[39] In particular,

Lewis believed that Roosevelt dilly-dallied with the coal industry and United Mine Workers (UMW) leader John L. Lewis. In 1943, after the president had ordered workers to return to the mines, John Lewis had called another strike, and while Roosevelt eventually asserted federal control over the mines, he stopped short of calling John Lewis a traitor. Nell Lewis did call the UMW leader a traitor and argued that labor strife compromised soldiers who were in a war for Christian and democratic civilization. She printed comments from soldiers who believed John Lewis should hang. In a departure from her 1920s condemnation of the greed of textile owners, she raised questions about American workers who would let greed supersede the need for a greater good. They were not the only ones pinched by wartime price hikes, she noted, as many Americans suffered from the rising cost of living. She worried that soldiers might hear about John Lewis orchestrating strikes in the coal fields and lose their will to "defend a country in which Labor can be free—to knife the defenders of that freedom in the back." For all these reasons, Lewis supported wholeheartedly the Smith-Connally War Labor Disputes bill passed by Congress that granted the president the power to seize war plants, banned political contributions by labor unions, outlawed strikes in government-run industries, and legalized strikes only after thirty days of "cooling off" and a secret ballot among union members. To her dismay, President Roosevelt, concerned by the excessive restrictions on labor, vetoed the bill—a veto that Congress quickly overrode. While Nell Battle Lewis condemned Roosevelt's leniency, she did not link the suppression of labor specifically to the maintenance of racial segregation.[40] In parts of the South, however, it was and remained difficult to separate discussions of labor unions and the rights of laborers from white supremacist politics and the segregated structure of much industrial work. The nearly simultaneous arrival of industrialization, Jim Crow laws, and broad disenfranchisement in the South resulted in white men seeking assurances that factory work would not put white women and black men together on the same factory floor. White southerners feared that an interracial work force would weaken white racial supremacy and allow interracial relationships to flourish outside the oversight of white fathers and husbands.[41] Segregated work forces also helped keep rates of unionization low by making a cross-racial labor alliance more difficult, and without unions, wages stayed low. Segregation also ensured a steady labor supply of agricultural and domestic workers often black, and millworkers often white, creating a system of "racial capitalism." The dictates of racial segregation in the workplace also meant that federal intervention on behalf of labor threatened not just the economic system but the entire political and social system as well. So when labor unions used wartime industrial needs to press for workplace reforms and when President Roosevelt signed an executive order barring employment discrimination in wartime industries, some white southern segregationist women collapsed labor agitation into efforts for racial equality.[42] In the absence of men, many white women equated protecting workplaces for their white sons, fathers, and husbands who would return from the war with the suppression of labor demands, the cessation of strikes, the demonization of union leaders, and the preservation of the Jim Crow order.

In the South Carolina low country, Republican and political activist Cornelia Dabney Tucker organized the National Defense Security League lobby to limit the power of organized labor, eliminate strikes, and create a national mediation board. Fresh from mobilizing a nation against the court-packing scheme, Tucker began writing to Franklin and Eleanor Roosevelt, John L. Lewis, Governor Olin D. Johnston of South Carolina, the Office of Production Management, the Department of Labor, the War Production Board, the CIO, and each senator on the Rules and the Foreign Relations Committees.[43] Invoking motherhood, Tucker told how strikes jeopardized her son serving overseas. As a concerned citizen, she argued that union tactics weakened the war effort in general. The National Defense Security League argued that if unions were patriotic, labor leaders would welcome a national mediation board. American Federation of Labor leaders reminded her of their no-strike pledge. While polls showed that 70 percent of union members supported parts of the Smith-Connally bill, some union leaders and members protested its scope, resenting group punishment for the actions of a few, namely, the UMW. Those responsible for America's entrance into the war, meaning President Roosevelt, Tucker claimed, should "put a stop to strikes in war production." If "they" lacked the political fortitude to do so, she noted, they would meet an "an outraged public" who would know of their "cowardly" and "feeble" efforts. Tucker worked hard to make that true. In just six days, she had received assurances of cooperation and support for Smith-Connally from politicians in forty-seven states.[44]

Anti-labor sentiment was vehement in Mississippi as well. Nellie Nugent Somerville attacked the New Deal leaders, Vice-President Henry Wallace in particular, for being too close to the Congress of Industrial Organizations, communists, and radicals.[45] Ogden seized on the moral authority of mothers to mobilize opposition to what she couched as FDR's leniency on labor. Mothers had sent their sons to war, paying the price for freedom. Left at home, Ogden argued, mothers had a wartime duty to "keep it safe, and hold it free." This meant preserving the status quo and preventing labor from using the war

FIGURE 5.1 A dress rehearsal for Tucker's anti-labor protest. During World War II, Cornelia Dabney Tucker pledged to picket in Washington, DC, if President Roosevelt did not stop the labor strikes. *Evening Post*, May 7, 1942, Charleston, South Carolina.

to seek monetary gains.[46] Adopting her hometown's white soldiers in a new wartime weekly column "My Dear Boys," Ogden insisted that Mothers' Day was a good time to remember that mothers "ask no special privileges for their sons, they expect no special privileges for any group or class." "It is a day for the Mothers of America to lift up their voices . . . and let them be heard. They have the power in their hands to stop strikes and delays if they but act and speak in unison."[47] Ogden believed that the mobilized mothers could change labor policies, and she instructed them to "demand that labor and industry cease their bickerings; that men work, not 40 hours but if necessary, until they fall exhausted as the boys on Bataan fell." Ogden counterpoised "unpatriotic" industrial laborers with a white Rosedale family who had sent four sons into war by 1944. What would that family think "of men striking . . . because they want 5 cents more an hour—one more beer—on their paychecks?"[48] Having "no patience with organized selfish minorities," mothers had a duty, an obligation to speak out since "the President has petted and spoiled labor until he is now like the parent who finds that the child he has indulged has grown defiant and completely out of his control."[49]

Acting as a kind of composite mother, Ogden used her weekly letter to assume the moral maternal authority that justified her oversight of economic, political, and social relations on the homefront. Knowing the editor of the *Bolivar County Democrat* sent the county's soldiers a copy of the weekly paper, Ogden reassured soldiers that they would return to a community that they recognized in part because white women had overseen racial segregation's wartime health. To remedy the homesickness of soldiers, she sent pictures of black laborers picking cotton and white children sledding on the levee, reminders of a system of white over black. While stories of white soldiers dominated her column, she did include some news of black soldiers, listing the names of those who left to train at Camp Shelby. She also quietly questioned their fitness for service by reporting the names of black soldiers, not white ones, who failed to pass the physical requirements and returned home.[50] She reminded her readers that black soldiers served in segregated units or in service to white units as cooks, stevedores, or waiters.[51] Telling these Jim Crow stories even in wartime, Ogden ensured that "her boys" came home to the Delta they had left— one where Jim Crow still ruled.

If Ogden's condemnation of labor strife and her "My Dear Boys" column reflected a popular position among Delta whites to secure segregation in the midst of war, her attribution of organized labor's allegedly bad behavior to the ethnicity of their workers was less mainstream.[52] With little concern for actual facts, Ogden argued that union members were simply not real Americans and they could not help it, for "love of a country is bred into peoples."[53] These industrial workers, whom she described as Eastern European immigrants, lacked the most basic qualification for American citizenship— whiteness. Ignoring immigration patterns and World War I–era restrictions, she contended that "most of them have come here within the last 30 years . . . and while many of them have lived in this country and enjoyed its freedom . . . they cannot love it as we do who were born here." Strikes served as proof enough, for Ogden, of their shaky nationalism and inferior ethnic background.[54] The fact that first- (or second- or third-) generation working class and black Americans received more consideration from a Democratic-controlled administration than "real" Americans galled her, and revealed how far the president and Democratic Party had strayed.[55]

Opposition to labor unions might not mean support for white suprema-cist politics, but for Ogden, the cozy relationship between the Democrats and labor leaders meant one thing: by 1943, "the party which kept the South solid for seventy-five years" no longer existed, and "not even Southern Democrats can doubt that America is a labor government." In Bolivar County, with a black population of 73 percent, any government protection of labor chal-lenged the Jim Crow order. The Fair Employment Practices Committee (FEPC), which prevented hiring discrimination in businesses receiving fed-eral contracts, was a perfect example of a new Democratic Party that served other masters. Rather than the party of "your grandfather who rode with Forrest, or who charged with Pickett at Gettysburg," Ogden believed that urban elites now ran her political party and had forsaken rural, agricultural, southern, and white Americans. The Democratic Party's favoritism toward labor and urban areas had resulted, Ogden wrote, in a disproportionate num-ber of rural Americans serving in the military. She claimed that in promot-ing racial equality the national Democratic Party had acted "like a heathen mother who throws her child to the crocodile."[56] The war-time domestic and political changes, Ogden complained, had threatened white supremacy and effectively destroyed her allegiance to the Democratic Party. But the changes were exposed another problem; Democratic men had failed to act as men, to behave as strong patriarchs, and to protect the privileges of white supremacy. This left white southern women to secure a segregated social order.[57]

Betrayed by the leadership of the Democratic Party, Ogden worked hard to convince white Mississippians to seek partisan homes elsewhere. She was not alone, nor was she first. By 1936, southern Democrats—Georgia's Eugene Talmadge, North Carolina's Josiah Bailey, and South Carolina's Cotton Ed Smith, most notably—made condemning the New Deal part of their daily ritual. But even amid their demagoguery and disdain for Roosevelt's poli-cies, they remained Democrats. Even though elected officials stopped short of switching political parties at this point, white southern women continued to talk about moving white southerners away from their routine support of the Democratic Party. Some, like Mississippian Mary Cain, had adopted the label of Jeffersonian Democrats to distance themselves from "New Dealers." For Cain, this departure aligned her with those on the right who shared a conservative political philosophy of which segregation was often a tenet. For Ogden, a former diehard New Dealer, the perceived capitulation of the

Democrats to a civil rights platform spurred her partisan break. For others, a partisan breakup might stem from their anti-labor politics, anti-communism, business conservatism, or vision of economic development, but these issues were infused with racial politics as well.

Largely exempt from party perks and election deals, white women had an easier time painting themselves as "true" Democrats. They criticized the Democratic National Committee without suffering significant repercussions, and even left the party. Nowhere was this more clear than in South Carolina. There, Cornelia Dabney Tucker had already reinvigorated the Republican Party before becoming an independent, and during World War II she sought to support conservative advocates of limited government and pro-business interests regardless of party affiliation.[58] While Tucker had been on the secret ballot crusade since her political baptism in 1937, the war years produced a host of policies and movements that alarmed white segregationist women like herself. The national capital pulsed with debates about legislation to abolish the poll tax, to pass anti-lynching legislation, and to exempt soldiers from voting restrictions. Challenges to the all-white primary made their way through the courts. The DNC moved to include a plank in their platform that called for racial equality, angering those who already resented having black northern convention delegates and a black chaplain lead a prayer. Faced with these issues, Tucker joined other segregationist women to mobilize white women to leave the Democratic Party.[59]

In Mississippi in 1944, the *Smith v. Allwright* decision declaring the all-white primary unconstitutional, precipitated partisan departures. Prior to the Supreme Court's decision, the Democratic primaries had been "private" elections exempt from constitutional challenges. With all-white primaries coming to an end, white Mississippians (who almost exclusively voted Democratic) faced the possibility of having their elections subjected to federal oversight, which they feared would open up voting to black participation. In the Supreme Court's decision, the majority of the justices held that the "United States is a constitutional Democracy," but former suffragist Nellie Nugent Somerville, writing in a pamphlet, argued that the constitution created a republic, not a democracy, and therefore not every voice had to be heard. In this pamphlet, which was serialized in the *Jackson Daily News*, she claimed that "from the earliest times in this Republic the exercise of the election franchise has been protected by qualifications and restrictions" (thus defending the poll tax and the white primary). She believed that elections should be regulated at the state level, as the US Constitution dictated. After federal intrusion into state-level election proceedings—abolishing the poll tax or the all-white primary—Somerville argued, federal control of elections would follow. She called on women in particular to protest changes to voting regulations and asked Florence Sillers Ogden to organize the DAR to begin educational programs that would spread the news that in a republic, disfranchisement was justified. Somerville also proclaimed herself "politically homeless."[60]

Ogden echoed Somerville's disillusionment with the Democratic Party, but she targeted Democratic congressman Vito Marcantonio to illustrate the partisan betrayal of the South and to explain her departure from the party. Harlem's representative, Marcantonio was a left-wing critic of the New Deal; a member of the American Labor Party; a communist sympathizer; the representative of a multi-racial political coalition of southern Italian immigrants, Jews, and African Americans; and the leader of the anti-poll tax crusade. In addition, he had defended labor interests and often advocated foreign policy that favored the Soviet Union.[61] Marcantonio's politics represented a multi-pronged attack on racial segregation, as he was in favor of potentially expanding the franchise for black southerners, eroding labor practices that kept black and white workers apart, and praising the Soviet Union's rejection of racial hierarchies. For Ogden, he embodied the Democratic Party's efforts to erode states' rights, state control, and national sovereignty. "Even the Republican Party," she wrote, "[had] never tried to take the constitutional right to provide the requirements for the franchise away from the states."[62]

The same year brought debates on how to enable more active duty soldiers to vote, raising alarms about black soldiers casting their votes via absentee ballots. In North Carolina, Nell Battle Lewis understood that the federally sponsored Soldier Voting Act threatened state control of elections, but she did not see it as a revolutionary measure. North Carolina's poll tax had been abolished in the 1920s, and minimal black voting in the state had not sapped racial segregation of much power. But by the 1940s, the landscape of electoral reform had changed. On the grounds of states' rights, Lewis opposed the Soldier Voting Act, arguing that "States themselves should say in war as well in peace who is to vote." But she felt southern opposition to the act played into Republican hands, and she distrusted the Republicans' convenient use of states' rights rhetoric to oppose the bill. Lewis believed the Republicans feared the act because "the more soldiers who vote, the more votes there will be for Commander in Chief," and she remained supportive of the president.[63]

Across the South, however, white southern women, who had positioned themselves as guardians of the homefront and protectors of the status quo, remained willing to deny active-duty soldiers the right to vote. Staunch defense of state regulation of voting overcame even Ogden's devotion to her Delta soldiers. Despite sending "lotions of love" to Delta soldiers each week in her "My Dear Boys" column, she did not defend their voting rights. She remained an opponent of the Soldier Voting Act even when her brother Walter Sillers, Speaker of the Mississippi House, authored a state-level version of the bill.[64] When legislation came before Congress, she claimed that Roosevelt's support was sheer political opportunism. While the New Dealers believed it would "prevent discrimination against our soldiers," Ogden understood it as an act that infringed on states' rights and one that would permit black soldiers serving out of the state to cast ballots free from white intimidation.[65] Ogden's congressman John Rankin told *Time* reporters that two reasons to oppose the act were to preserve "white supremacy" and to keep "the Negro from voting." Mary Cain agreed with Rankin, as did a Neshoba County soldier who affirmed to Cain his support of states' rights, the poll tax, white supremacy, and his regard for white womanhood. Speaking for his troops, he said that they trusted the home front to run the political situation. Other soldiers disagreed, and one white soldier called Cain a white supremacist; he believed in equality for all.[66]

As a result of the Democratic Party's wartime policies, white Mississippi women oversaw a dramatic attempt at state-level partisan realignment. In 1944, Ogden claimed that "the reason to vote the Democratic ticket no longer exists. . . . [T]he tie that binds the South is broken."[67] Moving to counter the betrayal of the Democratic Party and to break the partisan loyalty of some Mississippi Democrats, white women seized a more central role in the state meeting to discuss Mississippi's Democratic Party procedures for serving as a state convention delegate. Not one of the women at the meeting understood the process, so Ogden took it upon herself to find out, published her findings, and "notified the ladies who had been in on the discussion" about the precinct's delegate selection process. She also "modestly let it be known that I would like to continue my course in political science." And she did, leading the Rosedale precinct's ticket because, she mused, "I was the only one who voted for myself." At the Bolivar County convention, the delegates adopted a resolution offered by Somerville that charged the county delegates to "uphold the principles of government of the Republic." This resolution was shorthand for preserving Mississippi's right to control elections and to collect a poll tax. The county convention also elected Ogden to serve as a delegate at Mississippi's State Democratic Convention.[68]

In a bizarre state Democratic convention, the anti-Roosevelt forces, which included Ogden, controlled the floor and elected a slate of anti-Roosevelt delegates for the national convention. "Our fearless leaders of today stood up and demanded the preservation of their race, the retention of the ideals and traditions of the South and America, and their rights guaranteed under the constitution," wrote Ogden. She reassured her readers that Mississippi's Democrats were dedicated to white supremacist politics and that Delta men were "guided by statesmanship" and participated in "no kindling of hatred, no prejudices." For decades, race relations in Mississippi had been based on "mutual understanding, confidence, and respect between whites and Negroes . . . [but] the New Deal has done much to destroy this mutual confidence."[69] She told her Delta neighbors:

> There may be dark days ahead, but I know that some day unselfish, fearless men and women like those in Mississippi will rise in every hamlet, every cross road of America and demand that the people of the United States remain free and untrammeled; that they throw off this yoke of petty bureaucracy . . . of subservience to alien creeds . . . this threat to the preservation of the white race.[70]

After the convention, Ogden hoped to return home with renewed confidence that the white men of Mississippi would stand up for white supremacy at the national convention, but she wanted to make sure that she would be there to watch over them.

As Ogden prepared for the convention in Chicago, she remained convinced that Mississippi men, like women, would vote on a matter of principle, not party politics. On the eve of her trip to witness "the Democrats and the New Dealers perform," she disingenuously wondered "being just a woman . . . what it is that binds a person behind the prison bars of a party." From the press galley, Ogden watched as her state's delegates voted for presidential candidate Harry Byrd, as her brother seconded the nomination for vice-presidential nominee John Bankhead, the senator from Alabama, and as her state's delegation then voted for Harry Truman upon Bankhead's withdrawal.[71] The anti-Roosevelt sentiment of the Mississippi delegation was not widespread, however, and Mississippi's delegates returned home knowing that the incumbent would be the party's nominee. But they soon knew that three of the nine Mississippi electors pledged not to vote for FDR, no matter the popular vote. While Governor Thomas Bailey averted such a disaster by printing a pink ballot with pro-Roosevelt electors chosen by the legislature, the seeds of discontent among Mississippi Democrats grew.[72]

After 1944, Ogden never again voted for a Democrat in presidential elections. While it would be eight years before she voted Republican, she noted that the Republican Party's support for presidential term limits, free enterprise, and fierce anti-communism had more to offer, even with its stand on race, than what she called the "New Deal Party." While she admitted to having benefited financially from the New Deal, she contended that her political loyalty was not measured "in dollars and cents." By voting solidly Democratic, the South, she believed, had lost its bargaining power. For lessons in the value of bargaining, she pointed to the fact that "the Negroes no longer belong to any one party," and their escalating political influence was a result of partisan races for their votes.[73]

Ogden had come to a position on partisan realignment that Cornelia Tucker had reached prior to the war. Having already cast aside her allegiance to Democrats, Tucker sought to reinvigorate citizenship education to meet Cold War challenges. Only with a concerted educational program, Tucker believed, could capitalism and democracy be sustained. Women's authority over the home and its natural extension, the schools, meant that policing public education was part of their contribution to national defense. In South Carolina, Cornelia Dabney Tucker undertook a civic education campaign by calling for every South Carolina public school student to study civics and government through a single newly adopted "modern" textbook. Capitalizing on her networks in the American Association of University Women, the Business and Professional Women's Club, the DAR, the Republican Party, and Charleston's summer residents, Tucker repackaged the important national, political, and patriotic role white women held over curriculum for the anti-communist crusade. To guard against a "highly specialized foreign government propagandist," she targeted national groups, local politicians, and statewide women's organizations interested in making public school education the first line of defense in the battle against communism.[74] In 1944, she asked a state education official to endorse a plan entitled "Educating for World Peace."[75] She also communicated with the Business and Professional Women's Clubs, the American Association of University Women, the State Department, John Foster Dulles, and independent groups like the National Americanism Commission, the American Legion, and later the Chicago-based conservative organization, We the People, asking them to accelerate their efforts in civic, anti-communist education. She spoke to DAR chapters and the Children of the American Revolution and worked with male leaders in the Exchange and Service Clubs. And once again, she began a letter-writing campaign.[76] Women's supervision of schools, their efforts to shape curriculum, and their vigilance in combating the creep of communism into the minds of schoolchildren became central to the entire Cold War project. For Tucker, foreign policy dominated her politics in 1944, but once

segregationists so effectively linked African American resistance to communist subversion, women like Tucker, already mobilized to protect their public
schools from a red tide, would easily collapse civil rights activism into communist machinations and move against them both.[77]

In North Carolina, Nell Battle Lewis reacted joyfully to Roosevelt's 1944
reelection as she trusted his foreign policy. Lewis had spent much of the
World War II–era speaking to women's book clubs across the state about the
need for international cooperation, believing that principle, not partisan loyalty, guided women's political activism.[78] Hoping that the election stymied
the Republican hawkish cold warriors, she attributed Roosevelt's fourth
term to "The Good Wimmin [who] really straightened out and flew right
this time . . . voting against future wars even more than for the Democratic
candidate himself."[79]

When Lewis turned to domestic rather than foreign policy issues, her confidence in the Democratic leadership stood on shakier ground. Her assump-
tion that either the Democratic Party or white liberals could continue to
control the pace of racial change was dealt two heavy blows in 1944. Lewis
was so committed to the gradual strides of North Carolina's progress in race
relations that she was unwilling to imagine a South where black southerners did not welcome white charity, wisdom, and employment; as a result, she
was stunned at the publication of *What the Negro Wants*. In the University
of North Carolina Press essay collection, fourteen black leaders expressed a
desire for economic and political equality, despite their ideological differences. Each author opposed racial segregation, and five authors even discussed interracial marriage. In his essay, Langston Hughes painted the white
South as uncivilized and perhaps unredeemable.[80] Shocked by the consensus,
William T. Couch, director of the University of North Carolina Press, contradicted this broad agreement in a publisher's preface and asserted that the
solution to American race relations was the guiding hand of the white man.
Nell Lewis believed that most "intelligent, well-disposed, white readers in
the South" would agree with Couch. Assuming what was in 1944 a moderate
stance for white southerners, she also noted that most would find "much with
which he has to agree" in the essays. But reiterating her role as the storyteller
for white supremacy, Lewis supplanted the arguments of the essayists with
her own as she questioned whether Negro intellectuals "speak for the average
man and woman of their race, for the Negro . . . in Wake County, the Negro
cook in Raleigh?"[81]

When Georgia author Lillian Smith published *Strange Fruit* that same
year, Lewis responded with rancor, attacking Smith for writing about

interracial sex, segregation, and violence.[82] Criticizing white women reformers as "South-Savers," Lewis noted, "the female of the species is very deadly." Smith had returned from missionary work in China and written a novel that Lewis claimed was the result of "a well-born Southern white woman who romanticizes a case of miscegenation in the South." Lewis said that Smith's novel was one "I never expected to live to see" and one she greeted with "unmitigated disgust." She disparaged Smith for crossing racial boundaries and sexual boundaries in her book, calling it "a psychopathic exhibit." Smith wrote and acted in a manner that Lewis, also an unmarried white woman, deemed inappropriate for her sex. For "Southerners of balance, good feeling, and good sense in whose hands adjustment of racial relations is safest," Smith's publication seemed to exacerbate already tense race relations, and Lewis said whites could "do nothing but condemn it."[83] A year later, Lewis defended her review and cast aside any thought that her outrage was that of a reactionary southerner when a Massachusetts court had upheld Boston's ban on sales of *Strange Fruit* due to its obscenity.[84]

Lewis's condemnation of the 1944 publications was minor compared with the regionwide outrage among white southerners upon the release of "To Secure These Rights," the 1947 report from the President's Committee on Civil Rights. This document informed Truman's subsequent civil rights speech, which recommended a Ten Point Program that included calls for federal anti-lynching, anti-poll tax, and school desegregation legislation. The report also called for a permanent Fair Employment Practices Committee and the desegregation of the armed forces. While some black southerners received the report with a skepticism born of unfulfilled paper promises, many white southerners rallied to denounce it. Ogden called the report "the most vicious edict in the history of our nation." [85]

In North Carolina, Lewis noted "the ugly possibilities for the South from heated controversy regarding it," while the editorial pages of the *News and Observer* responded with headlines such as "The Remedy Is Worse than the Disease." Rather than commenting directly on the report, she wrote a nostalgic column about her black acquaintances in Raleigh's Oberlin neighborhood who had worked for her father and "had a very good name for respectability and industry." Later she paid tribute to her childhood mammy and a housekeeper as well as two black cooks who were "great friends of mine." Again, she used her black friends for what she termed "a mute rebuke" to white southerners who denied opportunities to black southerners. Lewis's opinions mirrored that of her paper's editor, Jonathan Daniels, who believed that it was the responsibility of white citizens, not the federal government, to take the lead in reforming race relations.[86] For Lewis, "To Secure These Rights" demanded that white citizens respond to such federal measures with increased state-level efforts to treat black southerners more fairly and humanely and to provide better educational, medical, and transportation facilities. But in her storytelling for white supremacy, she returned to celebrate only those black women who served white communities, not those who worked for the equality affirmed in the committee's report.

If North Carolinians responded with outrage, white Mississippians responded with a dramatic departure. In the Mississippi Delta, President Truman's civil rights stance served as an impetus for both Ogden and Democratic women to escalate their efforts to affect partisan realignment. In early 1948, a recruitment letter from Mississippi's State Democratic Party announced that "for the first time in the history of our State, the women of Mississippi are being given an opportunity to make their voices heard collectively." Organized by Mrs. William Kendall and Mrs. O. H. Palmer, chairs of the State Women's Committee, the first meeting took place on April 15 in Jackson. The invitation letter stressed that while "ONE MAN" might attend "we have served notice that the women of Mississippi will conduct this gathering and will make all the 'key-note speeches' necessary." Women, they felt, would play a key role in the fight for "State's rights" because:

> during the last few years we have taken a more active interest in the affairs of government, we have helped elect men to office of whom we are justly proud—we have made our influence felt where it has meant much, and now we must make our voice heard at a time when it will mean much to our children and grandchildren.[87]

While stressing a woman's duty to future generations, Ogden reiterated that women had "demonstrated that you are willing to assume your full responsibility as a citizen interested in the welfare of your country."[88]

Ogden delivered the meeting's keynote address entitled "Civil Rights" to the 800 women assembled. She began with the claim that "We, the women, have a big stake in these issues." She then attacked the president's Civil Rights Committee, noting that it included a left-wing attorney, black men, labor leaders, members of communist organizations, and Franklin Delano Roosevelt Jr. Speaking to the power of maternal influence over the young Roosevelt, Ogden suggested "IF you read 'My Day,' there is no need for me to say more about him." Noting that only two of the committee members were from the South, she painted both Dorothy Tilly and Frank

Porter Graham as traitors, deriding Tilly's work as a non-segregationist in the Methodist Church and Graham's participation in the purported communist-front organization, the Southern Conference for Human Welfare. She also noted the resemblance between the report and Mrs. Roosevelt's politics, extending the former First Lady's influence into the Truman White House. In her summary, Ogden suggested that the report attacked private affairs, white American children, and American heritage. Most critical was the anti-school segregation plank that would affect, in a familiar Ogden refrain, "you and your children and your children's children" and would institute an irreversible process of "mongrelization." Drawing on erroneous race science, Ogden suggested, "Segregation comes straight to us from our ancestors" and "race-preservation is self-preservation." White women, she demanded, must defend segregation in the name of white motherhood.[89]

Ogden delivered numerous speeches to Mississippi women encouraging political action for the maintenance of white supremacy, which meant leaving the Democratic Party. Speaking to the State Assembly of the Daughters of the American Colonies, Ogden delivered "Ancestors," a speech that stressed the inherent and immutable nature of race and linked racial purity to the social order. Speaking of her own ancestors, Ogden declared, "I'm glad mine were white and American." To the audience she proclaimed, "I know every woman around this table is proud of her ancestors . . . [who] gave us America," but "they did not give it to use to exploit, or to give away—either its natural resources . . . nor its white blood." The most "dangerous and far-reaching [threat]" facing Americans in 1948, she claimed, "is the threat to the white race." If science or history did not satisfy her audience, she asserted that segregation was "the way God planned it, and I still think He is a better planner than President Truman and his Civil Rights Committee—or even Mrs. Roosevelt."[90]

Her campaign for white supremacy targeted other female-dominated forums. At the Gunnison Parent-Teachers Association, Ogden celebrated the states' rights movement that had originated in Jackson. After offering praise for the male leaders of the movement, she noted that white women also participated in the meeting. In a PTA address, Ogden attacked Truman's program as the most significant threat to civil rights since the failed Reconstruction Acts of 1867 and suggested that his measure would be no more successful. More insidious, according to Ogden, was school integration, which unlike the other measures, would produce "the end of the Southern way of life." While she attacked the anti-lynching and school desegregation proposals in the report, the provision for the permanent establishment of the FEPC especially rankled Ogden. The FEPC, she contended, would "tell you whom to employ and whom not to employ. . . . [T]his committee will be packed against you." "And it will be black," she said. Moreover, the FEPC will "have the power to send FBI agencies into your place of business to spy upon you." The committee, not the judiciary, would interpret the law, she warned. She hypothesized that the makeup of the committee might reflect "some crackpot's conception of the law, or some communist's idea, or some Negro's." In an updated version of rumors of Eleanor Clubs, Ogden insisted that black men and women would soon run businesses with "white American girls" serving as their secretaries. In her opposition to the FEPC, Ogden had linked wartime concerns over labor, communism, and civil rights into attacks on racial segregation.[91]

As Ogden rallied white Mississippians to oppose the candidacy of Harry Truman and the policies of the national Democratic Party, she called on white women to be central actors. By focusing on the end of school segregation, the employment of young white female secretaries by black male bosses, and the increased intrusion of the federal government into private affairs, Ogden implied that the federal government would inhibit white women's ability to teach and to reinforce white racial supremacy. New workplace hierarchies, Ogden argued, would endanger the white racial purity that many southern communities had guarded for decades. White parents would be unable to protect their children. In these instances, Ogden appealed to maternal duty in an effort to uphold white supremacy, and her efforts to preserve the white southern way of life dovetailed with the rebellion brewing among southern Democrats who were unwilling to accept the civil rights agenda of their party.

After solidifying his reputation as a Cold Warrior on the international and domestic fronts, President Truman severely tested the loyalty of many southern Democrats when he vetoed the anti-union Taft-Hartley Act and pushed for civil rights legislation. Pressured by A. Phillip Randolph, former Brotherhood of Sleeping Car Porters union leader and activist central in the creation of the FEPC, and gauging the political expediency of civil rights legislation, President Truman issued executive orders that barred discrimination in federal employment and that desegregated the armed forces. Southern reactionaries bolted from the Democratic Party, formed the Dixiecrats, and looked for their own presidential candidate.[92] Ogden's wishes had been granted.

North Carolina did not participate in the Dixiecrat revolt, but Henry Wallace's Progressive Party candidacy provided Lewis with the perfect platform to exploit connections between labor rights, Cold War politics, and civil rights. By 1947, the former Secretary of Agriculture and FDR's third term vice-president had adopted a softer stance on the Soviet Union and the Cold War and a hardline demand for racial integration and equality. When Wallace first toured North Carolina in 1947, he had spoken to an integrated audience in Raleigh and advocated "human brotherhood and non-segregation."[93] At that time, Lewis scoffed at his racial idealism and ridiculed his relationship with the Soviet Union, implying that his accommodation was in part a failure of his masculinity. Seizing the opportunity, Lewis molded the menace of integration and communism into a unified force that threatened North Carolina homes, churches, schools, and government.

As the 1948 presidential race began to take its shape, Nell Battle Lewis no longer felt that a weekly column in the more liberal *Raleigh News and Observer* was enough to support the Cold War and segregation. She sought a newspaper more aligned with her segregationist and anti-communist politics and took a new position at the conservative *Raleigh Times*. In June 1948, the summer of the Democratic National Convention, she left behind writing her nearly thirty-year-old column.[94] At the *Times*, she joined editor and publisher John Park to create a daily campaign against the Progressive candidacy of Henry Wallace. Under Lewis's guidance, the editorial page became an amalgam of anti-communist, anti-black, anti-civil rights, and anti-liberal rhetoric. A few of Lewis's editorials continued to highlight the benefits of some interracial cooperation, to lobby for better health care for North Carolinians, and to praise women's accomplishments, but far more frequently she intertwined communism and civil rights in editorials entitled "Party Shot to Pieces by Civil Rights Issues," "South: Like a Mother Kicked out of Home," "Issue Whether States Settle Their Affairs," "Civil Rights a Term to Conjure with Now," and "A New Red Look for Fo'ty Acres an' Mule."[95] Cartoons depicted communists crouched behind an American flag dangling from a flagpole named civil rights. Others placed an effeminate-looking Henry Wallace behind the wheel of a car filled with communists, African Americans, labor organizers, and Joseph Stalin. As Wallace's red-ridden vehicle drove through the South, its occupants challenged the sexual, racial, and class order, wreaking havoc reminiscent of the stories white supremacists told of Reconstruction. One editorial claimed that Truman would lose the election because of his civil rights policies. Most suggested that Truman, Henry Wallace, communists, and civil rights activists were outside agitators and challenged the power of white southerners to direct North Carolina's race relations. By the time Wallace returned on his presidential tour in 1948, angry North Carolinians led by Lewis's former *News and Observer* editor Jonathan Daniels greeted Wallace with so much hostility that Governor Gregg Cherry had to provide police protection throughout the rest of his abbreviated North Carolina tour.

Though not a serious contender for the presidency, Wallace raised the ire of North Carolinians simply by virtue of his views on foreign policy and race relations.[96]

At the beginning of World War II, the most committed segregationist southern women had attacked the First Lady, as the embodiment of threats to racial segregation and white supremacy. However, as the war drew to an end, it was not just the First Lady or even President Roosevelt who had betrayed the white South, but the political party they represented. Particularly in the Deep South states, the national Democratic Party no longer embraced and actually threatened the racial and ideological agenda of many whites. In the two election cycles before the rise of the Dixiecrats, Cain had begun to self-identify as a Jeffersonian Democrat; Tucker had left the Democratic Party; and Ogden ended the war as a States' Rights Democrat. At war's end, only Nell Lewis remained a Democrat in the national sense, although she would leave the party in 1952. Massive support for racial segregation had shifted into massive resistance with conservative white women at the helm.[97]

Elections, campaigns, voting, and state and federal legislation, however, were only part of the white supremacist agenda. White segregationist women had bred and fed the Jim Crow system at other levels as well. They recognized that it was in the "everydayness" that racial identity gained meaning and in their grassroots efforts they translated postwar domestic and foreign policy into the most local and quotidian of actions. With the Democratic Party's weakening support for racial segregation, children would be seduced by communist propaganda promoting racial integration. Young white women, they insinuated, would suffer under the leering eyes of black male employers; soldiers voting would upend state authority of elections; integrated entertainment for military personnel would mean school integration in Louisiana. The quiet rudeness toward Eleanor Roosevelt by Salisbury's white women, the published columns of Mary Cain, the letters of South Carolina women, the discussions of schoolchildren in Louisiana, and the stories Nell Battle Lewis told about her black neighbors illuminate the multiple terrains on which white women defended the Jim Crow order.[98] By the end of the war years, white segregationist women remained scattered along the political spectrum, some reaching out to national conservatives while others criticized the Democratic Party's shift in race relations but remained supportive of its other domestic and foreign policies. These years had solidified the intertwining of civil rights and communism in the minds of segregation's gardeners. They critiqued political and social changes that diluted the ultimate power of white people to direct and to control racial change. In doing so they reinforced the architecture of massive resistance, making sure that it would take hold in homes, schools, at the polls, and in the stories white southerners continued to tell. In talking about the Democratic Party's betrayal as a betrayal of states' rights and an unconstitutional expansion of federal power, segregationist women found that their ideas and politics appealed to organizations beyond those specifically committed to white over black, broadening the scope of their networks. With small steps, white southern segregationist women cultivated their ties to national conservative organizations, giving massive resistance a national audience.

# 6

## Jim Crow's International Enemies and Nationwide Allies

IN 1948, when the frustrated southern delegates marched out of the Democratic National Convention, they finally did what some white southern women had been advocating—broke with the national Democratic Party.[1] The 1948 walkout most obviously resulted from the Democratic Party's domestic civil rights platform, Truman's order to desegregate the military, and his support for the 1947 report from the President's Committee on Civil Rights, "To Secure These Rights." However, southern delegates literally left their seats and the convention when Minneapolis Mayor Hubert Humphrey suggested that the United States should "walk . . . into the bright sunshine of human rights."[2] The United Nations Charter had defined human rights as fundamental rights due to all people "regardless of race, sex, language or religion." For southern segregationists, "human rights" was an internationalized euphemism for racial equality and a harbinger of attacks on domestic racial segregation. When the Democratic Party advocated these, it announced to a national and an international audience that the South's system of segregation violated basic human rights. "Human rights" also gave black civil rights activists a channel to take their grievances to the international stage. The National Negro Congress and the NAACP had petitioned the UN to condemn lynching, rape, and other human rights abuses in the American South. The interracial home-grown Southern Conference for Human Welfare had called for a broad platform of human rights, and their mere presence contradicted the oft-told fiction that outsiders, not native southerners, were pushing a politics of equality. To some, Humphrey's speech was another odious offspring of Eleanor Roosevelt, who served as the inaugural chairman of the United Nations' Commission on Human Rights. And those already wary of the UN could point to the organization's infiltration into American domestic policy-making. Just a year before the 1948 Democratic convention, the report from the President's Committee on Civil Rights had listed as one of its eleven constitutional justifications for federal intervention in civil rights Articles 55 and 56 of the UN's Charter. In this context, a call for "human rights" expressed regional, national, and international threats to the segregated South and evoked the possibility of a global campaign against segregation, racist violence, and political repression.[3] It was also, segregationists argued, a direct encroachment on national sovereignty.

For many southerners, white and black, international and national attention to Cold War civil rights had the potential to raze white political authority in the Jim Crow South.[4] Few white southerners initially realized that the Cold War culture actually narrowed civil rights activism by making economic critiques of capitalism and unionization subversive. Instead the South's most dedicated segregationists saw only challenges to states' rights and white supremacist politics in a human rights platform. Those who had always worried that apathetic and unaware whites imperiled the Jim Crow South now worried that the Jim Crow stories they told would be countered by those that emphasized the equality of people across the world and that had the global sanction of the UN.[5] As a result, parental authority would be challenged and the ability to reproduce and preserve racial segregation and white supremacy through public education would be diminished. The UN joined the list of challengers to the Jim Crow order, keeping company with a number of former allies of segregationists—the federal government; the executive branch under Roosevelt; and the Democratic Party that supported him. White segregationist women believed that the new international order threatened their communities and their local racial practices. Where some saw a truncated civil rights agenda, they saw an ever-widening road.

As threatening as postwar international affairs may have seemed, it came bearing its own political plenty. The emergent Cold War had moved foreign policy concerns about Soviet expansion onto America's home turf resulting in an internal campaign to police homegrown communists. The domestic anti-communist crusade offered opportunities to link conservatives across the nation in support of national security. Specifically, the gendered politics of domestic anti-communism offered women a political language in which home protection, oversight of their children's education, and the policing of seemingly benign outsiders polluting communities with incendiary ideas required their vigilance. Housewives, seeing themselves as domestic political vigilantes, organized in the name of civil defense, child protection, and anti-communism, forming the grassroots groundswell of the postwar right.[6]

Fearing a world populated by new, independent nations in Asia and Africa susceptible to Soviet machinations, others replaced a language of overt racial fears with one of economic and geographic development, elevating industrial nations above those that had just cast off colonial authority and economic control. Conservatives of various strands worried that the new emphasis on internationalism embodied by the United Nations meant an erosion of national sovereignty and economic superiority as the United States found itself collaborating, on equal footing, with the communist members of the Security Council—the Soviet Union and China. Caught between international organizations and state and local governments, the federal government would opperate, conservatives feared, as a portal for a liberal internationalist agenda to infiltrate their nation.[7]

Americans across the ideological spectrum also watched the Soviet Union approve the UN's Declaration of Human Rights and Genocide Convention and repeatedly publicize to the world the racist atrocities committed on American soil. Spurred in part by their horror over the lynching and torture of black veterans in the South, President Truman's Cold War policy team called for the desegregation of the military, a permanent FEPC, and a committee to study civil rights. Wary of such change, white southerners, among other Americans, claimed that Truman had capitulated to communist pressure. Rather than shoring up American democracy, some claimed, his steps toward racial justice undermined states' rights and individual freedoms. As homegrown black voter registration drives, employment rights campaigns, and crusades against racist sexual violence all intensified in the postwar South, it was easy for vehement anticommunists to see a Soviet imprint in civil rights activism. Thus anticommunist and white supremacy campaigns merged and allowed segregationists to collapse distinctions between communist-front and civil rights organizations. The Cold War had made increasingly visible a newly rehabilitated version of a domestic subversive—anyone who campaigned for both (or either) racial equality and the rights of laborers.[8]

Consequently, both anticommunists and anti-internationalists expressed their opposition to the UN and to human rights in ways that stoked the right and had broad appeal in the Jim Crow South.[9] While most southern segregationists remained Democrats, most also continued to believe in a racial hierarchy that upheld racial segregation at home and the supremacy of the United States abroad.[10] These hierarchies and beliefs about race were not out of line with the broader Cold War discourse which offered Jim Crow's defenders a language of international diplomacy, ideological differences, and global brinkmanship to defend American hegemony. Repackaging the language of white supremacy for the Cold War, segregationists tried out an early version of a "color-blind" conservatism.

For segregationists the spread of internationalism meant the erosion of states' rights, the condemnation of the Jim Crow order, the rise of integrated labor unions, and the proliferation of multicultural curricular materials. This was as true in southern California as it was in southern Mississippi. When the UN's educational wing—United Nations Education, Scientific and Cultural Organization (UNESCO)—created school curricula, teaching materials, and educational programs, anti-internationalists believed that they promoted collectivism, elevated the status of nonwhite nations, and eroded white supremacist beliefs. Making sure that public education supported white supremacy and the Jim Crow order had long been on the to-do list of many southern white women, so the oversight called for by the anti-internationalists overlapped with the authority white women already wielded over public schools. This broader political conversation encouraged Ogden, Tucker, and Cain to intensify their involvement and visibility in national conservative and even far-right organizations. Conservative segregationists feared the waning of national sovereignty, the replacement of red-blooded, individualistic Americans with those who celebrated the international brotherhood of man, and a diminution of American global authority. In their opposition to UNESCO, the UN and human rights, they could call on their fellow segregationists to preserve states' rights, small federal government, and constitutional liberties instead of highlighting their devotion to a white supremacist state, perhaps finding willing allies among more mainstream segregationists and conservatives.[11]

The postwar global order resulted in transposing anxieties about the world into threats to women's authority over their home, children, and schools. Segregation's activists responded, using club meetings, newspaper columns, and local politics to translate a debate about US foreign policy into grassroots concerns that ranged from changes in marriage and labor practices to the citizenship goals of school curriculum and teacher education. The international threats to racial segregation meant that segregationists could keep burying black homegrown civil rights activism behind majority white, outsider-inspired change, giving the fiction of satisfied black southerners its last gasp. White PTA mothers, historic society members, and churchgoers could be both Cold Warriors and guardians of the Jim Crow South. Anti-internationalism refracted through opposition to the UN enabled them to both defend the segregated order and to build coalitions and political networks with organizations opposing international collaboration and internationalist ideals.

Even a few years before 1948, no one had realized that the United Nations would be the focal point of the political mobilization of white women seeking to preserve the segregated social order. Initially, Americans supported the creation of the United Nations, rejected isolationism, and hoped international collaboration would prevent another genocide.[12] In 1945, the organization did not seem like a threat to those building support for massive resistance to civil rights.[13] In fact, the South showed the least inclination for isolation of any region in the nation, with 90 percent of southerners supporting the UN.[14] Even Mississippi's conservative newspaper, the *Jackson Clarion-Ledger*, applauded the US ratification of the UN Charter.[15] Florence Sillers Ogden was not enthusiastic about the UN but did not see it as a threat to white supremacist politics. Cornelia Dabney Tucker had sought an invitation to the United Nations Conference on International Organization in San Francisco, and Nell Battle Lewis called on her readers to support the new organization.[16] Lewis did not see international cooperation or diplomacy as a threat to her home, the order of her domestic world, or the enlightened role that her class could play in racial politics and social reform. Nor did she see it as a threat to white supremacy. In fact, Lewis believed, like the nationally syndicated columnist Dorothy Thompson, that for women "the center of life is the home; the duty of life is to children; the necessity of life is peace . . . [and] they are now called upon to exert in dynamic demonstrative energy for the salvation of mankind" and that meant global cooperation.[17]

Lewis's initial position aligned with those of other women who responded to the Cold War with a new commitment to end racist violence, to equalize schools, to build a more democratic nation, and to work toward disarmament. Events in 1947, however, both challenged the South's support for the UN and escalated the anti-internationalism of segregationist women. President Truman had affirmed his reputation as a Cold Warrior when he instituted the Truman Doctrine. When he called for loyalty oaths among federal employees, he legitimated the belief in the presence of homegrown communists and the domestic threat they posed. The language of containment traveled easily between the diplomatic and the domestic front. In Raleigh, Lewis watched as the Carolina District of the Communist Party purchased substantial advertising space in the *News and Observer* and used it to call on "labor, the farming population, the Negro people, professionals, and small business men" to push for the repeal of the sales tax, the advent of racial integration, and the defeat of an anti-strike bill. Claiming that her column "gave me a channel through which I could save my state," Lewis noted that the communist support for the sales tax repeal made her question her opposition to such a tax. In North Carolina, news of communists in her home state alarmed her and began to erode her moderation.[18] She made clear to her readers that the Communist Party did not represent North Carolina's labor leaders or its black leaders who had rejected the overtures of the communists; still she worried that the connection had been reinforced, and "the red paint smeared by this ad will stick."[19]

In North Carolina, this Cold War intrusion into southern white homes, Nell Lewis observed, came not from outsiders but from homegrown and misguided activists at their flagship university in Chapel Hill. Lewis discovered that North Carolina's chapter of the Communist Party was not only trying to organize interracial workers' unions, but was also seeking converts in the state's public universities. There they found support among some of Lewis's former friends who foregone calls for gradualism in race relations for a position of immediate racial equality. In HUAC hearing transcripts, Lewis read testimony about a "group of Communist party members at the University" who worked under the leadership of Greensboro native, World War II veteran, former vice president of the Southern Negro Youth Congress, and communist organizer Junius Scales. The newspaper of the North Carolina branch confirmed her suspicions that the state's youth were being misled and being encouraged to embrace racial equality. Taking aim at the University of North Carolina, Lewis claimed that North Carolinians never intended to pay taxes "on a nest for Muscovite fledglings." Frank Porter Graham, president of the university, had allowed an invasive "pinkish curtain of liberalism" to corrupt the state's youth and replace gradualism with a more radical path which, she believed, had hurt her state.[20]

Communists at Chapel Hill confirmed for Lewis that the state's most revered institution was fertile ground for the ideological seduction of young white southerners. Comparing campus conversations of the Communist Party at Chapel Hill with fireplace chats in her home, Lewis raised the specter of communist infiltrators in the midst of southern families.[21] Quoting the virulent anti-communist J. Edgar Hoover, director of the Federal Bureau of Investigation, she noted that "Communists and fellow travelers under the guise of academic freedom can teach our youth a way of life that eventually will destroy the sanctity of the home." Lewis framed her red-baiting in terms of a woman's responsibility to the home which connected her to other white women—segregationists and conservatives—who willingly assumed responsibility for preserving the domestic order and for policing their public schools.[22] Newspapers across the state picked up Lewis's concern and echoed her claim that one communist professor could influence "50 or more young men and women which was certainly more dangerous than 'red' government clerks who do not have access to the minds of the state's youth."[23] Locating the threat of communist subversion among public schools and teachers under-mined the very roles that they played in a democratic society and equated cri-tiques of them with expressions of anticommunism, patriotism and national security. Lewis's concern, however, came from more than alleged collegiate communists. She blamed Graham's refusal to "curb the commies" on his par-ticipation in the interracial Southern Conference for Human Welfare, which put him in the company of fellow travelers who wanted a different educa-tion for the South's white youth. Pinkish liberalism meant racial equality, and Graham's university leadership promoted an education that threatened the lessons about "racial integrity" taught in southern homes and the institution-alized white supremacist education that white women had worked so hard to maintain.

Lewis, a former southern liberal, was so alarmed by this domestic betrayal that she moved decidedly to the right, turning on North Carolina's beloved son and her former friend, Frank Porter Graham.[24] After a year spent strug-gling with recurring health problems, she returned to the *Raleigh News and Observer* just in time to help ignite opposition to Graham's 1950 Senate race. Folks across North Carolina celebrated the return of her column, "Incidentally," and Graham sent her a note of congratulations, hoping their old friendship offered ground for more congeniality than animosity.[25] At that time, he may have believed what many North Carolinians did—that his Senate election was a given. Graham's closest challenger in the Democratic primary was the political newcomer and conservative banker Willis Smith. Initially, Lewis con-ducted a restrained campaign for Smith by criticizing Graham as a member of Truman's civil rights committee, the Southern Conference for Human Welfare and as a permissive former president of the UNC. For Lewis, he epitomized the confluence of liberal forces attacking the status quo—communists, advo-cates of racial equality, and internationalists.[26] At the time of the first primary in May, her boss Jonathan Daniels had used the *News and Observer* to promote Graham's campaign. Lewis wrote to Smith, "I have not been free to write the column as I wished and to come out for you unequivocably [sic]." After Smith's narrow loss in the first primary, Lewis assured him that she had "used whatever personal influence I have in your behalf" and promised "redoubled efforts" in the next round.[27] Knowing that Lewis's column had a wide following, Smith supporters begged her to come out for him as "it will carry so much weight."

Vehement anti-communist and segregationist Stella K. Barbee asked Lewis to help her get the story out about Graham's alleged involvement with the University of Moscow.[28] Lewis responded by excoriating Graham's weak defense of white supremacy.

Her storytelling for segregation became central to the election as she tried to turn North Carolinians away from a more liberal political program. She was joined by Raleigh's WRAL television commentator Jesse Helms and the grassroots mobilization of North Carolina's conservative segregationist white women. In June 1950, her efforts were made easier when the US Supreme Court released decisions on three graduate school integration cases, in each instance siding with black challengers of segregated graduate public education. In an excerpt entitled "Ominous, Indeed," Lewis responded that "no white Southerner who loves his land could, it seems to me, have read of the recent U.S. Supreme Court decisions against [for] non-segregation of the races in education without the very gravest concern." Painting the white South as a weary martyr in its efforts to sort out the problem that "we have been cursed and afflicted with," Lewis praised the white South's efforts at racial justice and ignored the findings of the President's Committee on Civil Rights which had claimed the very opposite.[29] In light of the desegregation cases, Lewis's implication was clear. Graham's work with the federal government, his enervating effect on white officials to direct change, and his false liberalism threatened racial segregation and would make white youth the first victims of a new integrated order.

Other Smith supporters echoed Lewis's denunciation of Graham. While urging Smith to call for a second primary, Helms described Graham as both a communist and an integrationist.[30] In the second primary, Lewis described Smith as a man who would not cater to northern, liberal, or black opinions. He believed in "the southern way of life," and that meant opposition to reviving the FEPC, extending federal civil rights legislation, and capitulating to socialism. Smith contended that churches, schools, fraternal groups, and civic organizations could direct social change; the federal government could not. Striking such a stance, he protected white supremacy, states' rights, and in many ways, white women's roles in directing reform from local institutions. His advocacy for limited government guaranteed that conservative white women would continue to wield power.[31] It also guaranteed that they would support his campaign.

On the eve of the second primary, Lewis preceded Smith to the podium at a Wake County rally. Lewis observed that "it has been at least a half a century since the vote of a North Carolina Democrat has had as much significance as it will have in tomorrow's Senatorial primary," suggesting that the race was important "to the nation as well, and . . . to the world." Rather than celebrating Smith's conservative credentials, Lewis's opening words invoked the 1898 white supremacist campaign in North Carolina, the same one that had staged a violent political coup d'état in Wilmington, had destroyed the black press, and had escalated the state's embrace of racial segregation. Then, Lewis shifted away from the state's most infamous white supremacist campaign and painted the current contest as one about "ever-tightening state control over the lives of the citizens of this country."[32] Despite her later disclaimer that the Senate contest was not about race, the campaign tactics of Lewis and Smith supporters indicated that it was most certainly about white supremacy. The *Christian Science Monitor* reported that Graham could overcome accusations of communist sympathy alone but not when they were coupled with his reputation for racial moderation.[33] Throughout July, letters in the *News and Observer*'s "People's Forum" indicated that Smith's defeat of Graham arose from North Carolina's deep devotion to white supremacy.[34] During the Smith-Graham campaign, Lewis had moved the threat of integration into the deepest recesses of the home. At one point she screamed at her pro-Graham editor, Jonathan Daniels, "I hope all your daughters have nigger babies." As Lewis discussed it, the campaign for civil rights—political and economic—could be reduced ultimately to sex.[35] Maintaining white supremacy was both a family and a political matter.[36]

Lewis's editorials contemplating the connections between the spread of communism and a broader civil rights agenda and her campaign for Smith played into a conversation occurring in family rooms in Houston, Texas; Los Angeles, California; Rosedale, Mississippi; Chicago, Illinois; Atlanta, Georgia; and other communities across the nation. At meetings of the DAR, Minute Women, and Women for America as well as the more moderate General Federation of Women's Clubs, clubwomen emphasized their fundamental duties in the emerging Cold War world.[37] Just as Lewis had repackaged the states' rights argument for a new day, women across the nation decried the erosion of national sovereignty by the United Nations and the links between an expanding federal government and communist subversion.[38] Lewis's southern-style conservatism had connections to the anti-statism and anti-internationalism that was coalescing nationwide to form the nascent right.

As the senatorial campaign solidified Lewis's political work against integration and internationalism, conservative white women also focused on UNESCO and its development of school curriculum. In 1950, UNESCO issued a statement that said "'race' is not so much a biological phenomenon as a social myth." Since "all men belong to the same species," the pamphlet continued, "anti-miscegenation laws had no legitimate or scientific basis." For white supremacist women, school segregation and curriculum control helped them make interracial marriage taboo and thereby reproduced white supremacy intellectually and physically. Yet here was an international organization that published materials widely used in American schools countering the "natural order" of races. If race science was not a basis for anti-miscegenation laws, then certainly science could not be stretched to justify school segregation. Setting off a political storm, UNESCO recanted this statement, but it was too late. UNESCO had already established itself as a conduit through which an education that celebrated multiculturalism and, some felt, socialism would reach white children. Far from dealing with only international issues, many feared, that the UN's programs had designs on reordering daily life.[39]

White segregationist and conservative women responded. By condoning UNESCO, the United Nations reaffirmed the rumors that it threatened everyday matters for everyday people. By the end of 1951, the DAR had reasserted its opposition to world government and rescinded its former support for the United Nations. In 1948, the UN's passage of the the Universal Human Rights resolution and the Genocide convention had troubled DAR members. Two years later, the national DAR convention passed a resolution on "International Agreements," registering concern about the potential interference in domestic affairs made possible by the Human Rights Declaration and the Genocide Convention. Then, in 1951, *Perez v. California* challenged the state's prohibition on persons of Japanese ancestry owning land and cited the UN's Charter as part of their constitutional challenge. The DAR's earlier concern that the UN possibly could interfere in domestic affairs had come to fruition. The *DAR Magazine* ran articles warning its members that UN conventions could be invoked to overturn anti-miscegenation laws just as the Human Rights Declaration had been used to overturn racially exclusive property legislation in the California. Across the nation, DAR chapters spent much of 1951 studying the problems with the UN and the Genocide Convention. The Illinois DAR sponsored a statewide essay contest on why the United States should not belong to a world government organization. Mississippi chapters crafted a year-long study on world government and the Genocide Convention. The DAR state regent for Texas reported that 65 percent of its local programs focused on the UN or world government.

As more and more organizations adopted study plans like those of the DAR, support for the UN waned.[40]

After a year of study the DAR passed formal resolutions against the United Nations, world government, and the Genocide Treaty.[41] Arguing that the United Nations was a threat to private property, Christianity, and minority rights (in this case, the DAR noted that whites were a minority of the world's population), Ogden attacked the Genocide Treaty specifically because it defined genocide as a "crime which does mental or bodily harm to a member of a racial minority." As Florence Ogden stated, in the context of Mississippi, this meant (using minority rights to mean black southerners in this case) that it would be illegal to make derogatory statements about the NAACP. She also argued that under the treaty:

> a Negro, a Chinese, or a member of any racial minority, could insult you, or your daughter. Your husband might shoot him, knock him down, or cuss him out. If so he could be tried in an international court. It would also make it a crime to prevent racial intermarriage and inter-marriage would destroy the white race which has brought Christianity to the world.[42]

In what would soon become standard Ogden fare, she argued that the UN would further intrude in "other numerous matters that will affect your daily life," since under the auspices of its cultural programs, it influenced teaching and textbooks in American schools. Ogden believed that a communist block bent on an interracial order would eventually control the United Nations. The link between communism and black civil rights made the United Nations, in Ogden's mind, a likely ally in the growing effort to dismantle racial segregation. She raised doubts that American leadership in the United Nations, influenced by Eleanor Roosevelt and including African Americans Ralph Bunche and Archibald Carey, could represent white America's inter-ests.[43] Again noting that it would be the children and grandchildren who would suffer from communism, racial intermarriage, and a new brand of politicized schooling, she told the white women that "it is you who must rise up and lead the way."[44]

In their opposition to the UN and UNESCO, southern white women made common cause with conservative women and women on the far right across the nation who parlayed their opposition to the United Nations into local school curriculum and administration decisions. Women on the far right like those involved in earlier mothers' organizations had found willing publishers for their anti-UN editorials at *Spotlight*, the publication of the New York–based Committee for Constitutional Government, and the *The Cross and the Flag*, edited by former Nazi sympathizer and leader of the Christian Nationalist Crusade Gerald L. K. Smith. In Smith's publication isolationism, anticommunism, and white supremacy served as the three pillars of the United States. Former DAR officer Frances Lucas's research was featured in an article "UNESCO Campaign against Schools" in *The Cross and the Flag*. Lucas had published pamphlets accusing UNESCO of providing curriculum materials that destroyed patriotism and nationalism and indoctrinated students with the idea of becoming "world citizens" which appealed to the far right. She also had alerted her readers to the UN's attempts to conduct a "sinister and systematic campaign to poison the minds of American school children by indoctrinating their teachers, and by censoring and revising their textbooks."[45] UNESCO materials, Lucas and others argued, aimed to insult American mothers and "to correct many of the errors of home training." Mothers in Houston, Texas, who belonged to the Minute Women responded to these insults by electing two candidates for school board who opposed the use of UNESCO teaching materials.[46]

Women of the far right made strides in their campaigns against the UN because they found mainstream conservatives who agreed with them on this matter, even though they disagreed with their other anti-Semitic and fascist beliefs. Middle- and upper-class conservative white women in Los Angeles and Pasadena feared the influence of the UN and denounced the evils infiltrating their public schools—progressive education, desegregation, and communism. One of these women was Frances Bartlett, an Ogden and Cain correspondent who had grown up in Laurel, Mississippi, before she moved to the West Coast. Bartlett was involved in Pro-America, a women's organization founded in Seattle in the 1930s to protest New Deal liberalism. While the early founders were Republican, members of Pro-America rejected partisan labels and invited women who held conservative principles above party affiliation. Bartlett's focus was the evils of progressive education and the "invisible" threats to American society propagated by new curricular practices. She alerted parents to these issues in her newsletter, "FACTS in Education." FACTS was an acronym for Fundamental issues, Americanism, Constitutional Government, Truth, and Spiritual Values, and key to those causes, Bartlett made clear, were the connections between communism and the American civil rights campaign. In 1950, Bartlett and other women of both Pro America and Pasadena's School Development Council, a parent group, gathered to push out the very esteemed school superintendent,

Willard Goslin for being "too progressive when it came to pedagogical and racial issues."[47]

While Bartlett was more conservative than most, her fellow critics of certain progressive school reforms ranged across the conservative spectrum. For the School Development Council, Goslin's sins were many. First, he advocated sex education which they felt eroded parental authority. Second, he advocated learning about "foreign" nations and peoples which they felt detracted from learning about "American history and 'heritages.'" This failure became salient upon review of the textbooks used in the schools which Bartlett and others claimed eroded the loyalties of students to the United States. Goslin lobbied for summer camps that parents felt replaced more traditional options. He also tried to end the practice of busing white children out of their neighborhoods to white majority schools and instead have them attend their neighborhood school. Ironically, given the future of anti-busing campaigns, white families resisted an end to busing and condemned Goslin for that suggestion. Finally, Goslin had authorized the viewing of a short animated film, "The Brotherhood of Man," that advocated racial tolerance and made a scientific case against racism. While the League of Women Voters, the NAACP, a labor organization, and the Rotary Club supported the acclaimed administrator, they could not overcome accusations that Goslin participated in communist and civil rights activities. The school board finally succumbed to pressure and sent Goslin a telegram asking for his resignation. He received it while attending a United Nations committee meeting in New York.[48] The successful efforts of the particularly vocal women of the School Development Council exposed their power in deposing a nationally known and respected school administrator. Watched from afar, the anti-Goslin campaign offered southern female segregationists validation for their connection between communism, subversive curriculum materials, and racial integration. Pasadena's conservative women had used their local organizations and institutions to challenge the federal government, just as segregationists did in their opposition to the UN.[49] The national uproar against UNESCO teaching materials and "progressive" pedagogy affirmed that segregationists were part of a national, not a regional movement, and their allies could be found in cities and suburbs from the Black Belt to the Sunbelt. It also made sex education and multicultural education soft threats to segregated schooling in the South as both eroded parental authority.

From 1948 to 1952, conservative and segregationist white southern women had made public education central to their political identities and to their political work. Entering the debate from vastly different vantage points—anti-communism, school equalization campaigns in the South, anti-internationalism, anti-UNESCO, or states' rights—southern female conservatives used local, national, and international politics to harden white women's political authority over schools, curriculum, and schoolchildren. They also used such rhetoric to align themselves with various political iterations of white supremacy. Alert to subversive forces infiltrating their schools, white southern segregationist women joined white conservative women (also segregationist) nationwide in their vigilant oversight of public schools. These women enjoyed school board victories, the thrill of working for successful political campaigns, grassroots organizing, publishing, and the benefits of an increasingly national network of white conservative women Beyond the politics of public instruction, women activists also shaped racial segregation, specifically, and southern and national politics, more generally, through formal elections and campaigning, capitalizing on a rhetoric built as much on international affairs as state and local concerns.

Energized by her contacts with conservatives across the nation, Mary Dawson Cain decided to enter Mississippi's primary race for governor in 1951. She hoped that her central role in the state's Democratic Party in 1944 and 1948 and her roles as publisher, editor, and columnist of the *Summit Sun* would increase her chances of winning the statehouse. She commanded the attention of many of the women's civic and professional organizations in the state—the Mississippi Federation of Women's Clubs, with a membership of 8,000; the Business and Professional Women, with a membership of 2,000; the Mississippi branch of the American Poetic Association, and the Mississippi Federation of Press Women.[50] Her campaign was also of great interest to conservatives outside of Mississippi, including the Jeffersonians of Chicago; Phoebe and Kent Courtney, right-wing activists and future publishers of the far right newspaper in Gulfport, Mississippi, *Free Men Speak*; and Francis Bartlett of Pro-America.

Cain entered the race as a foe of the "Welfare State" and an unrelenting advocate of states' rights. She characterized her platform as "predicated on one idea: a restoration to the people of Mississippi of their sovereign rights as citizens of Mississippi and the United States." While calling for Mississippi to stop accepting any federal grants in aid, she called on the state specifically to resist "bowing the knee to socialism by accepting federal aid to education—the 'New Deal method of ending segregation in our schools.'" She also campaigned to abolish the Sixteenth Amendment that had established a progressive income tax. Three tenets of her platform spoke to her commitment to women's rights as she call for equal representation of women and men on all state Democratic

**FIGURE 6.1** Mary Dawson Cain for governor of Mississippi. In 1952, Cain ran on the Democratic ticket, conducting her own whistle stop campaign. Her bid for the state's executive seat failed, but she strengthened her conservative credentials. Robert Waller Photographs, McCain Library and Archives, University of Southern Mississippi. Hattiesburg.

committees, the appointment of women to policy posts, and jury service for women who were ready for it. She traveled constantly around Mississippi, sometimes giving three talks a day. She refused to take any campaign contributions. In the end, she finished fifth in the primary behind four seasoned politicians.[51]

Between her two runs for governor in 1951 and 1955, Mary Dawson Cain continued to expand her conservative credentials. She joined right-wing conservatives across the nation as a member of the Organization to Repeal Federal Income Taxes (ORFIT). Inspired and encouraged by Vivian Kellems, feminist, anti-income tax activist, and northeastern businesswoman, Cain also refused to pay Social Security tax. She had derided Social Security during her campaign for governor, claiming that it was unconstitutional and threatening to refuse to pay it. In 1952, the federal government sent two agents to padlock her newspaper office because she had not paid her Social Security taxes. In response, she dramatically marched to the offices and cut through the locks, earning the sobriquet "Hacksaw Mary." If her run for governorship had made her a household name in Mississippi, her Social Security protest earned her national attention. Included in her papers were over 7,000 letters of support for her refusal to pay Social Security. Hailing from every state across the nation, they attested to her conservative appeal on an issue not directly related to white supremacy.[52]

In the midst of this fight, she gave an address entitled "The Octopus of Socialism" to a well-attended ladies' luncheon in Pascagoula, Mississippi. Later published in pamphlet form, Cain's speech played on Elizabeth Dilling's 1940 tract "The Octopus," which accused the Anti-Defamation League of plans to create an atheistic, communist United States.[53] Both Cain and Dilling had been members of America First, an isolationist and anti-Semitic organization on the eve of World War II, and Dilling was known in far right circles as the leader of the wartime mother's movement. Dilling and Cain both put New Deal programs and communism in the same ideological basket and declared them Godless. For Cain's updated "Octopus" speech, she listed the eight arms of socialism that were bringing the United States to the brink of demise: taxation, public welfare, subsidies, public power, public housing, "the rotten dollar," foreign policy, and tax-exempt coops." In addition, she claimed that the Supreme Court and Congress had turned to communism, once seduced by the promises of the New Deal. The UN was also "Godless" and part of an effort to "sell our nation down the international river" in the name of "humanitarianism."[54]

Attempting to brake America's slide toward communism engendered by the New Deal, Cain also highlighted the work of the Marshall Housewives and the nineteenth-century New South booster, Henry Grady. An odd mix, Cain employed both to highlight her right-wing credentials while also situating segregation and white supremacist politics in a more national conservative tradition. She congratulated the Marshall, Texas, housewives on their refusal to pay Social Security taxes for domestic help. Founded at a bridge club, the Marshall Housewives claimed that the federal government forced them into "indentured servitude" when they were charged with collecting a 1.5% percent Social Security tax on their employees but received no just compensation for their accounting work. Refusing to deduct from their maid's wages, the Housewives' rebellion gained national attention. In newspaper coverage, reporters focused on the politicized white women, while largely ignoring their mostly black employees. Not addressing the role domestic service played in the segregated South, most newspapers ignored the racial implications of the protest, but not the *Dallas Morning News*. The Dallas paper ran an editorial that claimed, "Back under slavery, of course, every slave holder provided social security for his retired slaves. . . . Under the welfare state, Uncle Sam moves in to compel the colored help of East Texas to compel Negro workers to take it out."[55] The assertion that the social security of masters was better than the social security of Uncle Sam sustained the myth of white paternalism central to the maintenance of segregation. Cain referred to the employees as "domestic servants, babysitters, and yard boys," diminishing the age and skill of household workers. Cain also made clear that she believed the black workers benefited from the New Deal when she noted that the Texas housewives had refused to pay for their servants "if they can find one that isn't on de welfare rolls."[56]

Cain's "The Octopus of Socialism" speech represented just one of the moments that she publicized the Housewives' legal fight. To capitalize on the national noterity of the Marshall women, Cain and conservative women across the nation either came to Marshall, Texas, or invited the Marshall women to come to them to spotlight related conservative causes. In Shreveport, Louisiana, some of the Marshall housewives came to hear Cain talk. New England businesswoman Vivien Kellems, who had encouraged Cain's own Social Security protest, came to Marshall to convince the housewives to join in her battle to get the Sixteenth Amendment declared unconstitutional. While Kellems's appearance packed the local auditorium, the housewives maintained that their protest was about Social Security taxes, not the federal income tax. Cain constructed those middle-class white Texas women who could afford "yard boys" but who would not pay Social Security as principled but marginalized Americans, a kind of noble minority.[57] The housewives agreed and noted, "We, as mothers and housewives, cannot sit idly by and watch the gradual ensnarement of personal liberties without petitioning our government. . . . We want them [children] to inherit the great democracy that was our heritage, not a Socialistic welfare state where citizens become chattels of the Government." Others felt the same way, as the Marshall postmaster suffered under a deluge of mail addressed to "Housewives" and "Rebels." These letters, mostly from women, sought advice on how to start a rebellion in their towns.[58]

Along with Cain's attention to the Marshall Housewives, she also celebrated Henry Grady in an effort to highlight "true Americanism," as opposed to government intervention, programs, and entitlements. Resurrecting one of the 1890s most prominent spokesmen for racial segregation, Cain downplayed Grady's racial politics and called on women to remember his states' rights quote: "Exalt the citizen. . . . Let him lean on the state for nothing his arm can do, and on the government for nothing his state can do." She also implored her audience to revitalize Grady's call to "Teach him that his home is his castle and his sovereignty rests beneath his hat." She offered a particular view of individualism and the federal government without noting that Grady's statement on limited government became synonymous with the erosion of constitutional rights and state protections of African Americans during the rise of Jim Crow. Following her praise of Grady with a lament that Mississippi's women could hardly find anyone to work as a domestic servant since most were receiving welfare benefits, she noted when housewives (white) did find domestic help the struggle was not over. If they did not collect Social Security taxes, then "American mothers and wives!" she summarized, would be fined or imprisoned. Without mentioning segregation or even "Anglo-Saxon heritage," one of her pat phrases, Cain had used her fight against Social Security to connect seemingly disparate politics: the Marshall housewives' refusal to pay Social Security taxes on behalf of their domestic servants; the revival of Henry Grady, an architect of the New South's segregated system; a condemnation of the United Nations that had internationalized debates on southern-style racial violence and segregation. Taken together, these positions demanded that "true Americans" fight against New Deal programs, expansive federal government, communism, and the erosion of state-regulated segregation. All this, Cain argued meant that it was the duty of Christian women to vote to preserve "the hearth, the flag, the place of prayer." If women fought against the eight arms of socialistic encroachment, then she predicted a "strong America" would return, one built on "freedom and individual responsibility under God." And those eligible for real American citizenship and endowed with the duty to ensure freedom, those women were white.[59]

Henry Grady experienced a kind of renaissance in the 1950s and Cornelia Dabney Tucker joined Cain in reviving him for the civil rights era. In the late 1940s, Cornelia Dabney Tucker had moved from South Carolina to Georgia and had taken a post directing Governor Herman Talmadge's booster program, "Georgia Days." This program targeted schools, celebrated American history with pageants, and promoted the consumption of Georgia-made goods—all elements critical to America's mainstream efforts to stave off socialism and communism. As part of her educational crusade, Tucker urged all public schools to spend time teaching Henry Grady's New South speech—the very one that emphasized economic development coupled with social segregation and political disenfranchisement. In the midst of postwar violence toward African Americans and civil rights legislation, this was hardly a politically neutral celebration of one of Georgia's finest. While she commemorated Grady for bringing the South into a modern economy, others must have remembered slain African Americans piled up at the base of the Grady statue in the aftermath of the 1906 Atlanta riot or his advocacy for the Jim Crow order.[60]

The white supremacist message in the Grady celebration was subtle compared to another component of Georgia Days—the performance of a pageant called "The White Man's Magic." Written by Gertrude Ruskin, a Decatur resident fascinated by Cherokee history who also went by the name Princess Chewani, the play celebrated the accomplishments of Cherokee leader, Sequoyah, who developed the Cherokee syllabary. Harnessing Native American history to white supremacist politics, "The White Man's Magic" emphasized Anglo-Saxon superiority. The play suggested that the Cherokee believed that written language was the magic of white settlers, and Sequoyah's ability to bring a written language to the Cherokee resulted from his physical proximity to the white man. At the Georgia Products Spring Festival in 1953, Grady's New South speech was the theme and white children across the state watched historical pageants including "The White Man's Magic." As Tucker and other women claimed enthusiastically: "This is the age of visual education. Every loyal Georgian wants our younger generation to know and take pride in the history of the state. What better means is there toward this end than plays by our high schools depicting incidents in Georgia's history?"[61] Tucker had made schools central to several white women's postwar political crusades, and women's oversight of public schools and a broader public education continued to be contested political ground in the Cold War and segregationist project.

Amid the campaign to merge communism and civil rights, segregation's activists continued to shape stories for a Jim Crow world, but they also continued to turn to electoral politics to shore up the status quo. In the early 1950s, their political efforts centered on two campaigns: the 1952 presidential campaign and the ratification campaign for the Bricker Amendment—a proposal to change the treaty approval process. Both opportunities offered segregationists a chance to couch their political machinations in the language of constitutional government. For some white southern women, the 1952 presidential campaign offered them a chance to distance themselves once and for all from blind devotion to the Democratic Party, indicating that for many, the days of the Solid South, at least in presidential elections, had come to an end.

In 1952, Cain, Tucker, Lewis, and Ogden believed that the protection of their homes, nation, and Christianity meant that they had to cast their ballots for Republican presidential candidate Dwight D. Eisenhower.[62] Cain, along with many other conservatives, first had hoped that Douglas MacArthur would be the Republican candidate.[63] Ogden had even named her cat MacArthur, and Mississippi held a MacArthur Day with a DAR-hosted reception at Rosalie, a restored Natchez plantation home. Even after MacArthur failed to get the nomination, the DAR's national magazine asserted that the election was up to women and it was time for women to push for a different foreign policy platform. Noting that only 47 percent of eligible women voted in 1948, the DAR, the Minute Women, and other women's organizations orchestrated get-out-the-vote campaigns, believing they would swing the election.[64] During the Democratic National Convention, noted Ogden, "housewives have sat glued to the television while dust accumulated on the furniture" captivated as they tried to discern "the difference between a politician and a statesman." Among all the men who "needed a shoe shine and a hair cut," neither Ogden nor many other white southern women could find that statesman at the convention.[65] Conservative and anti-UN women announced "there was no longer any real distinction between domestic and foreign policy," encouraging their constituents to vote Republican. For many who condemned the UN, like conservative New Yorker Mrs. Enid G. Griswold, a vote for Eisenhower could distance the country from the UN and reassert "local control," the national synonym for "states' rights."[66]

The 1952 Democratic National Convention only affirmed for many of segregation's supporters that that the authority of white southern Democrats would be tossed aside. Ogden proclaimed, "I cannot follow these men and these policies." A vote for Democratic candidate Adlai Stevenson, she argued, was a vote for the CIO, the AFL, the NAACP, and for "many other organizations which most of us feel are un-American and which will carry us down the road to Socialism." Her litany of Democratic evils also included "Civil Rights, FEPC, the Brannan Plan, socialized medicine, federal aid for schools . . . that are anathema to most Mississippians." To her disgust, she noted that Mississippi's male leaders came home from Chicago professing allegiance to the national party and calling on Mississippians to support Stevenson to protect valuable committee assignments. For Ogden, no committee assignment could compensate for the capitulation to internationalism.[67] Disappointed with white Democratic men, many southern white women turned to Eisenhower, believing he would bring a sterner attitude toward communists, an end to the Korean War, and halt the Democratic Party's slide toward racial liberalism.[68]

In Mississippi, Ogden joined the Democrats for Eisenhower movement and pledged to "elect Ike all by myself—with the help of women." Fed up with the Democratic Party's "disregard for constitutional government," their "benign attitude toward subversives," and their promotion of "hatred between the races and classes," Ogden organized the Bolivar County Women for Eisenhower. The Bolivar women's committee sent telegrams, campaigned from door to door, and called on women from other counties to organize. In speeches around the Delta, Ogden claimed that a Republican president was the only hope they had for the defeat of the FEPC. If women were unmoved by their duties as citizens and white supremacists, she called on them to vote Republican in the name of their children. To protect their sons from war, women should help her elect Eisenhower. "They [women] don't care whether it is via the Republican ticket or the Democrats for Eisenhower, just so their votes count," Ogden remarked. As true patriots, women, Ogden said, believed in "putting their country above party or expediency."[69] In October, Ogden attended an integrated Memphis rally for Eisenhower that included "lots and lots of women." Energized by the meeting, Ogden claimed that "the women can carry this election for Ike, if they will, and I believe they will," since "the men have messed it up long enough."[70] Despite black voters' support for Eisenhower, Ogden predicted that as a reward for a Republican victory, southerners would see a more vigorous effort in rounding up communists and in preserving states' rights, and in securing white supremacy.[71]

White women across the South and even the nation replicated Ogden's efforts. The DAR leadership had charged the national defense chairmen of local chapters to ensure that their members were registered to vote. Every DAR member was instructed to contact ten non-DAR friends to encourage them to register and vote—noting if they succeeded at home they would succeed in Washington.[72] Ogden's sister Evelyn Pearson also stumped for Eisenhower in Bolivar County while Marie Hemphill delivered speeches for him in Sunflower County. In neighboring Washington County, Margaret Wynn organized for Eisenhower and held a September rally attended by 400 to 600 people.[73] In October, a North Carolina woman in the Democrats for Eisenhower organization wrote Ogden, noting "you are a power-house in your State, and I well know your influence can mean a lot for us." Then the North Carolina woman said that she had already voted for "IKE."[74]

From August through November 1952, Mary Dawson Cain dedicated her time and talents to Eisenhower's campaign, capitalizing on her notoriety from the her Social Security fight to reach women and men across the United States. The *Summit Sun* became the first Mississippi paper to support him. She even forgave Eisenhower's support for Social Security for what she believed was the most important priority, the defeat of "the New Deal [which] is the monster of Communism." To do her part, Cain noted that "I'm on the go constantly these days" as "I realize fully how hard it will be to throw the election to the Republican Party in November." But hard work was nothing new for Cain, and she noted that "no effort shall be spared." Her commitment was in direct contrast to political men who were concerned about Democratic committee assignments and party favors. In this fight, she noted that the state's women were central since Mississippi's former "states righters" like Hugh White, James Eastland, and even Ogden's brother Walter Sillers proclaimed their support for the national Democratic ticket. While Eisenhower's campaign was "taking more out of me than my own campaign," she claimed, "it would be worth dying for." She spoke to Kiwanis Clubs, Minute Women meetings, farmers' organizations, and Federation of Women's Clubs in Alabama, Arkansas, Texas, Louisiana, and Mississippi. She conducted her own whistle stop campaigns in small towns like Jackson, Linden, Thomasville, and Demopolis in Alabama; in Natchez, Cleveland, Yazoo City, and Port Gibson in Mississippi; and in Bastrop and Lake Charles in Louisiana. Not limited to small towns, she also took the stage in New Orleans and Houston. At the request of students, she spoke at the University of Mississippi.[75]

From 1952 and 1953, correspondence from more than twenty states indicated a national audience for Cain's Social Security fight and a regional audience for her efforts for Eisenhower. From twenty-two states, people requested copies of her newspaper, expressing their admiration for her "Americanism." The editor of a small town South Carolina paper wrote Cain to tell her that his county went for Eisenhower. "In all its history," he said, it had never gone Republican. In small towns across Alabama, women's groups invited Cain to speak on behalf of the Eisenhower campaign. Cain talked to the Hale County Citizens for Eisenhower Club, and Olelia Goodale from Uniontown said that Cain's speeches for Eisenhower "did a big part in winning votes in Alabama." In Demopolis, white women celebrated that for "the first time in their history," they had a headquarters for the Republican Party.[76]

In the end, the work of Ogden, Wynn, and Cain failed to convince enough Mississippians to carry the state, but Eisenhower carried five southern states and had majorities in Black Belt districts. Pondering the defeat, Ogden asked: "Could it be that the Civil War destroyed something fundamental in us?" "I have wept bitter tears that my own state was weighed in the balance and found wanting," Ogden wrote. She felt that her efforts for Eisenhower provided a valuable service to her county. However, "As long as men are men, we are doomed to disappointments."[77] Mary Cain was less disappointed than Ogden, but her county went for the Republican. The *Summit Sun* followed

Eisenhower's victory with the headline: "'The New Deal' Is Killed; Ike to be President." Just below the headline, another said "Summit, Pike County Give Ike Fine Majority." Politically it was a huge majority, with Eisenhower gaining nearly 63 percent of the vote in Summit, Mississippi.[78] But as a Democratic woman explained her vote, "It was not so much . . . because we loved the Republicans more but because we loved the Democrats less."[79]

The credit for Eisenhower's votes, Ogden claimed, went to "the women and the young people." "This, I think," Ogden surmised, "goes for the nation."[80] And she was right. As historian Catherine Rymph revealed, southern white women left the Democratic Party in 1952 to vote Republican. Fifty-nine percent of white southern women voters cast their ballot for Eisenhower.[81] White southern women's support for Eisenhower outdistanced white southern men's by 18 percent. Political scientists Merle and Earl Black suggested that higher rates of college education among women, Stevenson's divorce, and higher-income pockets in more metropolitan districts accounted for Eisenhower's success among white women. But as historian Bruce Schulman showed, in addition to strength in southern cities, Eisenhower "triumphed . . . in the Black Belts of South Carolina, Louisiana, and Mississippi" as well as the traditional Republican enclaves in the mountain South and the hill country. While South Carolina had a strong Independents for Eisenhower movement, Mississippi did not. Yet, where white women worked, in the Delta and in Summit County, Eisenhower did well.[82] For white women, the election of 1952 was a clear step in partisan realignment. For many white women who voted Republican, the Solid South had come to an end.

Segregationist women had believed that Eisenhower could stop the "red" tide of civil rights and internationalism. In North Carolina, Nell Battle Lewis believed that Eisenhower's inaugural address informed the world that he was a Christian man. She also was pleased that it focused on foreign policy.[83] Lewis praised Eisenhower's commitment to an anti-communist policy and his decision to stop protecting communist China from Chiang Kai-shek's troops on Formosa. Ogden delighted in the Democrats' opposition to the address. That Ogden and Lewis applauded Eisenhower's address was in part due to diminished expectations. "We can't expect all of this and Heaven too, from the Republicans," Ogden later put it; "after all, they are men, too."[84]

Many white women had counted on Eisenhower to combat internationalism by supporting the Bricker Amendment, a proposal to limit the president's diplomatic power by moving the treaty approval process out of the Senate and into the state legislatures for ratification. Ohio Republican Senator John Bricker had introduced this amendment to a congressional committee in 1951 after the UN approval of the Human Rights and Genocide Conventions. He had the support of the American Bar Association, the DAR, the Minute Women, the Christian Parents for Better Education, and Pro-America. Many of these organizations believed that the two UN conventions gave the federal government power to intervene in matters reserved for the states.[85] A host of southern senators including North Carolina's Willis Smith, Richard Russell of Georgia, and Alabama's John Sparkman also expressed their support for the Bricker Amendment. Senator A. Willis Robertson, the Virginian who had represented the state in Rockbridge County's Racial Integrity case nearly three decades earlier, wrote that the nation had enough trouble with homegrown "do-gooders" and did not need the UN to add fuel to their fire.[86] For white conservative women across the nation, UN policies meant interference in public education and the messages they sought to instill in their children. They opposed a UN-inspired multicultural curriculum that decentered the American experience. In the South, these inroads into homes and schools meant the weakening of a segregationist ethos in general and of legalized school segregation specifically. As white southern segregationist women de-emphasized race in their rhetoric, they invoked states' rights as a fundamental foundation for national sovereignty and patriotism. The timing was perfect. By early 1953, many southern newspapers anticipated a decision on school segregation in the case lingering before the Supreme Court that would soon be known as *Brown*.[87] Thus, as the Bricker debates heated up in January of 1954, white conservative women, still energized from their Democrats for Eisenhower effort, mobilized their clubs and communities to participate in this nationwide crusade to change the US Constitution in order to protect the national sovereignty, state level-control over public education, and parental control over their children.

In 1954, the alarm over the UN enabled women working to prevent desegregation to remain relevant to conservative women's crusades across the nation. It also allowed them to link support for segregation to constitutional, patriotic, anti-communist, and anti-international crusades. Emphasizing that Congress and the states could refuse to implement international treaties if they found them in conflict with constitutional rights, Bricker attracted states' righters from across the country. Ogden riled up her DAR audience by asking, "Do you want to trust the freedom of your children to two-thirds of the Senate?"[88] To prevent this, Ogden encouraged them to write their congressmen and express their support for the Bricker Amendment. "Stop a Treaty from taking precedence over the U.S. Constitution," she charged. "The women can do it," she said. The question she posed was "will they?"[89]

She worked hard to assure that they would, speaking to PTA meetings across Mississippi in early 1954 and devoting numerous columns to support for Bricker and derision of his opponents.

In 1953, women in Wisconsin and Illinois had formed the Vigilant Women for the Bricker Amendment. Drawing on cross membership in the DAR and the Minute Women as well as other women's organizations that had grown leery of the UN, the organization quickly spread across the nation. In Mississippi, Mary Dawson Cain served as the state coordinator for Vigilant Women, circulating petitions and soliciting "wires and letters" to the state's senators. Working with American Bar Association president Frank Holman, the national leadership of Vigilant Women were warned that in their lobbying effort "powerful forces will be . . . weighing heavily against you." "These forces represent that new type of internationalism," Bricker Amendment supporters argued, "which believes that somehow the world can be saved if America and American rights are subordinated to international considerations and international control."[90]

Petitions and letters from women urging continued support for the Bricker Amendment poured into Senate offices on Capitol Hill. Over the course of a few months in early 1954, North Carolina Senator Clyde Hoey received 241 pieces of mail related to the Bricker Amendment. Men wrote 130 letters, most of them single-authored. Women sent 111 letters, but most of those included petitions with multiple authors, making women's organizations and women's signatures far more numerous in this letter-writing campaign. Dominated by North Carolina women, petitions also came from Illinois, Virginia, Missouri, Ohio, New York, and California. Chapters of the DAR, PTA groups, the American Legion Auxiliary, the Medical Auxiliaries, Pro-America, the Miami-based American Women's Council, and the Ohio-based Women's League for Americanism all petitioned Hoey to support Bricker. In his home state, the campaign illuminated the grassroots organizations in small towns and hamlets with letters arriving from Candler, Marion, Chapel Hill, Mooresville, North Wilkesboro, Monroe, Thomasville, Lillington, Southern Pines, Concord, Albermarle, Gastonia, Kinston, Dunn, Wilson, Rocky Mount, Farmville, and Kings Mountain, as well as Raleigh, Durham, and Charlotte. Some letters came from older women, members of the DAR, but others were young PTA members. One twenty-nine-year-old mother wrote that she "want[ed] my children to grow up under the Constitution, with no possibility of its being undermined or super-ceded by any treaty with any foreign power." For good measure, she also asked him to defend the right to deport subversives guaranteed by the McCarran-Walter Act.[91] Most of the petitions and letters included denouncements of "internationalism," spoke of the necessity of the amendment "as a means of preserving American freedom and the Constitution," or cast it as "a safeguard against an invasion on our American way of life." In North Wilkesboro, women noted that "proponents of world government are using this clause . . . to destroy our national sovereignty, states' rights, and individual rights."[92] Others condemned world government, communism, and socialism as outcomes of the current treaty approval process. Notably, the League of Women Voters chapters, Durham Women's Legion, the Women of the Winston-Salem Presbytery, and the United Church Women of Rocky Mount opposed the amendment, and one Democrats for Eisenhower woman noted that she had faith in her president and was unwilling to limit his abilities just one year into his presidency.[93] For Hoey, the most common was a standard petition that linked national sovereignty, states' rights, and individual rights, a configuration that would become standard fare for segregationists in the coming campaign against school desegregation.

In January 1954, over 600 Vigilant Women descended on Washington, lobbied weary and wavering congressmen, and presented petitions with more than 300,000 signatures. This trip gave conservative women a congressional audience. Three women arrived at the Capitol clothed in the petitions, reminiscent of Cornelia Dabney Tucker's 1938 Supreme Court protest. It was an important moment in the mobilization of conservative women nationwide, as women made arguments on the floor of Congress about restraining executive power, maintaining national sovereignty, and protecting states' rights. Among the Bricker activists was a young Phyllis Schlafly, future founder of the Eagle Forum, anti-feminist, and Goldwater supporter, calling on Congress to prevent "the United Nations from infecting our free American system with world government and international socialism by the devious device of treaty law." From 1953 forward, Schlafly emphasized that such UN treaties would "undermine individual freedom, trial by jury, and private property."[94] Observers could also have heard Frank Holman address the Vigilant Women and say, "If an Irish man got into an altercation with a colored man in Mississippi, he (the Irish man) could be transferred overseas for trial under the Genocide Convention."[95] Paeans to national conservative color-blind ideals could not bury the segregationist impulses that also undergirded this call for constitutional reform.

In February, the Bricker Amendment was defeated by one vote in the Republican-controlled Senate. Ogden praised Mississippi senators James Eastland and John Stennis for supporting Bricker, but she noted that sixty white men had failed to act in the best interests of future Americans. Ogden predicted that they "will live to rue the day, or if they do not, certainly their unfortunate children and grandchildren will."[96] Despite its failure, debates over internationalism, the un-American actions of the UN, and the repackaged doctrine of states' rights continued to be part and parcel of efforts to boost support for racial segregation and other conservative causes nationwide.

By 1954, southern white segregationist women had capitalized on the overlap between their white supremacist politics devoted to sustaining Jim Crow segregation and the white supremacist message embedded in the anti-international, anticommunist critique of the United Nations. For those segregationists who felt at home on the far right like Mary Dawson Cain, the anti-UN debates connected them to activists and organizations across the nation. For those grassroots activists concerned with more local issues, the debates about the UN and human rights had trickled into PTA meetings, school textbook debates, curriculum decisions, and commencement addresses. For them, the threats that communism and internationalism posed to national sovereignty and to racial segregation found their clearest expression in critiques of the curriculum materials of UNESCO. For Ogden, long primed to resist outsiders, conversations on internationalism allowed her to paint white southerners as part of a worldwide minority, under the thumb of a rapacious federal government at the same time that international governing bodies undermined national sovereignty and states' rights. Because their male elected officials had failed again and again to vote for principle over self or party preservation, white women had to become the first line of home defense against communist encroachment and increase their political authority on a local, state, and national level. These broader national debates had offered the mothers of massive resistance another political issue for which to mobilize their communities. When the Supreme Court handed down its decision in *Brown* on May 17, months after the defeat of the Bricker Amendment, white segregationist women were ready. Jim Crow's constant gardeners would expand their efforts to sustain segregation at home, at school, at the polls, and in the stories they told, even in the face of judicial defeat.

# 7

## *Threats Within*

### BLACK SOUTHERNERS, 1954–1956

FEAR, UNCERTAINTY, AND HOPE pervaded breakfast tables as southern families scanned their morning papers on Monday, May 17, 1954. Like so much else in the Jim Crow South, those emotions operated in segregated spaces. Many black families weighed their hope for better education and the equality and freedom it would bring against the fears of sending their children into hostile situations. Many white families responded in ways that pitted their fear of the loss of white supremacy and of exclusive educational opportunity against the hope that "the people" could prevent the destruction of school segregation. If a sense of justice, political resolve, and activism came from the seeds of one hope, resistance germinated from the seeds of another.[1]

"Black Monday" was the segregationist term that marked the day that Chief Justice Earl Warren released the unanimous Supreme Court decision dismantling the seventy-eight-year-old doctrine of "separate but equal." Some white southern newspapers declared a "miscarriage of justice," while others feigned surprise, even though southerners in the know had been anticipating the decision for several years.[2] Mary Dawson Cain buried the ruling on page 4, calling for "calm, level-headed—but absolutely determined and uncompromising" commitment to racial segregation.[3] In her column "Incidentally," Nell Battle Lewis lamented the fact that the Supreme Court was not accountable to the people. Two weeks later, she described the ruling as "together with the war of the 60s, one of the worst two things that has ever happened to the South."[4] Florence Ogden wrote, "My friends . . . you will know now how it feels to live in a country that is not free." She contended that "social gains cannot compensate any group, class, or section for the loss of their constitutional rights under a Republic."[5] In South Carolina, Cornelia

Dabney Tucker doubted the expert witness testimony and the validity of the psychological and sociological evidence employed as she dug out her 1937 Supreme Court Security League stationery for a new crusade. Some of the initial news focused on the case's constitutional demerits and the questionable qualifications of the justices who handed down such a decision. By the second week, letters to editors, governors, senators, and columnists emphasized that the real threat provoked by this decision lay in black southerners armed with rising hope.

White supremacist politics and paternalism had long collaborated to cloak black protest in the shadows of the South. As long as homegrown black resistance was cast off center stage, many white southerners had been able to say that "their" black folks were satisfied, that disaffection with the Jim Crow order was the work of subversive outsiders, and that they knew best how to conduct race relations. Until 1954, massive support for racial segregation most often meant minimizing collective resistance, refusing to acknowledge it, or simply being blind to the political organizing of black southerners. The *Brown* decision exposed the outcomes of decades of black organizing, damaging "the foundational truths" of Jim Crow society and the political identities that white segregationist women had cultivated.[6] The repercussions of *Brown*, unlike all the other threats—apathetic whites, the executive branch, the Democratic Party, the UN—supported the direct challenge of their black neighbors and eroded the most fundamental fiction of the Jim Crow system, that white southerners knew best what was good for black southerners. With black parents and children petitioning over sixty southern communities for their children to walk up the steps of white schoolhouses in August, the stories segregationists told of black contentment were no longer possible.[7] *Brown* had also diminished the possibility of a liberal white supremacist agenda that stressed gradualism or equalization efforts when the decision extended racial equality in education to all African Americans, not just those considered the most deserving or most accomplished. Segregationist women, liberal or conservative, could no longer profess to represent the best interests of the black community or claim the authority to direct southern race relations. They could, however, continue to contest the decision.

The two years following *Brown* were high-water marks for a vibrant segregationist movement—even amid internal discord on the strategies of resistance.[8] For a time, *Brown* brought the discourse of segregationists to focus on a single institution—each community's public schools. Because of the Court's decision to forbid class action suits for violating *Brown*, each community would craft and implement desegregation one district at a time, leaving much power at the local level. The decision pulled to the center of the political debate the very institution where white women had generational, complex, and multilayered authority. Schools were repositories of their efforts as mothers, educators, citizens, and cultural guardians. Faced with this new onslaught, white segregationist women made the family the center of political life and political ideology. To preserve families now threatened by a a leviathan federal government that had overtaken public education, they offered a version of racialized family values. Opening up their political ranks to those women who were not political activists but who were wary about losing authority over their families, *Brown,* in part, had feminized massive resistance.

Over the next two decades, white southerners would respond in myriad ways as the Court's ruling engendered desultory and sporadic implementation. Many white southern women emerged as moderates. They advocated a middle road between fully integrated education and closed schools, arguing for token desegregation of public schools—for "accommodation not capitulation."[9] Other moderates announced their commitment to maintaining state funding for public schools. They rejected a hardline, but not uncommon, stance to cease state support of public education and prevent any crossing of the color line. Casting around for other solutions, others proposed a different institution—charter schools—that could maintain state funding but limit the "publics" they served. An even smaller minority, white liberals publicly considered a full embrace of school desegregation and racial equality, but in 1954 they lacked any real visible allies—institutional or otherwise. Faced with the unknown in terms of implementation, moderates gained visibilty later when communities confronted the reality of integrating their schools and when ending public education altogether had come to constitute the most extreme reaction. But in years just following *Brown I* and *Brown II*, which called for implementation at the indeterminate pace of "all deliberate speed," moderates were not particularly visible, vocal, or public.[10]

The voices dominating the early years were those of the opponents of school desegregation. These were the people who would not consider the practicalities of integration but spent their energy denouncing its erosion of their families, their schools, their politics, and their daily lives. Their voices drowned out the response of moderates. The clamor of obstructionist voices would be identified with the movement of massive resistance. Those southern white women calling for segregated schools revealed their layered investment in the white supremacist order. They invoked their roles as mothers, Christians, citizens, anticommunists, protectors of the constitution, conservatives, and government reformers. Continuing to adopt the bankrupt position as spokeswomen for black communities, some contended that black southerners really wanted equal facilities, not integrated ones, and pointed to scattered black signatures on petitions to uphold segregated schools. Some claimed that the presence of black children would harm their white schools, changing the lessons they taught their children and the dictates of white motherhood that defined their lives. Not only were white women's identities as partisan political actors or as citizens based on a segregated social order, but the ideology of white supremacy also had racialized their understanding of the responsibilities of motherhood. With so much that they had worked for on the line, they became the mass in massive resistance.

The *Brown* decision also resonated beyond the region and beyond the South's segregationists. It offered conservatives nationally a rich opportunity to weigh in on the erosion of parental, local, and states' rights and the influence of communism in American politics, diminishing the attention paid to white supremacy. In one of her first letters on the decision, Florence Sillers Ogden reached out to Californian Frances Bartlett who had led the anti-communist, anti-UN, and white supremacist campaign in the Los Angeles public schools. With no overt discussion of black and white children learning together and the perceived chaos that would cause, Ogden described the decision as "the most outrageous seizure of power in all the history of our country" and contended that it was "absolutely a movement inspired by the Communists."[11]

If Ogden and Bartlett focused on constitutional fiat, many white mothers saw *Brown* as a decision as much about interracial consensual sex and marriage as it was about education. Homes were early sites where racial lines were policed, and schools functioned as extensions of that domestic space. For many, segregated schools were necessary to reinforce the lessons taught in white homes about racial distance. Historically, segregation and white supremacist politics had been ushered in with rhetoric about the alleged rape of white women by black men, but many white southern women protesting desegregation worked as if interracial marriage was a more likely threat. Rather than invoking inflammatory rhetoric about sexual violence, they spoke in more mundane language, categorizing people to prevent interracial marriage and worrying about consensual sex and romantic attraction.[12] In Virginia, interracial marriage remained illegal in 1954 as it was in all southern states. Montana and Oregon had just repealed prohibitions on interracial marriage, but fifteen states outside the South still outlawed it. In Louisiana, the registrar of the Bureau of Vital Statistics of New Orleans, Naomi Drake, amped up her efforts and chased down obituaries, researched family trees, changed thousands of residents' racial classifications, and publicized likely interracial surname lists, sorting out the Jim Crow order even in its dying days.[13] Yet despite the legal and cultural prohibitions on interracial marriage, white women who protested *Brown* predicted such marriages as an outcome of integrated schooling. White mothers believed that the Court's decision would change their homes and their families by changing whom their children chose for sexual and marriage partners. This decision about public education was really a challenge, they contended, to private family life.

Many letters from white women painted schools as hothouses for consensual sex and breeding grounds for marriage. From Asheville, North Carolina, a young mother wrote, "We who have young children . . . do we want them to grow up and mix socially with Negroes, maybe marry them?"[14] In the *Raleigh News and Observer*, another affirmed that "if you start them together in early grades they will certainly marry."[15] One mother pledged to protect her girls, four and six years old, "who are just the right age to feel the full consequences of the thing [racial integration]."[16] In the *White Sentinel*, a far-right St. Louis newspaper, an Arizona woman penned an article "What Do You Think?" in which she instructed her readers to "Draw the blood line and see that rigid segregation is practiced when it comes to marriage or social matters." A year later, she continued, "We have no right to expose our helpless children to the danger of race-mixing, which is bound to occur when we accept blacks as being our social equals."[17] Other white women wrote letters asserting that "race mixing," not equal access to education, was the objective of school integration. In the rural North Carolina paper, the *Zebulon Herald*, one mother feared that integrated schools would lead her daughter to marry a black man, something, she claimed, God did not want.[18] A Mississippi DAR member insisted that "integration brings about intermarriage."[19] Sara A. Thompson, chairman of "a Segregation Movement," compiled a petition that she sent to seventeen governors that said "the citizens of Maryland are making an effort to subdue, eliminate and eradicate this decision, that would compel white children and negro children to attend school together, which would terminate in social equality and interracial marriage."[20] Intermarriage dominated the concerns of Virginia women who wrote to Governor Thomas Stanley in 1954. In the hundreds of letters sent to the governor, women authored the majority and most frequently justified their opposition to *Brown* with the phrase: "integration encourages miscegenation."[21] In one example, a Virginia woman predicted "in less than ten years we will face the problem of intermarriage."[22]

Far less common were letters that suggested unwanted sexual aggression from young black men. One Richmond woman noted that "white girls would feel humiliated by having colored boys make insulting remarks to them in school rooms.... [T]hey would naturally feel resentment in having to discontinue their social activities such as dancing and giving plays."[23] Fearing that her daughters would be influenced more by promiscuous black classmates than their own mothers, a North Carolina woman wrote that "in fact in a negro school close to where I taught school a few years ago seven of the negro girls had babies.... [I]t makes me shudder to even think of my girls being thrown in with negroes."[24] Focusing on sex again, and perhaps not marriage, another woman wrote, "I tell you, I did not grow up going to school with the negros. [*sic*] Don't visit them or make love to them. I am a white woman not a mixed breed. I won't see my children go into the negro race."[25] In harsher terms, North Carolinian Raymond Price, who was an early petitioner for absolute segregation, told Governor William Umstead that interracial "mating" should carry the same punishment as armed robbery, manslaughter, or breaking and entering.[26] And in cruder language, another petition proclaimed that the "grave danger is a little white girl and a little colored boy being together at school . . . [w]hich will bring mixed races, mongrels, curs, and everything in general."[27] The use of "danger" and "fear" and "mating" suggested the deep concerns over sex and alluded to a more aggressive sexuality among black boys and racialized sexual mores, but even those letters departed from the salacious, voyeuristic and alarmist black-on-white rape narratives that had underwritten the birth of the Jim Crow order. While proponents of integration observed that going to school together did not translate into interracial sex, segregationists saw sex and marriage as the most obvious and unavoidable outcome of racial integration.

An education in white supremacy had clearly taken hold in several high school students who echoed the positions of their elders. Jackie Robinson, a female high school student, claimed that school integration "could never take place in the near future in North Carolina." "The difference," she continued, "is not only our skin, but our manner of speaking, thinking, and our ideals." "Segregation has too long been established in the South for people . . . to demolish it," she concluded.[28] In Virginia, one high school girl claimed that "many high school students are mature enough to have arrived at the sensible conclusion that it is best for both races to keep to themselves."[29]

From New Hanover County, North Carolina, came a sixty-page report documenting the deleterious effects of racial integration on schools and schoolchildren. Akin to the 1924 publication *Mongrel Virginians,* quantitative data was used to "prove" black "intellectual inferiority." In the context of integration, this alleged intelligence gap would hinder the academic and vocational development of white and black children and create insurmount-able obstacles for teachers. It would also lower property values, infiltrate the nation with communist subversives, and breed racial enmity. Repeatedly, the report credited segregation with maintaining "white supremacy by discour-aging interracial contact, friendship, and ultimately consensual interracial sex." As a result of segregation, blacks and whites had lived together har-moniously in the South, in direct contrast, the report noted, to northern communities where "parents continuously teach racial hatred in order to counteract the influence of pro-amalgamation teachers." In an exercise in historical distortion, amnesia, and imagination, the document highlighted selective successes of black-only schools. The report praised segregated schools for instilling race pride among black girls who had learned to spurn "overtures from ... debased ... whites." Ignoring overwhelming historic evi-dence of the liaisons, so often forced, of "respectable" white men—planta-tion owners, modern cotton farmers, senators, business owners—with black women and girls, the report claimed that the white fathers of black children were the "crude, moronic, and beastly whites—not ... men of brains and cul-ture." Moreover, because black boys developed "sexual awareness at a surpris-ingly young age," the New Hanover document claimed, even integration at the elementary school level would put "little white girls" with "more mature negroes" and lead to racial amalgamation.[30]

In the segregationist discourse, it was hard to unravel the sexual from the sacred. Some women and men protested school integration on the grounds that physical segregation and anti-miscegenation laws were God's will. A North Carolina woman blamed the Supreme Court for questioning God's authority and creative handiwork. Just as God made different species of birds, he made distinctions among humans, suggested another.[31] "God made eve-rything of its kind and it was good," wrote another, and "he made the birds of the air, but he didn't make them all alike. ... [T]hey do not mix, yet they all fly in the same air."[32] Mississippi's Florence Ogden also noted the divine sanction of racial segregation when she compared it to the segregation of spe-cies of birds. "To do away with it [segregation]," another woman suggested, "would be breaking God's law." And an Anderson, South Carolina, woman wrote a letter to the editor in which she asserted that it was "strange that God never revealed to the great saints of our past, how wrong they were about segregation, and now, He reveals it all to nine old men."[33] But for some white women, God's will was not found in the church. In a letter to the *Citizens' Council*, one woman wrote that only "the influence of mothers" could coun-teract "the propaganda fed them in church and Sunday School literature."[34]

If some churches preached brotherly love and equality across the color line, most southern churches echoed the larger regional resolve to resist school integration. A member of North Carolina's Methodist Women's auxiliary replied to a church query on integration. She endorsed Christian gradualism and paternalism in the wake of *Brown*. "We can tax ourselves far harder to provide them with better separate schools, give them more separate hospitals and churches, build them better houses," she wrote, and "look after them when they are ill and in trouble, and allow them equal business and professional opportunity as they become educated to it." Integrated schools, however, she felt, would produce a "polyglot population to the sordid detriment of both races."[35] In her response, Mrs. Thompson was not much different from Baptist and Presbyterian women across the South. Ignoring centuries of an intertwined and integrated history, segregationists cited God as their authority to defend the political, economic, and social oppression of their black brothers and sisters.

At times, even religious events had to bend to segregationist politics, censoring spiritual leaders who had supported civil rights organizations. One of the more publicized interactions between religion and segregation arose around invited lecturers at the 1956 Religious Emphasis Week at the University of Mississippi wherethe Reverend Alvin Kershaw was slated to speak. When Florence Ogden got word of his invitation, she helped organize a petition drive, alerted state newspapers, and wrote Chancellor J. D. Williams to cancel Kershaw's appearance. Since Mississippi had been attacked by the NAACP, a reputed communist-front organization, and Kershaw supported the NAACP, then having him speak "would be a repudiation of all our State stands for," she noted. Kershaw's invitation was withdrawn, and in protest all the other invited ministers declined to participate in Ole Miss's Religious Emphasis Week.[36] For white Mississippians adherence to segregation trumped Christian service, devotion, and education. No religious leaders at Religious Emphasis week was better than using university funds to bring a contributor to the NAACP to Oxford.

Integrated schools also threatened to disrupt the intellectual reproduction of segregation. Textbook censorship, control of curriculum, and whitewashed citizenship instruction had all been central to the reign of Jim Crow. Integration promised to bring to schools black students instructed in a history taught by black men and women perhaps exposed to the curriculum developed by the Association for the Study of African American Life and History but certainly armed with stories from their pasts. White teachers who had been sponsored by the DAR and the UDC, and instructed in southern summer schools might find their authority questioned by black students or even black teachers who had different training, had alternative experiences with racial segregation, or who had been exposed to the UNESCO curriculum materials. Integrated schools would also bring white and black students who looked to their teachers, white or black, for similar treatment. When Pat Watters's lone black second grade student stood in line for his hug on the last day of school, Watters's remembered being stunned that a black seven-year-old would expect a hug just like his white classmates.[37] In this integrated climate, how could the lessons offered in essay contests about the nobility of the Confederacy or the benefits of racial segregation work?[38]

Segregationist women also argued that the academic preparation of their white children would suffer in newly integrated schools. The leader of the District of Columbia Public Schools Association sent a treatise to South Carolina's Cornelia Dabney Tucker noting that in just one year of integration "only 39% of children in schools are white" and that some have "3 or 4 white children in all 'negro schools' with 'negro faculty.'" As a result, white children's "education is being impaired."[39] The New Hanover report claimed that on IQ tests given to 5,946 students, 71 percent of black children were "morons" and that North Carolina's median IQ of black sixth grade pupils was between 77 and 83.[40] In Mississippi, Cain opposed equalization efforts in the aftermath of *Brown*, claiming that "most of our colored friends are getting just about all the education they can absorb."[41] White teachers of South Carolina issued a statement claiming that segregated education was the best route to educate children. While more extreme segregationists thought the South Carolina Education Association was too moderate, professional educators denying the plausibility of the Court's decision spoke to the depths of opposition to school integration.[42] In a 1955 poll, some white female teachers were more blunt. "Mix Negroes and whites . . . and they are at a disadvantage intellectually and never able to rise to their capacity." Another teacher claimed that black students in their late teens would "crowd the sixth and seventh grades."[43] And the president of the South Carolina League of Women Voters echoed the teachers' concerns, noting in 1955 that integration would hurt white students who were the intellectual superiors of their future black classmates.[44] White students would also suffer from the integration of teaching staffs, some predicted, as black teachers would reflect their experiences in teaching substandard students. For example, one report erroneously stated that black teachers had less education and taught at a pace aligned to the slow intellect of their students. Moreover, unlike white teachers, "the negro teacher," it concluded, "has been subjected to such a continuous volume of subversive propaganda that it has warped her viewpoint of life."[45]

School textbooks served as another front for opposition to *Brown*. In her March 1956 column, Ogden suggested subverting the Supreme Court decision by adopting "such textbooks in Mississippi schools as we see fit." Noting that unless "we understand the past, we cannot hope to understand the present, much less look to the future." Ogden called for "sound" textbooks that "would show something of the development of the races." Ogden was aware that maintaining control of the curriculum fell below federal oversight and remained largely controlled by local and state committees when she encouraged combatting racial equality through textbook selection. "Even the Supreme Court will surely find . . . [that] difficult to prevent," she concluded. For the rest of the century and into the next, activists from Texas to West Virginia sought to control textbook content, often minimizing nonwhite contributions to American society and recasting historical events from Reconstruction through the civil rights movement to uphold white supremacy.[46] In South Carolina, Cornelia Dabney Tucker maintained her work for students' education in Jim Crow citizenship. Far from being out of step with national trends, her work echoed that of Columbia University's president who praised his institution's Citizenship Education Project, noting that with such education, "There would . . . be far less need for teacher's oaths, Communist banning, and textbook inquiries when pupils are engaged in [a] powerful program of Americanism"[47] Given the association of racial equality with communism, states that adopted history textbooks starkly contrasting Americanism and communism served the segregationist's purpose well.

Merging opposition to integration with anti-communism, segregationists argued for the need to shore up the free market and secure states' rights, parental authority, and local control. One indignant female taxpayer wrote that "I see no reason to pay taxes . . . to fight a Communist nation if we are going to allow the Supreme Court to take over the duties of the legislative branch."[48] Another suggested that "if the communists can break down the churches and the schools they can control America."[49] A female farmer blamed the communists for integration, while another condemned communist propaganda that "contend[ed] that we are hiding some of our people in bondage or slavery, meaning the Negroes. . . . [T]his is untrue, and . . . a propaganda blast on the part of Russia and her satellites."[50] Across the South, white women implicated the NAACP in the domestic infiltration of communism, and others blamed America's new course on the "sinister aims of the Jewish Communist revolutionaries . . . [working for] a world government."[51] In South Carolina, the newly formed Women's States Rights Association muted its overt segregationist politics and came out for "constitutional government" and against "socialism and communism."[52] A member of the American Association of University Women noted that *Brown* was part of "a Socialistic-Communistic scheme to aid eventual federal control of local community living."[53] By this formulation, resistance to segregation became a badge of patriotism and the latest method of domestic containment. It allowed conservative segregationist women to downplay the racist underpinnings of their political language and instead to continue in a more palatable Cold War discourse.

Segregationist women across the South encouraged white women to work with male political leaders and organizations but to also build ties with national conservative groups like West Coast–based Pro America, Chicago-based We the People, and the Minute Women as well as more local, grassroots organizations. To combat *Brown*, Ogden called on white southerners to speak up and to meet the federal betrayal with open, strong, and civilized opposition. She warned against meeting it by "slipping up a dark alley or wearing a hood," and instead encouraged white southerners to courageously and " openly endorse a way of life that has existed from the day of the inception of the United States."[54] Fellow Mississippian Wilma Sledge, a state legislator, responded from the statehouse floor urging whites to support the newly formed Citizens' Council.[55]

In North Carolina, Nell Lewis had feared that apathy and resignation would overcome her state's white citizens and that they would not resist integration. Her concern seemed misplaced. In the immediate aftermath of *Brown*, many North Carolinians were already mobilized to oppose the decision. Within days, seven women signed the letter that Mrs. Preston Andrews of Charlotte, the mother of a two-year-old boy, wrote to Governor Umstead claiming that the Supreme Court's decision betrayed "States' Rights" and cultivated the rise of a dictatorship. She suggested that the taxes she paid were "for our own children," not all the children in the state. Until the "Negroes can pay their own way," she continued, "they have no right to say what will be done with our money." She did not want her son "to go [to school] with Negroes." Anticipating the proliferation of segregationist academies, she wrote, "It is an outrage that we have to support them [public schools] and then have to enter our children in private schools—bearing this additional expense." She also predicted race riots and claimed that "you can't get Negroes to work at all." Finally, she accused integrationists of being communists. Packed with numerous reasons to oppose *Brown*, Mrs. Andrews's letter was unusual only in its ability to cram so many reasons on one neatly typed page.[56]

Between May and October, North Carolina Governor Umstead received eighty-one petitions signed by over 28,000 citizens who opposed *Brown*. Seventy-five percent of the petitions arrived in the first two months, suggesting that resistance did not need time to coalesce. It was immediate and widespread. The first protest petition with fifty-four signatures was sent to the governor's office on May 18, the day after the decision. The first sizable petition came from a small town outside of Winston-Salem and arrived in the first week, containing 457 signatures (265 of them from women) collected by Mr. and Mrs. Lawrence Hobson. Week after week, petitions poured in. They arrived from over 100 communities, stretching from the mountain town of Clyde to the coastal town of Burgaw. Of the larger urban areas, Greensboro had the most contributors. Petitioning organizations included the Pender County Association for the Preservation of Segregation, the North Carolina Association for the Preservation of the White Race, the PTA, the Magnolia Women's Civic Club, the Island Creek Baptist Church, a YWCA chapter, and the Session of the First Presbyterian Church of Fayetteville. The Mutual Association of Colored People, based in Memphis, Tennessee, also sent a petition supporting the maintenance of segregated schools. Initially, Raymond Price of Pender County distributed a set of petitions, and many seemed to copy his format. Most petitions began "We strongly recommend that the State maintain segregated schools regardless of the consequence." Other petitions were original letters with signature pages attached. The language in some took a harder stance. In June, one Winston-Salem mother suggested an abandonment of public schools entirely. A year later, the Durham United Political Education Council (DUPEC), an organization of over 300 white residents, pledged to get 10,000 signatures for the privatization of public education and the redistribution of state funds to support private segregated schools, a stance associated with hardline segregationists, then, and much later with conservatives nationwide.[57] Women signed or wrote cover letters for about thirty-seven petitions, telegrams, or letters; men circulated sixty-one others. Sixteen came from organizations or businesses. Mrs. Hugh Bell and the Pender County Association for the Continuation of Segregation collected the largest single petition containing over 4,500 signatures. The petitions indicated that white North Carolinians were neither ambivalent about the decision nor were they slow to respond. In 1954, they were opposed, and that opposition continued for some time.[58]

In the Mississippi Delta, white men formed the Citizens' Council to counter any efforts to promote racial equality in their state. Composed of white middle- and upper-class men, the Citizens' Council used economic boycotts and intimidation, political repression, and threats more often than violence to subdue civil rights activists and to try to insure that black Deltans remained outside of the burgeoning civil rights movement. The Councils initially banned women from membership, but white women could still support the organization. Ogden described the councils as "patriotic citizens, bent on preserving our way of life" and urged women to "talk . . . your husband" into joining.[59] When the Mississippi Citizens' Council undertook initiatives, Ogden was more than willing to support them, allowing them to distribute her articles, spreading the news of their work, and aiding them in their censorship campaigns.[60]

As the Citizens' Councils spread across the South, white women soon joined and did much grassroots work. In South Carolina, Council women conducted membership drives, served as social chairs, organized recruiting events, and planned meetings. On John's Island, white women "constituted more than one third of the chapter's membership" and served on the Political and Election, Membership and Finance, and the Legal Advisory Committees. Council literature encouraged women to vote, counting on them to support hardline segregationists for office. Independent organizations, local in reach, also formed among white women to organize against integration, such as the Women's States Rights Association in South Carolina. In some states these new clubs joined more established and ostensibly mainstream organizations that came out in one way or another against school integration— the Daughters of the American Revolution, the Business and Professional Women's Organization, the Women's Society of Christian Service, the South Carolina Educational Association, the UDC, the Alabama PTA, the Methodist Women's Auxiliary, and the Republican Party. [61]

Public opposition by women coincided with the growth of grassroots resistance and with the election of more dedicated segregationists. In North Carolina, Senator Sam Ervin emerged as a spokesman for segregation and earned the respect of Lewis and many others. But not all victorious politicians were as married to massive resistance as Ervin. Luther Hodges represented a more moderate resistance, and he won the gubernatorial election in 1954.[62] By 1956, however, Hodges had adopted a more defiant position. He had re-appointed the state's Pearsall Commission, which had created a local choice plan that implemented school integration with the least likelihood of any actual integration happening. He criticized the NAACP and used the word "nigra" in public speeches. Yet he did not call for the abolition of public schools or advocate violence as a tool of resistance like his opponent I. Beverly Lake. In many ways, Hodges's strategy worked. North Carolina maintained its "progressive" image, allowing the state to attract business investment from across the nation, avoiding confrontations with the federal government, and sidestepping meaningful integration. In 1964, the state still had less than 1 percent of black students in desegregated schools. While state officials touted the state's lack of racial violence, a white Greensboro attorney summed up North Carolina's racial politics: "We're just like Georgia and Alabama except we do it in a tuxedo and they wear suspenders."[63]

Beyond supporting segregationists in elections and drumming up membership for the Citizens' Councils, some women organized for more specific policies that aligned with massive resistance. Again using her 1937 Supreme Court Security League stationery, Tucker began another letter-writing campaign to change the nomination process for Supreme Court justices. As usual, she targeted United States senators, representatives, and all the governors. The choice of her old letterhead was a shrewd political move. Distancing herself from the most strident segregationists in the South, she placed her protest in a more politically palatable anti–New Deal tradition, aligning herself with national conservatives who opposed integration and a behemoth federal government. Tucker publicized what she deemed to be the arbitrary and unconstitutional testimony used in the *Brown* case and pushed for greater state control over Supreme Court nominees. Her solution—and one later absorbed into the anti-communist, ultra-conservative fringe organization, the John Birch Society--was to have each US Senator suggest a short list of candidates for federal judicial appointments, ostensibly representative of their state's interest.[64]

In her correspondence, Tucker denounced *Brown* as an invalid decision, part of a worldwide communist conspiracy and an indicator of the federal government's excessive power. She minimized her role as a mother and focused not on her domestic duties but on a clash between fundamentally opposed philosophies of government. Initially, she wrote a letter to Chief Justice Earl Warren protesting the segregation decision and passed on copies to other South Carolinians, including gubernatorial hopeful and anti-segregationist George Bell Timmerman. By the beginning of 1955, she had found a champion in Senator James Eastland from Mississippi. Eastland had been instrumental in encouraging the formation of the Citizens' Council and Mississippi's State Sovereignty Commission, a taxpayer-sponsored secret intelligence force targeting civil rights activists and their supporters. In August 1954, he had circulated a pamphlet entitled "To the Mothers and Fathers of Jackson" encouraging them to guarantee their children the same "social protection" that they had experienced. But amid this rancor, Eastland had come to realize that stressing states' rights and the *Brown* decision as an expression of communist subversion were better political strategies outside the South than cries to preserve segregation at all costs. Careful to balance his segregationist credentials in Mississippi with his conservative credibility outside the state, Eastland found Cornelia Dabney Tucker to be a valuable partner in shaping national support for massive resistance. On May 26, 1955, Eastland delivered on the Senate floor a speech calling for an investigation of the scientific authorities who had shaped the Supreme Court's desegregation decision. He charged them with being influenced by Karl Marx and "alien ideologies . . . not the Constitution."[65] Tucker was primed to seek support for Eastland's cause, and Eastland sent her over 500 copies of his speech to distribute with her letters and petitions. Two other South Carolina women, Mrs. Albert Taylor and Mary K. Mathis, joined her efforts. Eastland praised her powerful pen and her "hard and efficient work." He also encouraged her to continue "to try to reach as many people outside of South Carolina and the South as possible." By the end of July, Tucker had sent hundreds of letters with copies of Eastland's speech to governors and attorneys general; Sons of the American Revolution chapters in Texas, Wisconsin, and Illinois; newspapers and periodicals including the *Constitution Press*; and chapters of the DAR and American Legion. Her articles reached as far as the West Coast. In each case, Tucker told her readers that the Court's decision was an "example of the alarming march of communism."[66]

In North Carolina, Nell Lewis worked with upper- and middle-class leaders of the North Carolina Defenders of States Rights and the Patriots of North Carolina to encourage organizational resistance to the Supreme Court ruling. Led by University of North Carolina biologist and scientific racist Wesley Critz George, the Patriots of North Carolina included men and women who were lawyers, ministers, professors, teachers, textile magnates, and state politicians.[67] The Patriots pledged to enroll "every white man and woman . . . over 21 years of age" to frustrate desegregation plans. They also wrote families of black children admitted to white schools, suggesting that they reconsider their decision. Their first priority, however, was the defeat of the three North Carolina representatives who had refused to sign the Declaration of Constitutional Principles or Southern Manifesto. Attacking the *Brown* decision and proclaiming loyalty to the Jim Crow order, The Manifesto was signed by 19 of 22 southern senators and 77 of 105 southern congressmen. As home to 3 of the 28 congressional defectors, Lewis supported efforts to oust them from office. She publicized the Patriots' efforts, shared her research with them, and encouraged North Carolinians to become members. She also sent them lists of anti-integrationists to contact and allowed her columns to be used in a pamphlet by segregationist, textile owner, and Patriot member Erwin Allen Holt.[68]

In the aftermath of *Brown*, Nell Battle Lewis and other white women maintained their storytelling for segregation and white supremacy. In 1955, Lewis read Sarah Patton Boyle's "Southerners Will Like Integration," in the *Saturday Evening Post*. She could not believe a native white southern woman would dare to rewrite segregation's story.[69] But Boyle, a Charlottesville, Virginia, native, had been seeking advice on southern race relations from black newspaper man T. J. Sellers and had conducted surveys trying to gauge white attitudes toward racial integration. She had written letters to the *Richmond Times Dispatch* encouraging white southerners to embrace it. She believed that the silent majority of white southerners were not prejudiced and would accept racial equality if they knew that their neighbors felt the same way. When her views made it into the *Saturday Evening Post*, Boyle suffered the vitriol of a white South mobilized for massive resistance. Lewis responded to Boyle in her Sunday column and sent her comments to the editor of the *Saturday Evening Post*, encouraging him to print her response to "that dreadful drivel written by Mrs. Boyle." She attacked Boyle for posing with black medical students, for mistaking support for graduate school integration for support for broad public school integration, and for being "a half-baked reformer . . . [like] I used to be." Lewis's column served as a public denunciation of Boyle, and the amount of hate mail Boyle received sent her into a spiritual crisis and also shook her belief in any sort of a "silent South," willing to accept school integration.[70]

Not content to let the Sarah Patton Boyles of the world say otherwise, white segregationist women reinvigorated their effort to tell stories of segregation as a system that suited white and black southerners. Ogden offered her own version of an appropriate interracial family just a week after Boyle's article appeared. In several columns, Ogden wrote about an orphaned black boy whom her grandmother had raised and called Alex Sillers. In her hands, his story was one of interracial amity between white and black Sillers families. She published letters from his children, both of whom noted that they read Ogden's columns in the *Clarion-Ledger*. Ogden's celebration of relationships with the black Sillerses countered national and international versions of southern race relations that focused on political and economic inequities and violence. Her stories also emphasized that these relatives reached out to her, implying in her mind their approval of her columns and their deep connection to her grandmother, who most likely had owned Alex Sillers's ancestors. In this whitewashed version of history, Ogden held up a social order built on

a benevolent recognition of white superiority and a white supremacy practiced by the best white people. If left alone, Ogden's stories suggested, racial
segregation would produce appreciative, deferential beneficiaries of white
charity and guidance who would continue to love their white benefactors.[71]

Nell Battle Lewis turned once again to her black childhood neighbors in
the Oberlin section of Raleigh to tell an uplifting story of racial friendship
in the Jim Crow era. Speaking to Oberlin church women, Lewis praised the
historically good relationship between white and black Raleigh residents,
emphasizing the "basic good will toward the Negro" among native whites and
expressing a maternal-like desire "for their continual progress."[72] Resurrecting
her mammy for another political crusade, Lewis emphasized the goodwill
that flowed from the hierarchy of southern race relations. By insisting on a
carefully choreographed version of their relationships with black families,
Ogden and Lewis celebrated an old order that put white women in a nurtur-
ing but superior position to their black neighbors.[73]

If Boyle's article prompted an outpouring of interracial friendship stories,
the 1955 murder of Emmett Till in Money, Mississippi, and the subsequent
trial that resulted in a quick acquittal of the accused murderers exposed the
deadly realities of white supremacy—realities that both Lewis and Ogden
had tried to silence in their storytelling. Before *Brown*, the brutal murder of
a young black boy might have earned the condemnation of some of the more
moderate white supremacists. In the 1930s and even the 1940s, Lewis might
have used Till's murder to highlight the repressive nature of Mississippi's
race relations as opposed to North Carolina's more benevolent, humane, and
"progressive" system of segregation. Even Mary Dawson Cain might have
condemned the act or blamed it on Eleanor Roosevelt. But with school integration on the horizon in Mississippi, Emmett Till had shown a picture of his
girlfriend who looked "white" and then "wolf-whistled" at Carolyn Bryant,
the white store clerk. In the stories that described his last few days, Till came
to serve as a symbol of what white southern women had claimed would happen with school integration: their white daughters would go out with black
boys. While the wolf-whistle has served as the narrative arc of Till's story, the
affirmation of interracial relationships evidenced by the photograph spoke
to the pervasive fears that white women had articulated about integrated
schooling.[74]

Faced with defending the brutal murder of a black child, some female
segregationists turned to conspiracy theories, denying the body was Till's. In
North Carolina, Nell Battle Lewis doubted that the corpse pulled from the
river was in fact that of young Emmett Till. A Mississippi woman rationalized

the decision by claiming that if Till had been murdered, "every responsible white person would find it a horrid crime and miscarriage of justice"; since there was no outcry, it was not Till, her reasoning went, suggesting that there had been no murder.[75] Instead, Lewis and Ogden among others referred to the murder as an "alleged killing," and Lewis suggested that the whole set-up looked like an NAACP conspiracy. When *Look* magazine ran the confessions of the white men who murdered Till just a few months after they were acquitted, Lewis offered no comment.[76] Her nonchalant reaction to the Till murder was a long way from her fiery condemnation of the mistreatment of black prisoners Shropshire and Barnes in the 1930s. One North Carolina woman even applauded the events in Mississippi. "The boy in Mississippi was no child," she wrote; "he knew how to insult a woman." "Do you condone such conduct?" she asked. "Certainly the men in Mississippi do not," she concluded.[77] With white supremacy under fire, some white women no longer attempted to call for the white protection of any black citizens, even if they were children.[78]

Unable to shape the Till murder into an appropriate story for white supremacy, Ogden tried to silence any censure offered by the South's own white citizens, making a condemnation of the Till murder tantamount to heresy in white Mississippi. Thinking about profit more than politics, a Meridian, Mississippi, theater owner A. L. Royal had purchased the rights to dramatize the *Look* article. Ogden was outraged and excoriated him in in an article that ran in the *Jackson Clarion Ledger,* the *Delta Democrat Times,* and the *Memphis Press Scimitar.* "He [Royal] could not hurt his state worse," she had written, "if he turned atom bombs loose on it." In fact, "an atom bomb would be much better," she continued, because "if they [agitators] must destroy a race, let it be done quickly and absolutely." She asked Mississippians if they would stand "silently by and allow Mr. Royal or any other movie producer to show a film which will stir up racial fires, divide our people, render us impotent?" She repudiated Royal so soundly that he began proceedings to bring suit against her for libel and slander. Beyond impugning his character, he also blamed her column for declining attendance in his theaters.[79]

By 1956, after two years of concentrated efforts to organize against integration, Nell Battle Lewis reflected that since 1954 the "defeatism, which together with burning resentment undoubtedly was widespread in the South" had changed to "determination to stand up against judicial dictatorship."[80] The political defeat of two of the three representatives from the state who had refused to sign the Southern Manifesto, the rising prominence of Senator Samuel Ervin, and her increased correspondence all served as signs for Lewis that white southerners were ready to resist integration.[81] For Lewis, who died of a heart attack returning home one evening in late November 1956, the story of the white South was not moderation but resistance. Certainly the events of the next decade revealed the misplaced optimism of her prediction, but in 1956 the voices of moderation and of accommodation, even token accommodation, had not risen to prominence, and signs indicated that implementation would be delayed and difficult. Lewis could have died knowing that her work had contributed to the grassroots mobilization of segregationists.

The same month that Lewis died, Tom Etheridge, columnist for the *Jackson Clarion-Ledger*, observed: "One reason why the overall timetable of America's integrationists has gone haywire is that intelligent independent women of the South are not swallowing propaganda as readily as was hoped." White southern women's opposition to the National PTA's pro-integration platform inspired this statement. At its 1956 national convention, the PTA adopted a resolution endorsing integration and calling on local chapters to help implement it in their schools. While the policies of the national organization were not binding, the statement still engendered a protest in Alabama. Led by the state's PTA president, the state chapter sent a resolution to national headquarters demanding that the pro-integration resolution be amended. On September 27, 1956, the National PTA issued a revised statement that accommodated the minimum compliance, obstructionist stance of southern segregationists. Shorn of its former commitment to school integration, the new statement read: "The National Congress urges parent-teacher leaders, in cooperation with schools and other governmental authorities in each community to study and pursue effective means of working toward a just solution to the complex problem of segregation in the public schools." This reversal, Etheridge claimed, "was literally compelled by aroused Southern women." And it was just one example, Etheridge wrote, "of their [southern women's] resistance generally."[82]

By 1956, white segregationist women had organized effective and widespread resistance to integration. In fact, it was clear that the school integration crisis elevated their positions as the most experienced proponents and sustainers of white supremacist thought in public education. In the letters they wrote, they linked their authority over their children and their vision of motherhood to their political mobilization. While their diverse politics and political strategies manifested themselves differently across southern communities, hardline segregationists who advocated the abolition of public schools over any school integration and practical segregationists who worked on plans to delay and circumvent the ruling both found the politics of public education particularly receptive to their activism.[83] This link between maternal authority, public schools, and political mobilization also animated the white southern women who would join the open-schools movement, calling for an acceptance of at least token integration and the importance of continued state funding. . All along the political spectrum, white women invoked their gendered identities to justify their intervention in the politics of public education.

The South's female segregationists had long worked to maintain racial distance, to teach the lessons of white supremacy, and to cultivate the "naturalness" of Jim Crow segregation. Physically segregated schools were the most obvious expression of this work, but segregation's constant gardeners had repeatedly worked to tell the right stories, to approve the right textbooks, to craft the right kind of teacher training, and to ensure racial segregation in marriage and social life. The consensus that Lewis saw in 1956 hid cracks in the façade of massive resistance. With little pressure for implementation, however, the opposition, even hardline opposition, to desegregation dominated the discourse and the politics of resistance without having to confront the full economic, social, and political consequences of maintaining absolute school segregation. Soon the voices of those who were unwilling to sacrifice business investment and economic development would gain some ground, pointing to the diverse positions within the South's white supremacist politics and beyond it. Even then, white southerners committed to the Jim Crow order could point to their allies across the nation to make this fight one with national import—a fight about family autonomy and family values, and about states' rights to direct public education. And in the face of implementation, token or otherwise, they could continue to work to make sure social welfare, public education, elections, and the stories they told upheld an investment in white supremacy

# 8

## White Women, White Youth, and the Hope of the Nation

FOR SEGREGATIONISTS WHO were counting on avoiding *Brown*, the two years following the decision sent some hopeful signs their way. In North Carolina, local choice plans forced black parents to navigate a labyrinth of procedures to qualify their sons and daughters for integrated education. Interposition's advocates continued to test whether a state government could prevent the implementation of a federal policy it deemed unjust. Every southern state passed a pupil placement act that allowed local districts to establish subjective criteria such as "morals, conduct, health, and personal standards" but not race, to dictate individual school assignments, avoiding integration.[1] All but North Carolina investigated the NAACP and found legislative paths to erode its membership. In South Carolina, the founding of private schools outpaced the state's substantial pre-*Brown* trend, and a public referendum overwhelmingly approved deleting from the state's constitution the provision to provide public education. In Arkansas's state capitol, school board member Virgil Blossom developed a plan that delayed even token desegregation for three years and provided "the least amount of integration over the longest period," and he was a moderate. These plans and 450 new segregation laws coupled with violence and intimidation meant that the South's schools remained segregated.[2]

White segregationist women had taken leading roles spreading the news of resistance. Louisiana's Mrs. Frances Mims served as the editor of her state's Citizens' Council newsletter. In Texas, Ida Darden's *Southern Conservative* published a panoply of articles opposing civil rights, excoriating the federal government, and alerting it readers to communist infiltration. In Virginia, Mrs. Charles Reynolds was the secretary of the Defenders of States

Sovereignty and Individual Rights, and Charlottesville parents formed the Charlottesville Educational Foundation and hired biology professor and eugenics supporter Ivey Lewis to charter private schools. In South Carolina, white women of the Greenwood Citizens' Council formed the Women's States' Rights Association.[3] Working against more moderate or silent southerners and positioning themselves as underdogs in a fight against a rapacious federal government, those most dedicated to the Jim Crow order used their newspapers, newsletters, and periodicals to encourage sustained defiance.[4]

All was not well for the cause of segregation, however. Just as white southern women could point to successes in maintaining a Jim Crow order, they could also see challenges to their work intensify among black grassroots activists, an amplified federal commitment to civil rights and a liberal internationalist order. The internal threat of white southern moderates further thwarted the labor of the most inflexible opponents of racial integration. Moderates believed that limited, token integration was preferable to closing public schools. Even if they did not substantially challenge a larger white supremacist political project, they constituted a rising threat to a rigid Jim Crow order. Some moderates embraced tokenism, finding a middle road between absolute segregation and substantial racial integration. While this path might have resulted in very few actual integrated schools (constituting a victory of sorts for segregationists), it did reject violence and the end of public education. Many had recoiled at the racist violence engendered by an unyielding commitment to white over black. In part, white moderates advocated a restrained position that would keep the federal government out and business investment in. In many ways the moderate position contributed to sustaining a Jim Crow nation, but the most committed segregationists did not see it that way. They saw internal dissent as a lack of resolve and as their failure to combat white apathy.[5]

Added to the lukewarm commitment of white moderates, white segregationists had to combat black mothers and fathers who had responded to *Brown* by preparing their children for the unenviable job of integrating a local school. Every time black parents sent their children up schoolhouse steps, they undermined white pronouncements of widespread black contentment with segregation. After *Brown,* white southerners witnessed reinvigorated efforts to register black voters and persistent attacks on white supremacy's reign. In Florence Ogden's backyard, Mississippi, World War II veteran and NAACP leader Aaron Henry announced his intention to register 100,000 black Deltans. Black youth conducted their own Youth March for Integrated Schools and participated in early sit-ins, predating the southern birth of the

Student Non-Violent Coordinating Committee.[6] Among black southerners, widespread resolve rippled out across the region. Despite their best efforts, segregationists could still blame black grassroots mobilization on outsiders, but they could no longer mean it.

To make matters worse for segregationists on the legislative front, Democratic senator Lyndon Johnson seemed to have successfully shepherded through the Civil Rights Act of 1957. The proposed bill created a Civil Rights Division of the Justice Department and established an investigative committee on voter suppression. Under the new act, to interfere with the ability of an individual to vote became a crime subject to a trial by jury. Thurgood Marshall, who headed the NAACP Legal Defense fund, was skeptical and said: "It would take two or three years for a good lawyer to get someone registered under this bill."[7] Southern segregationists thought differently, claiming that the limited legislation was the "greatest threat to it [the Constitution]" since *Brown*. They insisted that Eisenhower would break his oath to uphold the Constitution if he signed it. Assuring southern whites that the bill was about voting, not schools, Eisenhower signed it into law on September 9, 1957.[8]

Just a few weeks later, Eisenhower's promise lost all credence in Little Rock, Arkansas. After years of vetting, nine black teenagers had been selected to integrate Central High School in 1957. On Labor Day, Governor Orval Faubus had announced that the Arkansas National Guard would obstruct the entrance of the Little Rock Nine on the first day of school, and he advised them to stay away.[9] A few days later a federal judge ordered Faubus to allow the black children in school, and he complied and removed the National Guard. On September 23, 1957, mobs of screaming, angry white men, women, and children threatened the black teenagers as they entered the high school. Their school day was short-lived as threats of lynching and other violence led the local police to sneak them out of the high school. Two days later President Eisenhower ordered soldiers from the 101st Airborne Division to take up posts outside the school. The US paratroopers pointed their bayonets at the white mob and escorted the black students into their classrooms. Witnessing this, Faubus declared, "Little Rock has been occupied." Amid national and international media attention, Little Rock became, for segregationists, the symbol of federal commitment to school integration and of federal betrayal of the rights of white southerners.[10]

Calling the armed protection of black students a "federal invasion" and "occupation," the South's segregationist women used what was clearly a loss for massive resistance to broaden their political and grassroots organizing for white supremacist politics. In the years after Little Rock, Tucker, Cain, and Ogden invigorated a vibrant segregationist conservative movement on a national level, creating organizations that were an outgrowth of the integration crisis but reached beyond debates over legal segregation—organizations that came to mirror the emergent political discourse of the New Right. The narrative of "occupation" harkened to the dominant (and well-known) historical interpretation of Reconstruction that the nation's whites had been taught for decades: Reconstruction was a failure and federal troops occupying the South protected corrupt state governments, purveyors of government graft, and former black slaves who would relied on federal aid rather than their own two hands. Recycled for a civil rights era, the narrative served dual purposes. It painted white southerners as victims of an overreaching federal government and military. It also dismissed the responsibility of the state or federal governments to ensure the political and civil rights of Little Rock's black or even its white residents willing to attend integrated public schools. Invasion and occupation became the rallying cries for anyone who wanted to invoke the image of a behemoth federal government, unresponsive to the wishes of its white citizens.[11]

Faced with what they saw as a wholesale attack on their values, politics, and cultural power, white segregationist women sought to stave off the invasion by extending their training for the next generation of Jim Crow's white activists. While the threat that black youth posed for integrated schools had commanded much of their attention in 1954, after the Little Rock crisis, their focus on white youth intensified. White children had always been central to upholding white supreamcy, and now faced with so many threats, segregationist women amped up their efforts to produce future political activists for white supremacist conservative politics nationwide. Embracing this responsibility, white segregationist women would be, as Florence Sillers Ogden declared, "the hope of the nation."[12]

In Little Rock, white working-class segregationist women inspired hope among Jim Crow's supporters as they encouraged student resistance, campaigned against those pushing for token integration, and took to the streets. They had a friendly audience. When Central High School closed for the 1958 summer break, 19,470 of 27,031 Little Rock residents voted to close schools rather than to continue desegregation. This was a victory for the working-class women of the Mothers' League who had led the resistance, eschewed physical violence, and practiced verbal harassment with particular acumen. The Mothers' League also took their politics to the streets, loudly, some said hysterically, and with much media attention. They produced fliers educating voters on school board elections, worked to unseat moderate school board members, and circulated petitions. They even infiltrated the Women's Emergency Committee (WEC) meetings, where white moderates charted how to revive public education and to most successfully integrate the public schools. Mothers' League members passed on on the license tag numbers of WEC members to the Arkansas state police who were friendly to the segregationists' cause. One Mothers' League member noted that they worked with little monetary support, without the political capital of middle-class husbands, and with no sleep. Perhaps their most important work, historian Karen Anderson has noted, was that they "mobilized children as political actors." Through their protests, they taught their own children that whites were victims of an alliance between "African Americans, the federal government, and local leaders." The other lesson that white students took away from the school closing was that preserving whiteness and racial segregation mattered more to their parents than a high school diploma, a college scholarship, or even Friday night football.[13]

Unlike their working-class counterparts, Little Rock's Women's Emergency Committee lobbied for the schools to reopen. The WEC was filled with middle-class white women who expected to be heard and to win. They argued that closing schools would erode economic investment in Little Rock, and they supported the "Stop This Outrageous Purge" effort to reinstate teachers fired for allegedly integrationist sympathies. They did not have to turn to their children or to the streets to wield their political influence. Instead, they could mobilize their civic organizations, their fellow club members, and their political capital. They drew on their experience lobbying, petitioning, and advocating for public education to build a movement, working with business leaders, the moderates on the school board, and whites zoned for other schools. In the short term, they lost when Central High School closed its doors for the 1958–59 school year but won when it reopened for good in September of 1959.[14]

Like their moderate counterparts, the more dedicated middle–class white segregationists also had plenty of political support at home and across the nation. They wielded their conservative credentials, and they too avoided the streets. In her *Clarion-Ledger* column, Florence Sillers Ogden couched the federal government's actions as a raid on constitutional principles and state's rights. She called on her readers, friends, and club members to speak out "against the tyrannical methods of the Reconstruction Era, and of the dictatorships of Hitler, Mussolini, and Stalin which are being used today in Arkansas." She denounced the 1957 Civil Rights Bill for breeding such a federal fiat and predicted that the First Amendment freedoms of white southerners would suffer when the federal government hijacked the Tenth Amendment.[15] But she also used the racialized language of segregationists. She accused Eisenhower of denying the "white citizens of Arkansas . . . free choice in a free country." And she resorted to Jim Crow storytelling: "We were living in peace and harmony with our colored neighbors . . . until the NAACP, the Federal courts, and now the Federal executives, came down here and raised the furore." Discounting homegrown black activists, she did not blame the Little Rock Nine, for they were "misled into a vale of tears and sorrow, of hatreds and misconception." "Forgive them," she wrote, "for they know not what they do."[16] However, Ogden believed that the federal government did know what they had done, and she repackaged her opposition to civil rights as a constitutionally conservative response to an unconstitutional federal overreach.

Not all protests were as dramatic as Little Rock, and in Virginia, some protests coalesced more peacefully around the PTA and the issue of compulsory school attendance. As segregationists there had feared, the more liberal state PTA leadership reflected the influence of white moderates when it advocated compulsory school attendance. At the local level, delegates and chapters disagreed. At Venable Elementary School, near Charlottesville, eight rogue PTA parents sent out their own poll to counter another poorly worded PTA poll that touted majority support for open schools. The carefully worded rogue poll revealed an overwhelming commitment to segregated schools.[17] At nearby Lane High School, 831 parents signed a petition that supported closing public schools. Further east, parents in Prince George County received anonymous letters that deemed open schools and compulsory attendance laws "the principal objectives of integrationists" and urged opposition. The Crewe PTA voted that no education was better than an integrated education. On the outskirts of Virginia's capital city Richmond, young, well-dressed, white PTA women voted 258 to 199 against compulsory attendance laws. One Richmond member said that home chapters had instructed their district delegates "to be unalterably opposed to race mixing in public schools." Smaller PTA chapters in Farmville, Southside, and Staunton River also rejected the state proposals while other school districts voted for open schools but against compulsory attendance.[18]

When the school year ended in 1959, neither the open schools nor the compulsory attendance proposal had the eighteen required district votes for formal adoption. The PTA's statewide initiative fell one district vote short for open schools and three district votes shy for compulsory attendance laws. By October, twenty of twenty-four districts favored continuing public education and eighteen had approved compulsory attendance—a victory for moderates and the open school movement.[19] But the marriage of open schools and minimal integration was an easy one, and the PTA reaffirmed its willingness to accept token integration when they approved maintaining local options for school desegregation. The General Assembly followed suit and kept school "free choice" laws strong.[20] Local option laws, free choice laws, and pupil placement plans gave local school district leadership the authority to close schools, create vouchers for private schools, or redefine public schools entirely. These local options meant that private homes in which groups of children attended makeshift classrooms could be considered public schools. Even amid the victory of white moderates on attendance and open schools, schooling was severed from schoolhouses, and 12,500 Virginia students still faced school closings in Norfolk, Charlottesville, and the rural Warren and Prince Edward counties. After 1959, all but Prince Edward would reopen their public schools. If proponents of massive resistance had wanted only absolute school segregation in every district, then open schools in most districts with limited integration in some would have meant their defeat. If massive resistance encompassed a broader political agenda of white supremacy that could continue with token integration, then its defeat appeared much less complete. The PTA meetings, characterized by parliamentary procedure and politeness had disguised what was really a way through for open school advocates and segregationists. Those who embraced moderate rather than absolute resistance continued their grassroots work for some racial segregation and integration.

The expansive vision of massive resistance held by the South's female segregationists became apparent when even with some white children attending integrated schools, white women continued to work for the educational production of a Jim Crow order. They touted white over black in textbooks, public history celebrations, and essay contests. In Mississippi, the Citizens' Council established the Women's Activities and Youth Work (WAYW), granting middle-class segregationist women a more formal role in the Council's educational outreach. Led by former high school history teacher Sara McCorkle, WAYW aimed to "indoctrinate the nation's youth" with "patriotism, states' rights, and racial integrity." The WAYW distributed handbooks for elementary schoolchildren, through her school visits in 1958 and 1959, McCorkle passed on these lessons to high school students. She called on the United Daughters of the Confederacy, the DAR, and the American Legion to help censor instructional materials, textbooks, and films, and to sponsor statewide essay contests on the benefits of racial segregation and anti-communist crusades. In 1959, the Citizens' Council Education Fund sponsored an essay contest for Mississippi's high school students, who wrote on the following topics: "Why I Believe in Social Separation of the Races of Mankind," "Subversion in Racial Unrest," "Why the Preservation of State Rights Is Important to Every American," and "Why Separate Schools Should Be Maintained for the White and the Negro Races." Over 8,000 students from 163 Mississippi high schools participated in the contest. The two state-wide winners each received $500, a sum that in 1959 would have financed tuition for four years at the University of Mississippi.[21] In 1960, the state winner of the female division, Mary Rosalind Healy of Madison, Mississippi, asserted that segregation was the best policy as it staved off "the threat of intermarriage and compromise of moral, physical, and cultural standards." Her concluding paragraph attested to the training of white youth embarked on by white segregationist women when Healy wrote: "It is up to ME as a product of the struggle of my forefathers, as a student of today, and as a parent of tomorrow to preserve my racial integrity and keep it pure."[22]

While the mass marches, sit-ins, and violence of the civil rights movement made nightly news, white segregationist women continued to maintain an education in white supremacy at both the state and community level. The Mississippi Historical Society called for a new history program in the public schools.[23] Ogden encouraged Mississippians to join the Historical Society in order "to become acquainted with the men and women who teach the youth of our state," suggesting that they might need oversight or assistance to ensure that appropriate history was being taught. In her hometown, Ogden explained how white Rosedale students were having trouble writing competitive essays for the UDC's statewide contest. Faced with essay prompts on Reconstruction in Mississippi or the Cabinet of the Confederacy, the students cited a lack of available history sources. Ogden had advised the superintendent of her local schools to purchase a series of titles that described Reconstruction as a failed experiment due to black incompetence, Yankee corruption, disenfranchised former Confederates, and an overweening federal government She recommended James Garner's 1901 history as required reading for "every high school student in Mississippi." Garner's book emphasized the corruption that black enfranchisement brought to the state—a lesson that Ogden believed was relevant to the 1960s.[24]

The revived emphasis on the history of the Civil War and Reconstruction tapped into the long-standing education in the chaos that would ensue if white southerners lost political and economic control. In her history campaign, Ogden could reach a wide swath of Mississippians. Most whites in the

# WINNING

# ESSAYS

IN THE

## 1960 CONTEST

Sponsored by

## The Association of Citizens' Councils of Mississippi

**FIGURES 8.1 AND 8.2** The Citizens' Council Essay Contest in 1960. Supported by state funds filtered through the State Sovereignty Commission, two Mississippi students received $500 dollars for the best essay. Mary Rosalind Healy of Madison won for her essay on the benefits of segregation. Anti-Communism and Civil Rights Collection, McCain Library and Archives, University of Southern Mississippi, Hattiesburg.

MARY ROSALIND HEALY

MADISON, MISSISSIPPI

## WHY I BELIEVE IN

## SOCIAL SEPARATION OF THE

## RACES OF MANKIND

Though the problem of race relations has existed for many centuries throughout the world, only recently has it become of main interest to us here in America. Ample evidence is available to show me beyond a doubt that segregation represents the best thinking of representative America and is a time-tested national policy based on morals, ethics and racial pride — not on blind unreasoning prejudice as many latter-day critics have charged.

I know that the social exposure of one race to another brings about a laxity of principles and a complacency toward differences which can only develop into an incurable epidemic of intermarriage. This malady has but one inevitable result — racial death. Thus I must believe in the social separation of the races of mankind because I am a Christian and must abide by the laws of

( 1 )

FIGURES 8.1 AND 8.2 Continued

state, even her liberal editor Hodding Carter, had been indoctrinated with
the powerful white myths of the Reconstruction era. So pervasive were those
myths that segregationists employed them in the 1960s as a metaphor for the
alleged perils of black political equality.[25] Ogden contended that the "truth"
about Mississippi history, in particular Reconstruction, would help students
refute the ugly propaganda about their home state.[26]

In 1961 the Civil War Centennial served as an opportune moment for Jim
Crow storytelling, allowing segregationists to weave tales of white supremacy
with those of national reconciliation. Following the United States Congress's
establishment of the Civil War Centennial Commission, Mississippi established a Commission on the War between the States, providing a rich opportunity to shape historical memory for contemporary segregationist politics.
Amid sit-ins, boycotts, and a rising student movement, federal and state
governments, historical societies, and clubs across the South made plans to
fund a centennial celebration in Mississippi to the tune of $2 million in state
tax dollars.[27] In March, Mississippi's Centennial commenced with a parade
through Jackson filled with white men marching in colonels' uniforms made
from Mississippi cotton cheered on by white women in "hoopskirts and
crinolines." "No Confederate belle," Ogden predicted, "will be able to resist
her man in uniform."[28] In addition to ignoring the emancipation of slaves
and the wartime contributions of black Americans, the Centennial, black
activists contended, really served as a promotional event for white supremacy and resistance to the federal government.[29] Ogden, a committee member, certainly saw it that way, hoping that amid rising racial tensions across
the nation, the commemoration of national dissolution could instead remind
white Americans of their common cause "to preserve this great Republic."[30]

The Centennial, a "public sanctioned affair for white self-indulgence,"
coincided with other efforts across the South to inscribe a whitewashed history on the civil rights South. During the annual Pilgrimage, the Natchez
Trace brought thousands of visitors to wander through restored antebellum
homes of the plantation South decorated with "pretty maidens, magnolias,
pickaninnies."[31] In Washington, DC, when "little chocolate frops; Negroes"
came on school trips to the American History Museum, a Smithsonian
docent emphasized "what the white people have done to build this country"
but "not in an offensive way."[32] In Rosedale, the restoration of the old Rodney
church with its slave balcony recreated the architecture of the slave South. In
each case, white women managed to either erase the history of slavery or to
render it benign. They offered idealized depictions of the South that Mildred
Rutherford had created in her *Scrapbook* and that publishing houses still

inscribed on the pages of the nation's textbooks. Even as historians tried to counter ideas of slavery at a school and to connect a rich history of black politics to civil rights activism, lay historians offered powerful, opposing, accessible, and state-funded interpretations to the nation. As the South's female historical legion commemorated the values of the Old South, reconstructed the physical forms of the slave plantation, and linked the tragic consequences of the *Brown* decision to the martyred image of the Lost Cause, they exercised their authority as white women and offered to a new generation the values of a society steeped in white supremacist policies.[33]

In New Orleans, the white women of the Ninth Ward offered a more direct lesson in white supremacy and the costs of racial transgression to the young Ruby Bridges and their white neighbors. When the courts forced the predominantly white Ninth Ward school William Frantz Elementary to integrate, white working-class women with babies on their hips and aprons tied around their shirtwaists stood outside their neighborhood school for nearly a year yelling at Bridges, a first grade girl, and the dwindling numbers of white students who climbed those stairs with her. Witnessing their protest, John Steinbeck called them "cheerleaders" and described them as "crazy actors playing to a crazy audience." They did not see themselves as crazy but as good mothers, protecting their children. Bridges was not their only target. White mothers harassed their white neighbors who continued to walk their white children to school, reported their transgressions of the color line to their employers, and encouraged their children to bully their former schoolmates who kept attending integrated schools. Bridges and her family suffered threats of violence, alienation, consistent harassment, and a lifetime of psychic scars. The few white parents who continued to send their children to school lost their city jobs, had their electricity cut off, and had their homes vandalized. The actions ensured that even whites willing to integrate might succumb to community pressure. As working-class women, the daily mob did not believe that they could change federal court decisions or even those of the statehouse. They knew that they lacked political capital, but they did act as if their political protest could affect their local school and neighborhood. Without the economic security or stability to escape to the suburbs , they protected their investment in white privilege where they could—in their homes, in their schools, and on the streets. In New Orleans as in Little Rock, white women demonstrated how invested they were in white supremacy at the same time they taught their own children that maintaining school segregation was worth more than their education or their neighborhood friendships.[34]

The ugliness of white southern mobs confronting black school children outside schools captured national attention as some segregationists more quietly continued to emphasize a color-blind conservatism, cultivated their national conservative credentials, and retooled white supremacist politics for the long civil rights era. They built organizations that served to secure segregation where it has always been maintained—marriage and home, social welfare programs, schools, politics, and culture. Using her teaching credentials and access to her state's high schools, Sara McCorkle developed programs to promote a national conservatism among Mississippi's white youth. In 1960 McCorkle enjoined thirty-one women to establish the Paul Revere Ladies who would "fight for our American way of life." The members included DAR and PTA women, church leaders, a former State Federation Clubs officer, a Girl Scout official, an editor, a doctor, a leader of the Business and Professional Women's Organization, an administrator for the Cancer Fund, and one from the State Sovereignty Commission. Invoking the crowds that protested the Little Rock Nine and Ruby Bridges, the Paul Revere Ladies adopted a "Battle Cry" that ended with the following:

The hour is late! There is no time to spare!
The enemy is upon us from land, sea, and air.
Washington has been taken, Little Rock has been occupied.
The battle of New Orleans is raging Nationwide.

As the price of freedom,
In the graves our fathers lie.
We in turn must save our children—
We must stand, and fight, or die.[35]

In one of their first attempts to "save their children," the group decided to sponsor pro-segregation and states' rights speakers to lecture in junior colleges and at mass meetings. Funded by taxpayers' dollars funneled through the State Sovereignty Commission, their first speaker was the noted anticommunist Myers Lowman who visited white universities (the University of Mississippi and Delta State) and historically black institutions (Jackson State and Alcorn College) informing them that racial unrest was simply one component of a communist conspiracy. Despite some dissent, particularly at Jackson State and Ole Miss, the speaker series earned accolades from the *Clarion-Ledger* and the *Summit Sun*. As a right-wing organization funded by a state committee dedicated to silencing civil rights activists, the Ladies linked massive resistance to the broader anti-communist crusade and grounded their work in the historical context of the American Revolution.[36] Amid the heightened Cold War tensions, an anti-communist education helped create a curriculum of white supremacy for Mississippi's youth.

"Teaching" white youth the values of a conservative and segregated society was also undertaken by another McCorkle-founded organization— Patriotic American Youth (PAY).[37] Focusing on cultivating young conservatives in the early 1960s, PAY avoided white supremacist language and told potential donors that the organization's intent was to get students to be "conservative-minded."[38] McCorkle used the annual week-long Girls' State meeting, which was made up of Mississippi's most civic-minded white high school students studying democratic government, as a recruiting ground for PAY. Mimicking reading groups so popular in southern California, McCorkle also sought to supply each school in Mississippi with eight to ten books on fighting communism to be used in designated PAY reading circles. By the 1970s, the PAY annual meeting had grown to a week-long event, with over twenty speakers including university faculty, veterans of World War II and Vietnam, military recruiters, pastors, intelligence officers, newspaper publishers, and the president of the international Christian Anti-Communism Crusade. PAY headquarters were in Jackson, Mississippi, for a time, where they shared office space with the John Birch Society and the conservative volunteer-run Freedom Bookstore.[39] Moving seamlessly from the Citizens' Councils to conservative organizations, McCorkle continued to cultivate Mississippi's youth for an array of conservative causes.[40]

Meanwhile, women on the right continued their censorship crusade to prevent students from having access to textbooks that promoted racial tolerance and communism. In 1959, the national DAR had made one of its goals "to encourage the proper teaching of American History in all public institutions of learning."[41] The *Clarion Ledger* also reported that in its campaign to purge school textbooks of subversive influence, the DAR was "expected to pull no punches in its war against desegregation."[42] The DAR released a list of 165 school textbooks deemed unsatisfactory for American schools, which meant that the book praised the United Nations, condoned "one-worldliness," included uncomplimentary pictures of poverty and slums during the Great Depression. They even objected to those that featured pictures of Hiroshima after the atomic bomb, because they might promote "fear and compromise" in attitudes toward the Cold War.[43] Mississippi's DAR chapter found that 44 of the 165 subversive texts were being used in the state's schools. Collaborating

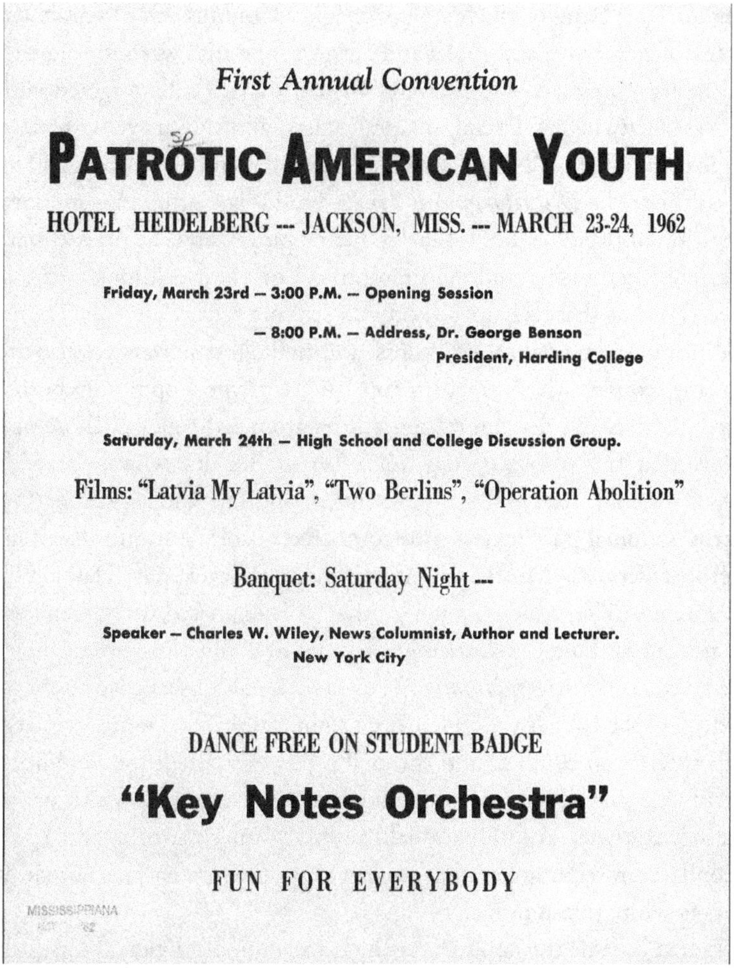

**FIGURE 8.3** 1962 Inaugural Patriotic American Youth (PAY) Meeting. Formed by Sarah McCorkle, PAY developed into week-long meetings of white youth schooled in conservative and anti-communist politics. Mississippiana Vertical File, McCain Library and Archives, University of Southern Mississippi, Hattiesburg.

with the American Legion, they prepared an exhibit of the textbooks with evaluations that indicated the level of racial tolerance and communism present. In response, one white woman suggested to Governor J. P. Coleman that history books were most guilty in promoting a "continual concerted attack on our form of Government, our social standards, on capitalism, and our Constitution . . . [and] introduce ways and means to improve social relations among the races." Nothing could be more dangerous, not even gun violence, she concluded, than "the books that have been placed in our schools."[44] Under

Governor Ross Barnett, the State Sovereignty Commission disseminated its own list of subversive textbooks and authors, one that was more restrictive than the list compiled by the DAR. Their list specifically targeted authors who were "leftwingers, liberal, integrationists, and subversive writers." This included a number of "Negro" writers, NAACP members, and even Ogden's own editor at the *Delta-Democrat Times*, Hodding Carter. Her support for segregation outweighed her loyalty to her employer, and she praised Barnett for textbook censorship and the appointment of a new textbook rating committee, claiming that he helped "keep our schools American."[45]

Securing America from communist and civil rights subversives also meant for many conservatives—mainstream and extreme—opposing both the United Nations and decolonization efforts around the globe. Those opposing included the *National Review*'s William Buckley who believed that Africans were not ready for self-government and Dr. Ruth Alexander in the Citizens' Council publication who compared decolonization in the Congo to Reconstruction in Mississippi. At the grassroots level, Mary Dawson Cain, and Florence Sillers Ogden, among others, disseminated the same views to their readers, and the *Clarion Ledger* kept up its copius coverage of the news in west Africa. Writing in *Human Events*, a national conservative publication, the editor of the Citizens' Council Texas publication, Mrs. Sam Davis, argued that both African conflicts and the civil rights movement were examples of a worldwide effort inspired by communists to subjugate white people.[46] Situating whites as an international minority, America's conservative activists conflated foreign policy that dealt with non-white nations abroad with threats to white rule at home.

Women became the conduit for the translation of foreign affairs to local matters in the South and across the nation, and foreign policy became a template on which they wrote a story of local resistance to the civil rights movement. In the late 1940s and 1950s, columns by conservative and segregationist women had demonstrated that attention to Africa and the United Nations mattered in local grassroots politics. In the segregation of even understanding, black Americans saw in African independence movements inspiration for struggle, while conservative whites saw in the rise of anti-colonialism the demise of their political supremacy. Citizens' Council publications devoted columns to the comparison of nation-building in Africa to the quest for racial equality at home, and across the South, white southerners used "another Congo" as shorthand for the outcomes of the civil rights movement.[47] In "Dis an' Dat," Ogden painted black Africans as utterly unfit to rule their homeland. The new president of Gabon, she reported, ate his mother-in-law, while a leader of the French Congo disappeared after he refused to eat a baby in a ritual feast.[48] Yet these were the nations, according to Ogden, that would rule the United Nations, rendering the United States voiceless "unless it caters to the racist . . . members of the African-Asian bloc." She claimed that "It won't be long now. It won't be long until the United States will be in the same position in the United Nations as the South is in the United States, with everybody playing against her for the African bloc vote, offering higher and higher bids or privileges. Some call it civil rights."[49] For segregationists, events in the Congo, Algiers, and Ghana became the subjects of conservative and Jim Crow storytelling, often earning more print space in southern newspapers than did the resistance of black southerners and civil rights protests.

Employing a more color-blind language, others critiqued the Peace Corps as an example of a misguided foreign policy that further eroded parental authority and replaced it with a nanny state. Segregationist women also disagreed with the education that Peace Corps volunteers received, knowing it countered the carefully crafted racial education cultivated in the Jim Crow South. When American missionaries to the Congo faced violence during the uprising for independence, Ogden asked, "Is that what we want for our daughters? Our sons?" More than violence, however, she feared that those involved in international aid and uplift, far away from teachings at home, would soon fall in love and get married. For those who resisted going "native" and refused to marry across the color line, Ogden resorted to a familiar white supremacist narrative of black on white sexual violence, wondering if they would be "abused and terrorized."[50]

Debates on international events had often allowed segregationists to employ a less racialized vernacular to reinforce white supremacy at home. While leading conservatives denounced the UN and the capitulation to decolonization as part of a liberal internationalist agenda, they also highlighted in national periodicals the inability of non-white nations to follow the rule of law. In local communities, southern segregationist and conservative white women took these issues to their local PTA chapters, garden clubs, and historic societies. For them, the UN had infiltrated so many facets of their life—school curricula, Hollywood films, the Republican and Democratic parties, and the celebration of Halloween and Christmas holidays. This multi-pronged attack only amplified how necessary a mother's oversight was to sustain national sovereignty and white supremacist politics. To a PTA chapter, Ogden warned mothers that United Nations Children's Fund (UNICEF) Christmas cards were a subtle challenge to the traditions of Christian nations and that they contributed to a worldwide anti-white movement. When children trick or treated for UNICEF, one segregationist organization advised its members to hand out the booklet "The Two Faces of Communism" instead of candy. This pamphlet informed the unaware children that by collecting for UNICEF they were "sponsor[ing] the murder of innocent men, women and children as committed in the Congo by the U.N."[51]

The responsibility of white mothers was central to segregation, anti-communism, and national sovereignty. When white children believed in racial equality, joined the Peace Corps, or considered being a peacenik instead of a hawk, they testified to the failures of white motherhood in the Jim Crow South. They had plenty of examples from which to choose. Ogden pointed out how communists were at work among young people as evidenced by the college students who rode the "Freedom Bus" and led the anti-HUAC demonstrations. The director of the FBI, J. Edgar Hoover had said that sit-ins were inspired by communists.[52] For segregationists, rearing children who believed in racial equality was the unintended result of waning parental influence and waxing governmental intrusion. With youth so susceptible to communist subversion and subsequent civil rights activism, the political responsibilities of white women grew.[53]

Even as white women organized, made stump speeches, voted, and watched over their schools in the name of white supremacy and anticommunism, their campaigns tilled the ground for an anti-feminist politics as well. As part of a national backlash against working mothers that had begun at the close of World War II, Ogden blamed mothers for the loss of values in American youth.[54] In addition to "losing the great privilege of making a home for their families," Ogden wrote that "they lose the opportunity to teach their children—subconsciously teach as well as consciously." Mothers must watch out for subversive influences in all institutions.[55] She claimed:

> It seems to me that what we need most in these United States today is more family life and less organization; more association of children with parents; more subconscious teaching of mother to child which comes from everyday association. Children cannot get it from schools, churches, or any other part of organized society. There is no substitute for parents in my book.[56]

For Ogden, the loss of maternal influence was just one of many threats to the Jim Crow order that upset what she believed was the very essence of American culture—white supremacist politics. Long a participant in the "culture talk" that explained American politics as a natural outgrowth of an organic racial hierarchy, Ogden responded by suggesting that the civil rights movement changed every aspect of society—including white womanhood. The federal government earned substantial blame for this upheaval and that accusation complemented the culture talk of the New Right.[57] When Ogden wrote that "Now that the Commies and the do-gooders have got the lady [black woman] out of the kitchen who is going to do all the civic improvement, P.T.A., garden club, patriotic society, and sweet charity work the lady [white women] in the parlor used to do?" she confirmed that for her the civil rights movement and the federal government had deracialized the term "lady," eroding the power of white women. White women could simply not be, Ogden wrote, "a Ladies-Aider and a kitchen maid too." Ignoring the vast church, social, and civic civil rights work undertaken by black women, Ogden questioned if "the former maids, released from domestic service, render the same community service once so freely given by the mistress of the House?" When she introduced a woman professor to the Mississippi Historical society, she commented that she hesitated to call her a lady because "when my cook comes in and says, Miss Flonce there's a lady in the kitchen to see you, I know this is someone seeking to get on the welfare roles [*sic*] of the ADC [Aid to Dependent Children] but when she says there's a woman in the parlor I know it is some Colonial Dame, UDC, DAR, or some historian or writer." Removing overt references to race, Ogden exposed both the threat that federal programs posed to white women's carefully constructed roles and the contested nature of women's power. Her comments also demonstrated how white supremacist language could be made color-blind with derogatory references to federal programs and federal legislation. "Lady," for Ogden was a term replete with racialized, class, and political meanings—meanings that no longer worked as black resistance challenged white cultural supremacy.[58]

Less concerned with challenges to the language of white supremacy, South Carolina's Cornelia Dabney Tucker targeted the men who handed down the *Brown* decision by calling for court reform. As the South's segregationists watched Congress take slow steps to address the nation's rising tide of civil rights activism, Tucker campaigned against judicial activism, constitutional erosion, and weakening standards for justices—all factors that she explained contributed to the Supreme Court's support of desegregation. She did not invoke racist tropes even as she turned to Mississippi Senator James Eastland. She focused on legislation supported by the American Bar Association, that restricted the appointment and confirmation of federal justices. Both Eastland and Tucker claimed liberal values, not core republican principles, swayed the justices who decided *Brown*. In her correspondence to organizations across the nation, she "divorced the issue of race integration from my presentation, not because I fail to emphatically oppose forced integration, but because to me the main issue is shall we calmly accept any decision come by in a way which marks the court itself as guilty of Un-American activity."[59] Tucker wrote letters to federal representatives, sent petitions to congressmen, and published articles. She reenacted her physical protest of 1937 by going to Washington, standing outside the Supreme Court building, and sporting a sash calling for "Supreme Court Security."[60] By 1958, Tucker celebrated that her proposal for an American Bar Association pre-approved list of potential nominees from each state to be used for US Supreme Court appointments was at that time "pending in the U.S. Senate Judiciary Committee."[61]

Tucker's attacks on the Supreme Court had pushed her further into national conservative circles. In 1957, Tucker had spoken at the annual meeting of We the People, Americans United for Patriotic Action.[62] We the People was a subsidiary group of the larger conservative umbrella organization, the Congress of Freedom, both of which believed in the abolishment of Social Security, the un-constitutionality of the income tax, the primacy of state governments over the federal one, the need to eliminate federal aid to education, the importance of domestic anti-communism, the ineffectiveness of the United Nations, and opposition to civil rights. At these meetings, leading national conservatives emphasized their belief in the existence of a worldwide communist conspiracy and linked the civil rights movement to that conspiracy. At the 1957 Chicago meeting calling for conservatives to lobby President Eisenhower, Congress, and the Supreme Court, Tucker received the endorsement for her plan to narrow the selection process of Supreme Court nominees.[63] Joining Tucker at the meeting was Florence Ogden, who delivered an address, "What the DAR Is Doing to Combat Communism and World Government" that praised the DAR for enrolling 300,000 children in Junior American Citizens' Clubs and for using its 184,108 members to disseminate thousands of pieces of literature that spoke to the communist menace.[64] At We the People, the DAR, Tucker, Ogden, and others had replicated what many segregationist women had done to secure Jim Crow—lobby elected officials, train white youth, and do the valuable work of storytelling—in order to invigorate a conservative political resurgence.

In 1959, Tucker returned to We the People's annual meeting as a featured speaker but this time took aim at public schools. Tucker argued that public school curriculum held a central place in the battle against communism and socialism. In her address, "An Education for World Peace," she called for required courses in "the fundamental economics of our free enterprise system of government" and "citizenship duties." Adopting a states' rights rhetoric employed in massive resistance, she reiterated that "in this government by federation of states, each state determines for itself all education policies for state supported schools and colleges."[65] Tucker hobnobbed with a slate of national conservative allies and authors including former Michigan congressman and member of HUAC, Kit Clardy, and "Mrs. GOP," Jessica Payne, a schoolteacher and former West Virginia state legislator. Harry Everingham, author of the widely read pamphlet "Will You Go Communist without a Fight?" served the organization as a vice-president while other officers came from Los Angeles, California; Lansing, Michigan; and Chicago, Illinois. Their institutional affiliations represented conservative groups as varied as American Progress, the National Committee for Economic Freedom, "United States Day" Committee, New Yorkers for the Constitution, and the Christian Crusade.[66]

These annual meetings also included Mary Dawson Cain who served on the board of directors of We the People and was a director and then president of the Congress of Freedom. Organized in 1952, the Congress of Freedom included members such as George Wallace, Utah Governor J. Bracken Lee, and Robert Patterson, founder of the Citizens' Council. For Cain, the Congress of Freedom was like a coming home party where she connected with people from across the nation who had been involved in an array of conservative issues. The organization sought to counter the influence of the United Nations, celebrate free market capitalism, encourage a limited government, and counter communist subversion. In 1959 president Cain started the Liberty Awards that were given to 500 leading conservatives, recipients included radio personality Paul Harvey, Arizona conservative Barry Goldwater, John Birch Society founder Robert Welch, and Florence Sillers Ogden. For decades, these awards continued to be given annually, honoring conservative thinkers, writers, and activists.[67] For segregationists, these annual meetings did not weaken their support for racial segregation; rather, they validated white supremacist politics in the language of a larger conservative framework. For Cain, Tucker, and Ogden, their participation in these organizations provided them additional expertise, institutional support, and national validation for their grassroots organizational efforts.[68]

Amid the storytelling, conservative organizing, protests on the streets, and mobilization of white youth, white female segregationists met the formidable forces of black men, women, and children dismantling legal segregation and white supremacy in one community after another. They watched

```
             Highlights of Program -- WE, THE PEOPLE!
         5th ANNUAL NATIONAL CONSTITUTION DAY CONVENTION

FRIDAY, Sept. 18, 1959 -- Grand Ballroom, LaSalle Hotel, Chicago
7:30 P.M. -- "A LESSON TO KHRUSHCHEV." RALLY -- (Free)

    People representing the 17 enslaved nations will describe "co-
    existence" with Communism and tell how they will revolt any time
    Khrushchev turns his back to start war.
    Bob Siegrist (Milwaukee, Wis.), Radio Commentator -- Interviews
    Harry T. Everingham (Chicago) -- "Something Worth Fighting For"
    Hon. Jessica Payne (Huntington, W. Va.) -- "Communist Influence
    on Our Children -- How to End it"
    Dr. Billy James Hargis (Tulsa, Okla.) -- "Communist Influence
    Through Church Organizations, the U.N., the NAACP, the Unions --
    A New Program to Combat It"

SATURDAY, Sept. 19, 1959 -- Grand Ballroom, LaSalle Hotel
9:00 A.M. -- Convention opens -- Hon. Ralph W. Gwinn (Pawling, N.Y.),
    Natl. President, WE, THE PEOPLE! -- "Statement of Purpose"
9:30 A.M. -- Dr. R. P. Oliver (Urbana, Ill.) -- "Communist Influence
    Within Our Federal Government"
10:15 A.M. -- Revelations by two former Communists: Joseph Z. Korn-
    feder (Detroit) and Ira Latimer (Chicago)
10:40 A.M. -- Mrs. Ray Erb, D.A.R. (Washington, D.C.) -- "What America's
    Women Must Do to Stop Communism in the U.S."
11:10 A.M. -- Willis E. Stone (Los Angeles) -- "How Business Can Get
    the Public to Combat Communism in the U.S."
11:45 A.M. -- Mrs. Cornelia Dabney Tucker (Charleston, S.C.) -- "The Best
    Education for World Peace"

12:30 P.M. -- Luncheon -- Century Room -- Judge John Unger presiding --
    Introductions -- Resolutions -- Program Plans
2:00 P.M. -- Senator Barry Goldwater -- "How to Win a Non-Partisan
    Victory for Freedom"
```

FIGURE 8.4 We the People 1959 program. Cornelia Dabney Tucker joined conservatives across the nation who believed that the civil rights movement was inspired by communists. She preceded Senator Barry Goldwater who was the keynote speaker. *News and Courier*, August 13, 1959, Charleston, South Carolina.

them organize sit-ins at Woolworths, Eckerds, and Howard Johnsons and carry their books into the Universities of Alabama, Georgia, and Virginia. They watched black men and women sit on Greyhound buses with white men and women and then read about them sleeping in southern jails. They saw their black neighbors register voters, attend Freedom Schools, and turn their beauty parlors into literacy workshops. They even saw some southern whites support these efforts.

Meanwhile, white moderates, many of them white women, worried about the loss of investment in the South, the decline of federal dollars, or the ugly violence that swept their communities. They moved to help implement desegregation, offering various degrees of support for open schools, compulsory attendance, token integration, voter registration, and an end to white supremacist-inspired violence. White moderate women, some who believed in white supremacist politics but not in the denial of public services or the dismissal of human rights, became a significant impediment to those who remained intransigent on the issue of integration. Women in the League of Women Voters, in PTA leadership roles, and in neighborhood councils like Atlanta's Help Our Public Education, Inc., tried to counteract the most extreme plans of segregationists, denouncing the violence levied on black civil rights activists.[69] Segregationists had always adapted to changing political winds, and as the civil rights movement gained momentum encouraging a wide swath of Americans that change must come, white segregationist women changed as well. The response of white segregationist women to James Meredith's arrival at the University of Mississippi exemplified the overlap between conservatism and segregationist politics.

Mississippi's hot summer of 1962 had been made hotter by the news that the University of Mississippi would integrate which inspired Governor Ross Barnett's incendiary speeches proclaiming that Ole Miss would remain all white. During a radio address and again at an Ole Miss football game, Barnett had pledged that "no school will be integrated in Mississippi while I am your governor" and "we will not drink from the cup of genocide."[70] Barnett's credentials as a segregationist were impeccable. In the summer of 1961, he had reinforced his reputation as a warrior for white supremacy when he greeted 323 freedom riders with jail sentences and subsequent imprisonment at Parchman Prison. White Mississippians expected him to take the same hard line against Air Force veteran and black Mississippian James Meredith who was slated to move onto the University of Mississippi campus on September 30, 1962.[71] Barnett's pledge did not hold. When Meredith arrived, a riot erupted, and white mothers and fathers across the state rushed to Oxford to get their children away from campus, federal troops, James Meredith, and white rioters. For many Mississippi segregationists, the armed integration of Ole Miss repeated the widespread evils of Little Rock—an intrusive federal government, a communist-inspired philosophy of racial equality, the betrayal of a region by its national government, and disregard for the white leadership of the state. For many white women, it was just one more example of the disregard for and erosion of their private and public authority over white youth.[72]

Incensed, South Carolina's Cornelia Dabney Tucker wrote to Attorney General Robert Kennedy that the Ole Miss riots resulted from federal force, not protest. Her segregationist sentiments shone through when she contended that the Ole Miss students were "motivated by what they believe to be a noble and heroic determination to preserve the integrity of the races." Rewriting recent history by replacing facts with falsehoods, she noted, "Before the era of forced mixing, Southern states were beginning to quietly admit negro students to their colleges and universities." She hoped the federal government could find faith in state officials and stop interfering in what were solely state matters.[73]

Closer to home, between 1,500 and 1,800 women from eight states, including California, organized the Women for Constitutional Government (WCG) to protest this "federal invasion" of Mississippi and the endangerment of the state's children.[74] These women did not take to the streets nor did they proclaim their devotion to racial segregation. Instead, they pledged to work for "free enterprise, the Christian faith, racial self-respect, and national sovereignty." The integration of Mississippi was just the most egregious example of how the federal government sought to take over women's business, but President Kennedy's "New Frontier" also posed a constant threat that included federal control of "the home, the schools, the prayers, the choice of association of our children." In speech after speech, WCG members stressed: "This is not an organization on racial issues. We believe in the separation of the races. But that is only one facet, a mere symptom of the disease."[75] The WCG carefully crafted a core list of seven goals that reflected their efforts to link southern segregationists to a broader national base. Including no specific mention of white supremacy, or even racial segregation, the WCG sought:

1. Defeat of communism.
2. The full recognition of the basic integrity, responsibility and individual initiative of the American people.
3. The full support of a free enterprise economic system at home and abroad . . .
4. Constitutional government, maintaining the separate integrity of the three Branches of government, executive, legislative and judicial . . .
5. A foreign policy that recognizes that is it not possible to buy friendship . . .
6. An economically and militarily strong America—recognizing that the free world could survive without the United Nations, but not without the United States.
7. A return to God in affairs and functions of American—regardless of the beliefs of other nations.[76]

They called on women to vote, to remove from office the men responsible for the federal invasion, and to eschew partisan loyalty to campaign for conservatives. It was a woman's responsibility to:

preserve the good life for her children—life, liberty, and the pursuit of happiness. Protection of the family. This is a woman's medium.

We have every right to fight for it; every incentive. If the men fail, we shall carry on. We are the mothers of men. We are the builders of the future. We have a duty to perform. Let's be up and about it![77]

Men had their uses, but women, the WCG claimed, needed to take the lead in preserving constitutional government. Womanly duties meant seeking men's input on a candidate's ideologies, asking men for money, and sometimes finding a man to carry out their agenda, but it also meant that as the majority of eligible voters, women needed to get out and vote, donate financially, and offer moral support. Their gender-specific duties also meant that white women had to forgo their "appointment at the Beauty Parlor, your Bridge Club meeting, your Garden Club convention," and study the Constitution, expose the UN as an organization that eroded American sovereignty, call for the reform of the electoral college, and begin a membership drive.[78] Ogden charged all these women to "organize, organize, organize . . . in every county, every city, every village, and every hamlet."[79] New chapters had only to accept the seven goals and then they could add others, preserving local autonomy and their devotion to states' rights.

And organize they did. As one member noted, "this Save the Constitution business" took a lot of work. Members delivered speeches, wrote columns and letters, telephoned, wired—"urging interminably."[80] Mary Dawson Cain, publicity chairman of WCG, sent out a public release about the organization to every daily, weekly, and county paper in Mississippi. She ran columns in the *Summit Sun* and began to collect inquiries and financial supporters from beyond the South.[81] WCG leaders encouraged their members to expand their contacts. With the assistance of a telephone operator, WCG organizers lined up ten women on the same line and talked for two to three minutes. The script encouraged "all women interested in preserving the Constitutional form of government" to come to a meeting, and the protocol advised phone tree recruiters not to mention the Kennedys by name and "try to stay off the racial problem except in our own localities." "If we get constitutional government, we will be able to handle all the rest," they advised.[82] Monthly chapter meetings involved reviewing books that exposed the actions of the State Department. After the book discussion, members were instructed to pass on their copy to other friends but before they left the WCG meeting they also had to write at least one letter to a congressman or senator on a current bill. What bills would be up to the discretion of each chapter. These segregationists believed that "women are capable of wielding unlimited power, especially when the welfare of their children is threatened." Organizational materials rejected partisanship, reminding members that the WCG "is not Republican or Democrat. We stand for CONSERVATIVE candidates." By 1964, that would mean Barry Goldwater, and if he was not the Republican nominee, then voting Republican would be no better than casting a vote for a Democrat. Stressing ideological purity over partisan loyalty, the WCG believed that "the women can save our country," and they expanded the rhetoric of massive resistance from women's role in white supremacy to women's duty to enact a certain vision of America.[83]

In 1963, the WCG kicked off their second year with a meeting in Montgomery, calling on "mothers of schoolchildren, believers in prayer, followers of the Christian faith" to join and "to perfect" the national organization.[84] The addition of religion drew on national conversations occuring in the aftermath of the Supreme Court's 1962 decision banning school prayer. Being "for prayer" was a way, as Cornelia Dabney Tucker put it, to unite "the Hillybilly and the city dweller, the Southern Bible Belt and Quaker New England, the Washfoot Baptist and the aristocratic Episcopalian" in a unified conservative movement.[85] The WCG capitalized on prayer as an issue to attract more members, but it also fit well with the segregationist argument that racial integration was against God's design. The same federal government and the same Supreme Court that embraced racial equality, they contended, also opposed Christianity.[86]

The 1963 meeting was attended by women from fourteen states—New York, Pennsylvania, Illinois, and Wisconsin as well as every southern state except Arkansas and Virginia. Those two states had formed similar organizations— in Arkansas, the Bi-Partisan Party for Constitutional Government and in Virginia, the Virginia Defenders of Individual Liberties and State Sovereignty. New chapters of the WCG began in Mississippi, Texas, Alabama, Arkansas, Florida, and Illinois. A Greenville, Mississippi, businesswoman volunteered to include propaganda in her business mailings to help spread WCG news to New York, Boston, and other northeastern cities. A Florida woman insisted that if women's organizations joined the cause of the WCG then "we could start something that would clean up this whole mess and get America back into patriotic hands."[87]

Part of the WCG's "Plan of Action" involved breeding distrust in the mainstream media. Liberals and communists, the WCG's study program said, dominated the mainstream news media. True Americans could not rely on it. Instead, WCG members should read the works of "patriots who believe in constitutional government" and invite speakers who could educate them on various constitutional violations. The WCG also distributed a newsletter with a recommended reading list that included the *Dan Smoot Report* out of Dallas; the DAR's National Defense Monthly Mailing, *Human Events* from Washington, DC; the publications of the American Coalition of Patriotic Society; the *Wall Street Journal*; and the Liberty Letter. They also marketed pamphlets by FBI director J. Edgar Hoover, and Dr. Orval Watts, a Harvard-educated economist who led one of the most important American free market think tanks of the twentieth century. In addition, the WCG advertised anti-communist literature such as "Roosevelt's Road to Russia," "No Wonder We Are Losing," and "America's Retreat from Victory." John Flynn's "While You Slept" was another sanctioned reading that exposed the overlap between segregationists and national conservatives. While Flynn abjured overt racism embodied in the KKK and other white supremacist organizations, he opposed federal civil rights legislation at home and the self-determination of many African nations because they were "not ready" for freedom.[88] It was an easy alliance between committed segregationists such as Cain, Ogden, and Tucker, who had long been arguing that black southerners thrived under white rule and were not ready for the freedoms that white southerners enjoyed, and conservatives, who invoked the "not ready" argument to deride those fighting to end colonial rule in Africa.

The reading list was meant to educate members and counter the alleged falsehoods of the mainstream media, but Cain, the publicist for the WCG, reminded members that constitutional arguments must be the root of all their calls for policy reform. For those who lived near Jackson, the WCG recommended going to the Freedom Bookstore where they could get materials to help them bolster their education in constitutional intent.[89] And WCG women elsewhere could get materials at a host of conservative bookstores, the American Opinion Library in Richmond or Poor Richard's in Pasadena.[90] Given the emphasis on constitutional arguments, Flynn's "not ready" argument against decolonization, while compelling to WCG members, could not be part of the organization's official policy. But sometimes WCG members strayed from their constitutional commitment and the party line and succumbed to white supremacist politics. As president of Mississippi's WCG branch, Cain sent out an open letter about the compliance measures in the 1964 Civil Rights Bill and called on women to "fight with all your might." "Our children's lives are at stake," she wrote, because the bill was "a deliberate attempt to break down MORALITY and the GENERAL WELL-BEING OF OUR PEOPLE by placing illegitimate Negro children side by side in classrooms of the State with white children whose parents have observed the State's moral and ethical codes, rearing theirs in wedlock."[91]

In 1963, the WCG sought to expand its regional base with a concerted effort in the Midwest. Hosting a national convention in Bensenville, Illinois, a suburb of Chicago, Cain served as the keynote speaker. WCG leaders hoped that the meeting would serve as a launch pad for regional growth. The Illinois chapters received assistance from WCG leader Margaret Peaster who had helped the Political Co-ordinating Committee of Chicago. Peaster left Chicago and continued organizing in Bismarck, North Dakota, and received additional requests for organizational materials from women in Missouri, Montana, Indiana, South Dakota, Oklahoma, Idaho, Pennsylvania, and Washington state.[92]

In May 1963 at the WCG's Dallas meeting, Ogden called the women who attended "dedicated, patriotic Americans." She celebrated their duties as mothers, insisting that their motivation was to preserve "the heritage of freedom for their children" and called on them to think about the world they were passing on to their children. She noted that they were needed to stop the US Congress and the United Nations from creating a "world government." Other speakers discussed the aims of the WCG, the dangers of disarmament, and the treachery of communism. One evening WCG members attended a reception at the home of General Edwin Walker who embodied the link between anti-communist and segregationist politics. A former military commander, in 1961 Walker resigned from the army after his attempts to politically indoctrinate his troops with far right anti-communist beliefs were the subject of a military hearing. A year later, Walker led a group of white Mississippi students who were protesting James Meredith's attempt to integrate Ole Miss. Evaluated at a psychiatric facility as part of his trial, rumors circulated that he was institutionalized for alleged mental illness as part of a government conspiracy to silence its critics, particularly those who linked communism and civil rights. Walker's defense of white rights at the University of Mississippi and his alleged persecution by the Justice Department had endeared him to conservatives and segregationists on the far right and the women of the WCG. For them, his actions and subsequent treatment made him an ally in their cause.[93]

By the end of 1963, the political agenda of the WCG was wide ranging, reflecting the organization's national focus. Repeated in much of their material was the reassurance that this organization was not simply about "the racial issue." Instead, constitutional government was their aim. Members would oppose sex education, public child care, and nationwide educational standards, often connecting these public policies to communist machinations and the abdication of maternal authority. In 1963, WCG leaders called on members to protest the Nuclear Test Ban Treaty and the Civil Rights bill.[94] The Civil Rights Bill, they claimed, interfered with states' rights and violated private property rights. In a speech in Starkville, Mississippi, Ogden used much of the WCG language to discuss the the impact of the future 1964 Civil Rights Bill. She called it the most damning piece of legislation "since Reconstruction." Her opposition emerged from its unconstitutional provisions that are in "violation of private property rights." She claimed that integration of facilities involved in interstate commerce would allow the US attorney general to represent members of the NAACP and Congress of Racial Equality (CORE), while citizens in "alleged" violation would have to pay for their own attorney. The bill also eroded the right of a citizen to "use his own property as he desires." The Public Schools section would allow the federal government to initiate desegregation in a school system, yet she noted "the Constitution gives no authority whatever to the Federal Government in public education." She also warned of its early steps "toward placing all elections under the absolute control of the Federal Government." Ironically, she also criticized the civil rights bill as a legislative open door for "any racist or irresponsible person [who] could, if you had fired an employee of another race, haul you into court, accuse you of violating the civil rights laws, and the attorney general would prosecute you."[95] Other than the NAACP or CORE, her opposition did not mention specifically the rights of African Americans, black leaders, or specific changes in her community.[96]

Far from working on the outskirts of society, the Women for Constitutional Government, the DAR, and other organizations connected white women of the Deep South to those female conservatives who had toppled progressive education in Los Angeles and were the "suburban warriors" of the New Right in southern California. By stressing conservative principles and discussions of the Constitution, however, the WCG had demonstrated how close the aims of the South's grassroots segregationists were to the goals of segregationists and conservatives in other regions. The WCG served as an example of how southern female segregationists helped make and shape the New Right in the 1960s.

The cross-pollination between southern segregationists and segregationist conservatives natiowide continued beyond the WCG. In 1963, when Frances Bartlett who had spearheaded the 1952 conservative reordering of the Los Angeles County School Board came to Mississippi to speak at a DAR National Defense luncheon. Advertised by Ogden as part of "Busy Weeks When Women Back Constitutional Rule," Bartlett delivered a lecture entitled "Crisis in Education: 'Testing' in Public Schools." Ogden had encouraged "many mothers of young children [who] are deeply concerned over the 'tests' being given in some schools," to come to Bartlett's address. Bartlett held reputable credentials—a graduate degree from the University of Chicago and more than a decade of leadership in patriotic education. Bartlett's critique of modern education was echoed by many conservative women particularly in southern California. There, parents had been called on to "wake up . . . there are some many things that we can and must do if our children are to remain ours." One woman gathered over a 1,000 signatures on a petition calling for Garden Grove, California, schools to "adhere strictly to traditional treatments of morals, religion, and patriotism in the classroom."[97] When Bartlett came to Laurel, she brought those organizing experiences with her.

Her return to Mississippi was in part a homecoming and in part a testament to the national network of segregationists. She had grown up in Laurel and left as part of the southern diaspora. With academic credentials and West Coast organizing experience, Bartlett drew on her expertise to connect her experiences in the urban, wealthy school districts of Los Angeles and Pasadena with those of rural, segregated Mississippi. In particular, Bartlett warned mothers about "hidden" statements unrelated to academics but inquisitive of home life that found their way into standardized tests. She noted that innocuous questions encouraged the erosion of respect for authority. For example, she listed statements where students could link and mark in agreement that patriarchal authority in the home was similar to teachers' authority in the schools. Most problematic, Bartlett contended, were questions about sex, conflict between religious beliefs and school subjects, and doubts about the existence of God that "should be alarming to conscientious, sensible parents." Focusing on schools, federal intervention into public education, and bureaucratic policies that intruded on parental authority, Bartlett reiterated local authority and parental control—both measures that white segregationist women had employed to maintain the Jim Crow order. Familiar with changing threats to white supremacist politics and to white women's authority in securing white over black, Bartlett's audience would have not been surprised that a new threat appeared cloaked in standardized testing.[98]

By 1963, the WCG and other segregationist organizations had articulated what would be the core talking points of the New Right—parental authority over the home, over matters of morals and sex education, and over academic education; and waning religious influence in public institutions. Like their counterparts in southern California, DAR and WCG meetings did not often express "harsh segregationist sentiments" but couched their opposition to civil rights in the language of parental and states' rights. But they held segregationist sentiments, forming after James Meredith's arrival at Ole Miss to sustain white supremacist politics. Southern segregationists shared key terrain with groups such as southern California's Citizens for Fundamental Education, who focused on public schools, public schoolteachers, and America's schoolchildren.[99] The years between Little Rock and the Voting Rights Act witnessed a continuation of the widespread and often woman-led resistance to school desegregation and the regular pollination of their white supremacist politics with the broader political discourse of national conservatism. If *Brown* had energized southern segregationist women, the years following Little Rock expanded their conservative political work by cultivating national organizations of white women like Women for Constitutional Government and strengthening their ties to the right nationwide.

White conservative segregationist women from the South and nation shifted to a more color-blind conservative political discourse that emphasized constitutional issues, and property rights. This meant campaigns to stop the fluoridation of water, limit mental health legislation, and stymy various urban renewal policies. It also meant opposing sex education. Politically, the women of the WCG joined conservative women nationwide to work for Barry Goldwater's campaign, urge the defeat of the Civil Rights Act, and encourage members to reject federal funding for public education. They also said that the Voting Rights Act violated the states' rights to control and to conduct elections and continued their opposition to federal aid to libraries and public schools. They lost on all counts.

For the politically astute workers for white supremacy and for those outside looking to the South, the death of Jim Crow seemed assured. White southerners, men and women, watched as the 1965 Voting Rights sent unprecedented numbers of black southerners into the electorate. Fifteen years later, Ogden's home county would have more black elected officials than any other county in the nation.[100] If maintaining segregation in schools, buses, and voting had been the only goals of segregationists, then the defeat of massive resistance and segregation could have been announced in the mid-1960s. But in the midst of what contemporaries and historians had come to call massive resistance, many white women had shifted their work, their political language, their strategies, and perhaps even their ideals. They might no longer mobilize their communities to sustain a rigid, legal segregation, but they could always continue to cultivate grassroots constituencies for a new conservatism that could house both their devotion to racial segregation and white supremacist politics. Having learned from the decades of their political activism, they accepted legislative defeats as an unpleasant, regrettable matter of course.

They also proceeded with the knowledge that white supremacist politics gained its strength from multiple fronts of which legislation was just one. They had remade segregation again and again, and they believed that they could do it again by stressing political conservatism, not race.

In the 1960s events—national and international—allowed them to continue to merge segregationist politics and an ideology of white supremacy into a larger conservative framework. In doing so, they helped to shape and structure the rise of the right. Decades earlier they had employed a color-blind language in DAR meetings and in campaigns against the United Nations. In the 1960s, decolonization; debates on school prayer, testing, and curriculum; and a growing national commitment to limit the federal government's efforts to make racial equality a reality provided fertile ground for segregationists nationwide to adjust their political rhetoric and strategies and for national conservative organizations to build their membership. Some segregationists had been active in national conservative circles for over thirty years. They knew that when white women in Chicago, Los Angeles, Washington, and New England faced substantial integration in their schools and watched the civil rights movement unfold in their communities, they would act much like white southern women had. They were segregationists too. In the face of apparent defeat, southern white segregationist women continued to educate and to encourage white youth to maintain a faith and a practice in white over black—in PAY, in WCG essay contests, in their move to white-only private schools. Facing a legislative end to white over black, they still maintained their domestic, educational, and cultural production for white supremacist politics, and mobilized their communities for another iteration of Jim Crow. Ogden, Cain, and Tucker understood the possibility of a national groundswell of support for racial segregation. Anticipating the northern trajectory of the the black freedom struggle, Ogden awaited what she imagined would be the unveiling of the national face of white supremacy. Anxious to see how those who had critiqued massive resistance and white southern segregationists would respond when they had to deal with their own system of segregation, Ogden noted wryly, "What is good for the chillun' is good for the grown folks."[101]

# Conclusion

# The New National Face of Segregation

## BOSTON WOMEN AGAINST BUSING

IN A 1964 column for Jackson, Mississippi's *Clarion Ledger*, Florence Sillers Ogden, predicted that when the North faced "forced" integration, northern whites would act much like their southern kin.[1] Her decades-long correspondence with women of the DAR, WCG, Congress of Freedom and We the People meant that she knew that women across the nation had mobilized their communities around a number of conservative causes, of which opposition to civil rights was just one. Her anticipation of national resistance to racial equality was not merely the bitter expression of an aging woman who watched her political efforts meet defeat nor the words of a white southern apologist, even though she was both. Her politics did not emerge from a distinctly anti-feminist agenda either. Her 1964 prediction emerged because she was a well-informed, politically connected, conservative female segregationist imbedded in national networks committed to various forms of segregationist politics. For the next eight years, Ogden continued to comment on the reactions of whites in northern places acknowledging that the civil rights movement threatened to reconfigure their daily lives.[2] She believed that massive resistance had a national following and that white supremacist politics operated on a national scale. For three decades, she had watched the language of overt racism transform periodically into new political expressions that subsumed segregationist agendas under the larger umbrella of parental authority, constitutional integrity, limited government, national sovereignty, or school choice. She expected that white women across the nation would rise up for conservative causes and in opposition to the next stage of the civil rights movement. When the busing crisis erupted, it was clear that her predictions were right. Massive resistance was national, and white women helped to make it so.

By the 1970s, the United States faced the intransigent problem of making school desegregation a reality in rural southern counties, and it also faced dilemmas in metropolitan areas from Charlotte to Detroit, and in urban centers like Boston. In the urban North and West, de facto segregation meant that some of those schools were close to being as segregated as those of the rural South. Over 90 percent of black students in Los Angeles, Chicago, Detroit, and Philadelphia attended schools that were more than 50 percent black.[3] In the Sunbelt South, the rise of the suburbs meant that residential patterns would ensure racially segregated schools even in the aftermath of legal integration unless federal or state courts intervened in new ways.[4] The faces of de jure segregation, that is, separation mandated by laws differentiating access and behavior based on race, and de facto segregation, that is, separation created by custom, residential housing patterns, and ostensibly race neutral laws and policies, had always been two sides of the same coin in the view of the South's segregationist white women. For decades they had known that maintaining racial segregation required work beyond dependence on merely laws. Reinforcing white supremacy at the level of culture was as necessary to sustain the system as canvassing for voters. Implementing race-neutral policies in ways that still differentiated based on race strengthened the laws that overtly segregated based on race.

White segregationist women knew what the national civil rights conversation often ignored, in the South de facto segregation existed alongside de jure segregation, working in tandem to support a system that required constant maintenance at various levels of society. The conversation that separated de facto and de jure segregation also minimized the municipal, county, state, and federal policies that undergirded de facto segregation in suburbs and cities. In fact, when Senator John Stennis of Mississippi proposed legislation to end segregation nationally, Senator Abraham Ribicoff of Connecticut joined him, claiming, "If segregation's bad in Alabama, it's bad in Connecticut." Ribicoff also noted, "A child in the third grade who goes to an all-black or all-white school—whether in Mississippi or New York City—has not the slightest idea that there is a difference between *dejure* and *defacto*." Unwilling to address the persistence of segregation, no matter the cause, in their own states, northern senators, liberal and conservative, dismissed Stennis, Ribicoff, and the proposal.[5]

The failed debate in the Senate mimicked the failure of many to address the role that policy as opposed to law played in shaping segregation in their communities. As a result, when the US Supreme Court handed down a series of decisions upholding busing and affirmative action as constitutional solutions to both de jure and de facto school segregation, national opposition erupted. In *Bradley v. Milliken*, a case involving Detroit's metropolitan area, Judge Seth Roth had written that school district lines were "simply matters of political convenience and may not be used to deny constitutional rights."[6] The initial *Bradley* ruling suggested that the desegregation of public schools could not be obstructed by residential segregation. The Supreme Court had already dismantled "freedom of choice" plans, a favorite approach in North Carolina, when the Supreme Court upheld Judge McMillan's busing decision in *Swann v. Mecklenburg*. In the *Swann* case, the NAACP had produced evidence that in Charlotte school assignment rules placed at least 10,000 white and black students in schools that were not the closest to their homes, eroding the "neighborhood school" theory invoked to maintain segregated schools. The widespread claim that merit and money, and not legally mandated segregation, shaped the racially segregated neighborhoods also faced refutation when Judge James McMillan stated that certain government policies made the quality of a student's education dependent on his or her racial and economic status.[7] McMillan had ordered busing in Charlotte-Mecklenburg schools when he could find no other reasonable way to achieve integration. The Charlotte case reverberated across the nation and earned the condemnation of many Americans who had supported an end to legal segregation but were opposed to "forced busing." The Court's decisions exposed the uncomfortable reality that what many Americans had claimed was "natural" or de facto segregation, rather than de jure, was in fact the product of local policies and legislation— redlining, federal loan policy, urban renewal plans, and highway development. Natural segregation, it turned out, was not natural at all.[8]

Amid a national outcry, a substantial number of Charlotte's white moderates worked to implement busing as peacefully as possible, but McMillan's reasoning fell on the relatively deaf ears of the newly formed anti-busing organization, the Concerned Parents Association (CPA). Led by three middle-class men, the CPA was sustained by the work of white mothers. One of those mothers, Mrs. Charles Warren, defended the neighborhood schools theory. She noted her willingness for black parents to buy in her neighborhood and send their children to school with her children which meant, by her own admission, that she was not opposed to racial equality. But, she continued, "if anyone thinks they're going to bus my children across town . . . without a fight, they're dreaming." Speaking at an anti-busing rally in September 1970, Jane Scott, wife of the vice-chairman of the CPA, said that a parent's duty to protect the innocence of her children superseded her responsibility to follow man's law, placing the unwritten rules of motherhood above the constitution. White motherhood carried with it responsibilities, anti-busing advocates argued, that negated their responsibility to follow government dictates. Neither Scott nor Warren nor the CPA stopped busing. Instead, Charlotte became a model for how municipal desegregation via busing could overcome residential segregation, at least for a while.[9]

Outside the South, integrated education could breed significant political backlash even where busing was not an issue. In the union-filled mining communities of southern West Virginia, a white Mississippi transplant, the middle-class "Sweet" Alice Moore capitalized on economic instability, opposition to more racially inclusive public school curriculum, and the rise of cultural conservatism to lead Kanawha County away from the Democratic Party and into the New Right. She did this as a member of the local school

**FIGURE C.1** Concerned Parents Association Meeting, Charlotte, North Carolina. Over 600 white middle-class parents meet to organize a boycott of metropolitan-wide busing. Courtesy of the *Charlotte Observer* and the Robinson-Spangler Carolina Room, Public Library of Charlotte and Mecklenburg County.

board. Focusing on new language arts textbooks and recommended reading lists, Kanawha County's white parents complained that the new curriculum was "anti-American" and inculcated their children with "ghetto language" and latent atheism. As the rebellion grew, white parents boycotted stores, kept 25 percent of the schoolchildren at home, attended anti-textbook rallies, joined wildcat strikes, and shut down the city bus system. In coal country, working-class and middle-class white women stood up for maternal authority and parental rights. Recognizing the Kanawha County protests as the next iteration in the fight against racial equality, the Citizens' Council periodical covered the controversy, reporting that "in the pages of their children's school books are false doctrines which will encourage their white sons and daughters to merge their racial identities with those of blacks in every phase of social life." The Kanawha County controversy capitalized on white supremacist ideas, evangelical conservatism, racialized construction of motherhood, and debates about American identity. The polyvocal nature of the politics of resistance, however, resulted some disturbing political alliances. The KKK was invited in. William Pierce, an anti-Semitic proponent of white armed revolution and the leader of the United States' own National Alliance (Nazi) organization, came to West Virginia to support the work of Kanawha's textbook boycotters. While these organizations were extreme, the connection between textbook controversies, anti-busing protests, and parental authority reflected more mainstream ideas. In Kanawha County, protestors believed that the outcome of the federal government's involvement in public education was the break down "traditional" values. They supported the inclusion of Booker T. Washington who had accommodated Jim Crow, but not Black Panther member Eldridge Cleaver, and they supported efforts to get black or "un-American" writers out of the school curriculum. The textbook controversy in West Virginia exposed at one level how school integration, even in terms of curriculum materials, meant to many the breakdown of racial difference, the loss of local school control, the erosion of parental autonomy, a betrayal by the Democratic Party, and, for some, the escalation of interracial sex and marriage.[10]

While women took the lead in both curriculum and busing protests, the political backlash against an integrated curriculum did not resonate across the nation in the way that busing to achieve school desegregation did. Most Americans, even those who had supported school integration, opposed the busing needed to achieve it. From Detroit, white working-class families who watched their economic possibilities attenuate in the 1960s feared that busing would erode the property values of their homes, further limiting their upward mobility. Busing, many believed, had rendered meaningless the financial sacrifices they made to send their children to "good schools," generated by residential segregation patterns. In 1972, the *New York Times* interviewed working-class whites who rejected labels of segregationist or racist. Instead, they explained their opposition to busing by emphasizing how hard work and hard economic choices made it possible for them to buy homes in good school districts which would make the American Dream possible for their children. Busing threatened to erode that dream and to violate their rights as property owners. As such, in 1972 many put their New Deal Democratic pasts behind them and voted for Alabama's George Wallace for president in Democratic primaries.[11]

In the Detroit suburb of Pontiac, a judicial decision to integrate schools via busing incited white women. Led by a young, attractive, and telegenic Irene McCabe, white women formed the innocuously named National Action Group (NAG) to protest busing their children. McCabe insisted that NAG's opposition to busing was not about race. Similar to the Women for Constitutional Government, she objected not to black children but to "the long arm of the federal government reaching into my home and controlling the children I gave birth to." In televised addresses she couched her protest as one to defeat communism, again minimizing her opposition to black children attending schools with her children. NAG women blocked buses with baby strollers, chained themselves to bus garage gates, and held a 620 mile "mothers' march" to Washington, DC, where they gathered at the Washington monument proudly wearing monogrammed aprons that attested to their roles as homemakers. In Pontiac, school buses were set on fire, and NAG invited George Wallace to be the keynote speaker at an anti-busing rally. When black children arrived at white schools, NAG protestors had organized pickets and other crowd members yelled "nigger, nigger, nigger" at the schoolchildren.[12] For those young children—white and black—walking into the schools, the lines between who protested due to constitutional overreach and those who objected out of a deep devotion to white supremacy were impossible to differentiate.

In Louisville, white women also led anti-busing forces. For several years, the school board had ignored mandates from the Department of Housing, Education, and Welfare to desegregate their schools. When their intransigence forced the issue into the courts, the circuit court judge developed a metropolitan busing plan that would begin in September 1975. The plan came up against those who had been cultivating opposition to integration via busing since 1972. In that year, as Jefferson County's all black Newburg Elementary planned to integrate, Joyce Spond, a white Jefferson County mother, had formed Save Our Schools (SOS). Within weeks she had 3,000 people on a mailing list who claimed to be against busing, not against integration. The timing of SOS belied such a claim. White women gathered in Louisville and Jefferson county and couched their protest in terms of parental duties, specifically their rights as mothers. Twenty thousand, Spond said, signed a petition to add an anti-busing amendment to Kentucky's state constitution. The anti-busing agitation had also energized white students who boycotted Fairdale High School and walked out of three other schools. Three years later, SOS would be just one among many anti-busing organizations with racially neutral, innocuous names—Concerned Parents, Parents for Freedom, Citizens against Busing, and United Labor against Busing. As the 1975 school term approached, another organization, the Kentucky's Taxpayers Association, invited the Klu Klux Klan to a local rally where anti-busers heard how busing was part of a concerted government effort to take away the rights of white people. Many parents kept their children out of school, fearing violence even as some white students tried to ignore the racial divide and welcome bused students to their schools. Civil rights activists and moderates feared another Boston, but middle-class and working-class anti-busing whites in Louisville often couched their opposition as animosity to government interference in their neighborhoods and schools. They contended that they, not the government, should have the power to shape the experiences of their children and families. But anti-busing advocates could hardly suppress the white supremacist rhetoric that characterized many of the protests. Many of the opponents of busing invoked the link between school integration, interracial relationships, and "miscegenation," as they destroyed property, blocked roadways, and chanted "Do away with nigs and pigs."[13]

Similar stories emerged across the nation from Milwaukee, Wisconsin, to Richmond, Virginia. Pictures splashed across the front pages of the nation's leading newspapers and reports of community meetings in smalltown weeklies showed mainstream middle-class and working-class white Americans rallying against their children's school assignments. As busing came to town, private church academies multiplied, parents kept their children home from school, and "For Sale" signs cropped up in affected neighborhoods. Petitions, rallies, and organizational meetings constituted one element of the resistance, but racist chants, taunts aimed at black students, and conflicts with police embodied another. Almost every anti-busing rally demonstrated the deep connections between property values, de jure and de facto segregation, and educational opportunity. And like the protests of white women of New Orleans' Ninth Ward in 1960, union support of Louisville's anti-busing movement suggested that busing plans exacted the greatest costs on working-class neighborhoods, often, but not always, leaving more middle-class suburbs out of what they derisively termed "social engineering."[14]

While resentment bubbled up across the nation, no urban protest gained more attention than in Boston. There, as Judge Wendell Arthur Garrity knew, the demarcation between black and white schools, black and white neighborhoods, and black and white families was the product of deliberate local, city, state, and federal policies. Even though racial lines in Boston closely adhered to parish and neighborhood boundaries, government policy had long shaped the city's residential patterns. South Boston was white; Roxbury was black; both were working class. By the time Judge Garrity issued his plan for desegregation of the city's schools and white Bostonians took to the streets, the city had witnessed over a decade of obstinance by the Boston School Committee that consisted of mostly middle-class citizens. Unlike Judge McMillan's plan in Charlotte, Judge Garrity's plan reflected the city's municipal, not metropolitan, boundaries and did not include the suburbs, even those of Brookline, Cambridge, and Winthrop whose lines carved deep into the city. For the most part, the plan spared the most elite neighborhoods, including Garrity's own, from busing.[15]

In 1965, the city had passed the Racial Imbalance Law, a measure intended to integrate schools. Boston's new law defined an imbalanced school as one with over 50 percent non-white pupils. City schools registering such an imbalance and showing no efforts at remediation could lose state funding. A school could delay the implementation of the law by requesting a judicial review, during which time parents were not required to bus their children. Counting on the slow pace of judicial time, the Boston School Committee stonewalled crafting a plan that instituted even "gradual" programs to meet the spirit of the law and ignored repeated court orders. While many white Bostonians supported the decision "to balance" the schools, by the time Judge Garrity handed down his ruling, Louise Day Hicks, John Kerrigan, and other members of the Boston School Committee had spent nearly a decade organizing the home and school associations across the city to obstruct the law.[16]

The Home and School associations had complied. In the years between RIL's passage and Judge Garrity's plan, the Boston School Committee and Louise Day Hicks, specifically, used the threat of busing to encourage their constituents to avoid compliance. Nine years of machinations set the stage for judicial intervention and served to foment grassroots rebellion among Boston's segregationist women. In 1972, several hundred mothers had lobbied to repeal the law; those who joined the Concerned Parents League of Boston also pressed city officials for a repeal. Often, they couched their opposition in terms of parental rights and "freedom of choice." They rarely stayed in the realm of constitutional arguments, however, and the more overt discriminatory language of white supremacy, white racial solidarity, and opposition to black students also defined their discourse. One Concerned Parents League mother remembered being startled "by the virulent racism which was expressed."[17]

If the language of "all deliberate speed" in *Brown II* had spurred resistance in the segregated South, the persistent flouting of the Racial Imbalance Law by the city's school officials had created space for a wide range of solutions for school segregation to circulate. While no integration was the goal of some, many white Boston women argued that black students could be bused into the white schools for educational quality; they just resisted the implementation of integration by the courts. In their letters to Judge Garrity, they explained that they did not want to bus their children out of their neighborhoods. Eschewing, for the most part, racist rhetoric, these letters of protest (a majority from women) spoke of constitutional rights, the rights of taxpayers and homeowners, and finally the authority of parents to choose their children's schools, their transportation, and the racial make up of their classrooms. Some of their solutions echoed those of white moderates in the post-*Brown* South who had resisted school closings and worked for strategic accommodation. In that vein, some white Bostonians crafted elaborate formulas about the optimal number of black students in white schools, claiming a willingness to move beyond individual racism as long as there were not "too many" black students. Others wrote in favor of "school choice." A young woman who attended South Boston High School echoed the language of Home and School Associations when she said that she was "for equal rights, but against busing," while another said "I am not a bigot or a racist. I believe in choice." Louise Day Hicks of the Boston School Committee rejected Garrity's decision wholesale; advocated compensatory, not punitive, programs in currently imbalanced schools; and claimed that busing unprepared black students to white schools would harm both black and white students.[18]

In the immediate aftermath of Garrity's decision, Hicks organized Restore Our Alienated Rights (ROAR), a group of mostly women committed to prevent integration via busing in Boston's city schools. Having formed an earlier group to hobble the Racial Imbalance Law, Hicks adopted the name ROAR to stress the alleged constitutional fiat posed by citywide busing. She claimed that "the issue of forced busing is a women's issue," and she identified ROAR members as "conservatives." Others would identify ROAR as a group of "militant mothers" as they justified their political activism in terms of their gendered responsibilities to protect their children. These mothers were white, and their defense of their children involved among other things invoking "virulent racist . . . language," and following prayer vigils at night with shouts of racial epithets at black students by day. Their conservatism included a deep investment in white supremacist politics and a commitment to racially segregated neighborhood schools, even if their more moderate spokeswomen buried those facts. Their goal was to continue the racial imbalance in the city's schools, to sustain Boston's version of segregation.[19]

Boston's residents repeatedly touted their segregated "neighborhood schools" as natural and organic compared with busing-created integrated ones or southern segregation which was created by law. They also lashed out at the early participants in Boston's white flight—white suburbanites who would be unaffected if citywide busing came to downtown neighborhoods. Sounding much like white southerners who had long used the proximity argument to claim particular authority over black-white relationships, some Bostonians argued that white suburbanites could not possible understand urban neighborhoods, black-dominated housing projects, or the plight of working mothers who would no longer be able to walk their children to school. One mother claimed: "Boston is not like the South. Colored people . . . were never forced to the back of anything in Boston." Espousing this sentiment again and again, many white Bostonian women defined themselves and their situation as fundamentally different from white southern segregationists. To some extent scholars have followed suit, trying to understand Boston's white resistance as separate, more complex, and distinct from the rabidly racist resistance in the South.[20]

If the differences between southern segregationists and northern anti-busers were salient to scholars and social critics, southern opponents of school integration and busing recognized in the urban uprising a common bond with their Boston counterparts. Southern radio and television stations offered advice and sympathy to their white Boston sisters and brothers, whom they believed were suffering similarly from government intervention, the reduction of parental authority, and the weakening of property rights. A North Carolina radio station invited Judge Garrity to call into their show. They told him that while "Charlotte-Mecklenburg may have put on party manners for the visiting Bostonians . . . even before the visitors left, it was back to the dreary grind of trying to cope." They continued, "The lesson Charlotte has to teach Boston and other communities is not how well busing works, but that, try as one will, it doesn't." In another program, Raleigh's TV station, WRAL, accused Garrity of bowing to the wishes of the NAACP and called those Bostonians who supported his busing decision "fanatics." WRAL commentators derided busing as "a utopian scheme" whose failings had been covered up by a conspiracy of silence among the media.[21] Addressed to the judge, the radio transcripts and accompanying correspondence suggested that North Carolinians both understood the situation in Boston and connected the events in Boston to their political struggles.

As commenters from North Carolina's WRAL focused on Boston's racial woes to paint school integration as a national failure, both Boston's anti-busers and busing advocates looked to the South for solutions. Bostonians visited Charlotte; they invited icons of the segregationist South into their homes. Louise Day Hicks refused to meet with presidential candidate George Wallace, even though she had taken a hardline stance against desegregation, but Wallace was warmly welcomed in South Boston neighborhoods. As had happened in the Kanawha Valley of West Virginia and suburban Detroit, white supremacist organizations also came to Boston. In early 1974, a Hyde Park woman, the leader of her neighborhood's anti-busers, invited the KKK to come to her home. As she later explained to the judge, it was not racism or bigotry that led to her invitation; rather it was "only through my own defiance of a law inimical to my beliefs." The presence of the KKK alarmed some citizens, and the Baptist Ministers Conference sent telegrams to Judge Garrity to protest the KKK presence. Another mother pled with Garrity to get federal troops into her Dorchester neighborhood because the children were unsafe with "too many KKK, Nazi Organizations here."[22]

While divisions among Boston's white women persisted, many formed the vanguard of the anti-busing movement and provided its daily workers. They chose titles for their grassroots organizations that espoused a political language emphasizing constitutional rights, freedom of choice and association, and the natural rights of parents. Under the auspices of ostensibly benign titles like the Dorchester Improvement Association or the West Roxbury Information Center, white women emerged as the central political actors in the grassroots resistance to busing. They conducted letter-writing campaigns soliciting the help of mothers, fathers, and even students. They worked on phone trees, prayer marches, and public protests. They even held impromptu parades, weaving their vehicles, decorated with anti-busing propaganda, in and out of neighborhoods. With some administrators friendly to their cause, they held meetings, in the public schools, and local businesses contributed money for copying and office costs. The more radical activists distributed literature from the John Birch Society and threw eggs at buses and children on the first day of school.

The anti-busing activism even prompted the formation of the Citywide Educational Coalition (CWEC), a group established to combat anti-busing propaganda. The CWEC included black and white men and women, mostly women, who helped implement the busing decision by serving as community liaisons, school volunteers, and staff at communication centers. CWEC members went undercover and attended anti-busing meetings, returning with transcripts. Communication center volunteers filled in harassment sheets that cataloged daily disturbances at schools and dozens of violent incidents. Volunteers collected copies of anti-busing flyers hung in high school hallways. They formed a rumor-control center aimed at investigating the anti-busers' often manufactured rumors of black-on-white violence, black male molestation of white females, and accusations of a racially defined two-tier discipline program that compromised successful integration.[23] While the presence of the CWEC highlighted the support for integration among some Bostonians, the volume of material recording the machinations of the anti-busers made clear the extent of resistance citywide.

In promotional material, flyers, and letters, Boston's anti-busing activists emphasized their status as mothers, sometimes working mothers, to separate their work in the name of child safety from that of rabid, unthinking racists. While they had looked to the South for strategies and inspiration, some imagined themselves as different, as less racist, than their southern sisters, even when their maternal and constitutional language resembled that of many southern segregationists in the 1970s. One ROAR mother and former Sierra Club member, Virginia Sheehy, spoke of her previous grassroots alliance with black women when they opposed the expansion of the airport. She insisted that her anti-busing efforts were about class, not race, yet she noted that the bond she had formed with black women over environmental concerns had been ripped apart by busing. Anti-busing might have been about class, according to Sheehy, but her interracial cooperation ceased, and her inability to see common cause with black Bostonians meant it was also certainly about race. The middle-class–dominated West Roxbury Information Center insisted again and again that their opposition to busing and their support of Restore Our Alienated Rights did not emerge from racism. In their publication "The True Paper," the West Roxbury Information Center explained their mission:

It has been erroneously reported that R.O.A.R. and the local anti-forced busing centers have been conceived to obstruct Judge Garrity's desegregation order, that we have been designed to promote racism, bigotry, and violence. This entire concept is without basis of fact. The

Constitution of the United States allows for freedom of speech and the freedom to protest peacefully. The forcible busing of children to desegregate our public schools is unconstitutional and as a citizen of the United States of America we are within our constitutional rights to protest this illegal act being perpetuated on us by a Federal judge, who has exceeded his judicial powers.[24]

A year later, the West Roxbury group sent its members guidelines for their continued resistance. It advised them to avoid biracial councils, to refuse to serve as school aides or bus monitors, and to avoid having their children attend the newly designed "neighborhood schools." Letting their children attend the schools with new district lines, the West Roxbury Information Center claimed, would be the equivalent of giving up their parental jurisdiction over their children. One working mother noted the predicament that busing introduced to her family. A later start time for her seven-year-old meant that while he was not being bused, she was no longer able to walk him to school and get to work on time. Walking her child to school was important to her, and she noted that if he were bused, she would move to avoid "possible violence or other influences of which I do not approve." Going to schools that were created by busing, others argued, meant an abdication of parental responsibility. Simply put, for the anti-busers, sending their children to schools affected by Garrity's ruling or even working with black mothers made them bad mothers.[25]

In the eyes of women protesting school integration and busing, the court decisions hindered their ability to protect and to mold their children. In Boston as in other places, the construction of motherhood could reach across class lines, but not always. Hicks was a member of the professional middle class, but she appealed to white South Boston's working-class women in the name of motherhood. On the other hand, working white mothers also resented suburban white mothers. Trapped in the city by low incomes, they were unable to move their families to the suburbs to "protect" them. They linked their ability to parent and to work to the ability of their children to walk to school, a concern that middle-class and professional women did not express Class resentment boiled over when one South Boston white woman pointed out the hypocrisy of middle-class suburban whites who kept "on telling us what we should do. They preach at us to take them [blacks] here and let them live there, and act this way to them, and that, and so on until you get sick hearing it all. Suddenly they're so kind, the suburban crowd."[26] They could be kind, she complained, because they were exempt from the very policies they supported. Middle-class privilege meant that they could remain good white mothers without taking their protests to the street. How could working-class whites, many wondered, be good mothers if they had to leave to go to work before their children caught the bus? In short, they justified their political work in part on their class and gendered identity and responsibilities. But by creating a grassroots political movement that married gender roles to a political platform of "family values," white working-class women offered a color-blind ideology that was easily portable to middle-class neighborhoods too. As they struggled in "an economically distressed city," their control over their families represented a shrinking island of authority.[27] Anti-busing became an outlet for expressing their commitment to their children. With echoes of New Orleans, anti-busers harassed and intimidated neighborhood mothers who joined biracial councils and who put their children on the bus. ROAR member Fran Johenne noted that you could not count on another mother to prevent your child from being bused. But the harassment experienced by mothers who complied with the court order suggested that there were plenty of other mothers "to protect" your child from busing whether you chose to or not.[28]

At times, Boston's white women who stressed their opposition to busing, not school integration, could not even pretend to reconcile opposition to busing with a rejection of racism. The various improvement associations, often affiliated with ROAR, placed women outside school playgrounds and at entrances to schools where they harassed Bostonians, white and black, who had volunteered to implement busing. Lucille Roberts and Zinia Porter, who were white, and Anna Mae Lewis, who was black, lived in the Maverick Street projects and had volunteered to work in school district eight to assist with the new student population. On the morning of September 8, at McKay Elementary School, Lucille Roberts met eighteen ROAR members, seventeen of them women, who came to protest in the name of "freedom of choice" and constitutional rights of assembly. One of the ROAR leaders, Elvira "Pixie" Palladino, future elected member of the Boston School Committee, hollered at Roberts, who was on the playground, "You fucking white trash, you fuck niggers, you're a nigger lover."[29] Palladino's actions were not isolated and trickled down to the next generation as Roberts and Lewis reported being harassed by white teenagers in their neighborhood. A few weeks after Palladino's verbal assault of Roberts, she found her car vandalized with slashed tires and broken windows. For the three volunteers, the racist message was clear, and it must have also been clear to the children gathered in the playground.[30] For teachers, parents, and students alike, Palladino, her fellow protesters, and even

ROAR served as spokeswomen for racial segregation and white supremacy far more convincingly than they did for the economic frustration of working-class white urbanites.[31]

The chants of ROAR volunteers posted outside the "busing" schools were aimed at the adults who supported busing, even if they inadvertently exposed Boston's elementary schoolchildren to crude racist language. Other anti-busing efforts, however, directly targeted high school students, extending an education in segregationist politics to the next generation. In Charlestown and Dorchester, anti-busing activists hung flyers in high school hallways that included specific directions on how students could skip school to attend rallies and protests at city hall. Students responded to such prodding. In one letter to Judge Garrity, a young high school student wrote, "I as an American citizen should have the right to legally to select the school that I feel will offer me the quality that I as a resident of Boston and one who will be forcabley [*sic*] bused and forced to give up my rights deserve to be given." He then asked if busing was related to communism.[32]

One letter to Judge Garrity from a white Hyde Park woman demonstrated how the anti-busing cause had filled her days. Claiming that she was not motivated by racial animosity, she had hosted meetings in her house and distributed literature from the John Birch Society. She had also written 245 registered letters per week, attended rallies, delivered speeches, participated in a prayer protest, put signs on her car, run the Home and School Association, awoken an hour earlier each morning to distribute anti-busing signs at schools outside her neighborhood, called up men and women to recruit them to the cause, answered strangers' calls to participate in a motorcade, and kept her kids home. As a result, she told the judge, her political activism had ruined her diet, which now consisted of potato chips on the run, her sex life which was now nonexistent, her housekeeping duties, and even her daily hygiene since she had lowered her weekly number of baths to save time for anti-busing organizing.[33]

On several levels, the very naming of the northern protestors—anti-busers—has created interpretive problems. Certainly, suburban, rural, and urban Americans resisted busing for many reasons, but in the absence of busing, what would have remained intact was segregated schools resulting from long-standing residential patterns and government policy. Busing was the means to create integrated schools and overcome residential segregation; anti-busing advocates were against busing, which meant they supported the persistence of racially imbalanced or segregated schools. Reliance on the terminology of anti-busing reveals a reluctance of northern whites, particularly northern white conservative women, to assign their actions—actions that exhibit a deep investment in white supremacist politics and policies—to racist motives. It separates the actions of southern segregationists from segregationists elsewhere. Those who protested busing in Boston upheld the color line, threatened black children, and denied the protections of whiteness to white adherents to the court's decision. They mobilized when and where their authority was challenged. The economic landscape of the city and the particular geographic lines of urban education shaped the place of their resistance, not the nature of it.

The anti-busing terminology also demonstrates a reluctance to look at how black families interpreted such actions. A group of black Roxbury parents wrote to Judge Garrity after white South Boston parents had refused to meet with them to discuss busing. Their letter spoke to the historical betrayal of black Bostonians and of the city's legacy that anti-busers had committed: "In a State of higher education which ran underground railroads for slaves; whose State was one of those who told the South that they were wrong, isn't it amazing that in modern times—the year 1974—we find that our City has residents who practice racism 100%, seven days a week?"[34] Many black Americans realized, "it's not the bus, it's us." When protestors attacked buses with black children on them, talked about oversexed black boys and interracial sex, and practiced verbal and sexual violence on school playgrounds, it was black parents and their children at McKay Elementary School who suffered the repercussions, not the bus. For black families, the economic concerns or complex class politics of the anti-busers were harder to discern.

By naming the protestors "anti-busers," however, opponents of school integration in Boston have operated in different historical and political space from those participating in massive resistance in the civil rights South, perpetuating a false divide in the historiography. Boston's segregationists insisted that they came to anti-busing from working-class concerns, and the scholarship has largely has reflected their own political rhetoric. Yet, their political work affected their white and black neighbors, not suburbanites. This intellectual segregation has rendered investment in property rights and parental rights expressed by northern white women fundamentally different from those same concerns among white southern women whose commitment to sustain and preserve the privileges of whiteness rendered invisible all their other political beliefs. By leaving segregationists sequestered in the South, scholars and policy makers have attenuated massive resistance to its narrowest thread—absolute school segregation—and ignored the political flexibility of segregationists and the diverse strategies they employed. In the end, the goal of anti-busers and segregationists was to prevent meaningful integration whether in rural Mississippi or the birthplace of the American Revolution.

The name "anti-busers," however, focuses on the mode of integration, not the outcome; it makes the bus central instead of the fate of the schoolchildren or the nation's public schools.

While the events in Boston were noteworthy, it is also worth remembering that they were not entirely new. In 1960, white working-class women in New Orleans had acted much like Boston's anti-busers. The primary battleground of resistance for the Ninth Ward cheerleaders and the West Roxbury ROAR members was where their children would meet black classmates, and their actions ensured that even whites willing to integrate might succumb to community pressure. Without the economic security or stability to escape to the suburbs or to take a loss on their property values that they feared integration might bring, they protected their investment in white privilege where they could—in their homes, in their schools, and on the streets. Their protest attested to the broad and long-standing appeal of massive resistance and the multiple fronts on which white privilege would and could be maintained.[35] Certainly the protests in New Orleans in 1960s, in Little Rock in 1957, and those in Boston in 1974 and 1975 were different—they occurred in a different political time and space, in a different legal and legislative atmosphere, and out of some different historical contexts. But they were not entirely different. The hard lines drawn between segregationists in the South and anti-busing advocates nationwide have obscured the continuities and relationships between the two. White women, segregationist and conservative in the South, and white women, segregationist and conservative in the North and West, practiced similar politics, invoked similar white supremacist tropes, capitalized on their identities as mothers, and tied themselves to a broader conservative political language. They participated in a movement long supported and shaped by white women. The Citizens' Councils in Mississippi, Concerned Parent Associations in Charlotte, and the Boston School Committee all guaranteed the persistence of sustained and diverse versions of racial segregation. They ensured that when Jim Crow died, segregation would remain.[36]

As it manifested itself in the early 1970s, anti-busing protests aimed at maintaining school segregation demonstrated how massive resistance to school desegregation had continued its widespread appeal. Expanding the history of massive resistance to anti-busing protests in Boston illuminates the importance of complicating or re-conceptualizing the story of those who resisted racial equality. By the 1970s, segregationists across the nation had orchestrated decades-long opposition to school integration. They had buried the persistence of structural racism behind a story of the legislative end of de jure segregation. They had elevated individual rights and made sacrosanct the rights of families

**FIGURE C.2**  September 2, 1970, protest at Charlotte-Mecklenburg Public School head-quarters. White students adopted the "freedom of choice" language that segregationists had invoked since the *Brown* decision. While black youth in the NAACP watched as white students pledged support for integration but not the busing that would accomplish it. Courtesy of the *Charlotte Observer* and the Robinson-Spangler Carolina Room, Public Library of Charlotte and Mecklenburg County.

to determine their children's education. They had seized the issue of "school choice" and taken it from its dissemination by southern states to circumvent *Brown* and applied it nationwide to the issue of busing. They had worked over decades to sidestep meaningful integration and the larger political agenda of racial equality. After arguing that the end of legal segregation was unconstitutional, they had continued to argue that customary segregation upheld by race-neutral policies was beyond the scope of judicial authority. Reconceived, massive resistance was not confined to the Jim Crow South; it did not die with the defeat of de jure segregation. Its fiercest proponents were not the silenced racist demagogues but the daily grassroots activists who continually reshaped their support for various versions of racial segregation. The national outcry created by busing might not mean that the antibusing protests of the 1970s were separate from the massive resistance, southern-style, in the 1950s and 1960s. Rather, the outrage over busing could be understood as the moment when massive resistance went undeniably national, becoming truly massive.

The meetings, letter-writing campaigns, neighborhood protests, and rural and urban organizing and national networks among white women have revealed several fault lines in the framing of massive resistance, fault lines that

FIGURE C.3 Faced with busing between white and black neighborhoods in Boston, white students and mothers lined the streets. Like suburban white students in Charlotte, these Bostonians claimed they were not against integration, just busing. They rejected identification with white southerners, arguing that their protests were not about racial segregation but about constitutional rights. Courtesy of Spencer Grant and Spencer Grant Collection, Boston Public Library, Boston, Massachusetts.

frustrate the nation's ability to address persistent inequality. Our regional focus and our periodization has limited our understanding of the sustained political work that created a broadly based political movement and that was rooted in what proved to be national opposition to school desegregation, a resistance that was and remains deep and wide. The language of constitutional fiat, of an activist judiciary, and of freedom of choice had long been part of the segregationists' litany, but in the continued resistance to the civil rights movement and the rise of the New Right, this rhetoric allowed dedicated segregationists to rehabilitate their image. This language employed by white women who wanted to secure racial segregation persists as do the institutions where they worked and continue to work. What these women have told us is that a political ideology that was ostensibly race neutral by the 1970s must be understood in the context of a history that reached well back into the 1920s and in conjunction with political involvement that was rarely race neutral. In fact, their political activism was often overt in its pursuit of white racial interest.

Boston's urbanites joined the Sunbelt South's suburbanites and the rural residents of the Deep South in espousing a color-blind political ideology that had been invoked since the 1930s to uphold parental autonomy, homeowners' rights, middle-class consumption, and states' rights. The political language of segregationists attested to the capability of white supremacist politics and systems of racial segregation to adapt to new political landscapes just as the New Right offered a political program that eschewed overtly racist language but that limited the reach of the civil rights movement and the scope of racial equality.[37] In the newly articulated commitment to end legal segregation, some segregationists had created a political home in the emerging New Right. There, they shaped a politics that emphasized breadwinner conservatism, economic growth, limited government, lower taxes, parental control over public schools, family values, and a broader anti-statist, anti-feminist, anti-busing, and anti-international human rights agenda.[38]

While the segregationists of the 1970s drew on the political language of the New Right, they also reached back to the deeper roots of those who supported racial segregation prior to *Brown*, those responsible for massive support of the Jim Crow order. Opposition to the Democratic Party and the United Nations; to the Supreme Court's alleged overreach in the 1950s; to federal involvement in education; and to the political, economic, and civil aspirations of black southerners were political positions that white female segregationists in the South had translated into grassroots, local politics for most of the twentieth century. In their opposition to these issues, southern segregationists had found nationwide allies who shared concerns and political language that de-emphasized overt racism and instead emphasized color-blind constitutional issues.[39] Florence Sillers Ogden, Mary Dawson Cain, Cornelia Dabney Tucker, and Nell Battle Lewis had all, at times, unleashed the language of white supremacy when working to shore up the Jim Crow South and then switched to a more race-neutral political language when they spoke to other audiences inside and outside the South. In doing so, they sought to celebrate common national goals and to reconcile the differences between the political needs of a Jim Crow South and a Jim Crow nation.

This long history of massive resistance has taught us that all segregationists do not look or act alike. At times even the most dedicated female segregationists had tried to strike a more moderate pose, professing to protect the rights of parents and states against an encroaching federal government. Emphasizing the principled and gendered politics of white women, Ogden once described the origins of a protest meeting:

> It called itself. It was what you might call spontaneous combustion—an involuntary and concerted stirring of women all over the State . . . an urge to meet and protest; to stand up and be counted. . . .

The Constitution of the United States . . . [has] been violated. . . . [O]ur children have been subjected to insult and mistreatment. . . . [W]e have been denied the freedom of choice. We have been denied the right to operate our own schools. . . . Many of our constitutional rights have been swept away. The racial issue is but one facet, a mere symptom of the disease. . . . Are we to live by the laws of the Constitution of the United States or by the rule of men? . . . [I]t breaks the heart of a true American woman to have her own country . . . tramp upon our rights and upon our children.[40]

Ogden's language resembled the language of female conservatives in Chicago, Pasadena, and Houston who emphasized a narrow vision of constitutional rights even if it meant that they also supported white supremacist politics. By the 1970s, Boston's anti-busing women offered very similar explanations, reflecting the maturation of massive resistance that pulled in those who supported a version of racial segregation but who would have rejected the label segregationist.

In the 1970s, segregation's activists emphasized their status as mothers, sometimes working mothers or even "militant mothers" as in Boston to separate their anti-busing work from that of unsophisticated, racist southerners. When protesting the ways court decisions hindered their ability to protect and to mold their children, some spoke of declining educational quality, of loss of parental oversight, and of public safety. Then they talked about protecting their daughters from interracial marriage, worrying that integrated schools would erode the cultural prohibitions on choosing black partners that they had instilled in their children. Fewer invoked the fear of oversexed and overly mature black boys seducing or assaulting their daughters, although instances of those remained. In each case, they justified their their political activism in the name of motherhood, attesting to the real power that particular gendered identities carried in the public realm. Often the assertion of "motherhood" was understood to elevate their concerns and grant them a kind of moral supremacy. Maternal politics could be invoked for liberal or conservative causes, but the motherhood claimed by segregationist women in Jackson, Mississippi, in the 1940s or Boston, Massachusetts, in the 1970s was tied to their whiteness and their class position. Their white motherhood meant teaching their children lessons in racial distance, in a racially determined place in society, and in white superiority. Whiteness had so infused definitions of motherhood in the Jim Crow South and a Jim Crow nation that they could hardly be separated.

At times the language of motherhood could paper over class differences and help build grassroots coalitions. In the Jim Crow South, a working-class white mother might not be the keynote speaker at a DAR meeting, but she could make sure that her child's teacher taught about the War between the States rather than the Civil War. At other times, as in the case of the white South Boston mothers, the different circumstances and greater political capital of middle-class white mothers meant conflict with a broader coalition of white working-class mothers. In either case, motherhood offered white segregationists paths to political activism in the very lessons they taught at home. Their identities as mothers were critical to creating a grassroots political movement that married gender roles and white supremacy to a political platform of family autonomy and parental rights. The invocation of "motherhood" further served to set them apart from more progressive women of the 1970s.[41]

When the feminist movement failed to embrace anti-busing as a women's issue or when liberal white women failed to participate in massive resistance, female segregationists looked elsewhere for political support, declaring the women's movement unfriendly to their vision of womanhood. Restricting their daughters' sexual partners was only one way they claimed to protect their children. Walking their children to school, having schools located in their neighborhood, and seeking to preserve their property values and school populations with residential segregation were other ways they could meet their obligations as white mothers. Appropriating traditional gender roles that stressed their child care responsibilities and capitalizing on motherhood to justify their political activism, white women invoked their gender identity to uphold their white privilege. White mothers working for a segregated state had played a central role in the national political mobilization of women and should be considered alongside women who mobilized for equal rights and a more responsive social welfare state.

For white women, massive support for segregation and later massive resistance to those who sought to dismantle it centered on their children's schools. From the hardline segregationists to the South's moderates to the nation's anti-busing women, the school functioned as the political epicenter of their mobilization. Many understood public schools to be an extension of themselves and thus an extension of their values. In many ways, schools were also feminized spaces where women had carved out islands of authority over curriculum, fundraising, textbooks, and teachers. Thus, schools functioned simultaneously as domestic and public institutions. They were both extensions of the home and thus of parental authority and repositories of government policies to create a democratic society. But, in the Jim Crow South, schools were where lessons in white over black were institutionalized and reproduced under state sanction, offering a white supremacist citizenship education. In their rejection of multicultural curriculum in Pasadena, white women achieved similar goals. When integrated public schools threatened their domestic values, segregationist white women moved to distance their families from them. White flight and later "school choice" became the political expressions of national attempts to continue to resist integrated education. The children who heard the shouts of "school choice" in the 1950s, 1960s, and 1970s became the parents on the left and the right who witnessed and supported the rise of "school choice" in the 1990s. Schools were central in the making of massive resistance, and white women's work was central to schools.

Stretching our understanding of massive resistance to address the persistence and shape-shifting qualities of the politics of white supremacy means understanding that the grassroots politics of massive resistance was also a women's movement. The stories of white segregationist women pull us to the local, demonstrating how white supremacist politics and the systems of segregation it sustained were enforced, sustained, and reproduced in communities across the nation. Confronted with white apathy, partisan realignments, Supreme Court decisions, black organizing, the United Nations, and NAACP litigation, white women had to work hard in all the places where white privilege was contested—in social welfare programs, in schools, in neighborhoods, in school board and PTA meetings, in the books they read and the stories they told, and on street corners and bus stops. In the eugenics movement, men did the talking but women cataloged their neighbors and turned in transgressors. When faced with the Democratic Party's new World War II coalition that undermined the Jim Crow order, white women moved away from the Democratic Party, made South Carolina's Republican Party lily white, and energized the Democrats for Eisenhower. In the campaign against the United Nations, women from southern California, Houston, Texas, and the Delta of Mississippi mobilized their PTAs, their reading circles, and their civic clubs to spread the word that internationalism meant the end of their control over the curriculum, over segregation, and over national sovereignty. As the Citizens' Councils faded, white women retooled their segregationist politics into the Women for Constitutional Government—an organization that stressed the need to rein in the federal government. Textbook censorship in the 1970s, echoed the campaigns of the 1920s and 1950s, each one making sure that stories of white over black remained entrenched in the minds of the nation's schoolchildren. And when white students wrote essays on the value of a segregated society in 1959 or picketed against busing in 1970, white women could claim that they had done their job, as a new generation acted out its lessons in white supremacist politics. White women's constant work at multiple levels of society, often took placed beyond the historic gaze and that remains so today. In legal segregation's dying days, its defenders sought to arm it for another political era, ensuring that segregation would outlive its legal collapse.

With white women at the center of the politics of Jim Crow, the silos separating de jure from de facto segregation move closer together. De facto segregation associated with the urban and suburban North had functioned in the South as well in conjunction with and in support of de jure segregation. After the legal dismantling of the South's Jim Crow system in 1964 and 1965, many expressions of customary and cultural segregation remained. The South's white segregationist women had always worked to sustain segregation in law and custom, in policy and practice. For them, customary segregation and legal segregation worked in tandem. De jure segregation distinguished the South for decades, but after its demise, de facto segregation persisted in the South and the nation. When opposition to busing defined the national landscape, the discussions of a racial segregation that developed naturally or even accidentally without government involvement or out of individual innocence were not unknown to white southerners who had long insisted and educated their communities on the naturalness of the Jim Crow system.

In the end, white women's work for massive resistance illuminated just how ubiquitous and enduringly seductive the politics of white supremacy remained decade after decade. Shaping ideas of sex, marriage, and motherhood as well as those about property rights, school curriculum, elections, and culture, legislation was never enough to sustain a Jim Crow South or nation, nor was it enough to destroy it. In the face of legislative defeat, segregationist women continued to craft a broader politics of white supremacy. The deep roots they had long nurtured continued to bear this particularly enduring and familiar fruit. Local policies and politics that continue to frustrate the quest for equality and the entrenched stories that shape American attitudes toward racial change have persisted and have made way for new ones. Grounded in such deep and fertile political soil, the politics of white supremacy and the segregationist women who made it so remain a powerful force in American politics. Where they live and where they work is the ground that still remains contested.

# Notes

INTRODUCTION

1. Pender County Association for the Continuation of Segregation Petition, September 22, 1954, Box 58.2, Folder P, Governor William B. Umstead Papers, North Carolina Division of Archives and History, Raleigh, North Carolina (hereafter cited as NCDAH); Mrs. Hugh P. Bell to Nell Battle Lewis, August 25, 1956, Box 40, Nell Battle Lewis (hereafter cited as NBL) Papers, NCDAH; "Non-Segregation Data for Study, New Hanover State of North Carolina," Box 40, Folder 3, NBL Papers.

2. On interposition, see George Lewis, *Massive Resistance: The White Response to the Civil Rights Movement* (London: Hodder Arnold, 2006), 62–65.

3. Francis Wilhoit, *The Politics of Massive Resistance* (New York: George Braziller, 1973); Numan V. Bartley, *The Rise of Massive Resistance: Race and Politics in the South during the 1950s* (Baton Rouge: Louisiana State University Press, 1969); George Lewis, *The White South and the Red Menace: Segregationists, Anti-Communism and Massive Resistance, 1945–1965* (Gainesville: University of Florida Press, 2004); Lewis, *Massive Resistance*; Clive Webb, ed., *Massive Resistance: Southern Opposition to the Second Reconstruction* (New York: Oxford University Press, 2005); Anders Walker, *The Ghosts of Jim Crow: How Southern Moderates Used Brown v. The Board of Education to Stall Civil Rights* (New York: Oxford University Press, 2009); Neil R. McMillen, *The Citizens' Council: Organized Resistance to the Second Reconstruction, 1954–1964* (Chicago: University of Illinois Press, 1971; reprint edition, 1994), 10.

4. On the end of massive resistance, J. Douglas Smith, *On Democracy's Doorstep: The Inside Story of How the Supreme Court Brought 'One Person, One Vote' to the United States* (New York: Hill and Wang, 2014), 71–98; McMillen, *The Citizens' Council*, 357–363; Jason Sokol, *There Goes My Everything: White Southerners in the Age of Civil Rights, 1945–1975* (New York: Vintage, 2006), 341–357; Lewis, *Massive*

*Resistance*, 167–176. Both Sokol and Lewis are careful to note that the end of massive resistance is hard to discern—multiple iterations of massive resistance shaped the South and nation. Some of those strands meshed with the rising conservative political agenda.

5. For multiple letters and petitions protesting school integration, see Boxes 58.1; Box 58.2; Box 58.3, Umstead Papers, NCDAH. On interposition, see Lewis, *Massive Resistance*, 62–66.

6. Peggy Pascoe, *What Comes Naturally: Miscegenation Law and the Making of Race in America* (New York: Oxford University Press, 2009), 137–140; Miroslava Chavez-Garcia, *States of Delinquency: Race and Science in the Making of California's Judicial System* (Berkeley: University of California Press, 2012), 79–111; Jennifer Ritterhouse, *Growing Up Jim Crow: How Black and White Southern Children Learned Race* (Chapel Hill: University of North Carolina Press, 2006), 55–107; Isaac William Martin, *Rich People's Movements: Grassroots Campaigns to Untax the One Percent* (New York: Oxford University Press, 2013), 113, 125; Ron Formisano, *Boston against Busing: Race, Class and Ethnicity in the 1960s and 1970s* (Chapel Hill: University of North Carolina Press, 1991), xi–xiv, 138–171; Anthony Lukas, *Common Ground: A Turbulent Decade in the Lives of Three American Families* (New York: Knopf, 1985); Tracy E K'Meyer, *Civil Rights in the Gateway to the South: Louisville, KY, 1945–1980* (Lexington: University Press of Kentucky, 2009); Robert Self, *All in the Family: The Realignment of American Democracy since the 1960s* (New York: Hill and Wang, 2012).

7. Donald Critchlow, *Phyllis Schlafly and Grassroots Conservatism: A Woman's Crusade* (Princeton, NJ: Princeton University Press, 2005); Michelle Nickerson, *Mothers of Conservatism: Women and the Postwar Right* (Princeton, NJ: Princeton University Press, 2012); Tom Sugrue, *Sweet Land of Liberty: The Forgotten Struggle for Civil Rights in the North* (New York: Random House, 2008); Kevin Boyle, *Arc of Justice: A Saga of Race, Civil Rights, and Murder in the Jazz Age* (New York: Holt, 2005); Tom Sugrue, *The Origins of the Urban Crisis: Race and Inequality in Postwar Detroit* (Princeton, NJ: Princeton University Press, 2005); Douglas Flamming, *Bound for Freedom: Black Los Angeles in Jim Crow America* (Berkeley: University of California Press, 2006). Arnold Hirsch, "Massive Resistance in the Urban North: Trumbull Park, Chicago, 1953–1966," *Journal of American History* 82 (September 1995): 522–550. For oral history projects that focus on Milwaukee, see http://recollectionwisconsin.org/civil-rights-milwaukee. Nathan D. B. Connolly, *A World More Concrete: Real Estate and the Remaking of Jim Crow South Florida* (Chicago: University of Chicago Press, 2014).

8. Alex Leidholdt, *Battling Nell: The Life of Southern Journalist Cornelia Battle Lewis, 1893–1956* (Baton Rouge: Louisiana State University Press, 2009).

9. Florence Sillers Ogden, "Biography," Florence Sillers Ogden Papers, Charles C. Capps Jr., Archives, Delta State University, Cleveland, Mississippi; hereafter cited as FSO Papers.

10. Lisa Speer, "'Contrary Mary': The Life of Mary Dawson Cain" (Ph.D. diss., University of Mississippi, August 1988).

11. Mary Badham Kittel, *Cornelia Dabney Tucker: The First Republican Southern Belle* (Columbia, SC: R. L. Bryan, 1969).

12. Quoted in Liva Baker, *The Second Battle for New Orleans: The Hundred-Year Struggle to Integrate the Schools* (New York: HarperCollins, 1996), 220; Lillian Smith, *Killers of the Dream* (New York: W.W. Norton; reissue, 1994), 77–79; Ritterhouse, *Growing Up Jim Crow*, 78–81.

13. Anna Krome-Lukens, "A Great Blessing to Defective Humanity: Women and the Eugenics Movement in North Carolina 1910–1940" (MA Thesis, University of North Carolina-Chapel Hill, 2009), 6–9; Gregory Dorr, *Segregation's Science: Eugenics and Society in Virginia* (Charlottesville: University of Virginia Press, 2008), 138–166.

14. Katherine Mellen Charron, *Freedom's Teacher: The Life of Septima Clark* (Chapel Hill: University of North Carolina Press, 2009), 3, 33, 40.

15. For work on schools as sites of reproduction of class, race, and sexual hierarchies, see Michael Apple, *Ideology and Curriculum*, 2nd ed. (New York: Routledge, 1990); Francis Fitzgerald, *America Revised: History Schoolbooks in the Twentieth Century* (Boston: Little, Brown, 1979); Diane Ravitch, *The Troubled Crusade: American Education, 1945–1989* (New York: Basic Books, 1983); and Diane Ravitch, *Left Back: A Century of Failed School Reforms* (New York: Simon and Schuster, 2000). For the specific role American history textbooks and curriculum have played in reflecting dominant social values, see Joseph Moreau, *Schoolbook Nation: Conflicts over American History Textbooks from Civil War to Present* (Ann Arbor: University of Michigan Press, 2004). While Moreau describes how a white southern interpretation became dominant in the first half of the twentieth century, he also demonstrates how textbooks and curriculum were often sites of conflict between groups competing for particular visions of the United States. For a more regional treatment, see Fred Bailey, "Textbooks of the Lost Cause: Censorship and the Creation of Southern State Histories." *Georgia Historical Quarterly* 75 (Fall 1991): 507–533; Adam Laats, *The Other School Reformers: Conservative Activism in American Education* (Cambridge, MA: Harvard University Press, 2015), 15, 19, 23.

16. Lorraine Gates Schuyler, *The Weight of Their Votes: Southern Women and Political Leverage in the 1920s* (Chapel Hill: University of North Carolina Press, 2006), 10–11.

17. The term "culture talk" comes from Mahmood Mamdani, *Good Muslim, Bad Muslim: America, the Cold War, and the Roots of Terror* (New York: Harmony, 2005), 17–20. He defines culture talk as conversation that "assumes that every culture has a tangible essence that defines it, and it then explains politics as a consequence of that essence." On Washington versus Cleaver, see Carol Mason, *Reading Appalachia from Left to Right: Conservatives and the 1974 Kanawha County Textbook Controversy* (Ithaca, NY: Cornell University Press, 2009), 21–22, 155–162.

18. James C. Cobb, *The South since World War II* (New York: Oxford University Press, 2011), 235; Hollinger Barnard, ed., *Outside the Magic Circle: The Autobiography of Virginia Durr* (Tuscaloosa: University of Alabama Press, 1985); Anne Loveland, *A Southerner Confronting the South: A Biography* (Baton Rouge: Louisiana State University Press, 1986); Catherine Fosl, *Subversive Southerner: Anne Braden and the Struggle for Racial Justice in the Cold War South* (New York: Palgrave Macmillan, 2002), 117–121.

19. Connolly, *A World More Concrete*; J. Douglas Smith, *Managing White Supremacy: Race, Politics, and Citizenship in Jim Crow Virginia* (Chapel Hill: University of North Carolina Press, 2002); Joseph Crespino, *In Search of Another Country: Mississippi and the Conservative Counterrevolution* (Princeton, NJ: Princeton University Press, 2007).

20. Lisa McGirr, *Suburban Warriors: The Origins of the New American Right* (Princeton, NJ: Princeton University Press, 2001); Nickerson, *Mothers of Conservatism*; Critchlow, *Phyllis Schlafly*; Kirsten Delegard, *Battling Miss Bolsheviki: The Origins of Female Conservatism in the United States* (Philadelphia: University of Pennsylvania Press, 2012), 85–112. For an approach that emphasizes not Sunbelt conservatives' commitment to white supremacist politics but southern whites' conservative beliefs beyond a commitment to segregation, see Joseph Crespino, "Strom Thurmond's Sunbelt: Rethinking Regional Politics and the Rise of the Right," in *Sunbelt Rising: The Politics of Space, Place, and Region*, ed. Michelle Nickerson and Darren Dochuk (Philadelphia: University of Pennsylvania Press, 2011), 60; Matthew D. Lassiter, "Big Government and Family Values: Political Culture in the Metropolitan Sunbelt," in *Sunbelt Rising*, 84–85.

21. Jason Morgan Ward, *Defending White Democracy: The Making of a Segregationist Movement and the Remaking of Racial Politics, 1936–1965*, (Chapel Hill: University of North Carolina Press, 2011)

22. On color-blind rhetoric, see Matthew D. Lassiter, *The Silent Majority: Suburban Politics in the Sunbelt South* (Princeton, NJ: Princeton University Press, 2006), 13–14; Lewis, *Massive Resistance*, 180–185; Crespino, *In Search of Another Country*, 8.

23. Charles Payne, *I've Got the Light of Freedom: The Organizing Tradition and the Mississippi Freedom Struggle* (Berkeley: University of California Press, 1995), 3, 426, 439, 441; John Dittmer, *Local People: The Struggle for Civil Rights in Mississippi* (Chicago: University of Illinois Press, 1994); Chana Kai Lee, *For Freedom's Sake: The Life of Fannie Lou Hamer* (Chicago: University of Chicago Press, 1999); Christina Greene, *Our Separate Ways: Women and the Black Freedom Movement in Durham, North Carolina* (Chapel Hill: University of North Carolina Press, 2005); Charron, *Freedom's Teacher*, 168; Glenda Gilmore, *Defying Dixie: The Radical Roots of Civil Rights, 1919–1950* (New York: W. W. Norton, 2008); Francoise Hamlin, *Crossroads at Clarksdale: The Black Freedom Struggle in the Mississippi Delta after World War II* (Chapel Hill: University of North Carolina Press, 2012).

24. Gwendolyn Mink, *The Wages of Motherhood: Inequality in the Welfare State, 1917– 1942* (Ithaca, NY: Cornell University Press, 1995), 5, 26. Mink argues that maternalist policies bred a type of racial liberalism. Most scholarship distinguishes between different ideological versions of maternalism but does not link it to regional variations. For discussions of maternalist politics in this period, see Molly Ladd-Taylor, *Mother-Work: Women, Child Welfare, and the State, 1890–1930* (Chicago: University of Illinois Press, 1994); Joanne L. Goodwin, "An American Experiment in Paid Motherhood: The Implementation of Mothers' Pensions in Early Twentieth Century Chicago," *Gender and History* 4 (Autumn 1992): 322– 342; Molly Ladd-Taylor and Lauri Umansky, eds., *"Bad" Mothers: The Politics of Blame in Twentieth Century America* (New York: New York University Press, 1998), 10–12; Seth Koven and Sonya Michel, eds., *Mothers of a New World: Maternalist Politics and the Origins of Welfare States* (Routledge: New York, 1993); Linda Gordon, ed., *Women, the State, and Welfare* (Madison: University of Wisconsin Press, 1990); Robin Muncy, *Creating a Female Dominion in American Reform, 1890–1935* (New York: Oxford University Press, 1991); Theda Skocpol, Marjorie Abend-Wein, Christopher Howard, and Susan Goodrich, "Women's Associations and the Enactment of Mother's Pensions in the United States," *American Political Science Review* 87 (September 1993): 686–701. For more recent work, see Nickerson, *Mothers of Conservatism.*

25. Patricia Sullivan, *Days of Hope: Race and Democracy in the New Deal Era* (Chapel Hill: University of North Carolina Press, 1996).

26. On World War II's effect on southern race and labor relations, see Patricia Sullivan, *Days of Hope*, 6–9, 134, 133–167; John Egerton, *Speak Now against the Day: The Generation before the Civil Rights Movement in the South* (Chapel Hill: University of North Carolina Press, 1995), 324–329; Barbara Griffith, *The Crisis of American Labor: Operation Dixie and the Defeat of the CIO* (Philadelphia: Temple University Press, 1988), 12–21; John Dittmer, *Local People: The Struggle for Civil Rights in Mississippi* (Urbana: University of Illinois Press, 1995), 1–18; Stephen Lawson, *Black Ballots: Voting Rights in the South, 1944–1969* (New York: Columbia University Press, 1976), 38–54, 65–78. On the Eleanor Clubs, see Bryant Simon, "Fearing Eleanor and the Wartime Racial Anxieties, 1940– 1945," in *Labor in the Modern South*, ed. Glen Eskew (Athens: University of Georgia Press, 2001), 83–101; Howard D. Odum, *Race and Rumors of Race: Challenge to American Crisis* (Chapel Hill: University of North Carolina Press, 1943), 67–89; note Robert R. Korstad, *Civil Rights Unionism: Tobacco Workers and the Struggle for Democracy in the Mid-Twentieth Century South* (Chapel Hill: University of North Carolina Press, 2003); Numan Bartley, *The New South, 1945–1980* (Baton Rouge: Louisiana State University Press, 1995), 1–37; Jeffrey J. Crow, Paul D. Escott, and Flora J. Hatley, *A History of African Americans in North Carolina* (Raleigh: Division of Archives and History, 1992), 145–152; Harvard Sitkoff, "African American Militancy in the World War II South: Another

Perspective," in *Remaking Dixie: The Impact of World War II on the American South*, ed. Neil R. McMillen (Jackson: University of Mississippi Press, 1997), 89–91; Egerton, *Speak Now*, 202–330; Joel Williamson, *A Rage for Order: Black-White Relations in the American South since Emancipation* (New York: Oxford University Press, 1986), 152–205; James C. Cobb, "World War II and the Mind of the Modern South," in *Remaking Dixie*, 5, 8–9. Morton Sosna, *In Search of the Silent South: Southern Liberals and the Race Issue* (New York: Columbia University Press, 1977).

27. Duane Tananbaum, *The Bricker Amendment Controversy: A Test of Eisenhower's Political Leadership* (Ithaca, NY: Cornell University Press, 1988).

28. On the link between racial segregation, anti-communism, and international politics, see Ann Ziker, "Race, Conservative Politics, and U.S. Foreign Policy in the Postcolonial World, 1948–1968" (Ph.D. diss., Rice University, 2008), and Margaret Nunnelley Olsen, "One Nation, One World: American Clubwomen and the Politics of Internationalism, 1945–1961 (Ph.D. diss., Rice University, 2007); Penny Von Eschen, *Race against Empire: Black Americans and Anticolonialism, 1937–1957* (Ithaca, NY: Cornell University Press, 1997); on a broader conservative movement, see Nickerson, *Mothers of Conservatism*. On southern conservatism, see Dan Carter, "More Than Race: Conservatism in the White South Since V. O. Key," in *Unlocking V.O. Key, Jr.: Southern Politics for the Twenty-First Century*, ed. Angie Maxwell and Todd G. Shields (Little Rock: University of Arkansas Press, 2011), 129–160.

29. Formisano, *Boston against Busing*, xi–xiv, 138–171; Lukas, *Common Ground*, 18–22; K'Meyer, *Civil Rights in the Gateway to the South*, 259–281.

30. At a national level, William Buckley and the *National Review* exhibited both; see David Farber, *The Rise and Fall of Modern American Conservatism: A Short History* (Princeton, NJ: Princeton University Press, 2010), 71–74, Donald Critchlow and Nancy MacLean, *Debating the American Conservative Movement 1945 to the Present* (New York: Rowman and Littlefield, 2010), 27, 32. Phyllis Schafly did not espouse such overtly white supremacist views but she believed that communists and communist ideology informed many civil rights activists.

31. McGirr, *Suburban Warriors;* Nickerson, *Mothers of Conservatism*; see Jonathan Schoenwald, *A Time for Choosing: The Rise of the Modern American Conservatism* (New York: Free Press, 2000); George H. Nash, *The Conservative Intellectual Movement in America since 1945* (New York: Basic Books, 1976).

32. Crespino, "Strom Thurmond's Sunbelt," 60.

33. My analysis here falls between historians who see the South as outside the normative narrative of American history and those who see the South and America as interchangeable after World War II. Southern segregationists as well as black civil rights activists spoke about particular southern experiences that defined their world. For a brief treatment of this debate, see Joseph Crespino and Matthew D.

Lassiter, eds., *The Myth of Southern Exceptionalism* (New York: Oxford University Press, 2009), 3–22.

CHAPTER 1

1. Walter Plecker to Mr. W. H. Clark, July 29, 1924, Box 41, Folder 10, Papers of John Powell, 1888-1978, n.d., Accession #7284, 7284-a, Albert and Shirley Small Special Collections Library, University of Virginia Charlottesville, Virginia; hereafter cited as John Powell Papers; Obituary, "Mrs. Reid McGuffin Henry," [1975?] Clipping File, Rockbridge Regional Library, Lexington, Virginia; Bobby Sue Henry, "Crossroads School," June 16, 1990, Clipping File, Rockbridge Regional Library, Lexington, Virginia. "Population Schedule for Amherst County, Virginia, South River District," Series 625, Roll 1906, page 238, Fourteenth U.S. Census, 1920, at http://o-persi.heritagequestonline.com; "Reid McGuffin 'Mike' Henry," *Rockbridge County Virginia Heritage Book, 1878–1997* (Rockbridge Area Genealogical Society, 1997), 222.

2. On eugenics in Virginia, see Paul Lombardo, "Miscegenation, Eugenics and Racism: Historical Footnotes to *Loving* v. *Virginia*," *University of California, Davis, Law Review*, 21 (1988), 451–452. For an overview of the rise of eugenics in the United States, see Daniel Kevles, *In the Name of Eugenics: Genetics and the Uses of Human Heredity* (New York: Alfred A. Knopf, 1985), 20–112; Dorr, *Segregation's Science*, 1–18; Ariela Gross, *What Blood Won't Tell: A History of Race on Trial in America* (Cambridge, MA: University of Harvard Press, 2008), 100; Phyl Newbeck, *Virginia Hasn't Always Been for Lovers: Interracial Marriage Bans and the Case of Richard and Mildred Loving* (Carbondale: Southern Illinois University Press, 2004), 52–56; Richard B. Sherman, "'The Last Stand': The Fight for Racial Integrity in Virginia in the 1920s," *Journal of Southern History* 54, no. 1 (February 1988): 69–92; Smith, *Managing White Supremacy*, 89–100; Peter Wallenstein, *Tell the Court I Love My Wife: Race, Marriage, and Law—An American History* (New York: Palgrave Macmillan, 2002), 139–141. Before 1912, in Virginia "black" meant a minimum of one-quarter "black blood." The last official census count of mulattos would be in 1920. See Joel Williamson, *New People: Miscegenation and Mulattos in the United States* (New York: Free Press, 1980), 97, 112–115.

3. Scott Nelson, *Steel Drivin' Man John Henry: The Untold Story of an American Legend* (New York: Oxford University Press, 2006), 4; Melanie D. Haimes-Bartolf, "The Social Construction of Race and Monacan Education in Amherst County, Virginia, 1908–1965: Monacan Perspective," *History of Education Quarterly* (November 2007): 391–415; "A Trip Down Irish Creek," August 17, 1939, clipping, Withrow Scrapbooks, vol. 5, Washington and Lee Special Collections, Washington and Lee University, Lexington, Virginia; "Irish Creek School Known in Far-Off Wisconsin," *LaFollette's Weekly*, (1915), Withrow Scrapbooks, vol. 3, Washington

and Lee Special Collections; Donna Huffer, "Irish Creek Had School," *News and Gazette* (Lexington, Virginia), November 6, 1985.

4. On Plecker, Pascoe, *What Comes Naturally*, 138–152.

5. For a discussion of this tri-racial history and how it manifested itself in Creek and Cherokee and Lumbee communities, see Claudio Saunt, *Black, White and Indian: Race and the Unmaking of an American Family* (New York: Oxford University Press, 2005); and Tiya Miles, *The Ties that Bind: An Afro-Cherokee Family in Slavery and Freedom* (Berkeley: University of California Press, 2005); Malinda Maynor Lowery, *Race, Identity, and the Making of a Nation: Lumbee Indians in the Jim Crow South* (Chapel Hill: University of North Carolina Press, 2010). On the Clarks, see Donna Huffer, interview with Mary Martin, 1985 (In possession of author); Donna Huffer, *Fare Thee Well, Old Joe Clark: History of the Clark Family of Rockbridge County* (2005) Typescript in author's possession.

6. For an early history of the area, see Samuel R. Cook, "The Monacan Indian Nation: Asserting Tribal Sovereignty in the Absence of Federal Recognition," *Wicazo Sa Review* 17, no. 2, (Autumn 2002), 96–97. "Mulatto" was a term used in the census from 1850 until 1920. For an early study of the development of this term, see Williamson, *New People*, xii, 25–26. In 1850, Virginia and Kentucky together had one-third of the entire southern mulatto population. Virginia had 80,000 mulattos of the total 350,000 southwide. In fact, Williamson argues that the upper south and in particular Virginia could have earned the designation "the mulatto belt" in contrast to the Deep South's "black belt." In Virginia, Maryland, the District of Columbia, Delaware, and North Carolina, 50 percent of the mulatto population was free. This is in deep contrast to the lower South and also the Upper south states to the west. In the upper South, the census suggests that "mulattoes" lived in rural areas more than urban areas. See Robert P. McNamara, Maria Tempenis, and Beth Walton, *Crossing the Line: Interracial Couples in the South* (Westport, CT: Praeger, 1999), 26. For broader works on mixed race identities and miscegenation, see John Inscoe, *Writing the South through Self: Explorations in Southern Autobiography* (Athens: University of Georgia Press, 2011); Williamson, *New People*, ix; Gary Nash, *Forbidden Love: The Secret History of Mixed-Race America* (New York: Henry Holt, 1999); Scott Malcomson, *One Drop of Blood: The American Misadventure of Race* (New York: Farrar, Straus and Giroux, 2000); Gayle Wald, *Crossing the Line: Racial Passing in Twentieth Century Literature and Culture* (Durham, NC: Duke University Press, 2000); Gross, *What Blood Won't Tell*; Pascoe, *What Comes Naturally*. See also essays in Martha Hodes, ed., *Sex, Love, Race: Crossing Boundaries in North American History* (New York: New York University Press, 1999); Allyson Hobbs, *A Chosen Exile: A History of Racial Passing in American Life* (Cambridge, MA: Harvard University Press, 2014), 23.

7. Charles Wynes, "The Evolution of Jim Crow Laws in Twentieth Century Virginia," *Phylon* 28, no. 4 (Winter 1967): 416–425.

8. Walter Plecker to Mr. W. H. Clark, July 29, 1924, Box 41, Folder 10, John Powell Papers; Walter Plecker to Mrs. Robert Cheatham and Mrs. Mary Giddon, April 30, 1924, Box 41,Folder 7 John Powell Papers.

9. W. A. Plecker to Aileen Goodman Henry, March 10, 1943, Box 42, Folder 15, John Powell Papers; on women's racial work for the Progressive Era state, Chavez-Garcia, *States of Delinquency*, 7; Pascoe, *What Comes Naturally*, 9.

10. Chavez-Garcia, *States of Delinquency*, 82–98; Pascoe, *What Comes Naturally*, 138–139.

11. Nyan Shah, *Stranger Intimacy: Contesting Race, Sexuality, and the Law in the North American West* (Berkeley: University of California Press, 2011), 163; Khalil Gibran Muhammad, *The Condemnation of Blackness: Race, Crime, and Making of Modern Urban America* (Cambridge, MA: Harvard University Press, 2010), 144.

12. Barbara Bair, "Remapping the Black/White Body: Sexuality, Nationalism, and Biracial Antimiscegenation Activism in 1920s Virginia," in *Sex, Love, and Race: Crossing Boundaries in North American History*, ed. Martha Hodes (New York: New York University Press, 1999), 410.

13. On women's particular perceived fitness for eugenics field work, see Hasian Arif Marouf, *The Rhetoric of Eugenics in Anglo-American Thought* (Athens: University of Georgia Press, 1996), 81–85.

14. Pascoe, *What Comes Naturally*, 139; Chavez-Garcia, *States of Delinquency*, 85–87; Michael Apple, *Teachers and Texts: A Political Economy of Class and Gender Relations in Education* (New York: Routledge, 1988), 60.

15. Walter Plecker to Harry Davis, October 4, 1924, Box 41, Folder 20, John Powell Papers; "Virginia Bureau of Child Welfare Help for Midwives," pamphlet (Richmond: State Publishing, 1924), www.encyclopediavirginia.org.

16. Bair, "Remapping the Black/White Body," 408, 412.

17. Chavez-Garcia, *States of Delinquency*, 7–13.

18. A sample of these writings include Madison Grant, *The Passing of the Great Race or the Racial Basis of European History* (New York: C. Scribner, 1918); Lothrap Stoddard, *The Rising Tide of Color against White World Supremacy* (New York: C. Scribner, 1920); and Earnest Cox, *White America* (Richmond: White America Society, 1923, 1925, 1937). Davenport published more often in scientific journals; see Joseph Spiro, *Defending the Master Race: Conservation, Eugenics and the Legacy of Madison Grant* (Burlington: University of Vermont Press, 2009), 423.

19. Muhammad, *The Condemnation of Blackness*, 10–11; Kevles, *In the Name of Eugenics*, 74–76.

20. Shah, *Intimate Matters*, 163.

21. Oren F. Morton, *A History of Rockbridge County, Virginia* (Staunton, VA: McClure, 1920).

22. James C. Scott, *Seeing Like a State: How Certain Schemes to Improve the Human Condition Have Failed* (New Haven, CT: Yale University Press, 1998), 2–6.

23. "Monacan Indian Tribal Association," typescript, [1990?] "Indians, Monacan, Local History" Vertical File, Rockbridge Regional Library; David I. Bushnell, "The Indian Inhabitants of the Valley of Virginia," *Virginia Magazine of History and Biography* 34, no. 4 (October 1926): 295–298; Cook, "The Monacan Indian Nation," 91–116. Rosemary Whitlock, *The Monacan Indian Nation of Virginia: The Drums of Life*, (Tuscaloosa: University of Alabama Press, 2008), 1–18.

24. Huffer, *History of the Clark Family of Rockbridge County* (2005).

25. Gross, *What Blood Won't Tell*, 111–139.

26. Huffer, *Fare Thee Well, Old Joe Clark;* Donna Huffer, "Irish Creek Had School," *News-Gazette* (Lexington), November 6, 1985, page 10.

27. In 1880, Amherst County had a 53 percent white, 36 percent black, and 10 percent mulatto population. Heritage Quest at Heritage Quest On-Line. Originally, I compiled the county level and family data from the Historical Census Browser from the University of Virginia, Geospatial and Statistical Data Center. That browser ended service in December 2016. The same census data can be accessed at the database, Steven Ruggles, Katie Genadek, Ronald Goeken, Josiah Grover, and Matthew Sobek, *Integrated Public Use Microdata Series: Version 6.0* [dataset] (Minneapolis: University of Minnesota, 2015), http://doi.org/10.18128/D010. V6.0, hereafter cited as IPUMS. In some census sheets, workers designated individuals with a T that perhaps meant tri-racial as it referred to individuals with surnames associated with mulatto or Indian identities. T was not a designation included in instructions to enumerators; Amherst County Census Data, 1880, 1900, 1910, 1920, IPUMS. For individual names, see Heritage Quest On-Line, https://www.ancestryheritagequest.com/HQA.

28. For examples of the racial categories in the census, see facsimiles of the "Enumerator Instructions" given to census takers," Steven Ruggles, J. Trent Alexander Katie Genadek, Ronald Goeken, Matthew B. Schroeder, and Matthew Sobek, *Integrated Public Use Microdata Series: Version 5.0* [Machine-readable database] (Minneapolis: University of Minnesota, 2010), http://usa.ipums.org/usa/voliii/. Instructions in 1890 listed distinctions between blacks, mulattos, quadroons, and octaroons. In 1900, no mulatto category was listed, nor did quadroon or octaroon appear. In 1910, the mulatto category reappeared and was defined as "some percentage of Negro blood." In 1920, the instructions defined mulatto as someone with "a percentage of white blood." The census of 1930 included mulatto but offered no definition that would characterize a person as such. The 1930 census did list "Mus" and "In" as possible descriptions but instruction number 151 said "A person of mixed and Negro blood should be returned as Negro, no matter how small the percentage of Negro blood. Both black and mulatto persons are to be returned as Negroes, without distinction. A person of mixed Indian and Negro blood should be returned as Negro, unless the Indian blood predominates and the status as an

Indian is generally accepted in the community." Instruction number 152. *"Indians.-* A person of mixed white and Indian blood should be returned as Indian, except where the percentage of Indian blood is very small, or where he is regarded as a white person by those in the community where he lives. (See par. 151 for mixed Indian and Negro.)"

29. "Inhabitants in South River District in County of Rockbridge in State of Virginia," Schedule 1, Series T9, Roll 1388, Page 226, 1880 United States Census; "Inhabitants in South River District in County of Rockbridge in State of Virginia," Schedule 1, Series T623, Roll 1726, Page 194, 1900 United States Census; "Inhabitants in South River District in County of Rockbridge in State of Virginia," Schedule 1, Series T624, Roll 1647, Page 193, 1910 United States Census; "Inhabitants in South River District in County of Rockbridge in State of Virginia," Schedule 1, Series 625, Roll 1906, Page 243, 1920 United States Census, Heritage Quest On-Line.

30. In Heritage Quest On-Line, the 1880 composite list of Johns included children and heads of household. In subsequent composite lists, the number listed was just heads of household and children in the Epileptic Colony in the county. All the census information is from Amherst County, Virginia, "Schedule 1—Population," 1880 United States Census, 1900 United States Census, 1910 United States Census, and 1920 United States Census. I double checked the racial categories on the composite lists against the names on the actual population schedule. Therefore, the numbers of each Johns head of household reflects the actual schedule and not the composite list for the county.

31. For Kate Johns, "Schedule 1, Population, Amherst Courthouse Township, Amherst County, Virginia," Series T623, Roll 1699, Page 3, 1900 US Census; "Schedule 1, Population, Amherst Courthouse Township, Amherst County, Virginia," Series T624, Roll 1621, Page 43, 1910 US Census; "Schedule 1, Population, Amherst Courthouse Township—Western District, Amherst County, Virginia," Series 626, Roll 2434, page 118, 1930 US Census.

32. In 1900, the categories seemed to include only black and white; however, in Amherst County there is a lone designation of I for an Indian woman. Before 1890, those who claimed Indian identity were most often designated as mulatto. On the census in this period and its role in segregation, see Pascoe, *What Comes Naturally*, 149. For broader treatment of the census, see Williamson, *New People*, 112–114; Hobbs, *Chosen Exile*, 23. For a general treatment of the relationship between the census and nation-building, see Benedict Anderson, *Imagined Communities: Reflections on the Origin and Spread of Nationalism* (New York: Verso, revised edition, 2006; Verso, 1983), 163–170.

33. Katherine M. B. Osburn, "The 'Identified Full-Bloods' in Mississippi: Race and Choctaw Identity, 1898–1918," *Ethnohistory* 56, no. 3 (Summer 2009): 424–425. For the relationship between racial segregation and Indian communities off reservation lands, see Lowery, *Lumbee Indians in the Jim Crow South*, 19–54, 213–250; Gross, *What Blood Won't Tell*, 138.

34. Bair, "Remapping," 403, 404; Smith, *Managing White Supremacy*, 102; Dorr, *Segregation's Science*, 145.

35. Derryn E. Moton, "Racial Integrity or 'Race Suicide': Virginia's Eugenic Movement, W. E. B. Du Bois, and the Work of Walter A. Plecker," *Negro History Bulletin* (April–September, 1999), 5; John Powell to *Negro World*, August 22, 1925 Box 39, Folder 62, John Powell Papers; Bair, "Remapping," 404, 408; Dorr, *Segregation's Science*, 111. Sherman, "The Last Stand: The Fight for Racial Integrity," 77; Gregory Michael Dorr, "Assuring America's Place in the Sun: Ivey Foreman Lewis and the Teaching of Eugenics at the University of Virginia, 1915–1953," *Journal of Southern History* 66, no. 2 (May 2000): 257–259, 265–270; Wynes, "The Evolution of Jim Crow Laws," 416–425. On the role of research universities in eugenics, see Edward Larson, *Sex, Race, and Science: Eugenics in the Deep South* (Baltimore, MD: Johns Hopkins University Press, 1995), 40–42. "Addresses of Women's Racial Integrity Club of Richmond, Virginia, 1926," Folder 3, Box 56, Plecker to Mrs. Augusta B. Fothergill, January 21, 1928, Folder 50, Box 41, Dr. Mary B. Baughman to John Powell, August 20, 1927, Box 39, Folder 102, John Powell Papers; Earnest S. Cox, White America (1925). Cox communicated with Nazi officials both before and after World War II. See Peter Hardin, "'Documentary Genocide' Families' Surnames on Racial Hit List," *Richmond Times-Dispatch*, March 5, 2000; Warren Fiske, "The Black and White World of Walter Plecker," *Virginian-Pilot*, April 2004.

36. For information on Davenport's lab at Cold Springs Harbor, see Dorr, *Segregation's Science*, 72–77; Hasian, *The Rhetoric of Eugenics*, 106–115; Kevles, *In the Name of Eugenics*, 45–48, 55–67; Dorr, *Segregation's Science*, 145.

37. Mary B. Baughman to John Powell, August 20, 1927, Box 39, Folder 102; "Addresses of W.R.I. Club of Richmond, VA, 1926," typescript, Box 56, Folder 3; Mrs, Smith Brockenbrough to John Powell, February 2, 1926, Box 4, Folder 10; Director to Mrs. Augustus B. Fothergill, January 21, 1928, Box 41, Folder 50; Walter Plecker to Arthur P. Gray, March 2, 1926, Box 41, Folder 45; John Powell Papers.

38. Arthur Estabrook, *The Jukes in 1915* (Washington, DC: Carnegie Institute of Washington, 1916); R. L. Dugdale, *'The Jukes': A Study in Crime, Pauperism, Disease, and Heredity* (New York: G. Putnam, 1891); Paul Lombardo, *Three Generations, No Imbeciles: Eugenics, the Supreme Court, and Buck v. Bell* (Baltimore, MD: Johns Hopkins University Press, 2010).

39. Louisa Hubbard to Arthur Estabrook, February 1, 1923, Box 1, Folder 2, Arthur Estabrook Scrapbook, Box 1, Folder 26, Arthur Estabrook Papers, M. E. Grenander Departments of Special Collections and Archives, University Library, University at Albany, State University of New York, Albany, New York, http://meg.library. albany.edu:8080/archive/view?docId=apapo69.xml. Also available at http:// www.eugenicsarchive.org/html/eugenics/index2.html?tag=1258.

40. Hasian, *The Rhetoric of Eugenics*, 82; Kevles, *In the Name of Eugenics*, 41–56; Amy Sue Bix, "Experiences and Voices of Eugenics Field-Workers: 'Women's Work' in Biology," *Social Studies of Science* 27 (1997): 649, 657, 658.

41. Kevles, *In the Name of Eugenics*, 50–55; Chavez-Garcia, *States of Delinquency*, 85; Muhammad, *The Condemnation*, 243.

42. "Field work for Mongrel Virginians in Amherst County, Virginia," Arthur Estabrook Scrapbook, Box 1, Folder 26, Arthur Estabrook Papers.

43. For a similar treatment of Mexican-American youth in California, see Chavez-Garcica, *States of Delinquency*, 85, 90.

44. Dorr, *Segregation's Science*, 113.

45. Huffer, "Irish Creek Had School," *News-Gazette*, November 6, 1985, page 2; Whitlock, *The Monacan Indian Nation*, 119.

46. Arthur Estabrook and Ivan McDougle, *Mongrel Virginians: The WIN Tribe* (Baltimore, MD: Williams and Wilkins, 1926), 161, 157.

47. "Original informant notes, Louisa Hubbard," field notes, handwritten, February 1, 1923; "Informant notes Miss Isabel Wagner (undated typescript), all in Box 1, Folder 25, Estabrook Papers.

48. Estabrook and McDougle, *Mongrel Virginians*, 161, 157; Chavez-Garcia, *States of Delinquency*, 99-102.

49. Estabrook and McDougle, *Mongrel Virginians,* 38–42.

50. Hardin, "'Documentary Genocide' Families"; Peter Hardin, "Eugenics Affected Va. Law: Theory Advocated Social Engineering," *Richmond Times Dispatch*, March 5, 2000; interview with William E. Sandidge in Whitlock, *The Monacan Indian Nation of Virginia*, 45–46.

51. Plecker to Graham, August 9, 1940, Box 41, Folder 90; Plecker to Mrs. Nancy Hundley, July 19 and July 27, 1943, Box 42, Folders 41 and 46, John Powell Papers.

52. "Virginia Has a New Color Law," *Dallas Express*, March 29, 1924, Reel 20, "Amalgamation—1924 Virginia," Tuskegee Institute News Clipping File (Division of Behavioral Science Research, Tuskegee Institute, 1976); Lombardo, "Miscegenation, Eugenics, and Racism," 421, 445.

53. Plecker to Miss Elise K. Graham, August 9, 1940, Box 42, Folder 41, John Powell Papers; Plecker to Local Registrars, Physicians, Health Offices, Nurses, School Superintendents, and Clerks of Courts (December 1942?), Walter Plecker Letters: A Series of Letters Relating to the Melungeons of Newman's Ridge, www.geocities.com/ourmelungeons/plecker.html.

54. Sherman, "The Last Stand," 70; Estimates by historian Gary Nash suggest that the practice of passing did increase during the Jim Crow Era. See Nash, *Forbidden Love*, 106; Gross, *What Blood Won't Tell*, 117; Plecker to Harry Davis, October 4, 1924, Box 41, Folder 20, John Powell Papers.

55. Plecker to John Powell, April 27, 1925, Box 41, Folder 40, Plecker to Major Earnest Cox, August 9, 1924, Box 41, Folder 16, John Powell Papers. Cook, *Monacans and Miners*, 107. Cook attributes the rumor's origin to Plecker but with little evidence.

56. On the Johns ancestry, see Samuel Cook, *Monacans and Miners: Native American and Coal Mining Communities in Appalachia* (Lincoln: University of Nebraska Press, 2000), 59–60; Sherrie McLeRoy and William McLeRoy, *Strangers in Their Midst: The Free Black Population of Amherst County*, rev. ed. (Berwyn Heights, MD: Heritage, 2009); Peter Houck, *Indian Island in Amherst County*, 2nd ed. (Lynchburg, VA: Warwick House, 1930).

57. *Lexington Gazette*, September 10, 1924; Pascoe, *What Comes Naturally*, 148.

58. *Rockbridge County News*, November 20, 1924; *Lexington-Gazette*, November 26, 1924. *County News*, November 27, 1924;

59. Plecker to John Powell, April 27, 1925, Box 56, Folder 2, John Powell Papers.

60. Plecker to Grace Davidson, October 4, 1935, Folder 59, Box 41, John Powell Papers.

61. Plecker to Lizzie Ware, October 2, 1935, Box 41, Folder 58, John Powell Papers.

62. Plecker to L. G. Moffatt, April 21, 1943, Folder 5, Box 56, John Powell Papers.

63. Haimes-Bartolf, "The Social Construction of Race and Monacan Education," 389–415; Hardin, " 'Documentary Genocide' Families."

64. Virginia led the country with this law, but similar laws would be enacted in all but eighteen other states. Louisiana and North Carolina followed Virginia. Louisiana passed a Racial Integrity Law preventing white and Indian intermarriage in 1920 and tightened the definition of white throughout the interwar period. In 1949, Naomi Drake took over Louisiana's Bureau of Vital Statistics and invoking the 1938 one-drop rule began to reclassify people based on a race list similar to Plecker's hit list. See Victoria Dominguez, *White by Definition: Social Classification in Creole Louisiana* (New Brunswick, NJ: Rutgers University Press, 1986), 36–46.

65. For the link between progressive liberalism and eugenics, see Dorr, *Segregation's Science*, 10–16.

66. Plecker to Aileen Goodman Henry, March 10, 1943, Box 42, Folder 15, John Powell Papers.

67. Donna Huffer interview with Mary Murray Martin, May 23, 1985. In possession of author. Some parts of this interview are included in Huffer, *Fare Thee Well, Old Joe Clark*.

68. Phyllis Branham Hicks interview in Whitlock, *The Monacan Indian Nation*, 67, 71.

69. Bertie Duff Branham interview, in Whitlock, *The Monacan Indian Nation*, 120.

70. Samuel R. Cook, "The Boundaries of Participatory Research: Lessons Learned in the Monacan Indian Nation," in *Participatory Development in Appalachia: Cultural Identity, Community, and Sustainability*, ed. Susan Keefe (Knoxville: University of Tennessee Press, 2009), 108–109.

71. Whitlock, *The Monacan Indian Nation*, 64, 65, 98, 111, 126, 135, 140.

72. It is not only residents who remember Plecker; he has been the focus of most historical treatments as well; see Smith, *Managing White Supremacy*, 89–104; Dorr, *Segregation's Science*, 147–154; and Pippa Holloway, *Sexuality, Politics, and Social Control in Virginia, 1920–1945* (Chapel Hill: University of North Carolina Press,

2006), 61–68. An exception to this is Barbara Bair, "Remapping the Black/White Body," 399–419.

73. On historical amnesia, see Michael Kammen, *Mystic Chords of Memory: The Transformation of Tradition in American Culture* (New York: Random House, 1993), 9–11, 280, 526–527.

CHAPTER 2

1. "Rutherford Committee," *Confederate Veteran* 28, no. 11 (November 1919): 405-6; "The Work of the Rutherford Committee," *Confederate Veteran* 29, no. 10 (October 1921): 327; Mildred Lewis Rutherford, "A Measuring Rod to Test Text Books, and Reference Books in Schools, Colleges, and Libraries," [1919], Pamphlet published at request of United Confederate Veterans, https://archive.org/details/measuringrodtootooruth. Bessie Pierce, *Public Opinion and the Teaching of History in the United States* (New York: Alfred A. Knopf, 1926), 158.

2. Fred Arthur Bailey, "Mildred Lewis Rutherford and the Patrician Cult of the Old South," *Georgia Historical Quarterly* 78 (Fall 1994): 509–535. Sarah Case, "Mildred Lewis Rutherford: The Redefinition of New South White Womanhood," in *Georgia Women: Their Lives and Times*, vol. 1, ed. Ann Short Chirhart and Betty Wood (Athens: University of Georgia Press, 2009), 272–296; Virginia Pettigrew Clare, *Thunder and Stars: The Life of Mildred Rutherford* (Atlanta: Oglethorpe University Press, 1941). Grace Elizabeth Hale, "'Some Women Have Never Been Reconstructed': Mildred Lewis Rutherford, Lucy M. Stanton, and the Racial Politics of White Southern Womanhood, 1900-1930," in *Georgia in Black and White: Explorations of the Race Relations of a Southern State, 1865–1950*, ed. John C. Inscoe (Athens: University of Georgia Press, 1994), 173–201; Elizabeth Gillespie McRae, "Caretakers of Southern Civilization: Georgia Women and the Anti-Suffrage Campaign, 1914–1920," *Georgia Historical Quarterly* 82 (Winter 1998): 801–828.

3. Charron, *Freedom's Teacher*, 3.

4. Charron, *Freedom's Teacher*, 40, 53; Eric Hobsbawm, "Introduction: Inventing Tradition," in *The Invention of Tradition*, ed. Eric Hobsbawm (London: Cambridge University Press, 1984), 1; Ritterhouse, *Growing Up Jim Crow*, 11–21; Joan Marie Johnson, *Southern Ladies, New Women: Race, Region, and Clubwomen in South Carolina,1890–1930* (Gainesville: University of Florida Press, 2004), 57; "Confederate Southern Memorial Association News," and Mildred Rutherford, "Loyalty to the South and Its Ideals," *Confederate Veteran* 30, no. 12 (December 1922): 476; Laats, *The Other School Reformers*, 15, 19, 23.

5. Delegard, *Battling Miss Bolsheviki*, 174–179; Kim Nielsen, *Un-American Womanhood: Antiradicalism, Antifeminism, and the First Red Scare* (Columbus: Ohio State University Press, 2001), 58–60.

6. On race scientists and the classification campaign, see Pascoe, *What Comes Naturally*, 116–119; Mildred Lewis Rutherford, "Our Textbooks—The South's Responsibility," undated clipping [1919?]. Mildred Lewis Rutherford Scrapbooks, Box 3, Hargrett Library, University of Georgia, Athens, Georgia; hereafter cited as MLR Scrapbooks. These are homemade scrapbooks, different from *Miss Rutherford's Scrapbook*, which was a serial publication.

7. William Link, *The Paradox of Southern Progressivism,1880–1930* (Chapel Hill: University of North Carolina Press, 1992); Daniel Singal, *The War Within: From Victorian to Modernist Thought in the South, 1919–1945* (Chapel Hill: University of North Carolina Press, 1982); Noralee Frankel, *Gender, Race, and Reform in the Progressive Era* (Lexington: University of Kentucky Press, 1991); Glenda Gilmore, *Gender and Jim Crow: Women and the Politics of White Supremacy in North Carolina, 1880–1920* (Chapel Hill: University of North Carolina Press, 1996).

8. Muncy, *Creating a Female Dominion in American Reform*, xii–xiv; Mink, *The Wages of Motherhood*, 5, 26. Mink takes the most care in discussing the racial views espoused by women. After 1930, Molly Ladd-Taylor argues that "the language of motherhood became the preserve of conservative politicians and organizers." See Ladd-Taylor, *Mother-Work*, 44. Paula Baker, "The Domestication of Politics: Women and American Political Society, 1780–1920," *American Historical Review* 89 (Fall 1984): 620–647. For scholarship on the postwar period, see Ruth Feldstein, "Antiracism and Maternal Failure in the 1940s and 1950s," in *"Bad" Mothers*, 148–152.

9. Ann Short Chirhart, *Torches of Light and the Coming of the Modern South* (Athens: University of Georgia Press, 2005), 82–91.

10. "Home Education at the South," *De Bow's Review*, n.s., 1: 655 (May 1855), quoted in Mary Elizabeth Carpenter, *The Treatment of the Negro in American History School Textbooks: A Comparison of Changing Textbook Content, 1826 to 1939 with Developing Scholarship in the History of the Negro in the United States* (Menasha, WI: George Banta, 1941), 9.

11. Ron Butchart, *Schooling the Freed People: Teaching, Learning and the Struggle for Black Freedom, 1861–1876* (Chapel Hill: University of North Carolina Press, 2010); James Leloudias, *Schooling the New South: Pedagogy, Self, and Society in North Carolina, 1880–1920* (Chapel Hill: University of North Carolina Press, 1996).

12. Laura Rose (Mrs. S. E. Rose), "Mississippi's Firsts" in *Miss Rutherford's Scrap Book: Valuable Information about the South*, vol. 2 (June 1924), 18–24; "Text-books Unjust to the South. Why Now Used in Schools?" *Miss Rutherford's Scrap Book*, vol. 1 (February 1923), 16–19.

13. On the prevalence of the Dunning school interpretation, see Francis Fitzgerald, *America Revised: History School books in the Twentieth* Century (New York: Vintage Books, 1979), 85–89; Nina Silber, *Romance of Reunion: Northerners and the South, 1865–1900* (Chapel Hill: University of North Carolina Press, 1993), 6, 11–12. On the

white supremacist beliefs that shaped imperialism, see Gail Bederman, *Manliness and Civilization: A Cultural History of Gender and Race in the United States, 1880–1917* (Chicago: University of Chicago Press, 1995), 25-27; Mary Renda, *Taking Haiti: Military Occupation and the Culture of U.S. Imperialism, 1915–1940* (Chapel Hill: University of North Carolina Press, 2001), 8, 16–21.

14. Laurence Reddick, "Racial Attitudes in American History Textbooks of the South," *Journal of Negro History*, 19 (July 1934): 255–265; Rolfe Lanier Hunt, "What Do We Teach about the Negro?" *Journal of the National Education Association* 28, no. 1 (January 1939): 11–12. Moreau, *Schoolbook Nation*, 125, 69, 79, 84–88; Fitzgerald, *America Revised*, 85–89; Pierce, *Public Opinion*, 163.

15. Moreau, *Schoolbook Nation*, 75, 88, 216, 90; Pierce, *Public Opinion*, 162.

16. Pierce, *Public Opinion*, 301–335; Bessie L. Pierce, *Citizens' Organization and the Civic Training of Youth: Part III Report of the Commission on the Social Studies* (New York: Charles Scribner's Sons, 1933), 112–129; Moreau, *Schoolbook Nation*, 176, 212, 239; Laats, *The Other School Reformers*, 17, 54-65.

17. Moreau, *Schoolbook Nation*, 1–25; Michael Apple, *Ideology and Curriculum*, 63–64. Moreau refers to textbooks as producers of "official knowledge" that represents the market, politics, and intellectual currents of the time period. He notes that the production of such knowledge is different from the consumption. Apple uses the term "legitimate knowledge" to reflect the knowledge that "we all must have." He notes that schools confer legitimacy on specific groups and contends that classrooms play a particular role in reproducing inequalities.

18. Julia Mickenberg, *Learning from the Left: Children's Literature, the Cold War, and Radical Politics in the United States* (New York: Oxford University Press, 2006), 29, 15, 49, 69.

19. Chirhart, *Torches of Light*, 79–87, 91; Fitzgerald, *America Revised*, 19, 50-51, 105

20. Pierce, *Citizens' Organizations*, 3; "Statement of Principles of the American Legion for the Writing of Their American History Textbook, as well as Their Attitude toward present-day Textbooks," in Pierce, *Public Opinion*, 331–332.

21. Pierce, *Public Opinion*, 269, 275.

22. Nielsen, *Un-American Womanhood*, 60.

23. For the links between anti-radicals and segregationists, see Francesca Morgan, *Women and Patriotism in Jim Crow America* (Chapel Hill: University of North Carolina Press, 2005), 143–150; for information on Margaret Robinson, see Delegard, *Battling Miss Bolsheviki*, 59, 50, 119. Delegard includes the UDC and DAR in her study of anti-radicals but does not address the linkages between anti-radical women's organizational platforms and their work for various manifestations of racial segregation. On anti-radical women's work in education in the 1920s and 1930s, see Christine Erickson, "'We Want No Teachers Who Say There Are Two Sides to Every Question': Conservative Women and Education in the 1930s," *History of Education Quarterly* 46, no. 4 (Winter 2006): 487–490; and Erickson, "'So Much for Men': Conservative Women and National Defense in the 1920s and

1930s," *American Studies* 45, no. 1 (Spring 2004): 85–102; Neilsen, *Un-American Womanhood*, 58–95.

24. "Confederated Southern Memorial Association News," *Confederate Veteran* 28, no. 8 (August 1920): 317.

25. Pierce, *Public Opinion*, 99, 109, 154–163; on southern textbook statewide committees, Moreau, *Schoolbook Nation*, 69, 71, 86, 90; Karen Cox, *Dixie's Daughters: The United Daughters of the Confederacy and the Preservation of Confederate Culture*, foreword by John David Smith (Gainesville: University of Florida Press, 2003), 160; Pierce, *Public Opinion*, 160–162; Fitzhugh Brundage, *The Southern Past: A Clash of Race and Memory* (Cambridge, MA: Belknap Press, 2005), 124.

26. Chirhart, *Torches of Light*, 18–19, 77, 81–92.

27. Chirhart, *Torches of Light*, 9, 105, 119; For more on the importance of black female teachers in propagating resistance to racial segregation, see Charron, *Freedom's Teacher*, 142–148.

28. Joan Marie Johnson, *Southern Ladies, New Women*, 54–56.

29. Micki McElya, *Clinging to Mammy: The Faithful Slave in Twentieth Century America* (Cambridge, MA: Harvard University Press, 2007), 143–164.

30. Ritterhouse, *Growing Up Jim Crow*, 213–215, 233, 178; Chirhart, *Torches of Light*, 60; Charron, *Freedom's Teacher*, 40.

31. Bailey, "The Textbooks of the 'Lost Cause,'" 517; Karen Cox, *Dixie's Daughters*, 161, 240.

32. "The Work of the Rutherford Committee," *Confederate Veteran* 29, no. 10 (October 1921): 397; Bessie Pierce, *Public Opinion*, 154–156.

33. Pierce, *Public Opinion*, 160, 256; Moreau, *Schoolbook Nation*, 151.

34. "The Work of the Rutherford Committee," *Confederate Veteran* 30, no. 7 (July 1922): 244.

35. Cox, *Dixie's Daughters*, 109, 171; Mary Poppenheim, *The History of the United Daughters of the Confederacy* (Raleigh, NC: Edwards and Broughton, 1956), 137, 141.

36. Mrs. Frank Wilson to Dr. Brooks, April 30, 1922; UDC Raleigh District Resolutions, April 22, 1921; Rutherford Committee to Supt. T. R. Forest, June 7, 1921; Dr. C. Z. Candler to Supt. T. R. Forest, June 6, 1921, Folder/Textbook Commission Minutes and Oath, 1921, North Carolina Department of Public Instruction/ Office of Supt. Textbook Correspondence, 1911–1922, NCDAH; "Approved High School Text-books," Folder-Report of Textbook Commission, 1922; Box DPI/Office of Supt. 1921–1922, NCDAH; To Hon. A. T. Allen (State Superintendent) from Houghton Mifflin Co., December 29, 1923, and Letters, Folder 1923 Correspondence Teaching of Americanism, Textbook Correspondence, 1923–1928, NCDAH.

37. Cox, *Dixie's Daughters*, 109; "UDC News," *Confederate Veteran* 29, no. 1 (January 1921): 73; Laura Rose, *The Ku Klux Klan: or, Invisible Empire* (New Orleans, LA: L. Graham, 1914), 1–80; Morgan, *Women and Patriotism*, 95–96. On the Union

Leagues, Steven Hahn, *A Nation under Our Feet: Black Political Struggles in the Rural South from Slavery to the Great Migration* (Cambridge, MA: Belknap Press, 2003), 177–179.

38. "Confederated Memorial Association News," *Confederate Veteran* 6 (June 1920): 231; "UDC News," *Confederate Veteran* 28, no. 8 (August 1920): 314.

39. "UDC News," *Confederate Veteran* 29, no. 2 (February 1921):74; "Confederate Veteran News," *Confederate Veteran* 29, no. 8 (August 1921): 285.

40. "UDC News," *Confederate Veteran* 29, no. 7 (July 1921): 272.

41. "UDC News," *Confederate Veteran* 28, no. 2 (February 1920): 73.

42. "Confederated Southern Memorial Association News," *Confederate Veteran* 30, no. 1 (January 1922): 36.

43. "UDC News," *Confederate Veteran* 27, no. 6 (June 1919): 233; "UDC News," *Confederate Veteran* 27, no. 7 (July 1919): 273.

44. Lucy McDonald to Mildred Rutherford, September 15, 1924, Box 1, Folder 16, Mildred Rutherford Papers, Hargrett Library, University of Georgia, Athens; hereafter cited as Mildred Rutherford Papers.

45. "UDC Historical Reports by Chapter, 1924," Louise Irwin to Mildred Rutherford, September 13, 1924, Box 1, Folder 18, Mildred Rutherford Papers.

46. "Committee Reports Education Bill," *Journal of the National Education Association* 10, no. 1 (March 1921): 41–44; John Keith, "Competent Teachers for the Nation: An Article Plank One of the Platform of the National Education Association," *Journal of the National Education Association* 10, no. 1 (March 1921): 46–48.

47. "Complete Schedule of University of Georgia Classes, Lectures, and Entertainment University of Georgia Summer School," *Athens Banner Herald*, June 26, 1923; "Summer School to Open June 25," *Athens Banner Herald*, Sunday, June 26, 1924; H. J. Rowe, *History of Athens and Clarke County* (Athens, Georgia: McGregor, 1923), 61, 72; "Waynesboro, GA, 1924, UDC Historian's Report," Folder 18, Box 1; "Hawkinsville GA UDC Division Report for 1924, Historical Report," Box 1, Folder 16; also Box 1, Folder 18, Mildred Lewis Rutherford Papers; Fran Thomas, *A Portrait of Historic Athens and Clark County* (Athens: University of Georgia Press, 1997), 154–155;

48. "Miss Rutherford," undated clipping, [1923?], Box 4, Folder 3, Mildred Lewis Rutherford Papers.

49. A list of advertisers in her periodical included numerous publishing houses, mostly southern. Others included the Lucy Cobb Institute, the Historical Department of the State of Mississippi, the American Book Company in New York, and the Georgia Railway and Power Company. For a complete list, see *Miss Rutherford's Scrapbooks*, 1923–1927; *Miss Rutherford's Scrapbook*, vol. 1 (August 1923), 16; "Faithful Servants," *Miss Rutherford's Scrapbook*, vol. 1 (August 1923), 14–16; *Miss Rutherford's Scrapbook*, vol. 1, no. 10 (October 1923), 1–2.

50. "Card of Thanks to Subscribers," *Miss Rutherford's Scrapbook*, vol. 1 (October 1923), 1.

51. "On the Freedmen's Bureau, Carpetbaggers, Scalawags," and "How Was the Civilization of the Old South Destroyed?" *Miss Rutherford's Scrapbook*, vol. 2 (February 1924), 9; Mrs. S. E. F. Rose, "Mississippi's Firsts," *Miss Rutherford's Scrapbook*, vol. 2 (June 1924), 18–24; "Don'ts of History," *Miss Rutherford's Scrapbook*, vol. 2 (May 1923), 2; "Social Equality," *Miss Rutherford's Scrapbook* vol. 2 (October 1925), 5.

52. Neilson, *Un-American Womanhood*, 91, 95, 108, 118; Margaret Robinson, "Why Massachusetts Beat Child Control New England Parents Believe They Can Manage Their Own Children," *Dearborn Independent*, March 7, 1925; Delegard, *Battling Miss Bolsheviki*, 120–128; "The Child Labor Amendment," *Miss Rutherford's Scrapbook*, vol. 12 (March 1925), 9

53. "The Child Labor Amendment," *Miss Rutherford's Scrapbook*, vol. 12 (March 1925), 9; Neilson, *Un-American Womanhood*, 91, 95, 108, 118: Delegard, *Battling Miss Bolsheviki*, 114–120.

54. On the South and the New Deal, see Sullivan, *Days of Hope*; Egerton, *Speak Now against the Day;* Harvard Sitkoff, "Impact of the New Deal on Black Southerners," in *The New Deal and the South*, ed. James C. Cobb and Michael V. Namorato (Jackson: University Press of Mississippi, 1984); Douglas Carl Abrams, *Conservative Constraints: North Carolina and the New Deal* (Jackson: University Press of Mississippi, 1992); Anthony Badger, *North Carolina and the New Deal* (Raleigh: North Carolina Department of Cultural Resources, 1981); Lawrence Nelson, *King Cotton's Advocate: Oscar G. Johnston and the New Deal* (Knoxville: University of Tennessee Press, 1999).

55. Poppenheim, *History of the UDC*, 141.

56. Johnson, *Southern Ladies*, 54–56; Brundage, *Southern Pasts*, 160–168; Ritterhouse, *Growing Up Jim Crow*, 183; *DAR Annual Proceedings, GA Division, 1930, Proceedings of the 32nd Conference of the Georgia Daughters National Society of the DAR*, 43, Georgia Room, Hargrett Library.

57. Carpenter, *The Treatment of the Negro*, 1–16.

58. Hunt, "What Do We Teach about the Negro?" *Journal of the National Education Association* 28, no. 1 (January 1939): 11–12; Dittmer, *Local People*, 58–62.

59. Hunt, "What Do We Teach about the Negro?" 11–12.

60. Erickson, "Conservative Women and Education in the 1930s," 487–502; Moreau, *Schoolbook Nation*, 1–25, 88, 217; Apple, *Ideology and Curriculum*, 63–64.

61. Brundage, *The Southern Past*, 49. Brundage argued that women's influence over the commemoration of the past waned in the aftermath of suffrage and in the wake of school centralization; however, his interpretation too quickly removes white women and women's organizations from positions of influence and authority in local schools. Bailey, "Textbooks of the Lost Cause," 507–533.

62. Hahn, *A Nation under Our Feet*, 479–480.

63. Middleton Harris, ed., *The Black Book* (New York: Random House, 1974); Dittmer, *Local People*, 60, 125, 225, 258–263; Chris Myers Asch, *The Senator and the*

*Sharecropper: The Freedom Struggles of James O. Eastland and Fannie Lou Hamer* (New York: New Press, 2008), 56–57.

CHAPTER 3

1. David Cohn, *Where I Was Born and Raised*, with a foreword by James Silver (Notre Dame, IN: University of Notre Dame Press, reprint 1967; originally printed 1935), 20.
2. Political scientist Robert Mickey recently described the politics of these states as "enclave rule." See Robert Mickey, *Paths Out of Dixie: The Democratization of Authoritarian Enclaves in America's Deep South, 1944–1972* (Princeton, NJ: Princeton University Press, 2015), 13, 25–27, 33–35.
3. Mickey, *Paths Out of Dixie*, 27, 28, 53–62, 90–91.
4. Schuyler, *The Weight of Their Vote*, 191–192, 212, 214, 222, 228; McRae, "Caretakers of Southern Civilization," 812; Elna S. Green, *Southern Strategies: Southern Women and the Woman Suffrage Question* (Chapel Hill: University of North Carolina Press, 1997), xi–xvii.
5. V. O. Key Jr., *Southern Politics in State and Nation* (New York: Alfred A. Knopf, 1949), 10–11.
6. Mickey, *Paths Out of Dixie*, 27.
7. Belmont's 1909 yearbook listed one student each from New York and Pennsylvania, and no students from the New England States. *Catalogue of Belmont School of Expression*, (n.d. but before the merger of Ward-Belmont in 1913), 7, 8, 15, Special Collections, Lila Brunch Library, Belmont University, Nashville, Tennessee; *Prospectus Belmont College for Young Women*, n.d., 5, Belmont College Prospectus, n.d.—approx. 1912, 46, Lila Brunch Library; *Milady in Brown*, 1909 Yearbook of Belmont College, Lila Brunch Library; "Florence Carson Sillers," Alumni Records, microfilm box 16 for Ward Seminary, Belmont College for Young Women, and Ward-Belmont School, Lila Brunch Library; *Belmont College: The Blue and Bronze*, June 1913, page 20, Lila Brunch Library; Herbert C. Baghart, *Work: The Soul of Good Fortune: Memoirs of a Love Affair with Belmont College* (Nashville, TN: Broadman Press, 1989), 31–33.
8. Morgan, *Women and Patriotism in Jim Crow America*, 127–152.
9. Kirsten Delegard, "Stopping Words: Female Anti-Radicalism and the Grassroots Censorship Campaign, 1924–1939," paper given at the 1999 Southern Historical Association Meeting, Fort Worth, Texas (in author's possession); Francesca Morgan, "Home and Country: Women, Nation and the Daughters of the American Revolution, 1890–1939" (Ph.D. diss., Columbia University, 1998), 415–434. For a discussion on the role of civic and ethnic nationalism in the United States and its intertwined history, see Rogers M. Smith, *Civic Ideas: Conflicting Visions of Citizenship in U.S. History* (New Haven. CT: Yale University Press, 1997), 5–12, 35–39.

10. Morgan, *Women and Patriotism,* 93–97, 137–146; "David Reese DAR Chapter, Rosedale and Bolivar County Yearbook, 1930–1931," Box 11, David Reese DAR Chapter Papers, J. D. Williams Library, University of Mississippi, Oxford, Mississippi.

11. Florence Sillers Ogden, "Immigration" speech to DAR group, 1928, Folder 13, FSO Papers; Ogden, "Excluded Chinese Form Rosedale School: Barred from White Classrooms by the Supreme Court, Orientals Organize Own Institution," *Commercial Appeal* (Memphis), November 19, 1933; "Bolivar County Has Public Schools for Four Different Races," *Daily Democrat Times,* Golden Jubilee Edition, September 1938; Choctaw Indians returned to the Delta in 1902 as potential laborers. Between 1885 and 1910, LeRoy Percy experimented with Italian laborers on his Mississippi and Arkansas plantations, even making a deal with the railroad to offer cheap passage to Italian immigrants willing to come to the Delta. See Lewis Turner Baker III, "LeRoy Percy, Delta Defender" (MA Thesis, Louisiana State University, 1977), 5–6, 40–44, 52–57.

12. Lyle Gardner of Palmer Literary Agency to FSO, May 7, 1926; Marjorie Woods Austin of the Federal Writers Project to FSO, September 22, 1936, FSO Papers.

13. "Dis an' Dat," *Delta Star* (Greenville, MS), February 14, 1937.

14. "Dis an' Dat," *Delta Star,* February 14, 1937. On the formation of the Dies committee, see Sullivan, *Days of Hope,* 104. See also Egerton, *Speak Now against the Day,* 172–174. John Rankin, Mississippi congressman from the First District, would serve on the Dies HUAC Committee in 1943. "Dis an' Dat," *Greenville Delta Democrat-Times,* April 21, August 4, September 1, 1940; June 1, June 8, June 22, October 12, November 23, 1941; James C. Cobb, *The Most Southern Place on Earth: The Mississippi Delta and the Roots of Regional Identity* (New York: Oxford University Press, 1992), 306–327.

15. "Dis an' Dat," *Greenville Delta Democrat-Times,* August 4, November 17, 1940.

16. "Dis an' Dat," *Delta Star,* February 14, 1937.

17. Will M. Whittington, Comments of Friday, September 6, 1940, *Congressional Record—Appendix,* 17721–17722; FSO to W. M. Whittington, January 30, 1941; FSO to Senator Pat Harrison, January 30, 1941, Folder 13, FSO Papers.

18. Roger D. Tate Jr., "Easing the Burden: The Era of Depression and New Deal in Mississippi" (Ph.D. diss., University of Tennessee, 1978), 6, 29. For a discussion of Mississippi's immunity from the consumer revolution of the 1920s, see 7–12. Cobb, *The Most Southern Place on Earth,* 63.

19. On the flood of 1927, see Pete Daniel, *Deep'n as It Come: The 1927 Mississippi River Flood* (New York: Oxford University Press, 1977); John Barry, *Rising Tide, the Great Mississippi Flood of 1927 and How It Changed America* (New York: Simon and Schuster, 1997), 200. For Florence Sillers Ogden's experience during the flood, see Mrs. Florence Sillers Ogden, interviewed by Henry Kline, MAETV, December 29, 1970, Mississippi Department of Archives and History, Jackson, Mississippi,

hereafter cited as MDAH; FSO to Harry Ogden's parents, April 1927, Folder 184, FSO Papers; Ogden, untitled typescript on the flood, Folder 184, FSO Papers.

20. "Dis an' Dat," *Greenville Delta Democrat-Times*, March 2, 1941, October 13, 1940; Ogden, "Depression in Cotton" Folder 139, FSO Papers.

21. "Dis an' Dat," *Greenville Delta Democrat-Times*, March 2, 1941, October 13, 1940; Ogden, "Depression in Cotton," Folder 139, FSO Papers.

22. Ogden, "Depression in Cotton," Folder 139, FSO Papers.

23. Mickey, *Paths Out of Dixie, 75–76*; Sillers, *History of Bolivar County*, 254–261.

24. George Tindall, *The Emergence of the New South, 1913–1945* (Baton Rouge: Louisiana State University Press, 1967), 24–25, 234; Chester Morgan, *Redneck Liberal: Theodore G. Bilbo and the New Deal* (Baton Rouge: Louisiana State University Press, 1985); William D. McCain, "The Triumph of Democracy, 1916–1932," in McLemore, *History of Mississippi*, 61, 84–96; Albert Kirwan, *Revolt of the Rednecks; Mississippi Politics: 1876–1925* (Gloucester, MA: P. Smith, 1964).

The Big Four controlled Mississippi's lower house and had constituted a powerful block against Bilbo's reform efforts. They included Walter Sillers Jr., who would be Speaker of the House from 1944 to 1965; Thomas L. Bailey of Lauderdale County, who was speaker from 1924 to 1936; Laurence Kennedy of Adams County who was chairman of the appropriations committee; and Joe George from Leflore County. During Governor Conner's term, they all supported the sales tax initiative. See McLemore, *History of Mississippi*, 104.

25. Ogden, "Speech to Bolivar County Women," 1931, Folder 101, FSO Papers. On the political factions in Mississippi, often oversimplified but nevertheless instructive, see Tindall, *The Emergence*, 229–234; Key, *Southern Politics*, 229–253; Morgan, *Redneck Liberal*; McCain, "The Triumph of Democracy, 1916–1932"; Cobb, *The Most Southern Place on Earth*, 148–150.

26. Ogden, "Speech to Bolivar County Women," 1931, Folder 101, FSO Papers.

27. FSO to Governor M. Sennet Conner, February 1, 1932; Folder 6, FSO Papers; Rueben W. Griffith, "The Public School 1890–1970," in McLemore, *History of Mississippi*, 397. On Conner's sales tax initiative, see William Winter, "Governor Mike Conner and the Sales Tax 1932," in *Mississippi Heroes*, ed. Dean Faulkner Wells and Hunter Cole (Jackson: University of Mississippi Press, 1980), 158–176. For more on white Mississippians's tax politics in the 1930s, see Martin, *Rich People's Movements*, 85–87.

28. Cobb, *The Most Southern Place on Earth*, 196–197. As supporters of the New Deal, Florence Sillers Ogden and Walter Sillers Jr. challenge, as James Cobb pointed out, V. O. Key's characterization of the Delta's response to the New Deal. See Key, *Southern Politics*, 243. For more on this point, see Pete Daniel, *Breaking the Land: The Transformation of Cotton, Tobacco, and Rice Cultures since 1880* (Urbana: University of Illinois Press, 1985), 100, 105–106, 109; Ogden, "Depression in Cotton," Folder 139, FSO Papers. Ogden's mother, Florence Sillers, was one

of the individual beneficiaries of AAA money when Wallace was forced to list who received payments. Ogden, "Dis an Dat," *Greenville Delta Democrat-Times*, October 27, 1940.

29. Sillers, *History of Bolivar County*, 246–247.

30. Sillers, *History of Bolivar County*, 359–361. "Golden Jubilee Edition," *Daily Democrat Times* (Greenville), August 31, 1938; the first mule races were such a success that holding a mule race became an annual event until World War II and then resumed after the war under the direction of the American Legion. On mule races, see Karen Glynn, "Running Mules: Mule Racing in the Mississippi Delta," *Mississippi Folklife* 28, No. 2 (Spring 1996): 1–12. Martha H. Swain, *Ellen S. Woodward: New Deal Advocate for Women* (Jackson: University Press of Mississippi, 1995).

31. "Dis an' Dat," *Delta Star*, May 9, February 8, 1937.

32. Bruce Schulman, *From Cotton Belt to Sun Belt: Federal Policy, Economic Development and the Transformation of the South, 1938–1980* (Durham, NC: Duke University Press, 1994), 49. Schulman notes that a Gallup Poll confirmed that southerners supported the court's expansion. "Dis an' Dat," *Delta Star*, March 14, 1937. By 1938, the *Delta Star* had merged with Greenville's *Daily Democrat Times*, and Hodding Carter remained the publisher and ran Ogden's column in the newly titled *Delta Democrat Times*.

33. "Dis an' Dat," *Greenville Delta Democrat-Times*, October 27, 1940.

34. John Ray Skates Jr., "World War II and Its Effects, 1940–1948," in McLemore, *History of Mississippi*, vol. 2, 130; Governor Paul B. Johnson, "Inaugural Message to the Joint Session Mississippi Legislature," Tuesday, January 16, 1940, Paul B. Johnson Papers, Mississippi Department of Archives and History, Jackson, Mississippi; hereafter cited as Paul Johnson Papers; Mickey, *Paths Out of Dixie*, 110.

35. "Dis an' Dat," *Greenville Delta Democrat-Times*, February 4, January 7, March 10, 1940. For the state of education in the South, see Tindall, *The Emergence*, 496–497. In Mississippi, see Reuben W. Griffith, "The Public School, 1890–1970," in *A History of Mississippi*, 402–403.

36. "Dis an' Dat," *Greenville Delta Democrat-Times*, March 10, 1940.

37. "Total Population, Negro Population, Farms in Acreage Increments from 10–14 acres to 1000+, acreage of white operated farms and acreage of land under non-white operators," United States Census, 1940 IPUMS, http://doi.org/10.18128/D010.V6.0.

38. Payne, *I've Got the Light of Freedom*, 113–120; Mickey, *Paths Out of Dixie*, 88.

39. Speer, " 'Contrary Mary,' " 36–38, 48; "Mary Dawson Cain," Principal Women of America, typed, undated transcript, Mary Dawson Cain Papers, hereafter cited as MDC Papers, MDAH; McComb Business and Professional Women's Club to MDC, May 17, 1934, Box 15, MDC Papers; Mississippi Business and Professonial Women's Clubp amphlet, May 17, 1936, Box 15, MDC Papers.

40. Mary Dawson Cain, "Prohibition Should Have Been Raped," *Plain Talk* [1932?], 26–27, 47–48; MDC to Senator Pat Harrison, November 15, 1932, Box 17, MDC Papers; Mississippi Division of the Women's Organization for National Prohibition Reform (WONPR) Letterhead, Box 1, MDC Papers; "Wet Leaders Hold Dr. Colvin Bigoted," *New York Times*, May 25, 1932, 3.

41. MDC to John Cain, May 30, 1933, Box 2, Mike Conner to MDC, May 6, 1933, Box 2, MDC Papers; MDC, "Prohibition Should Have Been Raped," 26–27, 47–48; MDC to Senator Pat Harrison, November 15, 1932, and Senator Pat Harrison to MDC, November 23, 1932, Box 17; MDC to Fred Sullens, August 15, 1932, Box 17; Vivian Franklin to Walter Sillers, March 9, 1933, Box 17; Mississippi Branch WONPR Letterhead [1932?], Box 1, MDC Papers.

42. "Races: Lynch and Anti-lynch," *Time Magazine*, April 26, 1937, http://www.time.com/time.

43. Key, *Southern Politics*, 330–334; MDC to May Thompson Evans, July 3, 1939, Box 17, MDC Papers. In this letter, Cain recounts an earlier exchange with Kendall.

44. On National Consumers Tax Commission (NCTC), see Landon Storr, *Civilizing Capitalism: The National Consumers' League, Women's Activism, and Labor Standards in the New Deal Era* (Chapel Hill: University of North Carolina Press, 2000); Lawrence Glickman, "The Strike in the Temple of Consumption: Consumer Activism and Twentieth Century American Political Culture," *Journal of American History* 88, no. 1 (June 2001): 104, 109; Mark Pendergrast, *Uncommon Grounds: The History of Coffee and How It Transformed Our World* (New York: Basic Books, 2000), 210.

45. Cain, "What Is Democracy?" [1939], Box 17, MDC Papers; MDC to May Thompson Evans, July 3, 1939, Box 17, MDC Papers.

46. MDC to W. E. Holcomb, March 5, 1943, Box 17, MDC Papers.

47. "Mary Cain's Column," *Summit Sun*, September 12, 1940, 1; Ward, *Defending White Democracy*, 23–30.

48. Cain to Mary L. Kendall, September 12, 1938, Box 9, MDC Papers; Speer, "'Contrary Mary,'" 84. "Dr. Jekyll of Hyde Park," *Summit Sun*, April 27, 1939; Ward, *Defending White Democracy*, 27–31.

49. Key, *Southern Politics*, 329; Kari Frederickson, *The Dixiecrat Revolt and the End of the Solid South, 1932–1968* (Chapel Hill: University of North Carolina Press, 2001), 4–6, 13–27; Sullivan, *Days of Hope*, 61, 100.

50. Stephanie Yuhl, "Rich and Tender Remembering: Elite White Women and an Aesthetic Sense of Place in Charleston, 1920s and 1930s," in *Where These Memories Grow: History, Memory, and Southern Identity*, ed. Fitzhugh Brundage (Chapel Hill: University of North Carolina Press, 2000), 227–248; for a discussion of the fight to get black teachers in black Charleston schools, see Charron, *Freedom's Teacher*, 40–45, 86, 95.

51. Albertine Moore, "Mrs Cornelia Dabney Tucker," typed transcript, 1944, Box 1, Cornelia Dabney Tucker Papers, 1939–1967, South Caroliniana Society, University of South Carolina, Columbia, SC; hereafter cited as CDT Papers.

52. "President Asked to Abandon Plan," February 20, 1937, [newspaper?], Microfilm, R263, Cornelia Dabney Tucker Scrapbooks, he South Caroliniana Library, University of South Carolina; hereafter cited as CDT Scrapbooks.

53. "Women Exhorted to Save Country," February 24, 1937, newspaper clipping, "Scrapbook, 194–1967," Microfilm R263, CDT Scrapbooks.

54. "The Grand Jury," letter to the editor, Cornelia Dabney Tucker, July 20, 1937, newspaper clipping, untitled; "Charleston Fires First Shot Again," *Charleston Evening Post*, February 19, 1937, Clipping; "Court Fight Is Kept Up," [1937?], undated clipping, "Petition Plan Spreading Out," [1937?], undated clipping; "Move Gaining in Momentum," [1937?], undated clipping, Microfilm, R174, CDT Scrapbooks. .

55. Mickey, *Paths Out of Dixie*, 28.

56. "Woman Works for Secret Ballot"; "New South Carolina Republican Party," *New York Herald Tribune*, Sunday, October 15, 1939; Microfilm R174, CDT Scrapbooks.

57. "Woman Works for Secret Ballot," *New Canaan Advertiser*, New Canaan, Connecticut, [1939?], Microfilm, R174, CDT Scrapbooks.

58. Walter Edgar, *South Carolina: A History* (Columbia: University of South Carolina Press, 1998), 546. Edgar attributes the rise of the new Republican Party in South Carolina to upstate citizens in the 1950s. He does note that Roosevelt's efforts in 1938 led to rising disaffection but does not mention this early effort to create a viable Republican Party. Charles Boineau was elected as a Republican to the state legislature in 1962 after that body had not had a Republican legislator for eighty years.

59. Kittel, *Cornelia Dabney Tucker*, 33–34.

60. Tucker, "The Dividing Line," letter to the editor, September 8, 1938, [clipping] Microfilm R174; Tucker, "Get Out of Hock," letter to the editor, *News and Courier*, [1938?], Microfilm R174; "State G.O.P. Woos Anti-New Dealers," July 19, 1939, [clipping] Microfilm, R174; "GOP IS Part of Peace, Speaker Tells Local Club," [September 1939?] clipping, Microfilm R174, CDT Scrapbooks.

61. Ward, *Defending White Democracy*, 20; Merle Black and Earl Black, *The Vital South: How Presidents Are Elected* (Cambridge, MA: Harvard University Press, 1992), 87–93; Kari Frederickson, *The Dixiecrat Revolt and the End of the Solid South, 1932–1968* (Chapel Hill: University of North Carolina Press, 2001), 24; in 1924 the southern block went 103 ballots to prevent the nomination of Al Smith. See also Richard E. Berg-Andersson, "Why Are They All Here Anyway?" at the Green Papers: History, http://www.thegreenpapers.com/Hx/NatDelegates2004.html.

62. Edgar, *South Carolina*, 507–508.

63. "Lincoln Democrats," letter to the editor, *Charleston News and Courier*, undated clipping [1939?], microfilm R174, CDT Scrapbooks.

64. "New South Carolina Republican Party," *New York Herald Tribune*, October 15, 1939; "Resolution Offered by Mrs. Messervy for State Rights," undated clipping, [1939?], Scrapbook, CDT microfilm R174, CDT Scrapbooks.

65. "Lincoln Democrats," letter to the editor, *Charleston News and Courier*, undated clipping [1939?], Tucker Scrapbook, 1928–1962, microfilm R174, CDT Scrapbooks.
66. "South Carolina: Palmetto Stump," *Time Magazine*, August 24, 1936.
67. "State's Republicans to Organize Women," 1939, microfilm R174, CDT Scrapbooks. ; for an explanation of Marion Martin's leadership, see Cynthia Rymph, *Republican Women: Feminism and Conservatism from Suffrage through the Rise of the New Right* (Chapel Hill: University of North Carolina Press, 2006), 67–97.
68. Address Delivered by Cornelia Dabney Tucker from rostrum of South Carolina Senate, March 3, 1939, typescript, 1928–1962, CDT Papers.
69. Address delivered by Cornelia Dabney Tucker from rostrum of South Carolina House of Representatives, March 15, 1940. typescript, CDT papers; "She Held the Floor" and "Did Not Realize Man Was Praying," clipping, [Thursday March 1940?], Microfilm R174, CDT Scrapbooks. .
70. Tucker, "Fundamental v. Radical Government," [1940?], , microfilm R174, CDT Scrapbooks.
71. Egerton, *Speak Now against the Day*, 280–302.

## CHAPTER 4

1. Lewis, "Incidentally," *Raleigh News and Observer*, November 18 and 25, 1923.
2. "Negro Folk Songs," *Smith College Weekly* (January 10, 1917), 5, Smith College Archives, Smith University, Northampton, Massachusetts.
3. Egerton, *Speak Now against the Day*, 58–61; Morgan, *Women and Patriotism*, 127–152; Darden Ashbury Pyron, "Nell Battle Lewis (1893–1956) and the New Southern Woman," in *Perspectives on the American South: An Annual Review of Society, Politics, and Culture*, vol. 3, ed. James C. Cobb and Charles R. Wilson (New York: Gordon and Breach Science, 1985), 65–66; Leidholdt, *Battling Nell*, 95–97; "Incidentally," *Raleigh News and Observer*, July 8, 1923.
4. Leidholdt, *Battling Nell*, 59–72; Marjorie Spruill Wheeler, *New Women of the New South: The Leaders of the Woman Suffrage Movement in the Southern States* (New York: Oxford University Press, 1993).
5. Lewis, "Incidentally," *Raleigh News and Observer*, September 24, 1921.
6. Lewis, "Incidentally," *Raleigh News and Observer*, January 4, 1925; November 18, 1923; November 21, 1921. About the Klan's resistance to the New Woman, see Nancy McLean, *Behind the Mask of Chivalry: The Emergence of the Second Klu Klux Klan* (New York: Oxford University Press, 1994), 98–124. For more on the Klan's reaction to the New South, see Tindall, *The Emergence*, 191–195.
7. John Inscoe, "*The Clansman* on Stage and Screen: North Carolina Reacts," *North Carolina Historical Review* 64, no. 2 (1987): 139–161.
8. While geographers use the term "cultural landscape" to "describe the influence of people on the places around them," my use of the term implies both a literal geographic place and mental terrain of human experience, to borrow

from Thomas Holt, "Marking: Race, Race-Making, and the Writing of History," *American Historical Review* 100, no. 1 (February 1995): 6. See also Owen J. Dwyer and Derek H. Alderman, *Civil Rights Memorials and the Geography of Memory* (Chicago: Center for American Places, Columbia College, 2008), 7, 17. For the term "affectionate segregation," see Micki McElya, "Commemorating the Color Line: The National Mammy Monument Controversy of the 1920s," in *Monuments to the Lost Cause: Women, Art, and the Landscapes of Southern Memory*, ed. Cynthia Mills and Pamela H. Simpson (Knoxville: University of Tennessee Press, 2003), 208.

9. Lewis, "Incidentally," *Raleigh News and Observer*, September 22, 1921; For the political role of storytellers, see Hannah Arendt, *Between Past and Future*, (New York: Viking Press, 1961; revised edition 1968), 63–75.

10. Holt, "Marking," 6–8; Joan Jensen, "The Contest over Southern Identity in Black and White Women's Clubs, South Carolina 1898–1930," *Journal of Southern History* 3, no. 66 (August 2000): 530; Ritterhouse, *Growing Up Jim Crow*, 9.

11. Muhammad, *The Condemnation of Blackness*, 9.

12. Gilmore, *Defying Dixie*, 235.

13. For a discussion of challenges to the Jim Crow order from African Americans and their allies in this period, see Gilmore, *Defying Dixie*; Robin D. G. Kelley, *Hammer and Hoe: Alabama Communists during the Great Depression* (Chapel Hill: University of North Carolina Press, 1990). On the link between progressive reforms and racial segregation, see Chavez-Garcia, *States of Delinquency*, 98, 118, 119, 145–146, 148, 175–5, 216; Pascoe, *What Comes Naturally*, 131–162; Muhammad, *The Condemnation of Blackness*, 90, 98. 100, 143–145; Sugrue, *Sweet Land of Liberty*, 5–12.

14. Sosna, *In Search of the Silent South*; Grace Elizabeth Hale, *Making Whiteness: The Culture of Segregation in the South, 1890–1940* (New York: Random House, 1998), 8.

15. For scholarship on the national reach of progressive era segregation, see Allen F. Davis, *Spearheads for Reform: The Social Settlements and the Progressive Movement, 1880–1914* (New York: Oxford University Press, 1967); Mina Carson, *Settlement Folk: Social Thought and the American Settlement Movement, 1885–1930* (Chicago: University of Chicago Press, 1990); Elizabeth J. Clapp, *Mothers of All Children: Women, Reformers and the Rise of Juvenile Courts in Progressive Era America* (College Station: Penn State University Press, 1998); Tomas Almaguer, *Racial Fault Lines: The Historical Origins of White Supremacy in California* (Berkeley: University of California Press, 2008). See also Ritterhouse, *Growing Up Jim Crow*, 14.

16. Key, *Southern Politics*, 205–228.

17. Evelyn Brooks Higginbotham, *Righteous Discontent: The Women's Movement in the Black Baptist Church, 1880–1920* (Cambridge, MA: Harvard University Press, 1994), 188; Michelle Alexander, *The New Jim Crow: Mass Incarceration*

*in the Age of Colorblindness* (New York: New Press, 2011), 212; Muhammad, *The Condemnation*, 10–11.

18. On the results of the 1898 disfranchisement campaigns in North Carolina that put "progressives" in political offices, see Stephen Kantrowitz, "The Two Faces of Domination in North Carolina, 1880–1898," in *Democracy Betrayed*, 95–111; Glenda Gilmore, "Murder, Memory and the Fight of Incubus," in *Democracy Betrayed*, 73–93. On North Carolina's progressive policies in the 1920s, see Hugh Talmadge Lefler and Alfred Ray Newsome, *North Carolina: The History of a Southern State* (Chapel Hill: University of North Carolina Press, 1954), 561–572. Lefler and Newsome note that annual state expenditures increased from $3.75 million in 1916 to $7.5 million in 1922, to $20.75 million in 1926 and $49.75 million in 1932. On progress in North Carolina and the possibilities and limits of the interracial movement there, see Link, *The Paradox of Southern Progressivism*, 257–267, 322. "Incidentally," *Raleigh News and Observer*, February 5, May 5, June 16, 1935. "Incidentally," January 5, 1936; Badger, *North Carolina and the New Deal*, 42–44; Smith and Wilson, *North Carolina Women*, 222; and Sarah Wilkerson-Freeman, "From Clubs to Parties: North Carolina Women in the Advancement of the New Deal." *North Carolina Historical Review* 68 (July 1991): 320–329; William D. Snider, *"Light on the Hill": A History of the University of North Carolina at Chapel Hill* (Chapel Hill: University of North Carolina Press, 1992), 179, 180, 205, 218.

19. Lewis, "Kiddies Corner," *Raleigh News and Observer*, January 9, 1921; "A Corner for Kids," *Raleigh News and Observer*, January 2, 1921, April 24, 1921. Lewis authored "Kiddies Corner," in the Sunday paper January through April of 1921. See "Incidentally," *Raleigh News and Observer*, June 2, 1940.

20. Lewis, "Kiddies Corner," *Raleigh News and Observer*, January 9, 1921,

21. Lewis, "Incidentally," *Raleigh News and Observer*, September 7, 1921, July 15, 1923

22. Lewis, "Incidentally," *RNO*, June 8, 1924; July 15, 1923; November 4, 1921.

23. Lewis, "Incidentally," *Raleigh News and Observer* September 7, 1921, January 1, 1921; Leidholdt, *Battling Nell*, 69.

24. McElya, "Commemorating the Color Line," 215; McElya, *Clinging to Mammy*, 154, 144, 117; Morgan, *Women and Patriotism*, 143–146; Cheryl Thurber, "The Development of the Mammy Image and Mythology," in *Southern Women Histories and Identities*, ed. Virginia Bernhard, Betty Brandon, Elizabeth Fox-Genovese, and Theda Perdue (Columbia: University of Missouri Press, 1992), 99, 108; Hale, *Making Whiteness*, 98–104, 111–113.

25. Lewis, "Incidentally," *Raleigh News and Observer*, December 2, 1923; Raymond Gavins, "The NAACP in North Carolina during the Age of Segregation," in *New Directions in Civil Rights Studies*, ed. Patricia Sullivan and Armstead Robinson (Charlottesville: University Press of Virginia, 1991), 108; Sullivan, *Days of Hope*, 3, 43–67.

26. Lewis, "Incidentally," *Raleigh News and Observer,* November 9, 1924.

27. Her scientific data were partially taken from her brother, University of Virginia biologist, and eugenics advocate, Ivey Lewis. "Incidentally," *Raleigh News and Observer*, December 28, 1924.

28. Lewis, "Incidentally," *Raleigh News and Observer*, March 29, 1925. As publicity chairman for the North Carolina Federation of Women's Clubs in 1921, Lewis noted that the Raleigh branch was entertained with black-face comedy. Lewis, "General Federation Director Sends Message to N.C. Clubs," *Raleigh News and Observer*, October 12, 1921.

29. Lewis, "Incidentally," *Raleigh News and Observer*, April 12, March 29, 1925.

30. Lewis, "Incidentally," *Raleigh News and Observer*, February 13, 1927, and February 27, 1927.

31. Muhammad, *The Condemnation*, 35–82.

32. Lewis, "Incidentally," *Raleigh News and Observer*, October 20, 1921; June 21, 1925; June 19, December 18, 1927.

33. Lewis, "Incidentally," *Raleigh News and Observer*, March 15, 1936. See also correspondence about the Society for the Abolition of Capital Punishment and the American League to Abolish Capital Punishment. N. C. Newbold to Lewis, January 18, 1935; Vivian Pierce (executive secretary of the American League to Abolish) to Lewis, January 29, 1953; Pierce to Lewis, February 13, 1936; Box 255.2, NBL Papers. Clarence Darrow was the president of the American League. "Incidentally," *Raleigh News and Observer*, March 3, 1938 and April 24, 1938.

34. Jacquelyn Dowd Hall, *Revolt against Chivalry: Jessie Daniel Ames and the Women's Campaign against Lynching*, rev. ed. (New York: Columbia University Press, 1993), 95–119. It does not appear that Lewis belonged to any interracial organizations. Her papers included substantial literature from both the Commission on Interracial Cooperation (CIC) and the ASWPL and requests to join Ames's campaign against lynching. She did not join and did not support the federal anti-lynching bill in the 1930s. "Incidentally," August 24, 1930. On Blease's brand of racism, see Bryant Simon, *The Fabric of Defeat: The Politics of South Carolina Millhands, 1910–1948* (Chapel Hill: University of North Carolina Press, 1998), 19–48.

35. The overwhelming majority of the state's textile workers were white. Women and children were the primary workers in the early textile industry. See Jacquelyn Dowd Hall, et al., *Like a Family: The Making of a Southern Cotton Mill World* (New York: W.W. Norton, 1987), xii, 56–57, 67–69; Lewis, "First District in Federation Has Very Successful Meeting," *Raleigh News and Observer*, October 16, 1921; Anastasia Sims, *The Power of Femininity in the New South: Women's Organizations and Politics in North Carolina, 1880–1930* (Columbia: University of South Carolina Press, 1997), 196; Lewis, "Incidentally," *Raleigh News and Observer*, November 20, 1927.

36. Lewis, "Incidentally," *Raleigh News and Observer*, January 4, March 15, 1925.

37. For Graham's prediction see, Lewis, "Incidentally," *Raleigh News and Observer*, November 20, 1927. For more detailed information on the Gastonia strike,

see John A. Salmond, *Gastonia 1929: The Story of the Loray Mill Strike* (Chapel Hill: University of North Carolina Press, 1995); Liston Pope, *Millhands and Preachers: A Study of Gastonia* (New Haven, CT: Yale University Press, 1942).

38. Salmond, *Gastonia 1929*, 67–90.

39. Lewis, "Incidentally," *Raleigh News and Observer*, April 28, 1929.

40. Lewis, "Incidentally," *Raleigh News and Observer*, April 28, August 18, July 21, August 4, 1929; Salmond, *Gastonia 1929*, 111–112.

41. Lewis, "Anarchy v. Communism in Gastonia," *The Nation*, September 25, 1929: 321–322; *Charlotte Observer*, September 16, 1929; Salmond, *Gastonia*, 51, 128.

42. Lewis, "Incidentally," *Raleigh News and Observer*, September 29, 1929; Smith and Wilson, *North Carolina Women*, 262–265; Salmond, *Gastonia 1929*, 130–131; Gilmore, *Defying Dixie*, 82–105,

43. Lewis, "Incidentally," *Raleigh News and Observer*, October 6, 1929. For Graham's support of the strikers, see Warren Ashby, *Frank Porter Graham: A Southern Liberal* (Winston-Salem, NC: J. F. Blair Press, 1980), 74–77.

44. Lewis, "Incidentally," *Raleigh News and Observer*, October 6, 1929.

45. Lewis, "Incidentally," August 28, 1929; Nell Battle Lewis, "Anarchy v. Communism in Gastonia," *Nation*, September 25, 1929, 321–322.

46. Lewis, "Incidentally," *Raleigh News and Observer*, April 28, 1929; *Labor Defender*, August 1929, September 1929, Folder 1, Box 255.30, NBL Papers. Nell Battle Lewis, handwritten chronology, Folder 1, Box 255.30, NBL Papers; "None Are So Blind," *Gastonia Gazette*, June 17, 1929; Leidholdt, *Battling Nell*, 149; *Southern Textile Bulletin*, April 10, 1930.

47. Nell Battle Lewis, "Anarchy v. Communism in Gastonia," *Nation*, September 25, 1929, 321–22.

48. Gilmore, *Defying Dixie*, 226.

49. Lewis, "Incidentally," *Raleigh News and Observer*, April 15, September 28, 30, October 7, October 14, 21, November 11, 1928. Linda Lou Green, "Nell Battle Lewis: Crusading Columnist, 1921–1938" (MA thesis, East Carolina University, 1969), 33; "To the Democratic Voters of Wake County," Petition, Folder 255.52, Nell Battle Lewis Papers, NCDAH. Her papers include two copies of this petition. Each is signed by several women, six in one case and ten in another. John Wertheimer, Brian Luskey, et al., "Escape of the Match-Strikers: Disorderly North Carolina Women, the Legal System and the Samarcand Arson Case of 1931." *North Carolina Historical Review* 75 (October 1988): 435–460; Samarcand Arson Case File, NBL Papers.

50. The poem was actually entitled "Christ in Alabama," but Kemp Lewis referred to it as "Black Christ." The poem was published for the first time in the December issue of *Contempo* that coincided with Hughes's visit to Chapel Hill. Anthony Buttita and Milton Abernathy published the magazine and had requested a poem about the Scottsboro boys in Alabama. On Langston Hughes's role in Scottsboro case, see Dan Carter, *Scottsboro: A Tragedy of the American South* (Baton Rouge: Louisiana

State University Press, 1979), 154, 166–167.0 Frank Porter Graham from Kemp
Plummer Lewis, November 28, 1931, and Governor O. Max Gardner to Kemp
Plummer Lewis, November 30, 1931, Kemp Plummer Lewis Papers, Southern
Historical Collection (SHC), Wilson Library, University of North Carolina at
Chapel Hill; hereafter cited as Kemp Lewis Papers, SHC.

51. Leidholdt, *Battling Nell*, 170–180.

52. Ashby, *Frank Porter Graham*, 125–130; NBL to Kemp Lewis, [1932?], NBL to Kemp
Lewis, September 1932, Folder 418, Box 32, Kemp Lewis to Governor O. Max
Gardner, November 7, 1932, Box 32, Folder 425, and Kemp Lewis to Professor
Francis Bradshaw, November 10, 1932, Box 32, Folder 425, Kemp Plummer Lewis
Papers, SHC. "Incidentally," *Raleigh News and Observer*, September, 18, 1932.

53. Lewis, "Incidentally," *Raleigh News and Observer*, July 21, 1935; Gilmore, *Defying
Dixie*, 224–227.

54. Lewis, "Incidentally," *Raleigh News and Observer*, July 21, 28, 1935.

55. Lewis, "Incidentally," *Raleigh News and Observer*, March 10, July 21, and July 28,
1935. As Koven and Michel contend, reformers and activists who employed an ideology of maternalism did not have to believe that the federal government needed
to intervene. They could be states' rights advocates and maternalists. See Koven and
Michel, "Introduction: Mother Worlds," in *Mothers of a New World*, 11.

56. For a discussion of organizations that challenged the Jim Crow order as it existed
in the 1930s, see Egerton, *Speak Now against the Day*, 64–81, 91–104, 121–167;
Sullivan, *Days of Hope,* 69–102. The belief that black southerners were satisfied
with a fair implementation of segregation was not completely misguided. Of course
black southerners were not satisfied with the Jim Crow order, but until the 1940s,
the NAACP attacked the Jim Crow system by attacking the lack of equal facilities,
not the unconstitutional nature of segregation itself. This was commonly called the
"Margold Bible." In the midst of World War II, Thurgood Marshall dismissed this
strategy and started an all-out attack on the principle of separate but equal. See
Robert Weisbrot, *Freedom Bound: A History of America's Civil Rights Movement*
(New York: Penguin, 1991), 8.

57. See Alain Locke, "Who and What Is 'Negro'?" *Opportunity: Journal of Negro Life*
20, no. 2 (1942): 36–42; 20–3, 83–87. See also Winona Fletcher, "Witnessing a
'Miracle': Sixty Years of 'Heaven Bound' at Big Bethel in Atlanta," *Black American
Literature Forum*, The Black Church and the Black Theatre, 25, no. 1 (Spring 1991),
83–92; William H. Wiggins, "Pilgrims, Crosses, and Faith: The Folk Dimensions of
*Heaven Bound*," *Black American Literature Forum* 25, no. 1 (Spring 1991), 93–100.

58. Lewis, speech to the congregation of St. Paul's AME Church, Raleigh, November
5, 1935, Box 255.44, NBL Papers.

59. Gilmore, *Defying Dixie*, 226–229; Dorr, "Assuring America's Place in the Sun,"
257–296.

60. Lewis, "Incidentally," *Raleigh News and Observer*, March 17, 1935. See Lewis,
"Speech on the Negro in the Art," (1925?), NBL Papers.

61. Nell Battle Lewis to Margaret Mitchell, Box 48, Folder 73, Margaret Mitchell Papers, Hargrett Library, University of Georgia, Athens.

62. Sarah Gardner, *Blood and Irony: Southern White Women's Narratives of the Civil War, 1861–1937* (Chapel Hill: University of North Carolina Press, 2004), 240–245; Lewis, "Incidentally," *Raleigh News and Observer,* September 13, 20, 1936; May 9, 1937; May 15, 1938.

63. Josiah Bailey, "Senator Bailey Goes into Detail about Who's Right about the Court," *Raleigh News and Observer,* April 25, 1937. Bailey contended that he was a true New Dealer and that Roosevelt and the rest of the Democratic Party had departed from its initial aims. The North Caolina General Assembly had asked Bailey to support the plan for the court, but Bailey refused on the grounds that the Democratic platform that North Carolinians voted for in 1936 did not include this provision. Therefore, despite petitions he received to support it, he argued that his opposition remained the truest representation of the people's wishes. See Julian Pleasants, *Buncombe Bob: The Life and Times of Robert Rice Reynolds* (Chapel Hill: University of North Carolina Press, 2000), 115–116; Badger, *North Carolina and the New Deal,* 76–80; Abrams, *Conservative Constraints,* 239, 241–248; Egerton, *Speak Now against the Day,* 104–114, 150–154; Sullivan, *Days of Hope,* 87–93.

64. Lewis, "Scarlett Materializes," *Raleigh News and Observer,* February 18, 1940; Lewis to Mitchell, March 14, 1940, Box 48, Folder 73 and Mitchell to Lewis, March 15, 1940, Box 48, Folder 73, Margaret Mitchell Papers, Hargrett Library, University of Georgia.

65. Gilmore, *Defying Dixie,* 67–105.

66. Micki McElya, "Commemorating the Color Line," 208.

CHAPTER 5

1. For scholarship on World War II and the political, economic, and social changes it engendered in the American South, see James C. Cobb, *The South and America since World War II* (New York: Oxford University Press, 2011), 1–15, 55; Morton Sosna, "More Important than the Civil War? The Impact of World War II on the South," in *Perspectives on the American South: An Annual Review of Society, Politics, and Culture,* vol. 4, ed. James C. Cobb and Charles R. Wilson (New York: Gordon and Breach, 1987), 145–161; Egerton, *Speak Now against the Day,* 201–341; Gilmore, *Defying Dixie,* 346–399; Neil R. McMillen, ed., *Remaking Dixie: The Impact of World War II on the American South* (Jackson: University of Mississippi Press, 1997); Schulman, *From Cotton Belt to Sunbelt,* 125, 88–116; Frederickson, *Dixiecrat Revolt,* 28–66; Ward, *Defending White Democracy,* 36–66. Sokol, *There Goes My Everything,* 1. For the use of the term "warfare state," see James T. Sparrow, *Warfare State: World War II Americans and the Era of Big Government* (New York: Oxford University Press, 2011), 4–8, 41–47.

2. On conservatism in wartime, see Cobb, *The South and America*, 5; Ward, *Defending White Democracy*, 66; Schulman, *From Cotton Belt to Sun Belt*, 127; Kim Phillips-Fein, *Invisible Hands: The Businessmen's Crusade against the New Deal* (New York: W. W. Norton, 2009), 31.

3. Sosna, *In Search of*, 19.

4. For a recent work that locates the origins of massive resistance in the five years prior to World War II, see Ward, *Defending White Democracy*, 1–8.

5. For various treatments on southern partisan realignment and the rise of the GOP in the South that locate the impetus later than World War II, see Crespino, *In Search of Another Country*, 75, 205–236; Ronald Keith Gaddie, "Realignment," in *The Oxford Handbook of Southern Politics*, ed. Charles S. Bulloch and Mark J. Rozell (New York: Oxford University Press, 2012), 296–311.

6. "U.S. at War, Salisbury Entertains," *Time Magazine*, August 24, 1942; Eleanor Roosevelt, "My Day," August 14, 15, 1942, Eleanor Roosevelt's Papers Project at https://erpapers.columbian.gwu.edu/my-day, hereafter cited as ERPP.

7. J. S. McRae to Eleanor Roosevelt (ER), June 22, 1943, Eleanor Roosevelt Papers, quoted in Tyler, "How Southern Women Viewed Eleanor," in *Lives Full of Struggle and Triumph: Southern Women, Their Institution, and Their Communities*, ed. Bruce Clayton and John Salmond (Gainesville: University of Florida Press, 2003), 186. Eleanor Roosevelt's "My Day" column did not mention the scorning. Most of her column described her visit to Cannon Mills and her time at Livingstone College, "My Day," August 15, 1942, ERPP. On the disturbance that Eleanor Roosevelt's racial politics caused among southerners, see Howard W. Odum, *Race and Rumors of Race: Challenge to American Crisis* (Chapel Hill: University of North Carolina Press, 1943), 81–89.

8. Eleanor Roosevelt, "My Day," February 10, 1941, ERPP; Ogden, "Dis an' Dat," *Greenville Delta Democrat-Times*, February 16, 1941, October 31, 1943. For evidence that Ogden believed Eleanor Roosevelt had led the president astray, see "Dis an' Dat," *Greenville Delta Democrat-Times*, July 4, 1943.

9. Ogden, "Dis an' Dat," *Greenville Delta Democrat Times*, February 16, 1941.

10. Oral History Interview with Virginia Foster Durr, March 13–15, 1975. Interview G0023-2, Southern Oral History Project #4007 in Southern Oral History Project Collection, Southern Historical Collection, Wilson Library, University of North Carolina, Chapel Hill; Morgan, *Women and Patriotism*, 155–156.

11. Tyler, "How Southern Women Viewed Eleanor," 186–200.

12. "Mary Cain's Column," *Summit Sun*, October 15, 29, 1942, November 5, 19, 1942; Ward, *Defending White Democracy*, 58.

13. John L. Thompson, "Dunjee, Roscoe (1883–1965)," in *Encyclopedia of Oklahoma History and Culture*" (Oklahoma Historical Society), http://digital.library. okstate.edu/encyclopedia/entries/d/du007.html; "Mary Cain's Column," *Summit Sun*, October 22, 1942 and November 5, 12, 19 1942.

14. "Mary Cain's Column," *Summit Sun*, November 12, 1942.

15. "Amity Is U.S. Task, First Lady Holds," *New York Times*, February 17, 1944. See Fedora Maria Carpenter to Eleanor Roosevelt, February 29, 1944, and Alma Valda Lester to Eleanor Roosevelt, February 29, 1944, Folder 190.1, Papers of Anna Eleanor Roosevelt, FDR Presidential Library and Museum, Hyde Park New York; hereafter cited as ER Papers.

16. Mrs. M. M. McConnell (Gallatin, Tennessee) to ER, March 10, 1944, Mrs. L. R. Standifer (Chattanooga, Tennessee) to ER, March 6, 1944, Marion M. Crisp (Elaine, AK) to ER, March 26, 1944, Folder 190.1, ER Papers.

17. Mrs. Paul Norris to ER, Folder 190.1, ER Papers.

18. Mrs. Paul Norris to ER, April 4, 1944, Folder 190.1, ER Papers.

19. Outraged woman (Lakeland, Florida) to ER, February 28, 1944, Folder 190.1, ER Papers.

20. Fedora Maria Carpenter to Eleanor Roosevelt, February 29, 1944, and Alma Valda Lester to Eleanor Roosevelt, February 29, 1944, Folder 190.1, ER Papers. See Folder 190.1, ER Papers, for a broader sampling of letters.

21. Black women did vote in the South after ratification of the Nineteenth Amendment, but they did so in relatively small numbers. See Gilmore, *Gender and Jim Crow*, 223–224; Schuyler, *The Weight of Their Votes*, 24–25; and Charron, *Freedom's Teacher*, 168.

22. Mrs. James C. Cowan, Orange, Virginia, to FSO, August 22, 1942, Folder 14, FSO Papers. While the exact nature of "servant question" is unclear in Cowan's letter, rumors of Eleanor Clubs were circulating around the South at this time; see Bryant Simon, "Fearing Eleanor: Wartime Rumors and Racial Anxieties, 1940–1945," in *Labor in the Modern South*, ed. Glen Eskew (Athens: University of Georgia Press, 2001), 83–101; James T. Sparrow, *Warfare State: World War II Americans and the Era of Big Government* (New York: Oxford University Press, 2011), 97–99; Odum, *Race and Rumors of Race*, 73–89.

23. At the University of Virginia, the lead academic was Ivey Lewis and at the University of North Carolina, Wesley Critz George continued to teach eugenics into the 1950s. See Gregory Dorr, "Assuring America's Place in the Sun: Ivy Foreman Lewis and the Teaching of Eugenics at the University of Virginia," *Journal of Southern History* 66, no. 2 (May 2000): 257–296; George Lewis, "Scientific Certainty"; Wesley Critz George, Racial Science and Organized White Resistance in North Carolina, 1954–1962," *Journal of American Studies* 38, no. 2 (August 2004): 227–247.

24. Miss Lillie M. Williams to Eleanor Roosevelt, March 6, 1944, Series 190.1, ER Papers.

25. Ogden, "Dis an' Dat," *Greenville Delta Democrat-Times*, July 4, 1943; March 8, 1942. Ogden's uncle Charles Clark studied with Ivey Lewis. See Charles W. Clark to Ivey Lewis, March 11, 1949, "C" Folder, Box 10, Dean's Papers 5119, Special Collections, Alderman Library, University of Virginia, Charlottesville; Dorr, "Assuring America's Place in the Sun," 257.

26. Ogden, "Dis an' Dat," *Greenville Delta Democrat-Times*, July 4, 1943; February 16, 1941; January 18, September 6, 1942; July 4, 1943.

27. Quoted in Tyler, "How Southern Women Viewed Eleanor," 196; W. H. Gordon, "Letter to the Editor," *Greenville Delta Democrat-Times*, July 6, 1943, Folder 15, FSO Papers. For a secondary treatment of the Detroit riots and the role of black southern immigrants, see Dominic J. Capeci Jr. and Martha Wilkerson, *Layered Violence: The Detroit Riots of 1943* (Jackson: University of Mississippi Press, 1991), 4. For broader treatments of Detroit, see Sugrue, *The Origins of the Urban Crisis;* Kevin Boyle, *Arc of Justice: A Saga of Race, Civil Rights, and Murder in the Jazz Age* (New York: Holt, 2004).

28. Loretta Carlisle to Eleanor Roosevelt, April 10, 1944, Mrs. M. M. McConnell to ER, March 10, 1944, Bertie Mae Loner (South Carolina) to ER, March 1, 1944, Folder 190.1, ER Papers. The blinding of black veteran Isaac Woodard outside Aiken, South Carolina, would bring to fruition what Loner had predicted.

29. Ogden, "Dis an' Dat," *Greenville Delta Democrat-Times*, November 7, 1943.

30. For a secondary treatment of the equalization campaigns in the South, see Harry Ashmore, *The Negro and the Schools*, with foreword by Owen J. Roberts (Chapel Hill: University of North Carolina Press, 1954), 107–139; Ravitch, *The Troubled Crusade*, 1–7. Ravitch notes that federal aid to education had been an issue visited periodically since 1870. She contends that aid bills had always foundered for three reasons: "race, religion, and fear of federal control." The debates on how or whether to fund segregated schools in the South were the key to the bill's failure.

31. Senator James Eastland to Mary Dawson Cain, April 26, 1944, Box 17, Mary Dawson Cain papers, Mississippi Department of Archives and History, Jackson, Mississippi. These are unprocessed with decades of materials scattered through the boxes with no archival guide.

32. Ogden, "Dis an' Dat," *Greenville Delta Democrat-Times*, July 25, 1943. On her opposition to federal aid to education, see also November 7, 1943; Ravitch, *The Troubled Crusade*, 5. The National Education Association's report in 1944 entitled "Education for All Americans" had called for public education, Ravitch argues, to be a "custodial institution" engaged in "preparing them for the existing social order." The report had remained silent on the issue of racial segregation. See Ravitch, *Left Behind*, 324–326.

33. Ogden, "Dis an' Dat," *Greenville Delta Democrat-Times*, July 25, 1943.

34. Laats, *The Other School Reformers*, 134–149.

35. ER, "My Day," February 14, 1944, ERPP.

36. Ogden, "Dis an' Dat," *Greenville Delta Democrat-Times*, July 25, 1943; August 1, 1943, November 7, 1943, November 21, 1943. Tindall, *The Emergence*, 496–497; Schulman, *From Cotton Belt to Sun Belt*, 193–194.

37. Tyler, "How Southern Women Viewed Eleanor," 196.

38. Lewis, "Incidentally," *Raleigh News and Observer*, October 25, 1942; September 27, 1942.

39. Korstad, *Civil Rights Unionism*, 55–57, 142–166.

40. Lewis, "Incidentally," *Raleigh News and Observer*, March 29, 1942; May 9 and May 30, 1943; Sparrow, *Warfare State*, 196–200.

41. On the relationship between racial segregation and labor segregation, see Korstad, *Civil Rights Unionism*, 100–113. On the relationship between labor, race, and Jim Crow, see also Michelle Brattain, *The Politics of Whiteness: Race, Worker and Culture in the Modern South* (Athens: University of Georgia Press, 2004), 47–48; Schulman, *From Cotton Belt to Sunbelt*, 28–30.

42. Korstad, *Civil Rights Unionism*, 5, 57–59.

43. United Mine Workers to Cornelia Dabney Tucker (CDT), May 28, 1941; Malvina Thompson to CDT, July 3, 1941; CDT to Thomas Connally, April 24, 1942; CDT to Senator Alvin Barkley, May 11, 1943; Sam Rayburn to CDT, June 2, 1943, Nathan Cowan to CDT, June 4, 1943, CDT to James Byrnes, June 6, 1943, William Green to CDT, June 6, 1943, Olin Johnston to CDT, Folder 2-19, Box 1, Cornelia Dabney Tucker Papers, South Caroliniana Library, University of South Carolina, Columbia.

44. Mercedes Daugherty of the CIO to CDT, June 12, 1943, Lloyd Garrison from the National War Labor Board to CDT, June 16, 1943; Folder 1, Box 1, CDT Papers.

45. Nellie Nugent Somerville to FSO, July 4, 1944, December 26, 1944, Folder 16, FSO Papers.

46. Ogden, "Dis an' Dat," *Greenville Delta Democrat-Times,* August 31, October 18, April 12, 1942.

47. Ogden, "Dis an' Dat," *Greenville Delta Democrat-Times*, May 10, 1942.

48. Ogden, "Dis an' Dat," *Greenville Delta Democrat-Times*, May 30, 1943.

49. Ogden, "Dis an' Dat," *Greenville Delta Democrat-Times*, May 10, April 12, 1942, June 20, August 8, October 17, 1943; January 16, 30, 1944; May 9, 1943.

50. Ogden was not the only Bolivar County woman to publish a weekly letter to soldiers. Mrs. Keith Somerville (Keith was her name, not her husband's.) did so in the other county paper but her tone was decidedly different, celebrating all the county's men in uniform. See Judy Barrett Litoff and David C. Smith, eds., *Dear Boys: World War II Letters from a Woman Back Home, by Mrs. Keith Frazier Somerville* (Jackson: University Press of Mississippi, 1991).

51. Florence Sillers Ogden, *Letters to the Boys* (Bolivar County, Mississippi: DAR, 1992), typescript copy in author's possession. "Dis and Dat," *Greenville Delta Democrat-Times,* May 10, 1942.

52. Sparrow, *Warfare State*, 190–200.

53. Ogden, "Dis an' Dat," *Greenville Delta Democrat-Times*, May 30,1943.

54. Ogden, "Dis an' Dat," *Greenville Delta Democrat-Times*, June 6, 1943.

55. For more on racial nationalism, see Gary Gerstle, *American Crucible: Race and Nation in the Twentieth Century* (Princeton, NJ: Princeton University Press, 2001), 1–13, 187–237.

56. Ogden, "Dis' an Dat," *Greenville Delta Democrat-Times*, June 6, 1943.

57. Numan Bartley emphasizes the role of the anti-communist crusade in wrecking the possibilities of liberalism in the postwar period. Bartley, *The New South*, 38–73.

58. Ward, *Defending White Democracy*, 9–37; Mrs. May Thompson Evan to MDC, July 1, 1939, Box 2, MDC Papers; Phillips-Fein, *Invisible Hands*, 22–23, 89. For connections between anti-communism and anti–civil rights, see Lewis, *White South, Red Menace*.

59. Albertine Moore, "Mrs. Cornelia Dabney Tucker," typed transcript, 1944, Folder 1, Box 1, CDT Papers; Steven F. Lawson, *Black Ballots: Voting Rights in the South, 1944–1969* (New York: Columbia University Press, 1976), 67–85.

60. Nellie Nugent Somerville to FSO, July 4, 1944, December 26, 1944, Folder 16, FSO Papers. Nellie Nugent Somerville, "Democracy and the Poll Tax," *Daily News* (Jackson, Mississippi), April 24, 1942. This was also printed in pamphlet form. A copy of the pamphlet is located in Folder 16, FSO Papers. Nellie Nugent Somerville, "Food for Thought," *Bolivar County Democrat* (Rosedale, Mississippi), April 27, 1944. For text on the Supreme Court's decision on the all-white primary, see *Smith* v. *Allwright*, 321 U.S. 649 (1944). For southern reactions to the decision, see Frederickson, *The Dixiecrat Revolt*, 39–42.

61. For information on Vito Marcantonio, see "Vito Marcantonio Falls Dead in Street," *New York Times*, August 10, 1954, Section L, 1. For a political biography, see Gerald Meyer, *Vito Marcantonio: Radical Politician, 1902–1954* (New York: State University of New York, 1989).

62. "Dis an' Dat," *Greenville Delta Democrat-Times*, June 6, 1943. In 1941, Mrs. Roosevelt delivered a speech in Virginia in which she called for the abolition of the poll tax. A few months later, Claude Pepper introduced such legislation into the United States Senate. For an article examining women's work to abolish the poll tax, see Sarah Wilkerson-Freeman, "The Second Battle for Women Suffrage: Alabama White Women, the Poll Tax, and V. O. Key's Master Narrative of Southern Politics," *Journal of Southern History* 68 (May 2002): 333–374.

63. "Incidentally," *Raleigh News and Observer*, February 13, 1944; Frederickson, *The Dixiecrat Revolt*, 36–37; Tindall, *The Emergence*, 726.

64. For an account of Walter Sillers and the Soldier Voting Act, see Thomas Melton, "Mr. Speaker: A Biography of Walter Sillers" (MA thesis, University of Mississippi, 1972), 62–63. George Tindall argued that the federal Soldier Voting Act was truncated by a states' rights block led by Mississippi senators Eastland and Rankin who demanded that the states' consent be required. See Tindall, *The Emergence*, 726; Lawson, *Black Ballots*, 74.

65. Ogden, "Dis an' Dat," *Greenville Delta Democrat-Times*, January 6, 1944.

66. "Two Strikes on Dewey," *Crisis*, April 1944, 104; Jerry Weir to MDC, March 12, 1944; Harry Cohan to MDC, February 4, 1944, Robert Hammond Murray to MDC, March 4, 1944, Lt. Robert Meredith to MDC, March 6, 1944, Lois Simpson to MDC, March 15, 1944, Box 17, MDC Papers.

67. Ogden, "Dis an' Dat," *Greenville Delta Democrat-Times*, May 7, 1944.

68. Ogden, "Dis an' Dat," *Greenville Delta Democrat-Times*, May 28, 1944.

69. Ogden, "Dis an' Dat," *Greenville Delta Democrat-Times*, June 11, 1944. Governor Thomas Bailey, resident of Sharkey County in the Delta, called a special session of the legislature that created a supplemental ballot excluding the bolting electors in order to avert an electoral vote that failed to represent 93 percent of Mississippi's votes. See Skates, "World War II and Its Effects," in *A History of Mississippi*, 130– 131. See also "Presidential Elector Revolt Best Mississippi News," *Greenville Delta Democrat-Times*, December 31, 1944; Mickey, *Paths Out of Dixie*, 154.

70. Ogden, "Dis an' Dat," *Greenville Delta Democrat-Times*, June 11, 1944.

71. Ogden, "Letter to the Boys in the Service," *Bolivar County Democrat*, July 20, 27, 1944.

72. On the convention and the elector controversy, see Roy H. Ruby, "The Presidential Election of 1944 in Mississippi: The Bolting Electors" (MA thesis, Mississippi State University, 1966), 39, 44–45. While three electors pledged not to cast their votes for FDR, two more did not say they would cast their votes according to the popular vote. Of the ten counties that cast between 9 percent and 23 percent of their votes for the bolting elector slate, five were in the Delta. Bolivar led the Delta in votes cast for the bolting electors. Of the counties casting the most votes for the bolting electors, only Grenada had a black population under 60 percent.

73. Ogden, "Dis an' Dat," *Greenville Delta Democrat-Times*, August 20, July 9, July 16, 1944.

74. CDT to Mary Fraser, June 14, 1945, Folder 2, Box 1, CDT Papers.

75. CDT to E. R. Stettinious, Acting Secretary of State, November 15, 1944 and J. M. Colton Hand to CDT, February 24, 1945, Folder 2, Box 1, CDT Papers.

76. Helen Dwight Reid, AAUW national headquarters, to CDT, March 17, 1945; Ruth Lawton to CDT, March 22, 1945; Mary Frayser to CDT, June 19, 1945. Evidently, CDT began a letter writing campaign to J. H. Hope, State Superintendent of Education. Hope to Mr. Harry G. Tobey; Hope to Mrs. James E. Malloch (noting endorsement of Your Country and Mine), Hope to Mrs. Henry Rutledge Buist, Governor Ransome Williams to Buist, Williams to CDT, June to August 1945, Box 1 Folder 2, CDT Papers; Edward Scheiberling to CDT, July 11, 1945; Francis F. Coleman to CDT, August 23, 1946, Box 1, Folder 3, CDT Papers.

77. On the relationship between the Cold War and civil rights, see Mary Dudziak, *Cold War Civil Rights: Race and the Image of American Democracy* (Princeton, NJ: Princeton University Press, 2000); Thomas Borstelmann, *The Cold War and the Color Line* (Cambridge, MA: Harvard University Press, 2001); Jonathan Seth Rosenberg, "'How Far the Promised Land?': World Affairs and the American Civil Rights Movement from the First World War to Vietnam" (Ph.D. diss., Harvard University, 1997); Penny Von Eschen, *Race against Empire: Black Americans and Anticolonialism, 1937–1957* (Ithaca, NY: Cornell University Press, 1997), 3, 82, 148– 150; Anderson, *Eyes Off the Prize*, 179–201.

78. As early as 1941, Lewis had indicated that her book club lectures were a source of income and were becoming fairly popular. See Nell Battle Lewis to Mrs. Ernest Cruikshank, March 27, 1941, "Nell Battle Lewis," File in St. Mary's School Archives, Raleigh, North Carolina. See also "Year Book of the Alma Club," Henderson, North Carolina, 1940–1941, Folder 255.6, Nell Battle Lewis Papers, NCDAH. The papers of Lewis include a list of eighty-one book clubs with 114 contact women across the state. The names of contacts in the Alma Club reflect the membership in 1941. See Folder 255.6, NBL Papers. Her advertised talks included "Background for Blitzkrieg," "True 'Ghost' Stories," and "Modern North Carolina Writers." By 1947, she had added "World Federation" to her list as book clubs contacted her about how to break down that subject into a year-long study group for the calendar year 1948. See Lucy Bosher of Fayetteville, North Carolina, to Nell Battle Lewis, May 27, 1948, Folder 255.6, Mary Hamilton Stephens, Montreat, North Carolina, to Nell Battle Lewis, July 14, 1948, Folder 255.6. Her advertising card listed summaries of her talks and fees. She charged a fee $25.00 for one lecture and $60.00 for a series of three plus travel, food, and lodging expenses. Folder 255.6, NBL Papers.

79. Lewis, "Incidentally," *Raleigh News and Observer*, November 12, 1944, February 20, 1944, October 22, 1944.

80. Gilmore, *Defying Dixie*, 378–380; Rayford Logan, ed., *What the Negro Wants* (Chapel Hill: University of North Carolina Press, 1944).

81. Lewis, "Incidentally," *Raleigh News and Observer*, November 5, 1944.

82. On reactions to Smith's novel, see Anne C. Loveland, *Lillian Smith: A Southerner Confronting the South, a Biography* (Baton Rouge: Louisiana State University Press, 1986), 69–76. While the novel received mixed reviews from both white and black audiences, Loveland noted that two renowned black communists—W. E. B. Du Bois and Paul Robeson—wrote and spoke favorably of the novel. Lewis also mentioned in her review that DuBois had given *Strange Fruit* a favorable review. Lillian Smith, *Strange Fruit: A Novel* (New York: Reynal and Hitchcock, 1944).

83. Lewis, "Incidentally," *Raleigh News and Observer*, August 4, 1946, April 9, 1944. Another woman wrote to Lewis and suggested that the reason Smith's book included so much filth was that it would sell in the North and "that a book that does not sell in the North has a poor sale." Quote by Francis B. Hays of Oxford, North Carolina, in "Incidentally," *Raleigh News and Observer*, April 16, April 9, 1944; January 20, 1946.

84. Lewis, "Incidentally," *Raleigh News and Observer*, September 23, 1945; Cobb, *The South since World War II*, 12–14.

85. Ogden, "Civil Rights" speech given to the Democratic Women of Mississippi, undated., 1947–8, Folder 103, FSO Papers; Frederickson, *The Dixiecrat Revolt*, 64–65.

86. Lewis, "Incidentally," *Raleigh News and Observer*, February 22, 1948. In an editorial on the same day entitled "Dixie Dictatorship," the writer praised North Carolina for abolishing the poll tax in the 1920s. It condemned the poll tax not as a racial

device but as a class device, contending that it disfranchised more whites than blacks. As evidence of its "progressive" nature, the editorial judged the poll tax "an anti-democratic institution wherever it exists."

87. Mrs. William Kendall and Mrs. O. H. Palmer to FSO, April 3, 1948, Folder 20, FSO Papers.

88. Mrs. William Kendall and Mrs. O. H. Palmer to FSO, April 3, 1948, Folder 20, FSO Papers.

89. Ogden, "Civil Rights," speech given to the Woman's Committee of the States' Rights Democratic Party, April 15, 1948, in Jackson, Mississippi, FSO Papers. For her account of the speech, see Ogden, "States' Rights," speech given to the Gunnison PTA, [1948?], Folder 119, FSO Papers.

90. Ogden, "Ancestors," speech delivered in Jackson, Mississippi, to the State Assembly of the Daughters of the American Colonies, undated [1948?], Folder 119, FSO Papers.

91. Ogden, "States' Rights," speech given to Gunnison Parent-Teachers Association, (underline in original), undated [1948?], Folder 119, FSO Papers.

92. Egerton, *Speak Now against the Day*, 500–505.

93. Lewis, "Incidentally," *Raleigh News and Observer*, June 8, 1947.

94. Lewis, "Incidentally," *Raleigh News and Observer*, June 13, 1948; *Raleigh News and Observer*, June 13, 1948; *Chapel Hill Weekly*, June 18, 1948.

95. For a listing of her editorials, see Folders 255.17, 255.18, NBL Papers. In a tally of editorials from June of 1948 through the fall, Lewis's notes indicate that she wrote forty-three of the sixty-one editorials published in that period.

96. Lewis, "Incidentally," *Raleigh News and Observer*, June 8, 1947; *Raleigh Times*, June 18, 19, July 15, 16, 1948; Bartley, *The New South*, 55–57.

97. Ward, *Defending White Democracy*, 41, 65–81; Cobb, *The South and World War II*, 235.

98. Holt, "Marking," 7.

CHAPTER 6

1. Ward, *Defending White Democracy*, 100–104; Frederickson, *The Dixiecrat Revolt*, 118–124; Gilmore, *Defying Dixie*, 409–414. In North Carolina, Tennessee, Arkansas, Georgia, and Alabama, the Democratic vote share rose 20 points in the New Deal and remained so for nearly two decades. See Gaddie, "Realignment," in *The Oxford Handbook of Southern Politics*, 298.

2. Ziker, "Race, Conservative Politics, and U.S. Foreign Policy," 27–28.

3. On the ways civil rights activists used the United Nations, see Gilmore, *Defying Dixie*, 2–3, 407–410. On the Dixiecrats, see Frederickson, *The Dixiecrat Revolt*, 118–129; Ziker, "Race, Conservative Politics, and U.S. Foreign Policy," 17, 22, 27, 41–48; Carol Anderson, *Eyes Off the Prize: The United Nations and the African American Freedom Struggle for Human Rights, 1944–1955* (Cambridge: Cambridge University

Press, 2003), 78; Duane Tananbaum, *The Bricker Amendment Controversy: A Test of Eisenhower's Political Leadership* (Ithaca, NY: Cornell University Press, 1988), 2–4; "To Secure These Rights: The Report of the Presidential Committee on Civil Rights," 1947, 110–111, http://www.trumanlibrary.org/civilrights/srights3.htm#110; Olsen, "One Nation, One World," 121. Other justifications for federal intervention in civil rights included a 1920 Supreme Court case, *Missouri* v. *Holland*, which decided that the international agreement between the United States and Great Britain to protect migratory birds trumped a state law that contested such protection, leading opponents of Article 55 and 56 of the UN Charter to say that the same reasoning could be used to extend federal control over social and economic matters. For the NAACP's petitioning of the UN, see also Danielle McGuire, *At the Dark End of the Street: Black Women, Rape, and Resistance: A New History of the Civil Rights Movement from Rosa Parks to the Rise of Black Power* (New York: Alfred A. Knopf, 2010), 142.

4. On the relationship between the Cold War and civil rights, see Mary Dudziak, *Cold War Civil Rights: Race and the Image of American Democracy* (Princeton, NJ: Princeton University Press, 2000); Thomas Borstelmann, *The Cold War and the Color Line* (Cambridge, MA: Harvard University Press, 2001); Jonathan Seth Rosenberg, " 'How Far the Promised Land?': World Affairs and the American Civil Rights Movement from the First World War to Vietnam" (Ph.D. diss., Harvard University, 1997); Penny Von Eschen, *Race against Empire: Black Americans and Anticolonialism, 1937–1957* (Ithaca, NY: Cornell University Press, 1997), 3, 82, 148–150; Anderson, *Eyes Off the Prize,* 179–201.

5. Ann Ziker argues that connections between southern segregationists and the more mainstream national conservative movement coalesced around opposition to anticolonialism. See Ziker, "Race, Conservative Politics, and U.S. Foreign Policy," 1–26; Nickerson, *Mothers of Conservatism,* 44–45, 69–102; Olsen, "One Nation, One World," 61, 86–88, 121.

6. For the best discussion of the impact of Cold War ideology on women's roles, ideas about sexuality, and the resurgence of the home as a woman's primary sphere, see Elaine Tyler May, *Homeward Bound: American Families in the Cold War Era* (New York: Basic Books, 1988), 58–134. See also K. A. Cuordileone, " 'Politics in the Age of Anxiety': Cold War Political Culture and the Crisis in American Masculinity," *Journal of American History* 87, no. 2 (September 2000): 515–545; Laura McEnaney, "He-Men and Christian Mothers: The America First Movement and the Gendered Meanings of Patriotism and Isolationism," *Diplomatic History* 18, no. 1 (Winter, 1994): 49.

7. Ziker, "Race, Conservative Politics, and U.S. Foreign Policy," 69; Michelle Brattain, "Race, Racism and Antiracism: UNESCO and the Politics of Presenting Science to the Postwar Public," *American Historical Review* 112, no. 5 (December 2007): 1386–1387.

8. Egerton, *Speak Now against the Day*, 448–460; Lewis, *The White South and the Red Menace*; Jeff Woods, *Black Struggle, Red Scare: Segregationists and Anticommunists in the South, 1948–1968* (Baton Rouge: Louisiana State University Press, 2004); Hollinger Barnard, ed., *Outside the Magic Circle: The Autobiography of Virginia Durr* (Tuscaloosa: University of Alabama Press, 1985), xx; Anne Loveland, *A Southerner Confronting the South: A Biography* (Baton Rouge: Louisiana State University Press, 1986); Catherine Fosl, *Subversive Southerner: Anne Braden and the Struggle for Racial Justice in the Cold War South* (New York: Palgrave Macmillan, 2002), 117–121; Robert Korstad, *Civil Rights Unionism: Tobacco Workers and the Struggle for Democracy in the Mid-Twentieth Century South* (Chapel Hill: University of North Carolina Press, 2003). On campaigns against sexual violence, see McGuire, *At the Dark End of the Street*, 28–65.

9. Tucker and Cain had long aligned themselves with business conservatives, advocates of limited government, and opponents of the New Deal state. Ogden had been an avid New Dealer, but the civil rights agenda of the wartime Democratic Party had moved her to embrace a broader conservative agenda in the postwar years.

10. Most white southerners did not question the reign of racial segregation, and if they did, they kept it to themselves. Support for segregation, however, in 1948 did not equal an embrace of a national conservative platform of small government or anti-New Deal sentiment. In the South, the label "segregationist" still had room for southern liberals, separate but equal liberals, and gradualists as well as conservatives.

11. Jason Morgan Ward emphasizes the efforts of Dixiecrats to make a states' rights platform the basis for the reinvigoration of a conservative national movement. Ward, *Defending White Democracy*, 92–120, particularly 106–108; Nickerson, *Mothers of Conservatism*, xx–xxii, 27–31, 91–97. On the rise of conservatism in general in this period, see Mary C. Brennan, *Wives, Mothers, and the Red Menace: Conservative Women and the Crusade against Communism* (Boulder: University of Colorado Press, 2008), 13–30; Critchlow, *Phyllis Schlafly*, 12–61; Nash, *The Conservative Intellectual Movement*; Schoenwald, *A Time for Choosing;* Dan Carter, *The Politics of Rage: George Wallace, the Origins of the New Conservatism, and the Transformation of American Politics* (New York: Simon and Schuster, 1995); McGirr, *Suburban Warriors*. On southern Conservatism, see Jane De Hart and Donald Mathews, *Sex, Gender, and the Politics of the ERA: A State and the Nation* (New York: Oxford University Press, 1990), 212–225; Elna Green, "From Antisuffragism to Anti-Communism: The Conservative Career of Ida M. Darden," *Journal of Southern History* 65, no. 2 (May 1999): 287–316; Sokol, *There Goes My Everything*, 37–47. On "color-blind" conservatism in a later era, see Matthew D. Lassiter, *The Silent Majority: Suburban Politics in the Sunbelt South* (Princeton, NJ: Princeton University Press, 2006), 13–14, 41–43, 323; Kevin Kruse, *White Flight: Atlanta and the Making of Modern Conservatism* (Princeton, NJ: Princeton University Press, 2005), 245–247.

12. Joseph Fry, *Dixie Looks Abroad: The South and U.S. Foreign Relations, 1789–1973* (Baton Rouge: Louisiana State University Press, 2002), 225–230.

13. Fry, *Dixie Looks Abroad*, 226; Alfred O. Hero Jr., *The Southerner and World Affairs* (Baton Rouge: Louisiana State University Press, 1965), 104–108; Ziker, "Race, Conservative Politics," 67–68; Lewis, "Incidentally," *Raleigh News and Observer*, March 10, June 30, September 29, 1946; Egerton, *Speak Now*, 45–45; Melvyn Lefler, *The Specter of Communism: The United States and the Origins of the Cold War, 1917–1953* (New York: Hill and Wang, 1994), 50–54.

14. Hero, *The Southerner and World Affairs*, 102–103. For information on other southerners who embraced a world organization, see Steven P. Moore, "The Shadow and the Spotlight: Ralph McGill and Liberalism in the New South, 1933–1950" (MA thesis, University of Georgia, 1988), 40; John Kneebone, *Southern Liberal Journalists and the Issue of Race, 1920–1944* (Chapel Hill: University of North Carolina Press, 1985), xviii; Nell Battle Lewis to Frank Porter Graham, August 12, 1943, Frank Porter Graham to NBL, August 17, 1943, Folders 1597–1606, Series 1.1., Frank Porter Graham Papers, Southern Historical Collection, Wilson Library, University of North Carolina, Chapel Hill; hereafter cited as Graham Papers.

15. Hero, *The Southerner and World Affairs*, 225–227. A majority of southerners, however, according to Hero, were opposed to changing the UN into a more all-encompassing world government of which Lewis was an early supporter. He found that in general a majority of southerners did not want a "supranational regime outside the UN."

16. Lewis, "Incidentally," *Raleigh News and Observer*, May 6, 1945; September 10, October 3, 6, 7, 21, 23; November 19, 26, 27; December 21; July 1, 1945. The headlines come from *Raleigh News and Observer*, September 10, 1945; October 3, 6, 23, 1945; November 19, 26, 27, 1945; and December 21, 1945. For her early interest in an international peacekeeping organization, see her columns on September 27, 1942, and October 1, 1943. See also Leidholdt, *Battling Nell*, 216.

17. Lewis, "Incidentally," *Raleigh News and Observer*, September 28, 1947.

18. Lewis, "Incidentally," *Raleigh News and Observer*, August 3, September 14, 21, 1947. These columns list the paper's headlines that related to communist expansion from August 1945 to July 1947; "Incidentally," *Raleigh News and Observer*, February 28, 1947.

19. Lewis, "Incidentally," *Raleigh News and Observer*, October 20, 1946, February 16, 17, March 23, 25, September 14, 21, 1947; Lefler, *The Specter*, 54–56; Egerton, *Speak Now against the Day*, 452–454; May, *Homeward Bound*, 19–39.

20. Lewis, "Incidentally," *Raleigh News and Observer*, August 3, September 14, 21, 1947. These columns list the paper's headlines that related to communist expansion from August 1945 to July 1947; "Incidentally," *Raleigh News and Observer*, February 28, 1947; Gilmore, *Defying Dixie*, 426–432.

21. Lewis, "Incidentally," *Raleigh News and Observer*, July 20, 27, August 31, September 7, 1947, June 13, 1948.

22. Olsen, "One World," 150–158; Nickerson, *Mothers of Conservatism*, 28, 73–78; Lewis, "Incidentally," *Raleigh News and Observer*, August 24, 1947.

23. Lewis, "Incidentally," *Raleigh News and Observer* July 27, September 1, 1947; *Sunday Star-News* (Wilmington), undated clipping in NBL Papers; *Savannah Morning News*, July 29, August 14, 1947; Mrs. L. B. Street, letter to the editor, *Raleigh News and Observer*, undated clipping, NBL Papers; three other newspaper editorials are included in this clipping file that applaud Nell Battle Lewis's efforts to save her university and her state from communist infiltration. See File 255.37, NBL Papers.

24. Nickerson, *Mothers of Conservatism*, 28; Ziker, "Race, Conservative Politics, and U.S. Foreign Policy," 6, 22.

25. Nell Battle Lewis to Frank Porter Graham, February 17, 1950; Frank Porter Graham to Nell Battle Lewis, February 17, 1950, Folder 255.6, Nell Battle Lewis Papers, North Carolina Division of History and Archives, Raleigh, North Carolina. On the 1948 and 1950 elections as moments of organizing for the right, see Ward, *Defending White Democracy*, 104.

26. Warren Ashby, *Frank Porter Graham: A Southern Liberal* (Winston-Salem, NC: John F. Blair, 1980), 257–271.

27. NBL to Willis Smith, May 29, 1950, NBL Papers.

28. Stella K. Barbee to NBL, February 8, 1950; Lily Park to NBL, June 21, 1950; and Mary Hilliard Hinton to NBL, June 10, 1950, NBL Papers.

29. Lewis, "Incidentally," *Raleigh News and Observer*, June 18, 1950. The following week she noted that her readers should have known that she meant "for" non-segregation, not against.

30. Frederickson, *The Dixiecrat Revolt*, 4–9, 119–149; Timothy Tyson, *Radio Free Dixie: Robert F. Williams and the Roots of Black Power* (Chapel Hill: University of North Carolina Press, 1999), 67.

31. Pleasants and Burns, *Frank Porter Graham*, 72–74, 89.

32. Talk by Nell Battle Lewis at Smith Rally, Wake County Court House, July 23, 1950, Folder 255.4, NBL Papers. She also refers to her speech in "Incidentally," *Raleigh News and Observer*, July 2, 1950. For a description of the rally and the *Raleigh News and Observer*'s support of Graham, see Pleasants and Burns, *Frank Porter Graham*, 49, 180–181. For information on the 1898 campaigns, see Gilmore, *Gender and Jim Crow*, 91–118; Timothy Tyson and David Cecelski, eds., *Democracy Betrayed: The Wilmington Race Riot of 1898 and Its Legacy* (Chapel Hill: University of North Carolina Press, 1998), 3–13.

33. *Raleigh News and Observer*, July 2, 1950. The editorial page ran a reprint from the *Christian Science Monitor*.

34. For examples, see "People's Forum," *Raleigh News and Observer*, July 3, July 10, 1950.

35. *Sweatt v. Painter*, United States Reports 339 (1950): 629; *McLaurin v. Oklahoma State Regents*, United States Report, 339 (1950): 637; *Henderson v. United States*, United States Reports, 339 (1950): 516; Nell Battle Lewis, untitled speech for Willis Smith, Wake County Court House, June 20, 1950; Lewis to Willis Smith, May

29, 1950, and Smith to Lewis, July 23, 1950; Mary Hilliard Hinton to Lewis, June 10, 1950; Lily Park to Lewis, June 21, 1950; Annie Avery to Lewis, December 3, 1950, NBL Papers; "Incidentally," *Raleigh News and Observer*, July 2, 1950; July 5, 1953; Paul Luebke, *Tarheel Politics: Myths and Realities* (Chapel Hill: University of North Carolina Press, 1990), 16–18. For a detailed discussion of the 1950 senatorial campaign in North Carolina and the quote to J. Daniels, see Pleasants and Burns, *Frank Porter Graham*, 117–118. For examples of her references to the 1898 white supremacist campaigns, see Lewis, "Incidentally," *Raleigh News and Observer*, June 25, 1950.

36. For examples of white supremacy being taught in white southern homes, see Anne Moody, *Coming of Age in Mississippi* (New York: Doubleday, 1968), 99–214; Melany Neilson, *Even Mississippi* (Tuscaloosa: University of Alabama Press, 1989), 7–34; Jacquelyn Dowd Hall, "'You Must Remember This': Autobiography as Social Critique," *Journal of American History* 85, no. 2 (Summer 1998): 439–465. For evidence of how white supremacy was taught in black schools, see Chana Kai Lee, *For Freedom's Sake: The Life of Fannie Lou Hamer* (Urbana: University of Illinois Press, 2000), 5.

37. Nickerson, *Mothers of Conservatism*, 1, 24, 28; Olsen, "One Nation, One World," 84–94; *Raleigh Times*, June 15, 1948.

38. Sullivan, *Days of Hope*, 242–247.

39. Ziker, "Race, Conservative Politics, and U.S. Foreign Policy," 69; Brattain, "Race, Racism and Antiracism," 1386–1387. This was covered in American papers; see "The Myth of Race," *New York Times*, July 19, 1950, 30. This was in the paper one day after the UNESCO statement was issued in Paris on July 18, 1950. See "UNESCO and Its Programme: The Race Question" (pamphlet) 1950.The statement was issued July 18, 1950, http://unesdoc.unesco.org/images/0012/001282/128291eo.pdf.

40. Olsen, "One Nation, One World," 132–139.

41. Ogden, "Dis an' Dat," *Greenville Delta Democrat-Times*, April 27, 1952.

42. Various versions of this quotation appeared in her speeches at Yazoo and Lake Village, 1954, Folder 105; Ogden, speech at State DAR Meeting and Madam Hodnett Chapter DAR Meeting, 1955, Folder 106, FSO Papers.

43. Ogden, "World Government and the United Nations," speech for the Yazoo Chapter and Lake Village Chapters of the DAR, January 1954, Folder 105, FSO Papers. On how the Soviet Press portrayed Bunche, see Dudziak, *Cold War Civil Rights*, 38–39.

44. Ogden, Lake Village DAR speech, 1954, Folder 105, FSO Papers. See also "Dis an' Dat," *Greenville Delta Democrat-Times*, March 14, 1954.

45. Edgar Waybright, "The U.N. Would Destroy Freedom," *Cross and the Flag*, March 1953, 14–16. This article reprints most of Frances Lucas's research, quoting liberally from several of her pamphlets. These periodicals were sent to Senator Richard B. Russell and are found in his papers. Folder 6, March 1952–1953, Box 242, Subgroup C. Congressional IX. Legislative L. Judiciary, General Correspondence

to 1956. Richard B. Russell Collection, Richard Russell Library, University of Georgia Libraries, Athens; Nickerson, *Mothers of Conservatism*, 24–25.

46. Nickerson, *Mothers of Conservatism*, 72; Olsen, "One Nation, One World," 165–167.

47. Nickerson, *Mothers of Conservatism*, 15–18, 72–79. By 1954, Bartlett and Ogden were in correspondence about *Brown* and Hodding Carter. See Francis P. Bartlett of Pasadena, California, to FSO, May 24, 1954, Folder 26 FSO Papers.

48. Laats, *The Other School Reformers*, 149–163; Nickerson, *Mothers of Conservatism*, 73–75.

49. Nickerson, *Mothers of Conservatism*, 70.

50. For organizational numbers, see Box 35a, MDC Papers.

51. "Work for Freedom's Champion!" campaign pamphlet for Mary D. Cain's run for governor, Box 1, MDC Papers; Curtis Wilkie, *Dixie: A Personal Odyssey through Historic Events That Shaped the Modern South* (New York: Scribner, 2002), 61.

52. Elliot Herbert, "Mary Cain, American," *Dixie Roto Magazine* of the *Times-Picayune*, May 3, 1953, 12–14, Box 2, MDC Papers; Martin, *Rich People's Movements*, 113, 125.

53. Mary Dawson Cain, "The Octopus of Socialism." Reprint of speech delivered [1952?] in Pascagoula, Mississippi, Box 2, MDC Papers. For the connection to earlier far right iterations, see Nickerson, *Mothers of Conservatism*, 19; Glen Jeansonne, *Women of the Far Right: The Mothers Movement and WWII* (Chicago: University of Chicago Press, 1996), 20–21; Ziker, "Race, Conservative Politics, and U.S. Foreign Policy," 21, 29. The octopus imagery was used again after *Brown*. See Cary Daniel, "Segregation's Archenemy: Hiss' United Nations, or Let's Get Out of the U.N.," [c.1955], File 13, Box, 138, Martin Dies Papers, Sam Houston Regional Library and Research Center, Liberty, Texas; cited in Ziker, "Race, Conservative Politics, and U.S. Foreign Policy," 21.

54. Mary Dawson Cain, "The Octopus of Socialism." Reprint of speech delivered [1952?] in Pascagoula, Mississippi, Box 2, MDC Papers.

55. Cain, "The Octopus of Socialism," MDC Papers; *Dallas Morning News*, May 4, 1951; Gail Beil, "Martin Dies and the Marshall Housewives," Marshall Housewives Clipping File, Harrison County Genealogical Society, Marshall, Texas.

56. Mary Dawson Cain, "Constitution Day 1952," *Summit Sun*, September 18, 1952.

57. "11 Housewives Fight U.S.," *New York Times*, February 15, 1952, 24; "10 Housewives Dun U.S.," August 22, 1951, 24; Bill Moyers, "This is Your Story—The Progressive Story of America. Pass it On," Speech to Take Back America Conference, June 4, 2003, https://www.commondreams.org/views/2003/06/10/your-story-progressive-story-america-pass-it; F. A. Whitmore, "Hacksaw Mary," *American Mercury*, October 1955, 147–150; "Editor Who Balked at Tax Cuts Way into Locked Plant," *New York Times*, January 7, 1953, 29.

58. Don Eddy, "They Gave Uncle Sam the Works!" *American Magazine*, June 1951, 35–114, quotation from 112; clipping file, "Marshall Housewives," Harrison County Genealogical Society, Harrison County, Texas.

59. Mary Dawson Cain, "The Octopus of Socialism," Box 2, MDC Papers.

60. David F. Godshalk, *Veiled Visions: The 1906 Atlanta Race Riot and the Reshaping of American Race Relations* (Chapel Hill: University of North Carolina Press, 2005).

61. A Memo to all Fulton County Principals from the Assistant Superintendent Douglas MacRae; "Educators Rally behind East Point's Mrs. Tucker, Ga. Products Festival," *Suburban Reader*, East Point, Georgia, paper, February 26, 1953; CDT, letters to the editor, "State Historical Play Would Boost Not Only our Profit But Also Pride," *Atlanta Journal*, September 11, 1952; "Reader Praises Visual Education," *Atlanta Journal*, December 3, 1951. From Mrs. C. C. Brock, "Letter to the Editors." Microfilm Reel---R284, CDT Scrapbooks, South Caroliniana Library, University of South Carolina.

62. Rymph, *Republican Women*, 110; Black and Black, *The Vital South*, 183.

63. Nickerson, *Mothers of Conservatism*, 18.

64. Henry Lesesne, "Legal Angles Complicate Politics in South Carolina," *Christian Science Monitor*, August 5, 1952, 1l. Ogden, "Dis an' Dat," *Greenville Delta Democrat-Times*, July 13, 1952; Nickerson, *Mothers of Conservatism*, 18. The quote is from Louise Ward Watkins, the Republican club leader of Southern California.

65. "Dis an' Dat," *Jackson Clarion-Ledger* , July 13, 1952; "Incidentally," *Raleigh News and Observer* January 25, February 8, 1953; "Dis an' Dat," *Greenville Delta Democrat Times*, January 11, 18; February 8, 1953.

66. Anderson, *Eyes Off the Prize*, 218; Ziker, "Race, Conservative Politics, and U.S. Foreign Policy," 70.

67. Ogden, "Dis an' Dat," *Greenville Delta Democrat-Times*, August 24, 31, 1952.

68. Lewis, "Incidentally," *Raleigh News and Observer* January 25, February 8, 1953; Ogden, "Dis an' Dat," *Greenville Delta Democrat-Times*, January 11, 18; February 8, 1953.

69. Ogden, "Dis an' Dat," *Greenville Delta Democrat-Times*, September 14, 1952.

70. "Mary Cain's Column," *Summit Sun*, October 30, 1952; Ogden, "Dis an' Dat," *Jackson Clarion-Ledger*. August 17, 1952.

71. Ogden, "Dis an' Dat," *Greenville Delta Democrat-Times*, October 19, 1952.

72. Olsen, "One Nation, One World," 162, 176.

73. Marie Hemphill to FSO, September 1952, Folder 24, FSO Papers. Other letters indicate a response to Ogden's efforts. William Wynn commented that in her campaigning for Eisenhower, she "functioned like a lady statesman and everyone was deeply interested in your talk." William Wynn to FSO, September 23, 1952, Folder 24, FSO Papers; Flora Haskins of Leland, Mississippi, sent several of Ogden's columns to the Federation of Republican Women's Clubs; see Flora Haskins to FSO, August 10, 1952, Folder 24, FSO Papers. See also telegram Sam S. Farrington to FSO. He was the state campaign manager for Mississippi's Democrats for Eisenhower, September 3, 1952, Folder 24, FSO Papers.

74. Gertrude to FSO, October 25, 1952, Folder 185, FSO Papers.

75. "Mary Cain's Column," *Summit Sun*, August 14, 21 September 4, 18, October 30, 1952; "Pike for Ike," *Summit Sun*, October 16, 1952; "Mary Cain's Column," *Summit Sun*, October 16, 1952.

76. "Mary Cain's Column," *Summit Sun*, October 16, 1952.

77. Ogden, "Dis an' Dat," *Greenville Delta Democrat-Times*, November 2, 1952, January 11, 1953; January 18 and February 8, 1953; Marie Hemphill to FSO, September 1952; Katie Dee to FSO, September 24, 1952; Ogden, untitled speech, September, 22, 1952; FSO to Mr. E. O. Spencer, June 10, 1953; FSO to Samuel Lumpkin, September 15, 1953, Ogden Papers. Lumpkin is mentioned as a leader in the Democrats for Eisenhower in Richard Aubrey McLemore, ed., *A History of Mississippi*, vol. 2 (Hattiesburg: University and College Press of Mississippi, 1973), 149. This brief account does not mention the role of Ogden or other women in the organization, nor does it note what happened to Lumpkin after the election. The letters between Ogden and Lumpkin, however, imply some sort of political retribution. For election results, see Tip H. Allen Jr., *Mississippi Votes: The Presidential and Gubernatorial Elections, 1947–1964* (State College: Social Science Research Center at Mississippi State University, 1967).

78. *Summit Sun*, November 6, 1952.

79. Ogden, "Dis an' Dat," *Greenville Delta Democrat-Times*, June 7, 1953; Lewis, "Incidentally," *Raleigh News and Observer*, February 8, 1953; "Dis an' Dat," *Greenville Delta Democrat-Times*, February 8, 1953.

80. "Dis an' Dat," *Greenville Delta Democrat-Times*, November 9, 1952.

81. Rymph, *Republican Women*, 110.

82. Black and Black, *The Vital South*, 180–183; Mickey, *Paths Out of Dixie*, 158–159; Schulman, *From Cotton Belt to Sun Belt*, 123.

83. Lewis, "Incidentally," *Raleigh News and Observer*, January 25, 1953.

84. Ogden, "Dis an' Dat," *Greenville Delta Democrat-Times*, June 7, 1953.

85. On organizations supporting Bricker, see Tananbaum, *The Bricker Amendment Controversy*, 119. Phyllis Schlafly made her first lobbying trip to Congress as a Vigilant Woman for Bricker Amendment. See Critchlow, *Phyllis Schlafly and Grassroots Conservatism*, 85.

86. Tananbaum, *The Bricker Amendment Controversy*, 30–31.

87. Editorial page, *Greenville Delta Democrat-Times*, January 12, 1953; "Time Getting Nearer for Supreme Court to Rule on Segregation for Nation's Schools," *Greenville Delta Democrat-Times*, May 31, 1953, 6; "Dis an Dat," *Greenville Delta Democrat-Times*, December 13, 1935. On organizations supporting Bricker, see Tananbaum, *The Bricker Amendment Controversy*, 119.

88. Ogden, "Dis an' Dat," *Greenville Delta Democrat-Times*, September 27, 1953; February 7, 1954.

89. Ogden, "World Government and the United Nations," speech for Yazoo Chapter of the DAR, [January 1954?], Folder 105, FSO Papers.

90. Letter to State Coordinator of the Vigilant Women for Bricker, January 6, 1954, Box 16, MDC Papers; Frank Holman, "Personal Message to the Vigilant and Patriotic Women of America Supporting the Bricker Amendment," Address January 6, 1954, Box 16, MDC Papers.

91. Mrs. Charles (Eleanor) Rice to Senator Clyde Hoey, February 8, 1954, Box 140, Folders 1, Subject Series, Bricker Amendment, Clyde Roark Hoey Papers, 1943– 1954, David M. Rubenstein Rare Book and Manuscript Library, Duke University, Durham, North Carolina; hereafter cited as Clyde Hoey Papers. Also quoted in Ziker, "Race, Conservative Politics, and U.S. Foreign Policy," 70.

92. "Petition for Action on the Bricker Amendment Limiting the Powers of Treaties," from North Wilkesboro women, [1954?], Box 140, Folders 1–4, Clyde Hoey Papers.

93. Nickerson, *Mothers of Conservatism*, 76–78, Box 140, Folders 1-4, Subject Series, Bricker Amendment, Clyde Hoey Papers.

94. Tananbaum, *The Bricker Amendment*, 120–121; Schlafly quoted in Critchlow, *Phyllis Schlafly and Grassroots Conservatism*, 85.

95. "Vigilant Women Endorse Bricker: Some 500 Visit Washington with Petitions Supporting Curb on Treaty Power," January 26, 1954, *New York Times*, 14. The article listed all the organizations represented by the Vigilant Women. Ninety-nine organizations were represented; sixteen of those were state branches of the American Bar Association; fifty-three of the organizations were solely women's organizations and included Pro-America, National Economic Council, Minute Women, DAR, Colonial Dames, and the auxiliary association of the American Medical Association.

96. "Dis an' Dat," *Greeneville Delta Democrat-Times*, March 14, 1954. Senator John W. Bricker to FSO, March 14, 1954, Folder 26, FSO Papers. This letter notes that one organization dedicated to securing favorable action on the amendment was "Vigilant Women for the Bricker Amendment" in Hinsdale, Illinois. James Eastland to FSO, January 21, 1954, Folder 26, FSO Papers. Senator Eastland comments on a petition in favor of Bricker that Ogden sent to him.

CHAPTER 7

1. James C. Cobb, *The Brown Decision, Jim Crow and Southern Identity* (Athens: University of Georgia Press, 2005), 48, 57, 65, 71.

2. On anticipation of the decision in Mississippi, Crespino, *In Search of Another Country*, 19.

3. "Mary Cain's Column," and "Southern Governors Calmly Make Plans for Maintaining Segregation," *Summit Sun*, May 20, 1954.

4. Lewis, "Incidentally," *Raleigh News and Observer*, May 23, 30, June 6, 1954.

5. Ogden, "Dis an' Dat," *Greenville Delta Democrat-Times*, June 6, 1954.

6. Jacquelyn Dowd Hall, "The Long Civil Rights Movement and the Political Uses of the Past," *Journal of American History* 91, no. 4 (March 2005): 1233–1263; Payne, *I've Got the Light*.

7. Cobb, *The Brown Decision*, 49; Ward, *Defending White Democracy*, 140–141.

8. On Massive Resistance, see Francis Wilhoit, *The Politics of Massive Resistance* (New York: George Braziller, 1973); McMillan, *The Citizens' Council*; Grace Elizabeth Hale, *Making Whiteness: The Culture of Segregation in the South, 1890–1940* (New York: Random House, 1998); Bartley, *The Rise of Massive Resistance*; Lewis, *The White South and the Red Menace*; Lewis, *Massive Resistance;* Clive Webb, ed. *Massive Resistance: Southern Opposition to the Second Reconstruction* (New York: Oxford University Press, 2005); Walker, *The Ghosts of Jim Crow*; Crespino, *In Search of Another Country*.

9. Mickey, *Paths Out of Dixie*, 179, 181

10. Mickey, *Paths Out of Dixie*, 184, 182; Bartley, *Rise of Massive Resistance*, 25; Cobb, *The South and America*, 50

11. FSO to Francis Bartlett, June 1, 1954, Folder 28, FSO Papers; For more on Frances Bartlett, see Nickerson, *Mothers of Conservatism*, 75–78.

12. On rape and the civil rights movement, see McGuire, *At the Dark End of the Street*. On crossing racial boundaries, see Martha Hodes, ed., *Sex, Love, Race: Crossing Boundaries in North American History* (New York: New York University Press, 1999).

13. Virginia Dominguez, *White by Definition: Social Classification in Creole Louisiana* (New Brunswick, NJ: Rutgers University Press, 1986), 36–51; Peggy Pascoe, *What Comes Naturally*, 243.

14. Mrs. Miriam F. Horne, "Letters to the Editor," Linville Falls, North Carolina, *Asheville Citizen Times*, May 23, 1954.

15. Mrs. Joe Baker, "People's Forum," *Raleigh News and Observer*, June 15, 1954.

16. News of this petition ran in the *Southern School News*, October 1, 1954. Their account emphasized the efforts of Pender County Attorney Lynn Corbett and did not mention Mrs. Hugh Bell.

17. Mrs. M. Conan, "What Do You Think?" 5:5 *The White Sentinel* (St. Louis, Missouri), January 1955 in Folder 1954–1960/Anti-Communist and Anti-Integration Newspapers, Box 28, Sarah Patton Boyle Papers, Albert and Shirley Small Special Collections Library, University of Virginia, Charlottesville; hereafter cited as SPB Papers.

18. Eloise Potter, "Potter's Patter," *Zebulon Record*, March 1, 11, 1955. The editorialist, Eloise Potter, wrote some pro-integration columns during her editor's absence in a column called Potter's Patter. When her editor returned, the columns stopped.

19. Mrs. James Patton to FSO, August 4, 1954, Folder 26, FSO Papers.

20. Mrs. Sara A. Thompson to Governor William Umstead, August 14, 1954, Folder T, Box 58.3, Governor William B. Umstead Papers, NCDAH; hereafter cited as Umstead Papers.

21. Jane Dailey, "Sex, Segregation, and the Sacred after *Brown*," *Journal of American History* 126, no. 7 (June 2004): 126–127.

22. Quoted in Daily, "Sex, Segregation and the Sacred," 113. She notes the letter is from Mrs. G. P. Smith to Governor Thomas Stanley, June 8, 1954, folder 1, box 100, General Correspondence, Stanley Executive Papers.

23. Mrs. W. R. Thomas, "Letter to the Editor," *Richmond Times Dispatch*, January 5, 1957, SPB Papers.

24. Mrs. REG to Governor William Umstead, May 31, 1954, Folder W, Box 58.1, Umstead Papers.

25. Mrs. Adele Townsend to Governor William Umstead, June 4, 1954, Folder T, Box 58.3. Umstead Papers.

26. Petition, July 12, 1954, compiled by Raymond Price, Raleigh, Folder P, Box 58.2. Umstead Papers.

27. Petition, May 22, 1954, from Beringer and Whitfield Furniture to Governor Umstead, Folder B, Box 58.2, Umstead Papers.

28. Jackie Robinson, "People's Forum," *Raleigh News and Observer* July 15, 1954.

29. Kate Patteson, letter to editor, *New York Times Magazine*, May 22, 1955, Folder "Letters to the Editor," SPB Papers.

30. Dailey, "Sex, Segregation, and the Sacred after *Brown*," 119–144; also see James T. Patterson, *Brown v. Board of Education: A Civil Rights Milestone and Its Troubled Legacy* (New York: Oxford University Press, 2002), 86–117; "New Hanover County Preliminary Report," or "Non-Segregation Data for Study, New Hanover County, State of North Carolina, July 1955," Box 40, Folder 3, NBL Papers; Mrs. Hugh Bell Jr. to NBL, August 25, 1955, NBL Papers. Attached to this letter was a copy of another letter that Bell sent to the Raleigh *News and Observer*. It criticized the paper's pro-integration stance and its unwillingness to expose the NAACP as an organization of "Jewish Communist revolutionaries." "New Hanover County: Preliminary Report to the State Advisory Committee on Non-Segregation," [1955?], NBL Papers. The concern over integrating elementary schools was not limited to Mrs. Bell. After a letter to the *Atlanta Journal-Constitution* suggested that starting integration in first grade would minimize problems, "a mother" wrote several letters contending that segregating first graders by making their classes racially mixed would be unfair. See "Pulse of the Public," *Atlanta Journal-Constitution*, July 8, July 12, and August 21, 1954. This concern was also reiterated when white women discussed the possibility of intermarriage.

31. Mrs. G. L. Rouse, "People's Forum, *Raleigh News and Observer* June 2, 1954; Mrs. R. M. Letchworth, Stantonsburg, "People's Forum," *Raleigh News and Observer*, June 17, 1954; Mrs. M. L. Jenkins, "People's Forum, *Raleigh News and Observer*, June 30, 1954; Mrs. H. T. Shaw, "People's Forum, *Raleigh News and Observer*, July 7, 1954.

32. Mrs. G. L. Rouse, "People's Forum," *Raleigh News and Observer*, June 2, 1954.

33. Mary E. Martin, letter to the editor, *Augusta Courier*, February 23, 1959. Quoted in John White, "Sara McCorkle and the Women of the White Citizens' Councils," paper delivered at the Southern Historical Association Annual Meeting, 2008 (in possession of author), 4.

34. John White, "Sara McCorkle and the Women of the White Citizens' Councils."

35. Undated statement of Mrs. Hugh A. Thompson, Files for 1955–56, NBL Papers.

36. Hugh V. Wall to FSO, November 9, 1955; FSO to J. D. Williams (Chancellor of the University of Mississippi) from Ogden, November 14, 1955; FSO to Hugh V. Wall, November 14, 1955; Folder 29, FSO Papers. For accounts of this censure of University of Mississippi speakers, see Bartley, *The Rise of Massive Resistance*, 229–230; James Silver, *Mississippi: The Closed Society* (New York: Harcourt, Brace, and World, 1966), 108–109. On the controversy surrounding Religious Emphasis Week, see Will Campbell, *Brother to a Dragonfly* (New York: Seabury Press, 1977), 113–124.

37. Cobb, *The Brown Decision*, 45–46.

38. Ritterhouse, *Growing Up*, 66–67; Mickenberg, *Learning from the Left*, 254–256.

39. From Gladyce G. Muse, secretary of District of Columbia Public Schools Association. July 7, 1955. A treatise called "Integration Impairs Education and Decreases Property Values," Folder 5, June 29–July 24, 1955, CDT Papers.

40. "New Hanover County: Preliminary Report to the State Advisory Committee on Non-Segregation," Folder 255.40, NBL Papers.

41. "Mary Cain's Column," *Summit Sun*, August 5, 1954.

42. John White, "White Women and 'Massive Resistance' in South Carolina," paper delivered at the Southern Women's History Association Tri-annual Meeting, 2008 (in author's possession).

43. For poll information, see the *News and Courier* (August 7, 1955), 4D. Cited in John White, "White Women and Massive Resistance."

44. White, "White Women and Massive Resistance," 9. White cites the South Carolina Council on Human Relations Collection, Harriet P. Simons to Alice Spearman, February 7, 1955, South Caroliniana Library, University of South Carolina, Columbia.

45. "New Hanover," NBL Papers.

46. Ogden, "Dis and Dat," *Greenville Delta Democrat-Times*, April 8, 1956; Mason, *Reading Appalachia from Left to Right*, 135, 171–172; Mickenberg, *Learning from the Left*, 252–253. Story Hinckley, "Texas: We Don't Need Academics to Fact-Check Our Textbooks," *Christian Science Monitor*, November 19, 2015, http://www.csmonitor.com/USA/Education/2015/1119/Texas-We-don-t-need-academics-to-fact-check-our-textbooks-video; Ellen Bresler Rockmore, "How Texas Teaches History," *New York Times*, October 21, 2015, http://www.nytimes.com/2015/10/22/opinion/how-texas-teaches-history.html.

47. Quoted in Mickenberg, *Learning from the Left*, 234.

48. Maud Wales, "Letter to the Editor," *Charlotte Observer*, May 23, 1954.

49. Mrs. Della Edwards, "Pulse of the Public," *Atlanta Journal-Constitution*, July 17, 1954.

50. Ms. A. S. Cowan, "The People's Forum," *Raleigh News and Observer*, July 2, 1954.

51. Unpublished letter to the editor of the *Raleigh News and Observer* from Mrs. Hugh Bell, Currie, North Carolina, August 25, 1955, Folder 255.4, NBL Papers; Francis P. Bartlett to FSO, May 24, 1954, Folder 26, FSO Papers.

52. John White, "Sara McCorkle and the Women of the White Citizens' Councils." The WSRA was formed in Greenwood, South Carolina.

53. White, "White Women," 9; *News and Courier*, December 3, 5, 1, 18, 22, 1955.

54. Ogden, "Dis an' Dat," *Greenville Delta Democrat-Times*, June 6, 1954, September 12, 1954; Lewis, "Incidentally," *Raleigh News and Observer*, February 13, 1955.

55. John White, "Sara McCorkle"; Steve Estes, *I Am a Man! Race, Manhood, and the Civil Rights Movement* (Chapel Hill: University of North Carolina Press, 2005), 47; for a different look at the role *Brown* played in the rise of massive resistance, see Michael Klarman, "How *Brown* Changed Race Relations: The Backlash Thesis," *Journal of American History* 81 (June 1994): 81–118. Klarman argues that *Brown* motivated massive resistance, but he does not mention the motivation and grassroots organization of white women.

56. Mrs. Preston Andrews to William B. Umstead, May 29, 1954, Folder A, Box 58.1, Umstead Papers. This petition was signed also by Mrs. W. Reid Caldwell, Mrs. A. J.Wilson, Mrs. Grady Ross, Miss Annie Lee Hayden, Mrs. Preston W. Adams, and Mrs. Walter C. Comer, all of Charlotte, North Carolina. For multiple letters and petitions echoing Mrs. Andrews's opinions, see Box 58.1, Box 58.2, Box 58.3, Umstead Papers. These boxes have files filled with letters regarding *Brown*, most from June, July, and August of 1954 in alphabetical order by name of letter writer or petition sender.

57. "County Segregation Organization Circulating Petition on Schools," August 27, 1955, *Durham Sun*, Clipping File, Division of Negro Education Office of Director, Newspaper Clippings, 1954–1962, Department of Public Instruction Papers, NCDAH.

58. Petitions and Letters to William B. Umstead about *Brown* in 1954 are in General Correspondence, Box 58.1, 58.2, and 58.3, organized alphabetically the name of the person or organization who signed the cover letter. Umstead Papers.

59. Ogden, Lake Village DAR Speech, 1954, FSO Papers. On Walter Sillers's involvement in the Citizens' Council, see Cobb, *The Most Southern Place on Earth*, 213–217, 227.

60. Cobb, *The Most Southern Place on Earth*, 227–228. On the Citizens' Councils, see McMillen, *The Citizens' Council*, 120–125; Bartley, *The New South*, 199–202; Bartley, *The Rise of Massive Resistance*, 82–107.

61. John White, "White Women and 'Massive Resistance.'"

62. Luther Hodges, *Businessman in the Statehouse: Six Years as Governor of North Carolina* (Chapel Hill: University of North Carolina Press, 1962). For Hodges's self-assessment of his leadership during the early years of massive resistance, see 107–125.

63. On moderates, see Lassiter, *The Silent Majority*, 120–128; for statistics on Hodges's election and the rise of women voters, see Earl Black, *Southern Governors and Civil Rights: Racial Segregation as a Campaign Issue in the Second Reconstruction* (Cambridge, MA: Harvard University Press, 1976), 106–108. On the rise in

women voting, see Harold W. Stanley, *Voter Mobilization and the Politics of Race: The South and Universal Suffrage, 1952–1964* (New York City: Praeger, 1987), 67. Stanley argues that women voting in increased numbers demarcates the 1950s South from V. O. Key's South. Some statistics reveal that the percentage of southern white females voting in presidential elections rose from 50 percent in 1952 to 51 percent in 1956 to 70 percent in 1960. See Carol Cassel, "Change in Electoral Participation in the South," *Journal of Politics* 41 (August 1979): 912. In presidential elections, the Democratic Party in 1956 failed for the first time since 1872 to win a majority of the southern electoral vote. See Earl Black and Merle Black, *The Vital South: How Presidents Are Elected* (Cambridge, MA: Harvard University Press, 1992), 189. On the positions of Hodges and Ervin on segregation, see Jack Bass and Walter DeVries, *The Transformation of Southern Politics: Social Change and Political Consequence since 1945* (New York: Basic Books, 1976), 228–230; Black, *Southern Governors*, 109; William Chafe, *Civilities and Civil Rights: Greensboro, North Carolina, and the Black Struggle for Freedom* (New York: Oxford University Press, 1980), 42, 49–61; Rymph, *Republican Women*, 131–159.

64. James A. Savage, "Save Our Republic: Battling John Birch in California's Conservative Cradle" (Ph.D. diss., University of Kentucky, 2015), 220–245. The John Birch Society conducted a wholesale attack on the Warren Court, campaigning against most of its decisions including *Brown*.

65. James Eastland to CDT, June 28, 1955, Folder 4, Box 1, CDT Papers.

66. Mrs. Albert Taylor and Mary Mathis to CDT, June 5, 1955; Senator Olin D. Johnston to CDT, July 14, 1955; Mrs. Frank Ramsey to Frank Hichborn, June 27, 1955; James Eastland to CDT, June 16, 1955, Folder 4, Box 1, CDT Papers; James A. Savage, "Save Our Republic: Battling John Birch in California's Conservative Cradle" (Ph.D. diss., University of Kentucky, 2015), 220–245.

67. George Lewis, "'Scientific Certainty': Wesley Critz George, Racial Science and Organized White Resistance in North Carolina, 1954–1962," *North Carolina Historical Review* 38, no. 2 (August 2004): 227–247.

68. "The Patriots of North Carolina," North Carolina Collection Clipping Files, Wilson Library, University of North Carolina, Chapel Hill; on the Southern Manifesto, see Bartley, *The New South*, 198–199; Egerton, *Speak Now against the Day*, 622–623.

69. Sarah Patton Boyle, "Southerners Will Like Segregation," *Saturday Evening Post* (February 19, 1955), 25, 133–134.

70. Sarah Patton Boyle, "Letters to the Editor," *Daily Progress*, [1953?], Box 24, SPB Papers; Jennifer Ritterhouse, "Speaking of Race: Sarah Patton Boyle and the 'T. J. Sellers Course for Backward Southern Whites,'" in *Sex, Love and Race*, 491–497; "Incidentally," *Raleigh News and Observer*, February 27, 1955, and March 6, 1955; Nell Battle Lewis to Ben Hibbs, March 1, 1955, Folder 255.9, Nell Battle Lewis Papers; Ritterhouse, *Growing Up Jim Crow*, 234–235; Cobb, *The Brown Decision*, 44.

71. Ogden, "Dis an' Dat," *Jackson Clarion Ledger and Greenville Daily-Democrat Times*, February 27, 1955.

72. Lewis, "Incidentally," *Raleigh News and Observer*, May 22, 1955. For a similar sentiment see Mrs. L. B. Street, "People's Forum," *Raleigh News and Observer*, August 20, 1955.

73. Ogden, "Dis an' Dat," *Greenville Delta Democrat-Times*, February 27, 1955.

74. For secondary treatments of the Till case, see Stephen J. Whitfield, *A Death in the Delta: The Story of Emmett Till* (Baltimore, MD: Johns Hopkins University Press, 1988), 107, 146–148. Whitfield argues that the Till case galvanized black resistance. He also suggests that the white South's response to the murder, and the outside condemnation that it engendered, also solidified white resistance to racial change. See also Timothy B. Tyson, *The Blood of Emmett Till* (New York: Simon & Schuster, 2017), 52.

75. Ogden, "Dis an' Dat," *Greenville Delta Democrat-Times,* January 29, 1956; Cobb, *The Most Southern Place on Earth*, 217–222; Cobb argues that the deluge of criticism led to increased defensiveness on the part of white Mississippians.

76. "Incidentally," *Raleigh News and Observer*, March 26, 1956. In this article, Lewis referred to *Look* magazine's biased representation of the South. She did not specifically mention the Till article here or in any of her other columns after the *Look* article appeared in January. William Bradford Huie, "The Shocking Story of Approved Killing in Mississippi," *Look*, January 24, 1956.

77. Nellie S. Young, "People's Forum," *Raleigh News and Observer*, September 13, 1955; for the Faulkner quote, see Joel Williamson, *William Faulkner and Southern History* (New York: Oxford University Press, 1993), 303, 307.

78. Lewis, "Incidentally," *Raleigh News and Observer*, October 2, 1955.

79. Ogden, "Dis an' Dat," *Greenville Delta Democrat-Times*, January 29, 1956. A similar article ran in the *Memphis Press Scimitar* on January 19, 1956, 29. Private correspondence attributes the article to Ogden but in the paper, there was no byline. For letters involving A. L. Royal's suit against Ogden, see Folder 30, FSO Papers; Huie, "The Shocking Story."

80. Lewis, "Incidentally," *Raleigh News and Observer*, May 13, 1956. This column along with five others by Lewis was reprinted in pamphlet form and distributed by Erwin A. Holt of Burlington, North Carolina. For the pamphlet, see Folder 255.40, NBL Papers.

81. *Chapel Hill Weekly*, November 30, 1956; *Raleigh News and Observer*, November 28, 1956.

82. Tom Etheridge, "Mississippi Notebook: Angry Rebels Made PTA Modify Integration Stand," *Jackson Clarion-Ledger*, November 4, 1956.

83. Crespino, *In Search of Another Country*, 19. Crespino differentiates between the hardline segregationist stance of the Citizens' Councils and the practical segregationist who advocated strategic accommodation to school integration. He argues that the practical segregationists were in fact much more successful in sustaining

white supremacist politics and the least federal interference than hardline segregationists. As evident in this book, white segregationist women were often hardline segregationists and practical segregationists as their work on multiple levels of society indicated.

CHAPTER 8

1. Patterson, *Brown v. Board of Education,* 100–101.
2. Crespino, *In Search of Another Country,* 172–173; Robin L. Gates, *The Making of Massive Resistance: Virginia's Politics of Public School Desegregation, 1954–1956* (Chapel Hill: University of North Carolina Press, 1962), 100–116; William Chafe, "Perspectives on Progressivism," in *Southern Businessmen and Desegregation,* ed. Elizabeth Jacoway and David R. Colburn (Baton Rouge: Louisiana State University Press, 1982), 42–69; Chafe, *Civilities and Civil Rights,* 72–82; Bartley, *The New South,* 187, 218, 221; Walter Edgar, *South Carolina: A History* (Columbia: University of South Carolina Press, 1998), 523; Elizabeth Jacoway, *Turn Away Thy Son: Little Rock, The Crisis that Shocked the Nation* (New York: Free Press, 2007), 56–57; Lewis, *Massive Resistance,* 86–87; Ravitch, *Left Back,* 372.
3. John White, "Sara McCorkle and the Women of the White Citizens' Councils," paper delivered at the Southern Historical Association Annual Meeting, 2008 (in author's possession), 4; Sokol, *There Goes My Everything,* 119; Earnest S. Cox to John and Louise Powell, February 23, 1959, Box 40: Folder 62, John Powell Papers.
4. On the silence of moderates, see Cobb, *The South and America,* 50; Sokol, *There Goes My Everything,* 120.
5. Crespino, *In Search of Another Country,* 18–19.
6. On NAACP numbers, see Mickey, *Paths Out of Dixie,* 88; Aaron Henry quoted in Dittmer, *Local People,* 46, 49–55, 70–89. For black efforts at racial change, see Weisbrot, *Freedom Bound,* 18; Aldon Morris, *The Origins of the Civil Rights Movement: Black Communities Organizing for Change* (New York: Free Press, 1984), 174–194; Sokol, *There Goes My Everything,* 117–181.
7. Ogden, "Dis an' Dat," *Jackson Clarion-Ledger,* March 20, April 24, 1960; Thurgood Marshall, quoted in Lawson, *Black Ballots,* 247.
8. Ogden, "Dis an' Dat," *Jackson Clarion-Ledger,* January 20, 27, 1957. For the best treatment of the negotiations between the attorney general and senators on the 1957 Civil Rights Bill, see Lawson, *Black Ballots,* 140–202. Lacking confidence in southern juries, the bill originally stated that violators would be tried by a judge, but senators on the left and the right opposed this measure, and the Senate compromised on a jury trial.
9. Bartley, *The New South,* 228.
10. Lawson, *Black Ballots,* 165–202. For the events at Little Rock, see Elizabeth Jacoway and C. Fred Williams, eds., *Understanding the Little Rock Crisis: An Exercise in Remembrance and Reconciliation* (Fayetteville: University of Arkansas Press, 1999); Bartley, *The New South,* 223–248; Lawson, *Black Ballots,* 204; Bartley, *The Rise*

*of Massive Resistance.* On women's involvement in preventing desegregation, see Graeme Cope, "'A Thorn in the Side'? The Mothers' League of Central High School and the Little Rock Desegregation Crisis of 1957," *Arkansas Historical Quarterly* 57 (Summer1998): 160–190; Cope, "'Honest White People of the Middle and Lower Classes'? A Profile of the Capital Citizens' Council during the Little Rock Crisis of 1957," *Arkansas Historical Quarterly* 61 (Spring 2000): 39–58.

11. "Statement by 936 Former Central High Students in Support of Purged Teachers," June 2, 1959, in Sondra Gordy, *Finding the Lost Year: What Happened When Little Rock Closed Its Public Schools* (Fayetteville: University of Arkansas Press, 2009), 199.

12. On various reactions among white southern women to desegregation and white college students, see Sokol, *There Goes My Everything,* 117–181; undated columns, Florence Sillers Ogden file, State Sovereignty Commission papers, MDAH; Beatrice Baldwin to FSO, November 2, 1963, Folder 54, FSO Papers; Ogden, Women for Constitutional Government (WCG) speeches, Jackson, October 30, 1962; Greenwood, March 5, 1963; Greenville, February 20, 1963, Folder 113, FSO Papers; Ogden, WCG Speech, Montgomery, Alabama, January 17, 1963, Folder 113, FSO Papers; WCG speech, Mobile, Alabama, February 11, 1965, Folder 114, FSO Papers.

13. Karen Anderson, *Little Rock: Race and Resistance at Central High School* (Princeton, NJ: Princeton University Press, 2010), 170–171. Gary Smith, "Blindsided by History," *Sports Illustrated,* April 9, 2007, at https://www.si.com/vault/2007/04/09/8404477/blindsided-by-history.

14. Anderson, *Little Rock,* 179, 235; Lorraine Gates Schuyler, "Power from the Pedestal: The Women's Emergency Committee and the Little Rock Crisis," *Arkansas Historical Quarterly* 55 (Spring 1996): 26–57; Cobb, *The South and America,* 49.

15. Ogden, "Dis an' Dat," *Jackson Clarion-Ledger,* September 15, 22, 29, 1957.

16. Ogden, "Dis an' Dat," *Jackson Clarion-Ledger,* September 29, 1957, September 21, 1958.

17. "Venable Parents to Conduct Second Poll on Integration," *Daily Progress,* Charlottesville, Virginia, June 25, 1958; "Venable School Poll Finds Heavy Segregation Vote," *Daily Progress,* July 12, 1958, Clippings, Folder 1957–1963, Materials Regarding Polls, Box 28, Sarah Patton Boyle Papers.

18. Jill Ogline Titus, *Brown's Battleground: Students, Segregationists, and the Struggle for Justice in Prince Edward County, Virginia* (Chapel Hill: University of North Carolina Press, 2011), 10–16; See also Lassiter and Lewis, eds., *The Moderate's Dilemma;* Smith, *Managing White Supremacy.*

19. On how moderates framed the choice of a desegregated South as one between closed schools and limited integration, see Lassiter, *The Silent Majority,* 39, 64–68; 80–93. On Virginia, see Andy Lewis, "Emergency Mothers: Basement Schools and the Preservation of Public Education in Charlottesville," 77–78.

20. "1959 Massive Resistance Folder," Box 1, and "PTA Folder," Box 11, Papers of Kathryn Stone, Albert and Shirley Small Special Collections Library, University of Virginia, Charlottesville.

21. McMillen, *The Citizens' Council*, 240–245; for the essay topics in 1959, see "Citizens' Council Essay Winners Told," *Jackson Clarion-Ledger*, July 24, 1959; The 1959–60 University of Mississippi catalog lists the total fees, apparently including tuition, for a full-time undergraduate at $127.50. At that rate, four years would have cost $510.00. See 1959–60 University of Mississippi Catalog, page 85, Special Collections, J. D. Williams Library, University of Mississippi, Oxford, Mississippi; hereafter cited as J. D. Williams Library.

22. Mary Rosalind Healy, "Why I Believe in the Social Separation of the Races of Mankind," in Winning Essays of the 1960 Contest Sponsored by the Association of Citizens' Councils of Mississippi, Special Collections, "Anti Communism and Civil Rights," University of Southern Mississippi, http://www.lib.usm.edu/legacy/spcol/exhibitions/anti-comm/civil_rights-3.html.

23. For a brief biographical sketch, see Folder 41, FSO Papers.

24. Ogden, "Dis an' Dat," *Jackson Clarion-Ledger*, February 8, 1959, March 17, 1957; James Garner, *Reconstruction in Mississippi* (New York: Macmillan, 1901).

25. Crespino, *In Search of Another Country*, 83. Included in her suggested reading list were Claude Bower's *The Tragic Era*, James Garner's *Reconstruction in Mississippi*, and Dunbar Rowland's *Mississippi, the Heart of the South*.

26. Ogden, "Dis an' Dat," *Jackson Clarion-Ledger*, April 28, 1957; FSO to Mr. Burrow (Superintendent of Rosedale School), November 26, 1960, Folder 43, FSO Papers.

27. For examples of women's earlier historical commemoration activities and their relationship to white supremacy, see Grace Elizabeth Hale, "Some Women Have Never Been Reconstructed: Mildred Lewis Rutherford, Lucy M. Stanton, and the Racial Politics of White Southern Womanhood, 1900–1930," in *Georgia in Black and White: Explorations in the Race Relations of a Southern State, 1865–1900*, ed. John C. Inscoe (Athens: University of Georgia Press, 1994), 179; Fitzhugh Brundage, "White Women and the Politics of Historical Memory in the New South, 1880–1920," in *Jumpin' Jim Crow: Southern Politics from Civil War to Civil Rights* (Princeton, NJ: Princeton University Press, 1999), 115–139; Robert Cook, "From Shiloh to Selma: The Impact of the Civil War Centennial on the Black Freedom Struggle in the United States, 1961–65," in *The Making of Martin Luther King and the Civil Rights Movement*, ed. Brian Ward and Tony Badger (New York: New York University Press, 1996), 131–145, particularly, 135–136.

28. Ogden, "Dis an'Dat," *Jackson Clarion-Ledger*, July 31, 1960; Barnett to FSO, May 23, 1960, Folder 42, FSO Papers.

29. Ogden, "Dis an' Dat," *Jackson Clarion-Ledger*, October 5, 1958, March 20, 1960. On Trumbell Park, see Arnold Hirsch, "Massive Resistance in the Urban North: Trumbell Park, Chicago, 1953–1966," *Journal of American History* 82 (September

1995): 522–550. On the Civil War Centennial, see Cook, "From Shiloh to Selma," 131–145. Cook contends that politicians realized the value of political theater when federal intervention was eroding their own ability to maintain a caste system. On the relationship between the Civil War, historical memory, and cultural politics, see David Blight, *Race and Reunion: The Civil War in American Memory* (Cambridge, MA: Belknap Press, 2001).

30. Ogden, "Dis an' Dat," *Jackson Clarion-Ledger*, April 12, 1959

31. Ogden, "Dis an' Dat," *Jackson Clarion-Ledger*, March 3, September 8, 1957; March 30, August 10, 1958; Jack Davis, *Race against Time: Culture and Separation in Natchez since 1930* (Baton Rouge: Louisiana State University Press, 2001), 52–82 (quote from 81); David Cohn, "Natchez Was a Lady," *Atlantic Monthly*, January 1940, 14.

32. U.S. Grant, III, to FSO, October 4, 1959; FSO to U.S. Grant III, October 15, 1959; James Silver to FSO, October 8, 1959, Folder 41, FSO Papers; "Dis an' Dat," *Jackson Clarion-Ledger*, March 16, 1958; FSO to Governor James P. Coleman, February 23, 1959; Governor James P. Coleman to FSO, [1959?], Folder 37; Ogden, "American History," Speech to Ralph Humphreys DAR Chapter, 1959, FSO Papers.

33. For more on how tourist sites and historic renovation teach racism or uphold the value of white supremacy, see Yuhl, "Rich and Tender Remembering," 227–248. For a more current example of the interplay between race, historical memory, tourism, and economic development, see Margaret A. Shannon with Stephen W. Taylor, "Astride the Plantation Gates: Tourism, Racial Politics, and the Development of Hilton Head Island," in *Southern Journeys: Tourism, History, and Culture in the Modern South*, ed. Richard D. Starnes (Tuscaloosa: University of Alabama Press, 2003), 177–195. On how tourist sites replete with certain images of femininity, such as Natchez, articulate racist values, see Tara McPherson, "Reconstructing Dixie: Race, Place, and Femininity in the Deep South" (Ph.D. diss, University of Wisconsin-Milwaukee, 1996), 24–39.

34. John Steinbeck, *Travels with Charley in Search of America* (New York: Viking Press, 1992); Baker, *The Second Battle for New Orleans*, 7.

35. Paul Revere Ladies Meeting, December 14, 1960, Serial Number 7-0-313, State Sovereignty Commission Files, Mississippi Department of Archives and History, Jackson, Mississippi.

36. Paul Revere Ladies Meeting, May 28, 1960, December 14, 1960, Serial Number 7-0-313, State Sovereignty Commission Files, MDAH; McMillen, *The Citizens' Council*, 240–245; Yasuhiro Katagiri, *The Mississippi State Sovereignty Commission: Civil Rights and States' Rights* (Jackson: University Press of Mississippi, 2001), 86–94. Lowman spoke at Mississippi Vocational College in Itta Bena, Jackson State College, and Alcorn Agricultural and Mechanical College to warn black students of the links between racial unrest and communist subversion; Crespino, *In Search of Another Country*, 58–59.

37. Nickerson, *Mothers of Conservatism*, 59–62, 142–148; McGirr, *Suburban Warriors*, 97–98, 113, 118.

38. The phrase "conservative-minded" came from an interview with Erle Johnston. Yasuhiro Katagiri, interview with "Erle Johnston," August 3, 1993, University of Southern Mississippi Center for Oral History and Cultural Heritage.

39. Erle Johnston, "Mississippi State Sovereignty Commission Memorandum," December 16, 1963, State Sovereignty Commission Online, http://mdah.state.ms.us/arrec/digital_archives/sovcom/result.php?image=images/png/cd09/071994.png. See http://www.lib.usm.edu/legacy/spcol/exhibitions/anti-comm/activism_pay.html On bookstores, see Nickerson, *Mothers of Conservatism*, 142–155; White, "McCorkle"; on McCorkle's access, see Erle Johnston Oral History, 38, http://digilib.usm.edu/cdm/fullbrowser/collection/coh/id/3987/rv/compound-object/cpd/4035.

40. "National Cleanest Town Achievement Awards Competition and Patriotic American Youth Scrapbook," 1960s, MF Roll #36597, Mississippi Department of Archives and History, Jackson, Mississippi.

41. Ogden, "Dis an' Dat," *Jackson Clarion-Ledger*, August 9, 1959. In this column, Ogden summarizes an article by the former chancellor of Mississippi, Alfred Hume. See also Mickenberg, *Learning from the Left*, 134–142, 252.

42. "Legion Will Take Textbook Action," *Jackson Clarion-Ledger*, September 6, 1959

43. "DAR and Legion to Display All Questioned Books," *Jackson Clarion-Ledger*, July 19, 1959; Crespino, *In Search*, 56–57.

44. M. N. Brown to Governor J. P. Coleman, June 24, 1959, Folder 39, FSO Papers.

45. Ogden, "Dis an' Dat," *Greenville Delta Democrat-Times*, March 14, 1954, March 11, 1956, April 8, 1956; Janice Neill to FSO, October 18, 1959, FSO Papers; list of textbook authors from the State Sovereignty Commission [postmarked October 2, 1960], Folder 42; FSO to Ross Barnett, May 9, 1960, Ross Barnett to FSO, June 13, 1960; and Ogden to Barnett, June 22, 1960, FSO Papers; Katagiri, *The Mississippi State Sovereignty Commission*, 86–94.

46. "Whose Drums in the Congo," *National Review*, March 26, 1959; Dr. Ruth Alexander, "Violence in the Congo Is Reminiscent of Tragedy of Reconstruction in South," *Citizen* (December 1962), 11–12; Mrs. Sam H. Davis, "Education to Prepare for 'The New World Order,'" *The Texas Councilor* 3 (January 25, 1961), series T12, reel 128, Right Wing Collection, University of Iowa. For a more sustained treatment of this collaboration, see Ziker, "Race, Conservative Politics, and U.S. Foreign Policy," 278–312.

47. Ziker, "Race, Conservative Politics, and U.S. Foreign Policy," 284.

48. Ogden, "Building Responsible Citizens through Knowledge and Appreciation of Our Country and Its History," speech to the Benoit PTA, February 20, 1961, Folder 111, FSO Papers.

49. Ogden, "Dis an' Dat," *Jackson Clarion-Ledger*, October 16, 1960.

50. Ogden, "Dis an' Dat," *Jackson Clarion-Ledger*, March 19, 1961.

51. "Newsletter," October 1963, Folder WCG, FSO Papers; Ogden, "Building Responsible Citizens through Knowledge and Appreciation of Our Country and

Its History," February 20, 1961, Folder 111; "The United Nations and Its Specialized Agencies," Grenada, Mississippi, October 19, 1962, Folder 114, FSO Papers; Olsen, "One Nation, One World," 415–453.

52. Ogden, "Dis an'Dat," *Jackson Clarion-Ledger*, August 27, 1961.

53. On the freedom rides in Mississippi, see Dittmer, *Local People*, 96–99.

54. Phillip Wylie, *Generation of Vipers* (New York, Toronto: Farrar & Rinehart, 1942). Eileen Boris, *Home to Work: Motherhood and the Politics of Industrial Homework in the United States* (New York: Cambridge University Press, 1994), 305–307; Cynthia Harrison, *On Account of Sex: The Politics of Women's Issues, 1945–1968* (Berkeley: University of California Press, 1988), 4–9, 24–29, May, *Homeward Bound*, 1–21.

55. Ogden, "Dis an' Dat," *Jackson Clarion-Ledger*, May 11, 1958.

56. Ogden, "Dis an' Dat," *Jackson Clarion-Ledger*, December 7, 1958. For the central role that families played in teaching values including white supremacy, see Ritterhouse, *Growing Up Jim Crow*, 55–107.

57. Ziker, "Race, Conservative Politics, and U.S. Foreign Policy," 307. See Mamdani, *Good Muslim, Bad Muslim: America, the Cold War, and the Roots of Terror* (Harmony, 2005), 17–20.

58. Ogden, Introduction at the Mississippi Historical Society, [1960?], Folder 119, FSO Papers. "Dis an' Dat," *Jackson Clarion-Ledger*, October 11, 1959. Black women had long resisted the long hours and seven-day week of domestic service. See Tera W. Hunter, *To 'Joy My Freedom: Southern Black Women's Lives and Laborers after the Civil War* (Cambridge, MA: Harvard University Press, 1997), 59–62.

59. To Mr. Barrslag from Cornelia Dabney Tucker, July 26, 1955, Folder 6, CDT Papers.

60. Cornelia Dabney Tucker, "Congressmen—Hear Ye! A Message to Our Honorable Congress of the United States," *Economic Liberty* [Oakland, California], January 1958, Folder 14, CDT Papers.

61. Christopher Myers Asch, *The Senator and the Sharecropper*, 157–166; 267–273; James Eastland Obituary, February 20, 1986, *New York Times*.

62. Harry T. Everingham to Cornelia Dabney Tucker, August 2, 1957, Box 1, Folder 12, CDT Papers.

63. "Time for Action," Program Advertisement, We the People, September 14 and 15, 1957, Box 1, Folder 12, CDT Papers.

64. Florence Sillers Ogden, "What the DAR Is Doing to Combat Communism and World Government," speech, April 20, 1957, FSO Papers.

65. Cornelia Dabney Tucker, "An Education for World Peace," 1959, Folder 5, CDT Papers (quotes were in all caps in original).

66. Harry Everingham, "Will You Go Communist without a Fight?" pamphlet (Chicago: Fact Finder, 1962). Willis E. Stone wrote a syndicated column "American Way," that ran in 3,000 newspapers, http://socialarchive.iath.virginia.edu/xtf/view?docId=stone-willis-e-willis-emerson-1899--cr.xml.

67. Speer, "'Contrary Mary,'" 257–259. In 1968, the 500 recipients of the Liberty Awards included Phyllis Schlafly, Ross Perot, and Ronald Reagan.

68. Barry Goldwater to CDT, July 16, 1960, CDT Papers.

69. On moderates, see Lassiter, *The Silent Majority*, 71–76; Paul E. Mertz, "'Mind Changing Time All Over Georgia': HOPE, Inc., and School Desegregation, 1958–1961," *Georgia Historical Quarterly* 77 (1993), 41–61; Adam Fairclough, *Race and Democracy: The Civil Rights Struggle in Louisiana, 1915–1972* (Athens: University of Georgia Press, 1995), 234–264;

70. Dittmer, *Local People*, 139, "Dis an' Dat," *Jackson Clarion-Ledger*, September 30, 1962.

71. Ogden, "Dis an' Dat," *Jackson Clarion-Ledger*, July 16, 23, 1961.

72. Mickey, *Paths Out of Dixie*, 209–214; Crespino, *In Search of Another Country*, 76–92.

73. CDT to Robert Kennedy, [1962] Box 2, Folder 23, CDT Papers.

74. "Executive Board of Women for Constitutional Government attending meeting at Jackson, October 30, 1962," typescript, Folder Women for Constitutional Government, FSO Papers.

75. FSO, Speech to WCG Greenville, February 29, 1963, page 13, FSO Papers, Folder 113, FSO Papers.

76. "Information Sheet Women for Constitutional Government," [1963?] Folder, Women for Constitutional Government, 1961–1972, FSO Papers.

77. Ogden, "Address to Chicago Branch of WCG," October 4, 1963, Folder 114, FSO Papers.

78. Ogden WCG Speech, Drew Mississippi, June 10, 1963, Folder 114, FSO Papers; Information Sheet, Women for Constitutional Government," [1963?] Folder, Women for Constitutional Government, 1961–1972, FSO Papers.

79. Ogden, "Dis an' Dat," *Jackson Clarion-Ledger*, November 11, 1962.

80. Ogden, "Dis an' Dat," *Jackson Clarion-Ledger*, May 5, 1963.

81. Margaret Peaster, Annual Report of WCG, October 29, 1963, Folder 114, FSO Papers.

82. Elsie Gill to FSO, January 24, 1963, and FSO to Gill, January 30, 1963, Folder 40, FSO Papers.

83. FSO to Sally Schooler, December 13, 1962, Folder 47, FSO Papers. Undated columns, Florence Sillers Ogden file, in the State Sovereignty Commission papers, MDAH; Ogden's WCG Speeches in Jackson, October 30, 1962; Greenwood, March 5, 1963; Greenville, February 20, 1963. Folder 113, FSO Papers; Ogden, WCG Speech, Montgomery, Alabama, January 17, 1963, FSO Papers; WCG Speech, Mobile, Alabama, February 11, 1965, Folder 113, FSO Papers. WCG Newsletter, October 1963, Folder 114, FSO Papers; For more on the Women for Constitutional Government, see Speer, "'Contrary Mary.'"

84. Ogden, "Dis an' Dat," *Jackson Clarion-Ledger*, January 6, 1963.

85. CDT to Senator Thurston Mortson, December 20, 1963, Folder 24, Box 2, CDT Papers.

86. Darren Dochuk, *From Bible Belt to Sunbelt: Plain-Folk Religion, Grassroots Politics, and the Rise of Evangelical Conservatism* (New York: W. W. Norton, 2011), 239–240.

87. Ziker, "Race, Conservative Politics, and U.S. Foreign Policy," 330.

88. Ziker, "Race, Conservative Politics, and U.S. Foreign Policy," 297; Crespino, *In Search of Another Country*, 77.

89. "Plan of Action," WCG, [undated], Folder, FSO Papers; *Newsletter from Women for Constitutional Government*, October 1963, Folder, WCG, FSO Papers.

90. Nickerson, *Mothers of Conservatism*, 59–60; Ziker, "Race, Conservative Politics, and U.S. Foreign Policy," 253.

91. Open Letter for Immediate Release, Mary Dawson Cain, [1965?], Folder WCG, FSO Papers.

92. Margaret Peaster, Annual Report of WCG, October 29, 1963, Folder 114, FSO Papers.

93. Ogden, "Dis an Dat," *Jackson Clarion-Ledger*, May 19, 1963. Mrs. Ross Barnett attended the reception as well as Mrs. H. L. Hunt, and Mrs. Tom Anderson (columnist of Nashville). See also Clive Webb, *Rabble Rousers: The American Far Right in the Civil Rights Era* (Athens: University of Georgia Press, 2010), 141–146; Crespino, *In Search of Another Country*, 79.

94. WCG Newsletter, October 1963, Folder 114, FSO Papers.

95. Ogden, "Dis an' Dat," *Jackson Clarion-Ledger*, May 24, 1964.

96. Ogden, "National Defense," speech given to the Hicashabaha Chapter DAR, December 5, 1963, Folder 114, FSO Papers.

97. McGirr, *Suburban Warriors*, 180–181.

98. Nickerson, *Mothers of Conservatism*, 75–78; Ogden, "Busy Weeks When Women Back Constitutional Rule," *Jackson Clarion-Ledger*, February 24, 1963.

99. McGirr, Nickerson, *Mothers of Conservativsm*, 150–160.

100. Frank Parker, *Black Votes Count: Political Empowerment in Mississippi after 1965* (Chapel Hill: University of North Carolina Press, 1990), 32, 205–209; Frank R. Parker, David C. Colby, and Minion K. C. Morrison "Mississippi," in *Quiet Revolution in the South: The Impact of the Voting Rights Act, 1965–1990*, ed. Chandler Davidson and Bernard Goffman (Princeton, NJ: Princeton University Press, 1994), 136–154. They argued that Mississippians diluted the Voting Rights Act by erecting barriers to black electoral power and participation. These efforts included deceit, intimidation, violence, and legislation such as the promotion of at-large municipal elections. The Supreme Court decided that at-large elections that attempted to reduce the power of the minority vote violated section 5 of the Voting Rights Act. Most Mississippi cities had adopted at-large voting prior to 1965 and thus were exempt from preclearance. The Mobile decision in 1980 decided that prosecutors had to prove that at-large systems had been adopted for discriminatory purposes and with discriminatory intent—a difficult burden of proof. Based on a study of 145 cities of 1,000 or more, the authors concluded that

black electoral power was significantly reduced in the aftermath of the Voting Rights Act. In addition, between 1965 and 1980, fourteen of Mississippi's eighty-two counties switched to at-large elections for county supervisors, twenty-two for school board members. Other disfranchising methods such as dual registration with county and municipal clerk were not abolished until 1984 and the party principles loyalty oath was not abolished until 1987. On Mississippi's elected officials, see US Bureau of the Census, *Statistical Abstract of the United States*, 1994, 114th edition, Washington, DC, Table 443. For information on the Voting Rights Act and its impact on the Mississippi Delta, see Benjamin E. Griffith, "The Impact of the 1982 Amendments to the Voting Rights Act of 1965 on Political Representation in the Mississippi Delta," at Public Hearing on Racial and Ethnic Tensions in American Communities—Poverty, Inequality, and Discrimination, before the United States Commission on Civil Rights, March 8, 1997, Greenville, Mississippi.

101. "Dis an' Dat," *Jackson Clarion-Ledger*, December 15, 1963, April 5, 1964. On the Civil Rights bill, see Lawson, *Black Ballots*, 292–300; Ogden was not the only one who believed that white northerners would support the civil rights movement only while it concentrated on the South; see Carter, *The Politics of Rage*, 349.

## CONCLUSION

1. Ogden, "Dis' an Dat," *Jackson Clarion-Ledger*, April 5, 1964.
2. Several works emphasize the constant and overt effort that white supremacist politics required and the individual actions that remade it over time. For example, see Stephen Kantrowitz, *Ben Tillman and the Reconstruction of White Supremacy* (Chapel Hill: University of North Carolina Press, 2000), 4–6; and Jane Dailey, Glenda Elizabeth Gilmore, and Bryant Simon, *Jumpin' Jim Crow: Southern Politics from Civil War to Civil Rights* (Princeton, NJ: Princeton University Press, 2000), 4; Nathan D. B. Connolly, *A World More Concrete: Real Estate and the Remaking of Jim Crow South Florida* (Chicago: University of Chicago Press, 2014), 277–290; Alexander, *The New Jim Crow*, 26; Ta-Nehisi Coates, *Between the World and Me*, (New York: Spiegel & Grau, 2015).
3. J. Harvie Wilkinson, *From Brown to Bakke: The Supreme Court and School Integration* (New York: Oxford University Press, 1978), 202–205, 216, 219.
4. Lassiter, *The Silent Majority*, 128–132.
5. "Ribicoff Attacks Schools in the North," *New York Times*, February 10, 1970, 1; "Stennis Rebuffed in School Aid Vote," *New York Times*, April 2, 1970, 1; Lassiter, *The Silent Majority*, 248–249.
6. *Swann v. Charlotte-Mecklenburg Board of Education*, 300 F. Supp. 1358 (1969), 1360–1372; *Swann v. Mecklenburg Board of Education*, 402 U.S., 1 (1971); Lassiter, *The Silent Majority*, 132–137; *Bradley v. Milliken*, 345 F. Supp. 914 (1972); *Milliken v. Bradley*, 418 U.S. 717 (1974), 733; Sugrue, *Sweet Land of Liberty*, 481–483.

7. Lassiter, *The Silent Majority*, 132–137.

8. Sugrue, *Sweet Land of Liberty*, 482; Connolly, *A World More Concrete*, 11–16, 239–275.

9. Lassiter, *The Silent Majority*, 153, 141, 167; *Charlotte Observer*, May 14, 1969. As Lassiter notes, it was also liberal white women in the League of Women Voters who expressed support for integration via busing.

10. Mason, *Reading Appalachia from Left to Right*, 3–5, 45–46, 53–55, 77–81, 97–99.

11. Jefferson Cowie, *Stayin' Alive: The 1970s and the Last Days of the Working Class* (New York: New Press, 2010), 1, 4; Carter, *The Politics of Rage*, 426–430; Sugrue, *The Origins of the Urban Crisis*, 267.

12. Sugrue, *Sweet Land of Liberty*, 479; Irene McCabe, ABC News, September 6, 1971, http://www.criticalcommons.org/Members/mattdelmont/clips/irene-mccabe-speaking-at-anti-busing-rally-pontiac/; Joe Darden, *Detroit: Race and Uneven Development* (Philadelphia, PA: Temple University Press, 1990), 231.

13. Tracy K'Meyer, *Civil Rights in the Gateway to the South: Louisville, KY, 1945–1980* (Lexington: University Press of Kentucky, 2009), 251–262; "8000 in Louisville March to Protest School Bus Order," *New York Times*, September 28, 1975, 59; Mrs. Joseph Phillips, letter to editor, *Louisville Times*, August 6, 1975; Carolyn Colwell and Ed Ryan, "Antibusing Speaker Renews Plan for Business Boycott," *Courier Journal* (Louisville), September 29, 1975; Sugrue, *Sweet Land of Liberty*, 479–483.

14. Liva Baker, *The Second Battle of New Orleans: The Hundred-Year Struggle to Integrate the Schools* (New York: HarperCollins, 1996), 393–409.

15. In the copious letters to Judge Garrity, Bostonians would point out that he would not experience the changes that he asked them to accept. See Box 49, Judge Garrity: Boston Schools Case Papers, Special Collections, University of Massachusetts, Boston; hereafter cited as Judge Garrity Papers.

16. Jeanne Theoharis, "'We Saved the City': Black Struggles for Educational Equality in Boston, 1960–1970," *Radical History Review* 81 (2001), 62–63. She notes that white Bostonians who complied with the decision have received little scholarly attention.

17. Formisano, *Boston against Busing*, 35–37, 58–59; "Louise Day Hicks Dies at 87: Led Fight on Busing in Boston," *New York Times*, October 23, 2003.

18. Michael Klarman, "How *Brown* Changed Race Relations: The Backlash Thesis," *Journal of American History* 81 (June, 1994): 81–118; Formisano, *Boston against Busing*, 37.

19. Kathleen Banks Nutter, "'Militant Mothers': Boston, Busing, and the Bicentennial of 1976," *Historical Journal of Massachusetts* (Fall 2010), 55–60, 66; Kathleen Kilgore, "Militant Mothers: The Politicization of ROAR Women," *Real Paper*, November 13, 1976, sec. 4, p. 6.

20. Older mother to Judge Garrity, September 1974, Folder 5, September 15–30, 1974, Mother of six from Ward 13 to Judge Garrity, April 1975, Folder 22, Judge Garrity

Papers. The names used in the correspondence are not to be used in citations per conditions of the collection agreement. Formisano and Lukas focus on the complexity of Boston's white resistance. Formisano, *Boston against Busing,* xi–xiii, 4; Anthony Lukas, *Common Ground,* 180; Jeanne Theoharis questions this distinction, wondering why white Bostonians turned to the language of white supremacy. See Theoharis, " 'We Saved the City,' " 61–62.

21. WRAL Channel 5 Broadcast from Raleigh, North Carolina, October 28, 1974, Folder 9– October 24–31, 1974, Judge Garrity Papers; Letter from William Cheshire at WRAL in Raleigh to Garrity, October 21, 1974. He attached an editorial from an October 16, 1974, program at 6:20 PM and on October 17, 1974, at 6:55 AM and offered WRAL facilities for the judge's response, Folder 8—October 1–23, 1974, Judge Garrity Papers.

22. Formisano, *Boston against Busing,* 192–195; Mrs. C of Hyde Park to Judge Garrity, October 10, 1974, Folder 7; Mrs. C of Hyde Park to Judge Garrity, September 1975, Folder 29, Sepember. 1–15, 1975; telegram from Baptist Ministers Conference, October 8, 1974, Folder 6; Mrs. S. of Dorchster to Garrity, September 19, 1974, Folder 5, Judge Garrity Papers.

23. For an overview, see the Citywide Educational Collection, Archives and Special Collections, Northeastern University, Boston, Massachusetts; hereafter cited as CWEC Papers.

24. West Roxbury Information Center, "The True Paper," vol. 1 [1975?], Folder 21, Box 3, CWEC Papers.

25. Ms. M of South Boston to Garrity, September 9, 1974, Folder 4, Garrity Papers.

26. Robert Coles, "The White Northerner: Pride and Prejudice," *Atlantic Monthly,* online (June 1966), http://www.theatlantic.com/politics/race/whitenor.htm.

27. Sugrue, *Sweet Land of Liberty,* 487.

28. "Massachussetts Citizens against Force Busing Newsletter," April 3, 1974, Folder 13, CWEC Papers. Fran Johenne's comments are written on the back of this newsletter.

29. Rumor Control Center: Field Harassment Reports, September 8, 1975, CWEC Papers.

30. Mary Ella Smith, "Rumor Control Center: Field Workers Harassment Reports," September 1975, Folder 19, CWEC Papers. The report was in the September file but otherwise undated. It did list in a follow-up that Roberts's car had been vandalized on October 1, 1975.

31. Rumor Control Center: Field Harassment Reports, September 8, 1975, Folder 19, CWEC Papers. For more on Pixie Palladino, see Formisano, *Boston against Busing,* 179–183.

32. Student to Judge Garrity, September 7, 1974, Folder 4, Garrity Papers.

33. Folder 13, CWEC Collection; Mrs. C of Hyde Park to Judge Garrity, Box 49, Folder 7, October 10, 1974, Garrity Papers.

34. "Press Release from the Parents of Roxbury," August 7, 1974, Folder 45, Box 6, CWEC Papers.

35. Baker, *The Second Battle of New Orleans*; John Steinbeck, *Travels with Charley*. On the comparison between New Orleans and Boston, Formisano notes the similar class background and the role of the Catholic Church. See Formisano, *Boston against Busing*, 20–21.

36. Connolly, *A World More Concrete*, 16; Thomas Holt, *The Problem of Race in the Twenty-first Century* (Cambridge, MA: Harvard University Press, 2000), 21.

37. Jacquelyn Dowd Hall, "The Long Civil Rights Movement: and Political Uses of the Past," *Journal of American History* 91, no. 4 (March 2005): 1233–1263.

38. Robert O. Self, *All in the Family: The Realignment of American Democracy since the 1960s* (New York: Hill and Wang, 2012), 352–355; Lassiter, *The Silent Majority*, 153; Carter, *The Politics of Rage*, 423–424.

39. Lassiter, *The Silent Majority*, 1–19; Florence Sillers Ogden, Yazoo and Lake Village speeches, 1954, Folder 105, Florence Sillers Ogden Papers, Capps Archives, Delta State University, Cleveland, Mississippi. On this political language and the connections between the positions of southern segregationists on the United Nations and conservatives with a more national audience, like William Buckley and the *National Review*, see Ann Ziker, "Race, Conservatives, and US Foreign Policy," 162–175, 197, 250–275.

40. Ogden, Women for Constitutional Government Speech, October 30, 1962, Folder 112, FSO Papers. See also Speer, " 'Contrary Mary.' "

41. This use of motherhood that stressed that identity over their political, racial, or even class identity meshed nicely with what Self called breadwinner conservatism. Self, *All in the Family*, 5–7. Rumor Control Center Reports, CWEC Papers, 1974–1975; New Hanover Schools Segregation Document, 1960, Box 40, Folder 3 NBL Papers, NCDAH.

# Bibliography

A. MANUSCRIPT COLLECTIONS
*Albany, New York*

M. E. Grenander Department of Special Collections and Archives, University Library, Albany, State University of New York
　Arthur Estabrook Papers


*Atlanta, Georgia*

State Department of Archives and History, Atlanta, Georgia
　Anti-suffrage Pamphlet Collection


*Athens, Georgia*

Hargrett Rare Book and Manuscript Library, University of Georgia, Athens, Georgia
　DAR Annual Proceedings, Georgia Division.
　Rebecca Latimer Felton Collection
　Margaret Mitchell Papers
　Mildred Lewis Rutherford (MLR) Papers
　*Miss Rutherford's Scrapbooks*
　Richard Russell Papers


*Boston, Massachusetts*

Special Collections, Northeastern University
　Citywide Educational Collection Records (CWEC), 1972–2001.
Special Collections, University of Massachusetts, Boston
　Judge Wendell Arthur Garrity Papers

### *Chapel Hill, North Carolina*

North Carolina Collection, Wilson Library, University of North Carolina
  Patriots of North Carolina Clipping File
  Defenders of States' Rights Clipping File
Southern Historical Collection (SHC), Wilson Library, University of North Carolina
  Wesley Critz George Collection
  Frank Porter Graham Papers
  Kemp Plummer Lewis Papers
  Southern Oral History Collection

### *Charlottesville, Virginia*

Albert and Shirley Small Special Collections Library, University of Virginia, Charlottesville, Virginia
  Sarah Patton Boyle (SPB) Papers
  John Powell Papers
  Kathryn B. Stone Papers

### *Cleveland, Mississippi*

Charles C. Capps Jr. Archives and Library, Delta State University, Cleveland, Mississippi
  Florence Sillers Ogden (FSO) Papers
  Walter Sillers Jr. Papers
  Florence Warfield Sillers Papers
Bolivar County Public Library, Cleveland, Mississippi
  Sillers Family Clipping File

### *Columbia, South Carolina*

The South Caroliniana Library, University of South Carolina
  Cornelia Dabney Tucker (CDT) Papers
  Cornelia Dabney Tucker Scrapbooks (CDT Scrapbooks) on Microfilm

### *Durham, North Carolina*

David M. Rubenstein Rare Book and Manuscript Library, Duke University
  Clyde B. Hoey Papers

### *Hattiesburg, Mississippi*

University of Southern Mississippi Special Collections, Hattiesburg, Mississippi

Anti Communism in Mississippi Digital Collection
http://www.lib.usm.edu/legacy/spcol/exhibitions/anti-comm/
Oral History Collection
  Erle Johnston
  http://digilib.usm.edu/cdm/compoundobject/collection/coh/id/4035/rec/3
  McClain Library and Archives, University of Southern Mississippi
    Robert Waller Photographs


*Hyde Park, New York*

Franklin Delano Roosevelt Presidential Library and Museum
  Anna Eleanor Roosevelt Papers (ERP)


*Jackson, Mississippi*

Mississippi State Department of Archives and History (MDAH)
  Mary Dawson Cain (MDC) Papers
  Paul B. Johnson Papers
  State Sovereignty Commission Papers
  Florence Sillers Ogden, Clipping File
  Textbook Commission Records


*Lexington, Virginia*

Rockbridge Regional Library
  Clipping File
  "Indians, Monacan, Local History," Vertical File
Washington and Lee Special Collections, Washington and Lee University Library,
  Withrow Scrapbooks


*Marshall, Texas*

Harrison County Genealogical Society
  Clipping File, Marshall Housewives


*Nashville, Tennessee*

Lila Brunch Library, Belmont University, Nashville, Tennessee
  *Catalogue of Belmont School of Expression*
  Collection of College Bulletins
  Alumni Card Catalog
  *MiLady in Brown*, Yearbook of Belmont College

## *Northhampton, Massachussetts*

Smith College Archives, Smith College
  *Smith College Weekly*

## *Oxford, Mississippi*

Special Collections, John D. Williams Library, University of Mississippi
  David Reese Chapter, DAR Papers
  University of Mississippi Catalog Collection

## *Raleigh, North Carolina*

North Carolina Department of Archives and History (NCDAH)
  Nell Battle Lewis (NBL) Papers
  Governor William B. Umstead Papers
  Gertrude Weil Papers
  North Carolina Department of Public Instruction/Office of Superintendent
  North Carolina Department of Public Instruction/Textbook Correspondence
  North Carolina Department of Public Instruction/Division of Negro Education
    Office of Director Papers
Special Collections, St. Mary's School, Raleigh, North Carolina
  Nell Battle Lewis Clipping File

### B. NEWSPAPERS AND PERIODICALS

*American Mercury*
*Atlantic Monthly*
*Boston Globe*
*Citizen-Council*, Jackson, Mississippi
*Citizen-Times*, Asheville, North Carolina
*Christian Science Monitor*
*Confederate Veteran*, Nashville, Tennessee
*Constitution, Journal*, and *Journal-Constitution*. Atlanta, Georgia
*Contempo*. Chapel Hill, North Carolina
*Crisis*
*Dearborn Independent*, Dearborn, Michigan
*DeBow's Review*, Washington, D.C.
*Athens Banner Herald*, Athens, Georgia
*Bolivar County Democrat*, Cleveland, Mississippi
*Charlotte Observer*, Charlotte, North Carolina
*Chapel Hill Daily*, Chapel Hill, North Carolina

*Commercial Appeal*, Memphis, Tennessee
*Gastonia Gazette*, Gastonia, North Carolina
*Daily Times*, Greensboro, North Carolina
*Dallas Morning News*, Dallas, Texas
*Daily Democrat Times*, Greenville, Mississippi
*Delta-Democrat Times*, Greenville, Mississippi
*Delta Star*, Greenville, Mississippi
*Daily News and Clarion Ledger*, Jackson, Mississippi
*Durham Sun*, Durham, North Carolina
*Lexington Gazette*, Lexington, Virginia.
*Look Magazine*
*Macon News*, Macon, Georgia
*Miss Rutherford's Scrap Book: Valuable Information about the South*, Athens, Georgia.
*News and Courier*, Charleston, South Carolina
*News and Gazette*, Lexington, Virginia
*News and Observer*, Raleigh, North Carolina
*New York Herald Tribune*
*New York Times*
*Perquimans Weekly*, Hertford, North Carolina
*Press Scimitar*, Memphis, Tennessee
*Times*, Raleigh, North Carolina
*Real Paper*, Boston, Massachusetts
*Richmond Times Dispatch*, Richmond, Virginia
*Rockbridge County News*, Lexington, Virginia
*Shreveport Times*, Shreveport, Louisiana
*Savannah Morning News*, Savannah, Georgia
*Southern School News*, Nashville, Tennessee
*Suburban Reader*, East Point, Georgia.
*Summit Sun*, Summit, Mississippi
*Time Magazine*
*Virginian Pilot*, Norfolk, Virginia
*Washington Post*, Washington, D.C.
*Zebulon Record*, Zebulon, North Carolina

### C. PUBLISHED PRIMARY

Boyle, Sarah Patton. "Southerners Will Like Segregation." *Saturday Evening Post* February 19, 1955. 25, 133–134.
Rockmore, Ellen Bresler. "How Texas Teaches History." *New York Times*. October 21, 2015, http://www.nytimes.com/2015/10/22/opinion/how-texas-teaches-history.html.
Cain, Mary Dawson. "Why I Am Proud to Be a Mississippian." *Mississippi Woman's Magazine* 26, no. 3 (May–June 1950).

Cain, Mary Dawson. "Mary Cain's Column." *Summit Sun*. Summit, Mississippi. 1936 to 1984.

Corbitt, David Leroy, ed. *Public Addresses, Letters, and Papers of Joseph Melville Broughton, Governor of North Carolina, 1941–1945*. Raleigh: Council of State, State of North Carolina, 1950.

Cox, Earnest. *White America*. Richmond: White American Society, 1923.

Cohn, David. "Natchez Was a Lady." *Atlantic Monthly*, January 1940.

Dugdale, R. L. *"The Jukes": A Study in Crime, Pauperism, Disease, and Heredity*. New York: G. Putnam, 1891.

Eddy, Don. "They Gave Uncle Sam the Works!" *American Magazine*, June 1951, 35–114.

Estabrook, Arthur. *The Jukes in 1915*. Washington, DC: Carnegie Institute of Washington, 1916.

Estabrook, Arthur, and Ivan McDougle. *The Mongrel Virginians: The WIN Tribe*. Baltimore, MD: Williams and Wilkins, 1926.

Hinckley, Story. "Texas: We Don't Need Academics to Fact-Check Our Textbooks," *Christian Science Monitor*, November 19, 2015. http://www.csmonitor.com/USA/Education/2015/1119/Texas-We-don-t-need-academics-to-fact-check-our-textbooks-video

Huie, William Bradford. "The Shocking Story of Approved Killing in Mississippi." *Look*. January 24, 1956.

Grant, Madison. *The Passing of the Great Race or the Racial Basis of European History*. New York: Scribner, 1918.

Keith, John. "Competent Teachers for the Nation: An Article Plank One of the Platform of the National Education Association." *Journal of the National Education Association* 10, no. 1 (March 1921).

Lewis, Nell Battle. "The North Carolina Conference for Social Service." *Journal of Social Forces* 1 (March 1923): 266–268.

Lewis, Nell Battle, and Kate Burr Johnson. "A Decade of Social Progress in North Carolina." *Journal of Social Forces* 1 (March 1923): 400–403.

Lewis, Nell Battle. "The University of North Carolina Gets Its Orders." *Nation* 122 (1926): 114–115.

Lewis, Nell Battle. "North Carolina." *American Mercury* 9 (May 1926): 36–43.

Lewis, Nell Battle. "Anarchy v. Communism in Gastonia." *Nation* (September 25, 1929): 321–322.

Lewis, Nell Battle. "North Carolina at the Cross-Roads." *Virginia Quarterly Review* (January 1930): 37–47.

Lewis, Nell Battle. "Incidentally." *News and Observer*, Raleigh, 1920–1956.

Lewis, Nell Battle. "Scarlett Materializes." *Raleigh News and Observer* (February 18, 1940).

Logan, Rayford, Ed. *What the Negro Wants*. Chapel Hill: University of North Carolina Press, 1944.

Lowell, Esther. "A Columnist with a Purpose." *Woman's Journal*, 14 March 1929, 24–25.

Ogden, Florence Sillers. "Dis an' Dat." *Greenville Delta Democrat*, 1938–1960.

Ogden, Florence Sillers. "Dis an' Dat." *Jackson Clarion-Ledger*, 1950–1970.

Percy, William Alexander. *Lanterns on the Levee: Recollections of a Planter's Son.* New York: Alfred A. Knopf, 1941.

Races: Lynch and Anti-lynch." *Time Magazine*. April 26, 1937.

Rose, Laura. *The Ku Klux Klan: or, Invisible Empire.* New Orleans: L. Graham, 1914.

Rowe, H.J. *History of Athens and Clarke County.* Athens, Georgia: McGregor, 1923,

Rutherford, Mildred. "A Measuring Rod to Test Text Books, and Reference Books in Schools, Colleges, and Libraries." Athens, GA: United Confederate Veterans, 1919.

Rutherford, Mildred. "Loyalty to the South and Its Ideals," *Confederate Veteran* 30, no. 12 (December 1922): 476;

Somerville, Nellie Nugent. "Food for Thought." *Bolivar County Democrat* (Rosedale, Mississippi), April 27, 1944.

Somerville, Nellie Nugent. "Democracy and the Poll Tax." *Daily News* (Jackson, Mississippi), April 24, 1942.

Smith, Lillian. *The Killers of the Dream.* New York: W.W. Norton, reissue, 1994.

Stoddard, Lothrap. *The Rising Tide or Color against White World Supremacy.* New York: Scribner, 1920.

Wylie, Phillip. *Generation of Vipers.* New York: Farrar and Rinehart, 1942.

Whitmore, F.A. "Hacksaw Mary." *American Mercury.* (October 1955): 147–150.

### D. COURT CASES AND GOVERNMENT DOCUMENTS

*Congressional Record*

*Henderson v. United States.* United States Reports, 339 (1950): 516.

*Lowery v. School Trustees of Kernersville.*

*McLaurin v. Oklahoma State Regents.* United States Reports, 339 (1950): 637.

*Public Laws of North Carolina*, 1933, 1935.

*Smith v. Allwright*, 321 United States Reports 649 (1944).

*Swann v. Charlotte-Mecklenburg*, 300 F. Supp. 1358 (1969).

*Sweatt v. Painter.* United States Reports 339 (1950): 629.

United States Census. 1880, 1900, 1910, 1920, 1930.

### E. DIGITIZED COLLECTIONS

Heritage Quest at *Heritage Quest On-Line*, http://o-persi.heritagequestonline.com. wncln.wncln.org/hqoweb/library/do/census/.

For oral history projects that focus on Milwaukee, see http://recollectionwisconsin. org/civil-rights-milwaukee.

Southern Oral History Project Collection, Southern Historical Collection, Wilson Library, University of North Carolina, Chapel Hill

"Walter Plecker Letters: A Series of Letters Relating to the Melungeons of Newman's Ridge," www.geocities.com/ourmelungeons/plecker.html. Accessed May 22, 2008.

Roosevelt, Eleanor. "My Day" columns. Eleanor Roosevelt Papers Project (ERPP) George Washington University. On-line Collection, https://erpapers.columbian. gwu.edu/my-day

Ruggles, Steven, Katie Genadek, Ronald Goeken, Josiah Grover, and Matthew Sobek, *Integrated Public Use Microdata Series: Version 6.0* [dataset] (Minneapolis: University of Minnesota, 2015), http://doi.org/10.18128/D010.V6.0,

Ruggles, Steven, J. Trent Alexander, Katie Genadek, Ronald Goeken, Matthew B. Schroeder, and Matthew Sobek. *Integrated Public Use Microdata Series: Version 5.0* [Machine-readable database]. Minneapolis: University of Minnesota, 2010. Available at http://usa.ipums.org/usa/voliii/.

Rutherford, Mildred. "Life Sketch of Mildred Rutherford," Clarke County, GA Archives, Biographies, http://www.rootsweb.com/~usgenweb/ga/gafiles.htm.

Truman Presidential Library, http://www.trumanlibrary.org/civilrights/srights3. htm#110.

F. PRIMARY DOCUMENTS IN AUTHOR'S POSSESSION

"My Dear Boys, 1942–1944."

SECONDARY SOURCES
*A. Books*

Abrams, Douglas Carl. *Conservative Constraints: North Carolina and the New Deal.* Jackson: University Press of Mississippi, 1992.

Alexander, Michelle. *The New Jim Crow: Mass Incarceration in the Age of Colorblindness.* New York: New Press, 2011.

Allen, Tip H. Jr. *Mississippi Votes: The Presidential and Gubernatorial Elections, 1947–1964.* State College: Mississippi State University, 1967.

Almaguer, Tomas. *Racial Fault Lines: The Historical Origins of White Supremacy in California.* Berkeley: University of California Press, 2008.

Anderson, Benedict. *Imagined Communities: Reflections on the Origins and Spread of Nationalism.* New York: Verso, 1983.

Anderson, Carol. *Eyes Off the Prize: The United Nations and the African American Freedom Struggle for Human Rights, 1944–1955.* New York: Cambridge University Press, 2003.

Anderson, Karen. *Little Rock: Race and Resistance at Central High School.* Princeton, NJ: Princeton University Press, 2010.

Apple, Michael. *Teachers and Texts: A Political Economy of Class and Gender Relations in Education.* New York: Routledge, 1988.

Apple, Michael. *Ideology and Curriculum,* 2nd ed. New York: Routledge, 1990.

Arendt, Hannah. *Between Past and Future.* New York: Viking Press, 1961; revised edition 1968.

Asch, Cristopher Meyers. *The Senator and the Share Cropper: The Freedom Struggles of James O. Eastland and Fannie Lou Hamer.* New York: New Press, 2008.

Ashby, Warren. *Frank Porter Graham: A Southern Liberal.* Winston-Salem, NC: John Blair, 1908.

Ashmore, Harry. *The Negro and the Schools.* Chapel Hill: University of North Carolina Press, 1954.

Ayers, Edward. *The Promise of the New South: Life after Reconstruction.* New York: Oxford University Press, 1992.

Badger, Anthony. *North Carolina and the New Deal.* Raleigh: North Carolina Department of Cultural Resources, 1981.

Baghart, Herbert C. *Work: The Soul of Good Fortune: Memoirs of a Love Affair with Belmont College.* Nashville, TN: Broadman Press, 1989.

Baker, Liva. *The Second Battle for New Orleans: The Hundred-year Struggle to Integrate the Schools.* New York: HarperCollins, 1996.

Barker, Hugh, and Yuval Taylor. *Faking It: The Quest for Authenticity in Popular Music.* New York: W. W. Norton, 2007.

Barnard, Hollinger, ed. *Outside the Magic Circle: The Autobiography of Virginia Durr.* Tuscaloosa: University of Alabama Press, 1986.

Barry, John. *Rising Tide: The Great Mississippi Flood of 1927 and How It Changed America.* New York: Simon and Schuster, 1997.

Bartley, Numan. *The Rise of Massive Resistance: Race and Politics in the South during the 1950s.* Baton Rouge: Louisiana State University Press, 1969.

Bartley, Numan. *The New South, 1945–1980.* Baton Rouge: Louisiana State University Press, 1995.

Bartley, Numan, and Hugh D. Graham. *Southern Politics and the Second Reconstruction.* Baltimore, MD: Johns Hopkins University Press, 1975.

Bass, Jack, and DeVries, Walter. *The Transformation of Southern Politics: Social Change and Political Consequence since 1945.* New York: Basic Books, 1976.

Bederman, Gail. *Manliness and Civilization: A Cultural History of Gender and Race in the United States, 1880–1917.* Chicago: University of Chicago Press, 1995.

Billingsley, William. *Communists on Campus: Race, Politics, and the Public University in Sixties North Carolina.* Athens: University of Georgia Press, 1999.

Black, Earl. *Southern Governors and Civil Rights: Racial Segregation as a Campaign Issue in the Second Reconstruction.* Cambridge, MA: Harvard University Press, 1976.

Black, Earl, and Merle Black. *The Vital South: How Presidents Are Elected.* Cambridge, MA: Harvard University Press, 1992.

Blight, David. *Race and Reunion: The Civil War in American Memory.* Cambridge, MA: Belknap Press, 2001.

Boris, Eileen. *Home to Work: Motherhood and the Politics of Industrial Homework in the United States.* New York: Cambridge University Press, 1994.

Borstelmann, Thomas. *The Cold War and the Color Line*. Cambridge, MA: Harvard University Press, 2001.

Bowers, Claude. *The Tragic Era: The Revolution after Lincoln*. New York: Houghton Mifflin, 1929.

Boyle, Kevin. *Arc of Justice: A Saga of Race, Civil Rights, and Murder in the Jazz Age*. New York: Holt, 2005.

Brattain, Michelle. *The Politics of Whiteness: Race, Worker and Culture in the Modern South*. Athens: University of Georgia Press, 2004.

Brennan, Mary C. *Wives, Mothers, and the Red Menace: Conservative Women and the Crusade against Communism*. Boulder: University Press of Colorado, 2008.

Brundage, Fitzhugh. *Lynching in the New South: Georgia and Virginia, 1880–1920*. Urbana: University of Illinois Press, 1993.

Brundage, Fitzhugh. *The Southern Past: A Clash of Race and Memory*. Cambridge, MA: Belknap Press, 2005.

Butchart, Ron. *Schooling the Freed People: Teaching, Learning, and the Struggle for Black Freedom, 1861–1876*. Chapel Hill: University of North Carolina Press, 2010.

Camhi, Janet Jerome. *Women against Women: American Antisuffragism, 1880–1920*. New York: Carlson, 1994.

Campbell, Will. *Brother to a Dragonfly*. New York: Seabury Press, 1977.

Capeci, Dominic J., and Martha Wilkerson. *Layered Violence: The Detroit Riots of 1943*. Jackson: University Press of Mississippi, 1991.

Carpenter, Mary Elizabeth. *The Treatment of the Negro in American History School Textbooks: A Comparison of Changing Textbook Content, 1826 to 1939 with Developing Scholarship in the History of the Negro in the United States*. Menasha, WI: George Banta, 1941.

Carson, Mina. *Settlement Folk: Social Thought and the American Settlement Movement, 1885–1930*. Chicago: University of Chicago Press, 1990.

Carter, Dan. *Scottsboro: A Tragedy of the American South*. Baton Rouge: Louisiana State University Press, 1979.

Carter, Dan. *The Politics of Rage: George Wallace, the Origins of the New Conservatism, and the Transformation of American Politics*. New York: Simon and Schuster, 1995.

Carter, Dan. *From George Wallace to Newt Gingrich: Race in the Conservative Counterrevolution, 1963–1994*. Baton Rouge: Louisiana State University Press, 1996.

Cash, Wilbur J. *The Mind of the South*. New York: Alfred A. Knopf, 1941; reprint, Vintage Books, 1991.

Caute, David. *The Great Fear: The Anti-Communist Purge under Truman and Eisenhower*. New York: Simon and Schuster, 1978.

Cecelski, David. *Along Freedom Road: Hyde County, North Carolina, and the Fate of Black Schools in the South*. Chapel Hill: University of North Carolina Press, 1994.

Cecelski, David, and Timothy Tyson, eds. *Democracy Betrayed: The Wilmington Race Riot of 1898 and Its Legacy*. Chapel Hill: University of North Carolina Press, 1998.

Chafe, William. *The American Woman: Her Changing Social, Economic, and Political Roles, 1920–1970*. New York: Oxford University Press, 1972.

Chafe, William. *Women and Equality: Changing Patterns in American Culture*. New York: Oxford University Press, 1977.

Chafe, William. *Civilities and Civil Rights: Greensboro, North Carolina, and the Black Struggle for Freedom*. New York: Oxford University Press, 1980.

Chafe, William. *The Paradox of Change: American Women in the 20th Century*. New York: Oxford University Press, 1991.

Charron Katherine Mellen. *Freedom's Teacher: The Life of Septima Clark*. Chapel Hill: University of North Carolina Press, 2009.

Chavez-Garcia, Miroslava. *States of Delinquency: Race and Science in the Making of California's Judicial System*. Berkeley: University of California Press, 2012.

Chirhart, Ann. *Torches of Light and the Coming of the Modern South*. Athens: University of Georgia Press, 2005.

Clapp, Elizabeth J. *Mothers of All Children: Women, Reformers and the Rise of Juvenile Courts in Progressive Era America*. College Station: Penn State University Press, 1998.

Clare, Virginia Pettigrew. *Thunder and Stars: The Life of Mildred Rutherford*. Atlanta: Oglethorpe University Press, 1941.

Clayton, Bruce L., and John A. Salmond, ed. *Lives Full of Struggle and Triumph: Southern Women, Their Institution, and Their Communities*. Gainesville: University of Florida Press, 2003.

Coates, Ta-Nehisi Coates. *Between the World and Me*. New York: Spiegel & Grau, 2015.

Cobb, James C. *The Most Southern Place on Earth: The Mississippi Delta and the Roots of Regional Identity*. New York: Oxford University Press, 1992.

Cobb, James C. *Redefining Southern Culture: Mind and Identity in the Modern South*. Athens: University of Georgia Press, 1999.

Cobb, James C. *The Brown Decision, Jim Crow and Southern Identity*. Athens: University of Georgia Press, 2005.

Cobb, James C. *The South and America since World War II*. New York: Oxford University Press, 2011.

Cobb, James C., and Michael Namorato, eds. *The New Deal and the South: Essays*. Jackson: University Mississippi Press, 1984.

Cohn, David. *Where I Was Born and Raised*. Foreword by James Silver. Notre Dame, IN: University of Notre Dame Press, 1967; original edition, 1935.

Connolly, Nathan D. B. *A World More Concrete: Real Estate and the Remaking of Jim Crow South Florida*. Chicago: University of Chicago Press, 2014.

Cook, Samuel R. *Monacans and Miners: Native American and Coal Mining Communities in Appalachia*. Lincoln: University of Nebraska Press, 2000.

Cott, Nancy. *The Grounding of Modern Feminism*. New Haven, CT: Yale University Press, 1987.

Cowie, Jefferson. *Stayin' Alive: The 1970s and the Last Days of the Working Class.* New York: New Press, 2010.

Cox, Earnest. *White America.* Richmond, VA: White America Society, 1923.

Cox, Karen. *Dixie's Daughters: The United Daughters of the Confederacy and the Preservation of Confederate Culture.* Foreword by John David Smith. Gainesville: University of Florida Press, 2003.

Crespino, Joseph. *In Search of Another Country: Mississippi and the Conservative Counterrevolution.* Princeton, NJ: Princeton University Press, 2007.

Crespino, Joseph, and Matthew D. Lassiter, eds. *The Myth of Southern Exceptionalism.* New York: Oxford University Press, 2009.

Critchlow, Donald. *Phyllis Schlafly and Grassroots Conservatism: A Woman's Crusade.* Princeton, NJ: Princeton University Press, 2005.

Critchlow, Donald, and Nancy MacLean. *Debating the American Conservative Movement 1945 to the Present.* New York: Rowman and Littlefield, 2010.

Crow, Jeffrey, Paul D. Escott, and Flora J. Hatley. *A History of African Americans in North Carolina.* Raleigh, NC: Division of Archives and History, 1992.

Curry, Constance. *Silver Rights.* New York: Algonquin, 1995.

Daily, Jane. *Before Jim Crow: The Politics of Post-Emancipation Virginia.* Chapel Hill: University of North Carolina Press, 2000.

Dailey, Jane, Glenda Elizabeth Gilmore, and Bryant Simon, Eds. *Jumpin' Jim Crow: Southern Politics from Civil War to Civil Rights.* Princeton, NJ: Princeton University Press, 2000.

Daniel, Pete. *Deep'n as It Come: The 1927 Mississippi River Flood.* New York: Oxford University Press, 1977.

Daniel, Pete. *Breaking the Land: The Transformation of Cotton, Tobacco, and Rice Cultures since 1880.* Urbana: University of Illinois Press, 1985.

Daniel, Pete. *Lost Revolutions: The South in the 1950s.* Chapel Hill: University of North Carolina Press for the Smithsonian, 2000.

Darden, Joe. *Detroit: Race and Uneven Development.* Philadelphia, PA: Temple University Press, 1990.

Davenport, Doris. *Madness like Morning Glories.* Baton Rouge: Louisiana State University Press, 2005.

Davies, David R., ed. *The Press and Race: Mississippi Journalists Confront the Movement.* Jackson: University Press of Mississippi, 2001.

Davis, Allen F. *Spearheads for Reform: The Social Settlements and the Progressive Movement, 1880–1914.* New York: Oxford University Press, 1967.

Davis, Jack. *Race against Time: Culture and Separation in Natchez since 1930.* Baton Rouge: Louisiana State University Press, 2001.

De Hart, Jane, and Donald Mathews. *Sex, Gender, and the Politics of the ERA: A State and the Nation.* New York: Oxford University Press, 1990.

Delegard, Kirsten. *Battling Miss Bolsheviki: The Origins of Female Conservatism in the United States.* Philadelphia: University of Pennsylvania Press, 2012.

D'Emilio, John, and Estelle B. Freedman. *Intimate Matters: A History of Sexuality in America.* New York: Harper & Row, 1988.

Dittmer, John. *Local People: The Struggle for Civil Rights in Mississippi.* Urbana: University of Illinois Press, 1995.

Dochuk, Darren. *From Bible Belt to Sunbelt: Plain-Folk Religion, Grassroots Politics, and the Rise of Evangelical Conservatism.* New York: W. W. Norton, 2011.

Dominguez, Victoria. *White by Definition: Social Classification in Creole Louisiana.* New Brunswick, NJ: Rutgers University Press, 1986.

Dorr, Gregory. *Segregation Science: Eugenics and Society in Virginia.* Charlottesville: University Press of Virginia, 2008.

Douglas, Davison. *Reading, Writing, and Race: The Desegregation of the Charlotte Schools.* Chapel Hill: University of North Carolina Press, 1995.

Douglas, Susan. *Where the Girls Are: Growing Up Female with the Mass Media.* New York: Three Rivers Press, 1994.

Dudziak, Mary. *Cold War Civil Rights: Race and the Image of American Democracy.* Princeton, NJ: Princeton University Press, 2000.

Dunbar, Anthony P. *Against the Grain: Southern Radicals and Prophets, 1929–1959.* Charlottesville: University of Virginia Press, 1981.

Dwyer, Owen, and Derek H. Alderman. *Civil Rights Memorials and the Geography of Memory.* Chicago: Center for American Places, Columbia College, 2008.

Edgar, Walter. *South Carolina: A History.* Columbia: University of South Carolina Press, 1998.

Egerton, John. *Speak Now against the Day: The Generation before the Civil Rights Movement in the South.* Chapel Hill: University of North Carolina Press, 1995.

Eschen, Penny Von. *Race against Empire: Black Americans and Anticolonialism, 1937–1957.* Ithaca, NY: Cornell University Press, 1997.

Estabrook, Arthur. *The Jukes of 1915.* Washington, DC: Carnegie Institution, 1916.

Estes, Steve. *I Am a Man! Race, Manhood, and the Civil Rights Movement.* Chapel Hill: University of North Carolina Press, 2005.

Fairclough, Adam. *Race and Democracy: The Civil Rights Struggle in Louisiana, 1915–1972.* Athens: University of Georgia Press, 1995.

Farber, David. *The Rise and Fall of Modern American Conservatism: A Short History.* Princeton, NJ: Princeton University Press, 2010.

Fitzgerald, Francis. *America Revised: History Schoolbooks in the Twentieth Century.* Boston: Little, Brown, 1979.

Flamming, Douglas. *Bound for Freedom: Black Los Angeles in Jim Crow America.* Berkeley: University of California Press, 2006.

Formisano, Ron. *Boston against Busing: Race, Class, and Ethnicity in the 1960s and 1970s.* Chapel Hill: University of North Carolina Press, 1991.

Fosl, Catherine. *Subversive Southerner: Anne Braden and the Struggle for Racial Justice in the Cold War South.* New York: Palgrave Macmillan, 2002.

Frederickson, Kari. *The Dixiecrat Revolt and the End of the Solid South, 1932–1968.* Chapel Hill: University of North Carolina Press, 2001.

Noralee. *Gender, Race, and Reform in the Progressive Era.* Lexington: University of Kentucky Press, 1991.

Fry, Joseph. *Dixie Looks Abroad: The South and U.S. Foreign Relations, 1789–1973.* Baton Rouge: Louisiana State University Press, 2002.

Gardner, Sarah. *Blood and Irony: Southern White Women's Narratives of the Civil War, 1861–1937.* Chapel Hill: University of North Caolina Press, 2004.

Garner, James. *Reconstruction in Mississippi.* New York: Macmillan, 1901.

Gates, Robin L. *The Making of Massive Resistance: Virginia's Politics of Public School Desegregation, 1954–1956.* Chapel Hill: University of North Carolina Press, 1962.

Gerstle, Gary. *American Crucible: Race and Nation in the Twentieth Century.* Princeton, NJ: Princeton University Press, 2001.

Gilmore, Glenda Elizabeth. *Gender and Jim Crow: Women and the Politics of White Supremacy in North Carolina, 1896–1920.* Chapel Hill: University of North Carolina Press, 1996.

Gilmore, Glenda Elizabeth. *Defying Dixie: The Radical Roots of Civil Rights, 1919–1950.* New York: Norton, 2008.

Godshalk, David. *Veiled Visions: The 1906 Atlanta Race Riot and the Reshaping of American Race Relations.* Chapel Hill: University of North Carolina Press, 2005.

Goldberg, Michael. *An Army of Women: Gender and Politics in Gilded Age Kansas.* Baltimore, MD: Johns Hopkins University Press, 1997.

Gordon, Linda, ed. *Women, the State, and Welfare.* Madison: University of Wisconsin Press, 1990.

Gordy, Sondra. *Finding the Lost Year: What Happened When Little Rock Closed Its Public Schools.* Fayetteville: University of Arkansas Press, 2009.

Grant, Madison. *The Passing of the Great Race or the Racial Basis of European History.* New York: C. Scribner, 1918.

Grant, Madison. *Southern Progressivism: The Reconciliation of Progress and Tradition.* Knoxville: University of Tennessee Press, 1983.

Grantham, Dewey W. *The Life and Death of the Solid South: A Political History.* Lexington: University Press of Kentucky, 1988.

Gray, William. *Imperial Bolivar.* Cleveland, MS: Bolivar Commercial, 1923.

Green, Elna. *Southern Strategies: Southern Women and the Woman Suffrage Question.* Chapel Hill: University of North Carolina Press, 1997.

Greene, Christina. *Our Separate Ways: Women and the Black Freedom Movement in Durham, North Carolina.* Chapel Hill: University of North Carolina Press, 2005.

Griffith, Barbara. *The Crisis of American Labor: Operation Dixie and the Defeat of the CIO.* Philadelphia: Temple University Press, 1988.

Gross, Ariel. *What Blood Won't Tell: A History of Race on Trial in America.* Cambridge, MA: University of Harvard Press, 2008.

Steven Hahn, *A Nation under Our Feet: Black Political Struggles in the Rural South from Slavery to the Great Migration* (Cambridge, MA: Belknap Press, 2003),

Hale, Grace Elizabeth. *Making Whiteness: The Culture of Segregation in the South, 1890–1940*. New York: Random House, 1998.

Hall, Jacquelyn Dowd. *Like a Family: The Making of a Southern Cotton Mill World*. New York: W.W. Norton, 1987.

Hall, Jacquelyn Dowd. *Revolt against Chivalry: Jessie Daniel Ames and the Southern Association for the Prevention of Lynching*. New York: Columbia University Press, 1993.

Hamlin, Francoise. *Crossroads at Clarksdale: The Black Freedom Struggle in the Mississippi Delta after World War II*. Chapel Hill: University of North Carolina Press, 2012.

Harris, Middleton, ed. *The Black Book*. New York: Random House: 1974.

Harrison, Cynthia. *On Account of Sex: The Politics of Women's Issues, 1945–1968*. Berkeley: University of California Press, 1988.

Henry, Aaron, with Constance Curry. *Aaron Henry: The Fire Ever Burning*. With an introduction by John Dittmer. Jackson: University Press of Mississippi, 2000.

Hero, Alfred. *The Southerner and World Affairs*. Baton Rouge: Louisiana State University Press, 1965.

Higginbotham, Evelyn Brooks. *Righteous Discontent: The Women's Movement in the Black Baptist Church, 1880–1920*. Cambridge, MA: Harvard University Press, 1994.

Hobbs, Allyson. *A Chosen Exile: A History of Racial Passing in American Life*. Cambridge, MA: Harvard University Press, 2014.

Hobsbawm, Eric. *The Invention of Tradition*. London: Cambridge University Press, 1984.

Hobson, Fred. *Serpent in Eden: H. L. Mencken and the South*. Foreword by Gerald W. Johnson. Chapel Hill: University of North Carolina Press, 1974.

Hodes, Martha. Ed. *Sex, Love, Race: Crossing Boundaries in North American History*. New York: New York University Press, 1999.

Hodges, Luther. *Businessman in the Statehouse: Six Years and Governor of North Carolina*. Chapel Hill: University of North Carolina Press, 1962.

Holloway, Pippa. *Sexuality, Politics, and Social Control in Virginia, 1920–1945*. Chapel Hill: University of North Carolina Press, 2006.

Holt, Thomas. *The Problem of Race in the Twenty-first Century*. Cambridge, MA: Harvard University Press, 2000.

Houck, Peter. *Indian Island in Amherst County*. Lynchburg. VA: Warwick House, 1993.

Hunter, Tera. *To Joy' My Freedom: Southern Black Lives and Laborers after the Civil War*. Cambridge. MA: Harvard University Press, 1997.

Inscoe, John, ed. *Appalachians and Race: The Mountain South from Slavery to Segregation*. Lexington: University of Kentucky Press, 2001.

Inscoe, John. *Writing the South through Self: Explorations in Southern Autobiography.* Athens: University of Georgia Press, 2011.

Jablonsky, Thomas J. *The Home, Heaven, and Mother Party: Female Anti-suffragists in the United States, 1868–1920.* New York: Carlson, 1944.

Jacoway, Elizabeth. *Turn Away Thy Son: Little Rock, the Crisis that Shocked the Nation.* New York: Free Press, 2007.

Jacoway, Elizabeth, and C. Fred Williams, eds. *Understanding the Little Rock Crisis: An Exercise in Remembrance and Reconciliation.* Fayetteville: University of Arkansas Press, 1999.

James, Thomas. *Exile Within: The Schooling of Japanese Americans, 1942–1945.* Cambridge. MA: Harvard University Press, 1987.

Jeansonne, Glen. *Women of the Far Right: The Mothers Movement and WWII.* Chicago: University of Chicago Press, 1996.

Johnson, Joan Marie. *Southern Ladies, New Women: Race, Religion, and Clubwomen in South Carolina, 1890–1930.* Gainesville: University of Florida Press, 2004.

Jones, Edward P. *The Known World.* New York: Amistad, 2003.

Kammen, Michael. *Mystic Chords of Memory: The Transformation of Tradition in American Culture.* New York: Random House, 1993.

Kantrowitz, Stephen. *Ben Tillman and the Reconstruction of White Supremacy.* Chapel Hill, NC: University of North Carolina Press, 2000.

Katagiri, Yasuhiro. *The Mississippi State Sovereignty Commission: Civil Rights and States' Rights.* Jackson: University Press of Mississippi, 2001.

Kelley, Robin D. G. *Hammer and Hoe: Alabama Communists during the Great Depression.* Chapel Hill: University of North Carolina Press, 1990.

Kevles, Daniel. *In the Name of Eugenics: Genetics and the Uses of Human Heredity.* New York: Alfred A. Knopf, 1985.

Key, V. O *Southern Politics in State and Nation.* New York: Alfred A. Knopf, 1949.

Kirby, Jack Temple. *Darkness at the Dawning: Race and Reform in the Progressive South.* Philadelphia: Lippincott, 1972.

Kirwan, Albert. *Revolt of the Rednecks: Mississippi Politics, 1876–1925.* Gloucester, MA: P. Smith, 1964.

Kittel, Mary Badham. *Cornelia Dabney Tucker: The First Republican Southern Belle.* Columbia, SC: R. L. Bryan, 1969.

Klarman, Michael J. *From Jim Crow to Civil Rights: The Supreme Court and the Struggle for Racial Equality.* New York: Oxford University Press, 2006.

K'Meyer, Tracy E. *Civil Rights in the Gateway to the South: Louisville, KY, 1945–1980.* Lexington: University of Kentucky Press, 2009.

Klatch, Rebecca. *Women of the New Right.* Philadelphia: Temple University Press, 1987.

Kneebone, John. *Southern Liberal Journalists and the Issue of Race, 1920–1944.* Chapel Hill: University of North Carolina Press, 1985.

Korstad, Robert. *Civil Rights Unionism: Tobacco Workers and the Struggle for Democracy in the Mid-Twentieth Century South*. Chapel Hill: University of North Carolina Press, 2003.

Koussser, J. Morgan. *Colorblind Injustice: Minority Voting Rights and the Undoing of the Second Reconstruction*. Chapel Hill: University of North Carolina Press, 1999.

Koven, Seth, and Sonya Michel, eds. *Mothers of a New World: Maternalist Politics and the Origins of the Welfare States*. London: Routledge, 1993.

Kraditor, Aileen. *Ideas of the Woman Suffrage Movement, 1890-1920*. New York: Columbia University Press, 1965.

Krueger, Thomas A. *And Promises to Keep: Southern Conference for Human Welfare, 1938–1948*. Nashville: Vanderbilt University Press, 1967.

Kruse, Kevin. *White Flight: Atlanta and the Making of Modern Conservatism*. Princeton, NJ: Princeton University Press, 2005.

Laats, Adam. *The Other School Reformers: Conservative Activism in American Education*. Cambridge, MA: Harvard University Press, 2015.

Ladd-Taylor, Molly. *Mother-Work: Women, Child Welfare, and the State, 1890–1930*. Chicago: University of Illinois Press, 1994.

Ladd-Taylor, Molly, and Lauri Umansky, eds. *"Bad" Mothers: The Politics of Blame in Twentieth Century America*. New York: New York University Press, 1998.

Larson, Edward. *Sex, Race, and Science: Eugenics in the Deep South*. Baltimore, MD: Johns Hopkins University Press, 1995.

Lassiter, Matthew D. *The Silent Majority: Suburban Politics in the Sunbelt South*. Princeton, NJ: Princeton University Press, 2006.

Lawson, Stephen. *Black Ballots: Voting Rights in the South, 1944–1969*. New York: Columbia University Press, 1976.

Lawson, Stephen. *Civil Rights Crossroads: Nation, Community, and the Black Freedom Struggle*. Lexington: University Press of Kentucky, 2003.

Lee, Chana Kai. *For Freedom's Sake: The Life of Fannie Lou Hamer*. Chicago: University of Illinois Press, 1999.

Lefler, Hugh, and Alfred Newsome. *North Carolina: The History of a Southern State*. Chapel Hill: University of North Carolina Press, 1954.

Lefler, Melvyn. *The Specter of Communism: The United States and the Origins of the Cold War, 1917–1953*. New York: Hill and Wang, 1994.

Leloudias, James. *Schooling the New South: Pedagogy, Self, and Society in North Carolina, 1880–1920*. Chapel Hill: University of North Carolina Press, 1996.

Lewis, George. *White South and the Red Menace: Segregationists, Anticommunism, and Massive Resistance*. Gainesville: University of Florida Press, 2004.

Lewis, George. *Massive Resistance: The White Response to the Civil Rights Movement*. London: Hodder Headline, 2006.

Leidholdt, Alex. *Battling Nell: Life of Southern Journalist Cornelia Battle Lewis, 1893–1956*. Baton Rouge: Louisiana State University Press, 2009.

Link, William. *The Paradox of Southern Progressivism, 1880–1930*. Chapel Hill: University of North Carolina Press, 1992.

Litoff, Judy Barrett, and David C. Smith, eds. *Dear Boys: World War II Letters from a Woman Back Home, by Mrs. Keith Frazier Somerville*. Jackson: University Press of Mississippi, 1991.

Lombardo, Paul. *Three Generations, No Imbeciles: Eugenics, the Supreme Court, and Buck v. Bell*. Baltimore, MD: Johns Hopkins University Press, 2010.

Loveland, Anne C. *A Southerner Confronting the South: A Biography*. Baton Rouge: Louisiana State University Press, 1986.

Lowery, Malinda Maynor. *Race, Identity, and the Making of a Nation: Lumbee Indians in the Jim Crow South*. Chapel Hill: University of North Carolina Press, 2010.

Luebke, Paul. *Tarheel Politics: Myths and Realities*. Chapel Hill: University of North Carolina Press, 1990.

Lukas, Anthony. *Common Ground: A Turbulent Decade in the Lives of Three American Families*. New York: Alfred A. Knopf, 1985.

Lumpkin, Katherine DuPre. *The Making of a Southerner*. Athens: University of Georgia Press, 1992.

Lynch, John R. *The Facts of Reconstruction*. Neale Press, 1913; new edition with preface by James McPherson, New York: Arno Press, 1968.

MacLean, Nancy. *Behind the Mask of Chivalry: The Making of the Second Ku Klux Klan*. New York: Oxford University Press, 1994.

Malcomson, Scott. *One Drop of Blood: The American Misadventure of Race*. New York: Farrar, Straus and Giroux, 2000.

Mamdani, Mahmood. *Good Muslim, Bad Muslim: America, the Cold War, and the Roots of Terror*. New York: Harmony, 2005,

Marable, Manning. *Race, Reform, and Rebellion: The Second Reconstruction in Black America, 1945–1990*. Jackson: University of Mississippi Press, 1991.

Marouf, Hasian Arif. *The Rhetoric of Eugenics in Anglo-American Thought*. Athens: University of Georgia Press, 1996.

Martin, Isaac William. *Rich People's Movements: Grassroots Campaigns to Untax the One Percent*. New York: Oxford University Press, 2013.

Mason, Carol. *Reading Appalachia from Left to Right: Conservatives and the 1974 Kanawha County Textbook Controversy*. Ithaca, NY: Cornell University Press, 2009.

May, Elaine Tyler. *Homeward Bound: American Families in the Cold War Era*. New York: Basic Books, 1988.

McAdam, Doug. *Freedom Summer*. New York: Oxford University Press, 1988.

McClymer, John F. *Mississippi Freedom Summer*. Belmont, CA: Wadsworth, 2004.

McElya, Micki. *Clinging to Mammy: The Faithful Slave in Twentieth Century America*. Cambridge, MA: Harvard University Press, 2007.

McGirr, Lisa. *Suburban Warriors: The Origins of the New American Right*. Princeton, NJ: Princeton University Press, 2001.

McGuire, Danielle. *At the Dark End of the Street: Black Women, Rape, and Resistance a New History of the Civil Rights Movement from Rosa Parks to the Rise of Black Power.* New York: Alfred A. Knopf, 2010.

McLemore, Richard Aubrey. *A History of Mississippi.* Vol. 2. Hattiesburg: University and College Press of Mississippi, 1973.

McLeRoy, Roy, and Sherry McLeRoy. *Strangers in Their Midst: The Free Black Population of Amherst County,* rev. ed. Berwyn Heights, MD: Heritage, 2009.

McMillen, Neil R. *The Citizens' Council: Organized Resistance to the Second Reconstruction, 1954–1964.* Urbana: University of Illinois Press, 1971.

McMillen, Neil R. *Dark Journey: Black Mississippians in the Age of Jim Crow.* Chicago: University of Illinois Press, 1989.

McNamara, Robert P., Maria Tempenis, and Beth Walton. *Crossing the Color Line: Interracial Couples in the South.* Westport, CT: Praeger, 1999.

McPherson, Tara. *Reconstructing Dixie: Race, Gender, and Nostalgia in the Imagined South.* Durham, NC: Duke University Press, 2003.

Meyer, Gerald. *Vito Marcantonio: Radical Politician, 1902–1954.* New York: State University of New York Press, 1989.

Mickenberg, Julia. *Learning from the Left: Children's Literature, the Cold War, and Racial Politics in the United States.* New York: Oxford University Press, 2006.

Mickey, Robert. *Paths Out of Dixie: The Democratiziation of Authoritarian Enclaves in America's Deep South, 1944–1972.* Princeton, NJ: Princeton University Press, 2015.

Miles, Tiya. *The Ties That Bind: An Afro-Cherokee Family in Slavery and Freedom.* Berkeley: University of California Press, 2005.

Mims, Edwin. *The Advancing South: Stories of Progress and Reaction.* New York: Doubleday, Page, 1926.

Mink, Gwendolyn. *The Wages of Motherhood: Inequality in the Welfare State, 1917–1942.* Ithaca, NY: Cornell University Press, 1995.

Moody, Anne. *Coming of Age in Mississippi.* New York: Laurelleaf, 1969.

Moreau, Joseph. *Schoolbook Nation: Conflicts over American History Textbooks from Civil War to Present.* Ann Arbor: University of Michigan Press, 2004.

Morgan, Chester. *Redneck Liberal: Theodore G. Bilbo and the New Deal.* Baton Rouge: Louisiana State University Press, 1985.

Morgan, Francesca. *Women and Patriotism in Jim Crow America.* Chapel Hill: University of North Carolina Press, 2005.

Morris, Aldon. *The Origins of the Civil Rights Movement: Black Communities Organizing for Change.* New York: Free Press, 1984.

Morrison, Toni. *Song of Solomon.* New York: Alfred A. Knopf, 1977.

Morton, Oren F. *A History of Rockbridge County, Virginia.* Staunton, VA: McClure, 1920.

Moynihan, Ruth Barnes, Cynthia Russell, and Laurie Crumpacker, eds. *Second to None: A Documentary History of American Women.* Vol. 2. Lincoln: University of Nebraska Press, 1993.

Muhammad, Khalil Gibran. *The Condemnation of Blackness: Race, Crime, and Making of Modern Urban America.* Cambridge, MA: Harvard University Press, 2010.

Muncy. Robyn. *Creating a Female Dominion in American Reform, 1890–1935.* New York: Oxford University Press, 1991.

Myrdal, Gunnar. *An American Dilemma.* New York: McGraw Hill, 1964.

Nash, Gary. *The Conservative Intellectual Movement in America since 1945.* Wilmington DE: Intercollegiate Studies Institute, 1996.

Nash, Gary. *Forbidden Love: The Secret History of Mixed-Race America.* New York: Farrar, Straus and Giroux, 2000.

Neilsen, Melany. *Even Mississippi.* Tuscaloosa: University of Alabama Press, 1989.

Nelson, Lawrence. *King Cotton's Advocate: Oscar G. Johnston and the New Deal.* Knoxville: University of Tennessee Press, 1999.

Nelson, Scott. *Steel Drivin' Man John Henry: The Untold Story of an American Legend.* New York: Oxford University Press, 2006.

Newbeck, Phyl. *Virginia Hasn't Always Been for Lovers.* Carbondale: Southern Illinois University Press, 2008.

Nickerson, Michelle. *Mothers of Conservatism: Women and the Postwar Right.* Princeton, NJ: Princeton University Press, 2012.

Nickerson, Michelle, and Darren Dochuk, eds. *Sunbelt Rising: The Politics of Space, Place, and Region.* Philadelphia: University of Pennsylvania Press, 2011.

Nielsen, Kim. *Un-American Womanhood: Antiradicalism, Antifeminism, and the First Red Scare.* Columbus: Ohio State University Press, 2001.

Odum, Howard. *Race and Rumors of Race: The American South in the Early Forties.* Chapel Hill: University of North Carolina Press, 1943; reprint, Baltimore, MD: Johns Hopkins University Press, 1997.

Oshinsky, David. *Conspiracy So Immense: The World of Joe McCarthy.* New York: Free Press, 1983.

Parker, Frank. *Black Votes Count: Political Empowerment in Mississippi after 1965.* Chapel Hill: University of North Carolina Press, 1990.

Pascoe, Peggy. *What Comes Naturally: Miscegenation Law and the Making of Race in America.* New York: Oxford University Press, 2009.

Patterson, James T. *Brown v. Board of Education: A Civil Rights Milestone and Its Troubled Legacy.* New York: Oxford University Press, 2011.

Payne, Charles. *I've Got the Light of Freedom: The Organizing Tradition and the Mississippi Freedom Struggle.* Berkeley: University of California Press, 1995.

Pendergrast, Mark. *Uncommon Grounds: The History of Coffee and How It Transformed Our World.* New York: Basic Books, 2000.

Phillips-Fein, Kim. *Invisible Hands: The Businessmen's Crusade against the New Deal.* New York: W. W. Norton, 2009.

Pierce, Bessie. *Public Opinion and the Teaching of History.* New York: Alfred A. Knopf, 1926.

Pierce, Bessie. *Citizens' Organization and the Civic Training of Youth: Part III, Report of the Commission on the Social Studies.* New York: Charles Scribner's Sons, 1933.

Pleasants, Julian. *Buncombe Bob: The Life and Times of Robert Rice Reynolds.* Chapel Hill: University of North Carolina Press, 2000.

Pleasants, Julian, and Augustus M. Burns. *Frank Porter Graham and the 1950 Senate Race in North Carolina.* Chapel Hill: University of North Carolina Press, 1990.

Pope, Liston. *Millhands and Preachers: A Study of Gastonia.* New Haven, CT: Yale University Press, 1942.

Poppenheim, Mary. *The History of the United Daughters of the Confederacy.* Raleigh: Edwards and Broughton, 1956.

Powdermaker, Hortense. *After Freedom: A Cultural Study in the Deep South.* New York: Viking Press, 1939.

Powell, William S., ed. *Dictionary of North Carolina Biography.* Vol. 4. Chapel Hill: University of North Carolina Press, 1991.

Puryear, Elmer L. *Democratic Dissension in North Carolina, 1928–1936.* Chapel Hill: University of North Carolina Press, 1962.

Ravitch, Diane. *The Troubled Crusade: American Education, 1945–1989.* New York: Basic Books, 1983.

Ravitch, Diane. *Left Back: A Century of Failed School Reforms.* New York: Simon and Schuster, 2000.

Reed, Linda. *Simple Decency and Common Sense: The Southern Conference Movement, 1938–1963.* Bloomington: Indiana University Press, 1991.

Renda, Mary. *Taking Haiti: Military Occupation and the Culture of U.S. Imperialism, 1915–1940.* Chapel Hill: University of North Carolina Press, 2001.

Ritterhouse, Jennifer. *Growing Up Jim Crow: How Black and White Southern Children Learned Race.* Chapel Hill: University of North Carolina Press, 2006.

*Rockbridge County Virginia Heritage Book, 1878–1997.* Lexington, VA: Rockbridge Area Genealogical Society, 1997.

Rowland, Dunbar. *History of Mississippi: The Heart of the South.* Jackson, MS: S.J. Clarke, 1929.

Rymph, Cynthia. *Republican Women: Feminism and Conservatism from Suffrage through the Rise of the New Right.* Chapel Hill: University of North Carolina Press, 2006.

Salmond, John A. *Gastonia 1929: The Story of the Loray Mill Strike.* Chapel Hill: University of North Carolina Press, 1995.

Saunt, Claudio. *Black, White, and Indian: Race and the Unmaking of an American Family.* New York: Oxford University Press, 2005.

Schoenwald, Jonathan M. *A Time for Choosing: The Rise of Modern American Conservatism.* New York: Oxford University Press, 2001.

Schulman, Bruce. *From Cotton Belt to Sun Belt: Federal Policy, Economic Development, and the Transformation of the South, 1938–1980.* Durham, NC: Duke University Press, 1994.

Schuyler, Lorraine Gates. *The Weight of Their Votes: Southern Women and Political Leverage in the 1920's*. Chapel Hill: University of North Carolina Press, 2006.

Scott, Anne Firor. *The Southern Lady from Pedestal to Politics*. Chicago: University of Chicago Press, 1970.

Scott, Anne Firor. *Natural Allies: Women's Associations in American History*. Chicago: University of Chicago Press, 1991.

Scott, James C. *Seeing Like a State: How Certain Schemes to Improve the Human Condition Have Failed*. New Haven, CT: Yale University Press, 1998.

Self, Robert. *All in the Family: The Realignment of American Democracy since the 1960s*. New York: Hill and Wang, 2012.

Shah, Nyan. *Stranger Intimacy: Contesting Race, Sexuality, and the Law in the North American West*. Berkeley: University of California Press, 2011.

Silber, Nina. *Romance of Reunion: Northerners and the South, 1865–1900*. Chapel Hill: University of North Carolina Press, 1993.

Sillers, Florence Warfield, compiler. *History of Bolivar County*. Jackson, MS: Hederman Bros., 1948.

Silver, James. *Mississippi: The Closed Society*. New York: Harcourt, Brace & World, 1966.

Simon, Bryant. *The Fabric of Defeat: The Politics of South Carolina Millhands, 1910–1948*. Chapel Hill: University of North Carolina Press, 1998.

Sims, Anastasia. *The Power of Femininity in the New South: Women's Organizations and Politics in North Carolina, 1880–1930*. Columbia: University of South Carolina Press, 1997.

Singal, Daniel. *The War Within: From Victorian to Modernist Thought in the South, 1919–1945*. Chapel Hill: University of North Carolina Press, 1982.

Smith, Douglas J. *Managing White Supremacy: Race, Politics, and Citizenship in Jim Crow Virginia*. Chapel Hill: University of North Carolina Press, 2002.

Smith, Douglas J. *On Democracy's Doorstep: The Inside Story of How the Supreme Court Brought 'One Person, One Vote' to the United States*. New York: Hill and Wang, 2014.

Smith, Margaret Supplee, and Emily Herring Wilson. *North Carolina Women Making History*. Chapel Hill: University of North Carolina Press, 1999.

Smith, Rogers. *Civic Ideas: Conflicting Visions of Citizenship in U.S. History*. New Haven, CT: Yale University Press, 1997.

Sokol, Jason. *There Goes My Everything: White Southerners in the Age of Civil Rights, 1945–1975*. New York: Vintage, 2007.

Sosna, Morton. *In Search of the Silent South: Southern Liberals and the Race Issue*. New York: Columbia University Press, 1977.

Sparrow, James T. *Warfare State: World War II Americans and the Era of Big Government*. New York: Oxford University Press, 2011.

Spencer, Elizabeth. *Landscapes of the Heart: A Memoir*. New York: Random House, 1998.

Spiro, Joseph. *Defending the Master Race: Conservation, Eugenics, and the Legacy of Madison Grant*. Burlington: University of Vermont Press, 2009.

Stanley, Harold W. *Voter Mobilization and the Politics of Race: The South and Universal Suffrage, 1952–1964.* New York: Praeger, 1987.

Steinbeck, John. *Travels with Charley in Search of America.* New York: Viking Press, 1992.

Stoddard, Lothrap. *The Rising Tide of Color against White World Supremacy.* New York: C. Scribner, 1920.

Storr, Landon. *Civilizing Capitalism: The National Consumers' League, Women's Activism, and Labor Standards in the New Deal Era.* Chapel Hill: University of North Carolina Press, 2000.

Sugrue, Tom. *The Origins of the Urban Crisis: Race and Inequality in Postwar Detroit.* Princeton, NJ: Princeton University Press, 2005.

Sugrue, Tom. *Sweet Land of Liberty: The Forgotten Struggle for Civil Rights in the North.* New York: Random House, 2008.

Sullivan, Patricia. *Days of Hope: Race and Democracy in the New Deal Era.* Chapel Hill: University of North Carolina Press, 1996.

Swain, Martha. *Ellen S. Woodward: New Deal Advocate for Women.* Jackson: University Press of Mississippi, 1995.

Tananbaum, Duane. *The Bricker Amendment Controversy: A Test of Eisenhower's Political Leadership.* Ithaca, NY: Cornell University Press, 1988

Taulbert, Clifton L. *Once Upon a Time When We Were Colored.* Tulsa, OK: Council Oak Books, 1989.

Terbourg-Penn, Rosalyn. *African American Women in the Struggle for the Vote, 1850–1920.* Bloomington: University of Indiana Press, 1998.

Thomas, Fran. *A Portrait of Historic Athens and Clark County.* Athens: University of Georgia Press, 1997.

Thornton, J. Mills. *Dividing Lines: Municipal Politics and the Struggle for Civil Rights in Montgomery, Birmingham, and Selma.* Tuscaloosa: University of Alabama Press, 2002.

Tindall, George Brown. *The Emergence of the New South, 1913–1945.* Baton Rouge: Louisiana State University Press, 1967.

Titus, Jill Ogline. *Brown's Battleground: Students, Segregationists, and the Struggle for Justice in Prince Edward County, Virginia.* Chapel Hill: University of North Carolina Press, 2011.

Tyler, Pamela. *Silk Stockings and Ballot Boxes: Women and Politics in New Orleans, 1920–1963.* Athens: University of Georgia Press, 1996.

Tyson, Timothy B. *The Blood of Emmett Till.* New York: Simon and Schuster, 2017.

Tyson, Timothy B. *Radio Free Dixie: Robert F. Williams and the Roots of Black Power.* Chapel Hill: University of North Carolina Press, 1999.

Von Eschen, Penny. *Race against Empire: Black Americans and Anticolonialism, 1937–1957.* Ithaca, NY: Cornell University Press, 1997.

Wald, Gayle. *Crossing the Line: Racial Passing in Twentieth Century Literature and Culture.* Durham, NC: Duke University Press, 2000.

Walker, Anders. *The Ghosts of Jim Crow: How Southern Moderates Used Brown v. The Board of Education to Stall Civil Rights.* New York: Oxford University Press, 2009.

Walker, Frank X. *Affrilachia: Poems by Frank X Walker.* Lexington, KY: Old Cove Press, 2000.

Wallenstein, Peter. *Tell the Court I Love My Wife: Race, Marriage, and Law—An American History.* New York: Palgrave Macmillan, 2002.

Ward, Jason. *Defending White Democracy: The Making of a Segregationist Movement and the Remaking of Racial Politics, 1936–1965.* Chapel Hill: University of North Carolina Press, 2011.

Webb, Clive. *Rabble Rousers: The American Far Right in the Civil Rights Era.* Athens: University of Georgia Press, 2010.

Webb, Clive. Ed. *Massive Resistance: Southern Opposition to the Second Reconstruction.* New York: Oxford University Press, 2005.

Weisbrot, Robert. *Freedom Bound: A History of America's Civil Rights Movement.* New York: Penguin, 1991.

Wells, Dean Faulkner, and Hunter Cole, eds. *Mississippi Heroes.* Jackson: University Press of Mississippi, 1980.

Wharton, Vernon. *The Negro in Mississippi, 1865–1990.* Chapel Hill: University of North Carolina Press, 1947.

Wheeler, Marjorie Spruill. *New Women of the New South: The Leaders of the Woman Suffrage Movement in the Southern States.* New York: Oxford University Press, 1993.

Wheeler, Marjorie Spruill, ed. *Votes for Women! The Woman Suffrage Movement in Tennessee, the South, and the Nation.* Knoxville: University of Tennessee Press, 1995.

Wheeler, Marjorie, Ed. *One Woman, One Vote: Rediscovering the Woman Suffrage Movement.* Troutdale, OR: New Sage Press, 1995.

White, Deborah Gray. *Ar'n't I A Woman: Female Slaves in the Plantation South.* New York: W.W. Norton, 1985.

Whitfield, Stephen J. *A Death in the Delta: The Story of Emmett Till.* Baltimore, MD: Johns Hopkins University Press, 1988.

Whitlock, Rosemary. *The Monacan Indian Nation of Virginia: The Drums of Life.* Tuscaloosa: University of Alabama Press, 2008.

Wilhoit, Francis. *The Politics of Massive Resistance.* New York: George Braziller, 1973.

Wilkie, Curtis. *Dixie: A Personal Odyssey through Historic Events That Shaped the Modern South.* New York: Scribner, 2002.

Wilkinson, J. Harvie. *From Brown to Bakke: The Supreme Court and School Integration.* New York: Oxford University Press, 1978.

Williamson, Joel. *New People: Miscegenation and Mulattos in the United States.* New York: Free Press, 1980.

Williamson, Joel. *A Rage for Order: Black-White Relations in the American South since Emancipation.* New York: Oxford University Press, 1989.

Williamson, Joel. *William Faulkner and Southern History*. New York: Oxford University Press, 1993.

Woods, Jeff. *Black Struggle, Red Scare: Segregationists and Anticommunists in the South, 1948–1968*. Baton Rouge: Louisiana State University Press, 2004.

### B. Articles

Arnenson, Eric. "Reconsidering the Long Civil Rights Movement." *Historically Speaking* 10, no. 2 (April 2009): 31–34.

Badger, Anthony J. "The White Reaction to *Brown*: Arkansas, the Southern Manifesto, and Massive Resistance." In *Understanding the Little Rock Crisis: An Exercise in Remembrance and Reconciliation*. Edited by Elizabeth Jacoway and C. Fred Williams. Fayetteville: University of Arkansas Press, 1999.

Bailey, Fred. "Textbooks of the Lost Cause: Censorship and the Creation of Southern State Histories." *Georgia Historical Quarterly* 75 (Fall 1991): 507–533.

Bailey, Fred. "Mildred Lewis Rutherford and the Patrician Cult of the Old South." *Georgia Historical Quarterly* 78 (Fall 1998): 22–44.

Bair, Barbara. "Remapping the Black/White Body: Sexuality, Nationalism, and Biracial Antimiscegenation Activism in 1920s Virginia." In *Sex, Love, and Race: Crossing Boundaries in North American History*. Edited by Martha Hodes. New York: New York University Press, 1999. 399-491.

Baker, Paula. "The Domestication of Politics: Women and American Political Society, 1780–1920." *American Historical Review* 89 (Fall 1984): 620–647.

Berg-Anderson, Richard E. "Why Are They All Here Anyway?"At thegreenpapers. com/Hx/Nat Delegates2004.htm.

Bix, Amy Sue. "Experiences and Voices of Eugenics Field-Workers: 'Women's Work' in Biology." *Social Studies of Science* 27 (1997): 625–668.

Boris, Eileen. "Reconstructing the 'Family': Women, Progressive Reform, and the Problem of Social Control." In *Gender, Class, Race, and Reform in the Progressive Era*. Edited by Noralee Frankel and Nancy S. Dye. Lexington: University Press of Kentucky, 1991. 73-86.

Boris, Eileen. "The Power of Motherhood: Black and White Activist Women Redefine the 'Political.'" *Yale Journal of Law & Feminism*, 2, no. 1, Article 3. Available at: http://digitalcommons.law.yale.edu/yjlf/vol2/iss1/3

Brattain, Michelle. "Race, Racism and Antiracism: UNESCO and the Politics of Presenting Science to the Postwar Public." *American Historical Review* 112, no. 5 (December 2007): 1386–1387.

Brundage, W. Fitzhugh. "White Women and the Politics of Historical Memory in the New South, 1880–1920." In *Jumping Jim Crow: Southern Politics from Civil War to Civil Rights*. Edited by Jane Dailey, Glenda Gilmore, and Bryant Simon. Princeton, NJ: Princeton University Press, 2000. 115-139.

Bushnell, David I. "The Indian Inhabitants of the Valley of Virginia." *Virginia Magazine of History and Biography* 34, no. 4 (October 1926): 295–298.

Carter, Dan. "More Than Race: Conservatism in the White South since V. O. Key." In *Unlocking V. O. Key, Jr.: Southern Politics for the Twenty-first Century.* Edited by Angie Maxwell and Todd G. Shields. Little Rock: University of Arkansas Press, 2011: 129-160.

Case, Sarah. "Mildred Lewis Rutherford: The Redefinition of New South White Womanhood." In *Georgia Women: Their Lives and Times.* Vol. 1. Edited by Ann Short Chirhart and Betty Wood. Athens: University of Georgia Press, 2009. 272-296.

Cassel, Carol. "Change in Electoral Participation in the South." *e Journal of Politics* 41 (August 1979): 907–917.

Chafe, William. "Perspectives on Progressivism." In *Southern Businessmen and Desegregation.* Edited by Elizabeth Jacoway and David R. Colburn. Baton Rouge: Louisiana State University Press, 1982. 42-69.

Cobb, James C. "World War II and the Mind of the Modern South." In *Remaking Dixie: The Impact of World War II on the American South.* Edited by Neil R. McMillen. Jackson: University Press of Mississippi, 1997. 3-20.

Coles, Robert. "The White Northerner: Pride and Prejudice." *Atlantic Monthly*, online. June 1966. http://www.theatlantic.com/politics/race/whitenor.htm.

Cook, Robert. "From Shiloh to Selma: The Impact of the Civil War Centennial on the Black Freedom Struggle in the United States, 1961–1965." In *The Making of Martin Luther King and the Civil Rights Movement.* Edited by Brian Ward and Tony Badger. New York: New York University Press, 1996. 131-145.

Cook, Samuel R. "The Monacan Indian Nation: Asserting Tribal Sovereignty in the Absence of Federal Recognition." *Wicaso Sa Review* 17, no. 2 (Autumn 2002): 91–116.

Cook, Samuel R. "The Boundaries of Participatory Research: Lessons Learned in the Monacan Indian Nation." In *Participatory Development in Appalachia: Cultural Identity, Community, and Sustainability.* Edited by Susan Keefe. Knoxville: University of Tennessee Press, 2009. 100-124.

Cope, Graeme. "'A Thorn in the Side'? The Mothers' League of Central High School and the Little Rock Desegregation Crisis of 1957." *Arkansas Historical Quarterly* 57 (Summer 1998): 160–190.

Cope, Graeme. "'Gordy and Lower Classes'? A Profile of the Capital Citizens' Council during the Little Rock Crisis of 1957." *Arkansas Historical Quarterly* 61 (Spring 2000): 39–58.

Cott, Nancy F. "What's in a Name? The Limits of "Social Feminism"; or Expanding the Vocabulary of Women's History." *Journal of American History* 76 (December 1989): 809–829.

Cuordileone, K. A. "Politics in an Age of Anxiety: Cold War Political Culture and the Crisis in American Masculinity, 1949–1960." *Journal of American History* 87 (September 2000): 515–545.

Crespino, Joseph. "Strom Thurmond's Sunbelt: Rethinking Regional Politics and the Rise of the Right." In *Sunbelt Rising: The Politics of Space, Place, and Region*. Edited by Michelle Nickerson and Darren Dochuk. Philadelphia: University of Pennsylvania Press, 2011. 58-81

Dailey, Jane. "Sex, Segregation, and the Sacred after *Brown*." *Journal of American History* 126, no. 7 (June 2004): 119–144.

Daniel, Pete. "Going among Strangers: Southern Reactions to World War II." *Journal of American History* 77 (Fall 1990): 886–911.

De Hart, Jane. "Gender on the Right: Meanings behind the Existential Scream." *Gender and History* 3. no. 3 (Autumn 1991): 246–267.

De Hart, Jane. "Second Wave Feminism(s) and the South: The Differences that Differences Make." In *Women of the American South: A Multicultural Reader*. Edited by Christine Anne Farnham. New York: New York University Press, 1997.

Deutsch, Sara. "Learning to Talk More Like a Man: Boston Women's Class-Bridging Organization, 1870–1940. *American Historical Review* 97 (April 1992): 379–404.

Dorr, Gregory. "Assuring America's Place in the Sun: Ivy Foreman Lewis and the Teaching of Eugenics at the University of Virginia." *Journal of Southern History* 66, no. 2 (May 2000): 257296.

Erickson, Christine. "'So Much for Men:' Conservative Women and National Defense in the 1920's and 1930's." *American Studies* 45, no.1 (Spring 2004): 85–102.

Erickson, Christine. "'We Want No Teachers Who Say There Are Two Sides to Every Question': Conservative Women and Education in the 1930's." *History of Education Quarterly* 26, no. 4 (Winter 2006): 487–490.

Evans, Sara. "Women's History and Political Theory: Toward a Feminist Approach to Public Life." In *Visible Women: New Essays in American Activism*. Edited by Suzanne Lebsock and Nancy Hewitt. Chicago: University of Illinois Press, 1993. 119-140.

Feldstein, Ruth. "Antiracism and Maternal Failure in the 1940s and 1950s." In *Bad Mothers: The Politics of Blame in Twentieth Century America*. New York: New York University Press, 1998, 148–152.

Fletcher, Winona. "'Witnessing a Miracle:' Sixty Years of Heaven Bound at Big Bethel in Atlanta. *Black American Literature Forum* 25, no.1 (Spring 1991): 83–92.

Frederickson, Kari. "As a Man I Am Interested in States' Rights: Gender, Race, and the Family in the Dixiecrat Party, 1948–1950." In *Jumpin' Jim Crow: Southern Politics from Civil War to Civil Rights*. Edited by Jane Dailey, Glenda Gilmore, and Bryant Simon. Princeton, NJ: Princeton University Press, 2000. 260-274.

Gaddie, Ronald Keith. "Realignment." In *The Oxford Handbook of Southern Politics*. Ed. Charles S. Bulloch and Mark J. Rozell. New York: Oxford University Press, 2012. 296-311.

Gavins, Raymond. "A 'Sin of Omission': Black Historiography in North Carolina." In *Black Americans in North Carolina and the South*. Edited by Jeffery J. Crow and Flora J. Hatley. Chapel Hill: University of North Carolina Press, 1984. 3-56.

Gavins, Raymond. "The NAACP in North Carolina during the Age of Segregation." In *New Directions in Civil Rights Studies*. Edited by Patricia Sullivan and Armstead Robinson. Charlottesville: University Press of Virginia, 1991. 105-125.

Gersen, Deborah. "'Is Family Devotion Now Subversive?' Familialism against McCarthyism." In *Not June Cleaver: Women and Gender in Postwar America, 1945–1960*. Edited by Joanne Meyerowitz. Philadelphia: Temple University Press, 1994. 151-179.

Gilmore, Glenda. "Murder, Memory and the Flight of Incubus." In *Democracy Betrayed: The Wilmington Race Riot of 1898 and Its Legacy*. Edited by David Cecelski and Timothy Tyson. Chapel Hill: University of North Carolina Press, 1998. 73-94.

Glickman, Lawrence. "The Strike in the Temple of Consumption: Consumer Activism and Twentieth Century Political Culture." *Journal of American History* 88, no. 1 (June 2001): 99–128.

Glynn, Karen. "Running Mules: Mule Racing in the Mississippi Delta." *Mississippi Folklife* 28, no. 2 (Spring 1996): 1–12.

Goodwin, Joanne L. "An American Experiment in Paid Motherhood: The Implementation of Mothers' Pensions in Early Twentieth Century Chicago." *Gender and History* 4 (Autumn 1991): 322–342.

Green, Elna. "From Antisuffragism to Anti-Communism: The Conservative Career of Ida M. Darden." *Journal of Southern History* 65, no. 2 (May 1999): 287–316.

Griffith, Rueben. "The Public School, 1890–1970." In *A History of Mississippi*. Edited by Richard McLemore. Hattiesburg: University and College Press of Mississippi, 1973. 395-410.

Haimes-Bartlof, Melanie. "The Social Construction of Race and Monacan Education in Amherst County, Virginia, 1908–1965." *History of Education Quarterly* 47 no. 4 (November 2007): 391–415.

Hale, Grace Elizabeth. "Granite Stopped Time: The Stone Mountain Memorial and the Representation of White Southern Identity." *Georgia Historical Quarterly* 82 (Spring 1988): 22–44.

Hale, Grace Elizabeth. "Some Women Have Never Been Reconstructed: Mildred Lewis Rutherford, Lucy M. Stanton, and the Racial Politics of White Southern Womanhood, 1900–1930." In *Georgia in Black and White: Explorations in Race Relations of a Southern State, 1865–1940*. Edited by John C. Inscoe. Athens: University of Georgia Press, 1994. 173-201.

Hall, Jacquelyn Dowd. "'The Mind that Burns in Each Body': Women, Rape, and Racial Violence." *Southern Exposure* 12, no. 6 (1984): 61–71.

Hall, Jacquelyn Dowd. "Partial Truths." *Signs: Journal of Women in Culture and Society* 14, no. 4 (Summer 1989): 902–911.

Hall, Jacquelyn Dowd. "Open Secrets: Memory, Imagination and the Refashioning of Southern Identity." *American Quarterly* 50 (March 1998): 109–124.

Hall, Jacquelyn Dowd. "'You Must Remember This': Autobiography as Social Critique." *Journal of American History* 85 (Summer 1998): 439–465.

Hall, Jacquelyn Dowd. "The Long Civil Rights Movement and Political Uses of the Past." *Journal of American History* 91, no. 4 (March 2005): 1233–1263.

Harris, Robin L. "To Illustrate the Genius of Southern Womanhood": Julia Flisch and Her Campaign for the Higher Education of Georgia Women." *Georgia Historical Quarterly* 80 (Fall 1996): 506–525.

Hewitt, Nancy. "Beyond the Search for Sisterhood: American Women's History in the 1980's." *Social History* 10 (October 1985): 299–321.

Hirsch, Arnold. "Massive Resistance in the Urban North: Trumbell Park, Chicago, 1953–1966." *Journal of American History* 82 (September 1995): 522–550.

Holt, Thomas. "Marking: Race, Race-Making, and the Writing of History." *American Historical Review* 100, no. 1 (February 1995): 1–20.

Hunt, Rolfe Lanier. "What Do We Teach about the Negro?" *Journal of the National Education Association* 28, no. 1 (January 1939): 2–12.

Inscoe, John. "The Clansman on Stage and Screen: North Carolina Reacts." *North Carolina Historical Review* 64, no. 2 (April 1987): 139–143.

Jensen, Joan Marie. "'Drill in to us . . . the Rebel Tradition': The Contest over Southern Identity in Black and White Women's Clubs, South Carolina 1898–1930." *Journal of Southern History* 66, no. 3 (August 2000): 525-562.

Kantrowitz, Stephen. "The Two Faces of Domination in North Carolina, 1880–1898." In *Democracy Betrayed: The Wilmington Race Riot of 1898 and Its Legacy*. Edited by David Cecelski and Timothy Tyson. Chapel Hill: University of North Carolina Press, 1998. 95-112.

Keith, John. "Competent Teachers for the Nation: An Article Plank One of the Platform of the National Education Association." *Journal of the National Education Association* 10, no. 1 (March 1921):46-48.

Klarman, Michael. "How *Brown* Changed Race Relations: The Backlash Thesis." *Journal of American History* 81 (June 1994): 81–118.

Kousser, J. Morgan. "Progressivism for Middle-Class Whites Only: North Carolina Education, 1890–1910. *Journal of Southern History* 46 (May 1980): 169–194.

Larson, Edward. "In the Finest Most Womanly Way: Women and the Southern Eugenics Movement." *American Journal of Legal History* 39 (April 1995): 119–147.

Lassiter, Matthew D. "Big Government and Family Values: Political Culture in the Metropolitan Sunbelt." In *Sunbelt Rising: The Politics of Space, Place, and Region*. Edited by Michelle Nickerson and Darren Dochuk. Philadelphia: University of Pennsylvania Press, 2011, 82-109.

Lebsock, Suzanne. "Women Suffrage and White Supremacy: A Virginia Case Study." In *Visible Women: New Essays on American Activism*. Edited by Suzanne Lebsock and Nancy A. Hewitt. Chicago: University of Illinois Press, 1993. 62-100.

Leonardo, Micheila di. "Moral, Mothers, and Militarism: Anti-Militarism and Feminist Theory." *Feminist Studies* 11 (1985): 599–617.

Lewis, Andy. "Emergency Mothers: Basement Schools and the Preservation of Public Education in Charlottesville." In *The Moderates' Dilemma: Massive*

*Resistance to School Desegregation.* Edited by Matthew Lassiter and Andy Lewis. Charlottesville: University of Virginia Press, 1998, 72–103.

Lewis, George. "'Scientific Certainty': Wesley Critz George, Racial Science and Organized White Resistance in North Carolina, 1954–1962." *Journal of American Studies* 38, no. 2 (August 2004): 227–247.

Lipsitz, George. "The Struggle for Hegemony." *Journal of American History* 75, no. 1 (June 1988): 146–150.

Locke, Alain. "Who and What Is 'Negro'?' Opportunity. *Journal of Negro Life* 20, no.2 (1942): 20-3, 36–42, 83–87.

Lombardo, Paul, "Miscegenation, Eugenics and Racism: Historical Footnotes to *Loving v. Virginia.*" *University of California, Davis Law Review* 21 (1988): 451–452.

MacLean, Nancy. "The Leo Frank Case Reconsidered: Gender and Sexual Politics in the Making of Reactionary Populism." *Journal of American History* 78 (December 1991): 917–948.

McCain, William D. "The Triumph of Democracy, 1916–1932." In *A History of Mississippi.* Vol. 2. Edited by Richard Aubrey McLemore. Hattiesburg: University and College Press of Mississippi, 1973. 61-96.

McElya, Micki. "Commemorating the Color Line: The National Mammy Monument Controversy of the 1920s." In *Monuments to the Lost Cause: Women, Art, and the Landscapes of Southern Memory.* Edited by Cynthia Mills and Pamela H. Simpson. Knoxville: University of Tennessee Press, 2003. 203-218.

McEnaney, Laura. "He-Men and Christian Mothers: The America First Movement and the Gendered Meanings of Patriotism and Nationalism." *Diplomatic History* 18 (Winter 1994): 47–57.

McGerr, Michael. "Political Style and Women's Power, 1830–1930." *Journal of American History* 77 (December 1990): 864–885.

McRae, Elizabeth Gillespie. "Caretakers of Southern Civilization: Georgia Women and the Anti-Suffrage Campaign, 1914–1920." *Georgia Historical Quarterly* 82 (Winter 1998): 801–828.

McRae, Elizabeth Gillespie. "Nell Battle Lewis: The Political Journey of a Liberal White Supremacist." In *North Carolina Women: Their Lives, Their Histories.* Vol. 2. Athens: University of Georgia Press, 2015. 120-143.

Mertz, Paul E. "'Mind Changing Time All Over Georgia': HOPE, Inc., and School Desegregation, 1958–1961." *Georgia Historical Quarterly* 77 (Spring 1993): 41–61.

Moton, Derryn E. "Racial Integrity or 'Race Suicide': Virginias's Eugenic Movement, W. E. B. Du Bois, and the Work of Walter A. Plecker." *Negro History Bulletin* (April–September 1999): 5.

Moyers, Bill. "This is Your Story—The Progressive Story of America. Pass it On." Speech to Take Back America Conference. June 4, 2003. https://www.common-dreams.org/views/2003/06/10/your-story-progressive-story-america-

Murray, Paul T. "Who Is an Indian? Who Is a Negro? Virginia Indians in the World War II Draft." *Virginia Magazine of History and Biography* 95, no. 2 (April 1987): 215–231.

Nasstrom, Kathy. "'More Was Expected of Us': The North Carolina League of Women Voters and the Feminist Movement in the 1920s.'" *North Carolina Historical Review* 68, no. 3 (July 1991): 307–319.

Nutter, Kathleen Banks. "'Militant Mothers': Boston, Busing, and the Bicentennial of 1976." *Historical Journal of Massachusetts* 38, no. 2 (Fall 2010): 52–75.

Ogden, Florence Sillers. "A Famous Indian Lawsuit." *Journal of Mississippi History* 8 (April 1946): 121–128.

Osburn, Katherine M. B. "The 'Identified Full-Bloods' in Mississippi: Race and Choctaw Identity." *Ethnohistory* 56, no. 3 (Summer 2009): 423–447.

Parker, Frank, David C. Colby, and Minion K. C. Morrison, "Mississippi." In *Quiet Revolution in the South: The Impact of the Voting Rights Act, 1965–1990*. Edited by Chandler Davidson and Bernard Goffman. Princeton, NJ: University of Princeton Press, 1994. 136-154.

Pyron, Darden Ashbury. "Nell Battle Lewis and the New Southern Woman." In *Perspectives on the American South: An Annual Review of Society, Politics, and Culture*. Edited by James C. Cobb and Charles R. Wilson. New York: Gordon and Breach, 1985. 70-91.

Quinn, Olive Westbrook. "The Transmission of Racial Attitudes among White Southerners." In *Social Forces* 33 (October 1954): 41–47.

Reddick, Laurence. "Racial Attitudes in American History Textbooks of the South." *Journal of Negro History* 19 (July 1934): 255–265.

Ritterhouse, Jennifer. "Speaking of Race: Sarah Patton Boyle and the 'T. J. Sellers Course for Backward Southern Whites.'" in *Sex, Love, and Race: Crossing Boundaries in North American History*. Edited by Martha Hodes. New York: New York University Press, 1999. 491-513.

Schuyler, Lorraine Gates. "Power from the Pedestal: The Women's Emergency Committee and the Little Rock Crisis." *Arkansas Historical Quarterly* 55 (Spring 1996): 26–57.

Shannon, Margaret A., with Stephen W. Taylor. "Astride the Plantation Gates: Tourism, Racial Politics, and the Development of Hilton Head Island." In *Southern Journeys: Tourism, History, and Culture in the Modern South*. Edited by Richard D. Starnes. Tuscaloosa: University of Alabama Press, 2003. 177-195.

Sherman, Richard B. "'The Teachings at Hampton Institute': Social Equality, Racial Integrity, and the Virginia Public Assemblage Act of 1926." *Virginia Magazine of History and Biography* 95, no. 3 (July 1987): 275–300.

Sherman, Richard B. "'The Last Stand': The Fight for Racial Integrity in Virginia in the 1920's." *Journal of Southern History* 54, no. 1 (February 1988): 69–92.

Simon, Bryant. "Fearing Eleanor: Wartime Rumors and Racial Anxieties, 1940–1945." In *Labor in the Modern South*. Edited by Glen Eskew. Athens: University of Georgia Press, 2001. 83-101.

Sims, Anastasia. "Beyond the Ballot: The Radical Vision of the Antisuffragists." In *Votes for Women! The Woman Suffrage Movement in Tennessee, the South, and the Nation*.

Edited by Marjorie Spruill Wheeler. Knoxville: University of Tennessee Press, 1995. 105-128.

Sitkoff, Harvard. "Impact of the New Deal on Black Southerners." In *The New Deal and the South*. Edited by James C. Cobb and Michael V. Namorato. Jackson: University Press of Mississippi, 1984. 117-134.

Sitkoff, Harvard. "African American Militancy in the World War II South: Another Perspective." In *Remaking Dixie: The Impact of World War II on the American South*. Edited by Neil R. McMillen. Jackson: University Press of Mississippi, 1997. 70-92.

Skates, John Ray. "World War II and Its Effects, 1940–1948." *History of Mississippi*, Vol. 2. Edited by Richard Aubrey McLemore. Jackson: University Press of Mississippi, 1973. 120–139.

Skocpol, Theda, Marjorie Abend-Wien, Christopher Howard, and Susan Goodrich. "Women's Associations and the Enactment of Mothers' Pensions in the United States." *American Political Science Review* 87 (September 1993): 686–701.

Smith, Gary. Gary Smith, "Blindsided by History," *Sports Illustrated*, April 9, 2007, at https://www.si.com/vault/2007/04/09/8404477/blindsided-by-history.

Sosna, Morton. "More Important than the Civil War? The Impact of World War II on the South." In *Perspectives on the American South: An Annual Review of Society, Politics, and Culture* vol. 4. Edited by James C. Cobb and Charles R. Wilson. New York: Gordon and Breach, 1987. 145-162.

Sugrue, Thomas. "Crabgrass Politics: Race, Rights, and Reaction against Liberalism in the Urban North, 1940–1964." *Journal of American History* 82 (September, 1995): 551–578.

Theoharis, Jeanne. "'We Saved the City': Black Struggles for Educational Equality in Boston, 1960–1970," *Radical History Review* 81 (2001): 61–93.

Thompson, John L. "Dunjee, Roscoe (1883–1965)." In *Encyclopedia of Oklahoma History and Culture*. Oklahoma Historical Society. http://digital.library.okstate.edu/encyclopedia/entries/d/du007.html

Thurber, Cheryl. "The Development of the Mammy Image and Mythology." In *Southern Women Histories and Identities*. Edited by Virginia Bernhard, Betty Brandon, Elizabeth Fox-Genovese, and Theda Perdue (Columbia: University of Missouri Press, 1992), 97-108.

Tyler, Pamela. "How Southern Women Viewed Eleanor." In *Lives Full of Struggle and Triumph: Southern Women, Their Institution, and Their Communities*. Edited by Bruce Clayton and John Salmond. Gainesville: University of Florida Press, 2003, 186-200.

Wall, Cheryl. "Toni Morrison, Editor and Teacher." In *The Cambridge Companion to Toni Morrison*. Edited by Justine Tally. Cambridge: Cambridge University Press, 2007.

Wertheimer, John, Brian Luskey, et al. "Escape of the Match-Strikers: Disorderly North Carolina Women, the Legal System and the Samarcand Arson Case of 1931." *North Carolina Historical Review* 75 (October 1988): 435–460.

Whites, LeeAnn. "Rebecca Latimer Felton and the Wife's Farm: The Class and Racial Politics of Gender Reform." *Georgia Historical Quarterly* 76 (Summer 1992): 354–360.

Whites, LeeAnn. "Rebecca Latimer Felton and the Problem of 'Protection' in the New South." In *Visible Women: New Essays on American Activism.* Edited by Suzanne Lebsock and Nancy Hewitt. Chicago: University of Illinois Press, 1994. 41-61.

Wiggins, William H. "Pilgrims, Crosses, and Faith: The Folk Dimensions of *Heaven Bound.*" *Black American Literature Forum* 25, no.1 (Spring 1991): 93–100.

Wilkerson-Freeman, Sarah. "From Clubs to Parties: North Carolina Women in the Advancement of the New Deal." *North Carolina Historical Review* 68 (July 1991): 320–339.

Wilkerson-Freeman, Sarah. "The Second Battle for Woman Suffrage: Alabama White Women, the Poll Tax, and V. O. Key's Master Narrative of Southern Politics." *Journal of Southern History* 68 (May, 2002): 333–374.

Winter, William F. "Governor Mike Conner and the Sales Tax, 1932." In *Mississippi Heroes.* Edited by Dean Faulkner Wells and Hunter Cole. Jackson: University of Mississippi Press, 1980. 158-176.

Wolfe, Brendan. "Racial Integrity Laws, 1924-1930." In *Encyclopedia Virginia.* Richmond: Virginia Foundation for the Humanities, 2015. http://www. EncyclopediaVirginia.org/Racial_Integrity_Laws_of_the_1920s.

Wynes, Charles. "The Evolution of Jim Crow Laws in Twentieth Century Virginia." *Phylon* 28, no. 4 (Winter 1967): 416–425.

Yuhl, Stephanie. "Rich and Tender Remembering: Elite White Women and an Aesthetic Sense of Place in Charleston, 1920s and 1930s." In *Where These Memories Grow: History, Memory, and Southern Identity.* Edited by Fitzhugh Brundage. Chapel Hill: University of North Carolina Press, 2000. 227-248.

## C. Theses and Dissertations

Baker, Lewis Turner, III. "LeRoy Percy: Delta Defender." MA thesis, Louisiana State University Press, 1977.

Billingsley, William. "Speaker Ban: The Anti-Communist Crusade in North Carolina, 1963–1970." Ph.D. dissertation, University of California at Irvine, 1994.

Boschert, Thomas. "A Family Affair: Mississippi Politics, 1882–1932." Ph.D. dissertation, University of Mississippi, 1995.

Cox, Karen. "Women, the Lost Cause, and the New South: The United Daughters of the Confederacy and the Transmission of Confederate Culture, 1894–1914." Ph.D. dissertation, University of Southern Mississippi, 1997.

Delegard, Kirsten. "Women Patriots: Female Activism and the Politics of American Anti-Radicalism, 1919-1935." Ph.D. dissertation, Duke University, 1999.

Green, Linda Lou. "Nell Battle Lewis: Crusading Columnist, 1921–1938." MA thesis, East Carolina University, 1969.

Krome-Lukens, Anna. "A Great Blessing to Defective Humanity: Women and the Eugenics Movement in North Carolina 1910–1940." MA thesis, University of North Carolina-Chapel Hill, 2009.

McPheron, Tara. "Reconstructing Dixie: Race, Place, and Femininity in the Deep South." Ph.D. dissertation, University of Wisconsin-Milwaukee, 1996.

Melton, Thomas. "Mr. Speaker: A Biography of Walter Sillers." MA thesis, University of Mississippi, 1972.

Moore, Steven. "The Shadow and the Spotlight: Ralph McGill and Liberalism in the New South, 1933–1950." MA. thesis, University of Georgia, 1988.

Morgan, Francesca. "Home and Country: Women, Nation, and the Daughters of the American Revolution, 1890–1939." Ph. D. dissertation, Columbia University, 1998.

Morris, Robin. "Building the New Right: Georgia Women, Grassroots Organizing, and Party Realignment, 1950–1980." Ph.D. dissertation, Yale University, 2012.

Olsen, Margaret Nunnelley. "One Nation, One World: American Clubwomen and the Politics of Internationalism, 1945–1961. Ph.D. dissertation, Rice University, 2007.

Rosenburg, Jonathan Seth. "'How Far the Promised Land?' World Affairs and the American Civil Rights Movement from the First World War to Vietnam." Ph.D. dissertation, Harvard University, 1997.

Roydhouse, Marion Winifred, "The 'Universal Sisterhood of Women:' Women and Labor Reform in North Carolina, 1900–1932." Ph. D. dissertation, Duke University, 1980.

Ruby, Roy H. "The Presidential Election of 1944 in Mississippi: The Bolting Electors." MA thesis, Mississippi State University, 1966.

Savage, James A. "Save Our Republic: Battling John Birch in California's Conservative Cradle." Ph.D. dissertation, University of Kentucky, 2015.

Sellers, Linda Williams. "South-Saver: Nell Battle Lewis in the 1920s." MA thesis, University of North Carolina at Chapel Hill, 1984.

Speer, Lisa. "'Contrary Mary': The Life of Mary Dawson Cain." Ph.D. dissertation, University of Mississippi, 1998.

Stewart, William Albert. "The North Carolina Speaker Ban Law Episode: Its History and Implications for Higher Education." Ph.D. dissertation, University of North Carolina at Greensboro, 1988.

Tate, Roger D. Jr. "Easing the Burden: The Era of Depression and New Deal in Mississippi." Ph.D. dissertation, University of Tennessee, 1978.

Wilkerson-Freeman, Sarah. "The Emerging Political Consciousness of Gertrude Weil: Education and Women's Clubs, 1879–1914." MA thesis, University of North Carolina at Chapel Hill, 1985.

Wilkerson-Freeman, Sarah. "Women and the Transformation of American Politics: North Carolina, 1898–1940." Ph.D. dissertation, University of North Carolina at Chapel Hill, 1995.

Ziker, Ann. "Race, Conservative Politics, and U.S. Foreign Policy in the Post-Colonial World, 1948–1968." Ph.D. dissertation, Rice University, 2008.

UNPUBLISHED PAPERS

Delegard, Kristen. "Stopping Words: Female Anti-Radicalism and the Grassroots Censorship Campaign, 1924–1939." 1999 Southern Historical Association Meeting, Fort Worth, TX.

White, John. "Sara McCorkle and the Women of the White Citizen's Councils." Paper Delivered at the Southern Historical Association Annual Meeting, Richmond, Virginia, November 2007.

White, John. "White Women and 'Massive Ressistance' in South Carolina." Paper Delivered at the Southern Historical Association of Women Historians Triennial Meeting, Univeristy of Maryland-Baltimore County, June 2006.

# Index